Essentia...

of **Psychological** ...

Everything you need to know to administer, score, and interpret the major psychological tests.

I'd like to order the following *Essentials of Psychological Assessment:*

- ❑ WAIS®-III Assessment / 978-0-471-28295-2 • $34.95
- ❑ WJ III™ Cognitive Abilities Assessment / 978-0-471-34466-7 • $34.95
- ❑ Cross-Battery Assessment, Second Edition (w/CD-ROM) / 978-0-471-75771-9 • $44.95
- ❑ Nonverbal Assessment / 978-0-471-38318-5 • $34.95
- ❑ PAI® Assessment / 978-0-471-08463-1 • $34.95
- ❑ CAS Assessment / 978-0-471-29015-5 • $34.95
- ❑ MMPI-2™ Assessment / 978-0-471-34533-6 • $34.95
- ❑ Myers-Briggs Type Indicator® Assessment / 978-0-471-33239-8 • $34.95
- ❑ Rorschach® Assessment / 978-0-471-33146-9 • $34.95
- ❑ Millon™ Inventories Assessment, Third Edition / 978-0-470-16862-2 • $34.95
- ❑ TAT and Other Storytelling Techniques / 978-0-471-39469-3 • $34.95
- ❑ MMPI-A™ Assessment / 978-0-471-39815-8 • $34.95
- ❑ NEPSY® Assessment / 978-0-471-32690-8 • $34.95
- ❑ Neuropsychological Assessment / 978-0-471-40522-1 • $34.95
- ❑ WJ III™ Tests of Achievement Assessment / 978-0-471-33059-2 • $34.95
- ❑ Evidence-Based Academic Interventions / 978-0-470-20632-4 • $34.95
- ❑ WRAML2 and TOMAL-2 Assessment / 978-0-470-17911-6 • $34.95
- ❑ WMS®-III Assessment / 978-0-471-38080-1 • $34.95
- ❑ Behavioral Assessment / 978-0-471-35367-6 • $34.95
- ❑ Forensic Psychological Assessment / 978-0-471-33186-5 • $34.95
- ❑ Bayley Scales of Infant Development II Assessment / 978-0-471-32651-9 • $34.95
- ❑ Career Interest Assessment / 978-0-471-35365-2 • $34.95
- ❑ WPPSI™-III Assessment / 978-0-471-28895-4 • $34.95
- ❑ 16PF® Assessment / 978-0-471-23424-1 • $34.95
- ❑ Assessment Report Writing / 978-0-471-39487-7 • $34.95
- ❑ Stanford-Binet Intelligence Scales (SB5) Assessment / 978-0-471-22404-4 • $34.95
- ❑ WISC®-IV Assessment / 978-0-471-47691-7 • $34.95
- ❑ KABC-II Assessment / 978-0-471-66733-9 • $34.95
- ❑ WIAT®-II and KTEA-II Assessment / 978-0-471-70706-6 • $34.95
- ❑ Processing Assessment / 978-0-471-71925-0 • $34.95
- ❑ School Neuropsychological Assessment / 978-0-471-78372-5 • $34.95
- ❑ Cognitive Assessment with KAIT & Other Kaufman Measures / 978-0-471-38317-8 • $34.95
- ❑ Assessment with Brief Intelligence Tests / 978-0-471-26412-5 • $34.95
- ❑ Creativity Assessment / 978-0-470-13742-0 • $34.95
- ❑ WNV™ Assessment / 978-0-470-28467-4 • $34.95
- ❑ DAS-II® Assessment (w/CD-ROM) / 978-0-470-22520-2 • $44.95

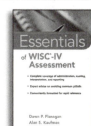

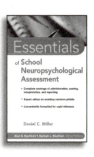

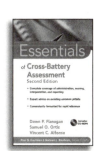

Please complete the order form on the back.
To order by phone, call toll free 1-877-762-2974
To order online: www.wiley.com/essentials
To order by mail: refer to order form on next page

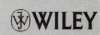

Essentials

of **Psychological Assessment** Series

ORDER FORM

Please send this order form with your payment (credit card or check) to:
John Wiley & Sons, Attn: J. Knott, 111 River Street, Hoboken, NJ 07030-5774

QUANTITY	TITLE	ISBN	PRICE
_____	_____	_____	_____
_____	_____	_____	_____
_____	_____	_____	_____
_____	_____	_____	_____
_____	_____	_____	_____

Shipping Charges:	**Surface**	**2-Day**	**1-Day**
First item	$5.00	$10.50	$17.50
Each additional item	$3.00	$3.00	$4.00

For orders greater than 15 items,
please contact Customer Care at 1-877-762-2974.

ORDER AMOUNT _____

SHIPPING CHARGES _____

SALES TAX _____

TOTAL ENCLOSED _____

NAME_____

AFFILIATION _____

ADDRESS_____

CITY/STATE/ZIP _____

TELEPHONE _____

EMAIL_____

❏ Please add me to your e-mailing list

PAYMENT METHOD:

❏ Check/Money Order   ❏ Visa   ❏ Mastercard   ❏ AmEx

Card Number _____ Exp. Date _____

Cardholder Name *(Please print)* _____

Signature _____

*Make checks payable to **John Wiley & Sons.** Credit card orders invalid if not signed.*
All orders subject to credit approval. • Prices subject to change.

To order by phone, call toll free 1-877-762-2974
To order online: www.wiley.com/essentials

 WILEY

Essentials of
DAS-II® Assessment

Essentials of Psychological Assessment Series
Series Editors, Alan S. Kaufman and Nadeen L. Kaufman

Essentials

of DAS-II® Assessment

Ron Dumont

John O. Willis

Colin D. Elliott

John Wiley & Sons, Inc.

Published by John Wiley & Sons, Inc., Hoboken, New Jersey.
Published simultaneously in Canada.

For general information on our other products and services please contact our Customer Care Department within the U.S. at (800) 762-2974, outside the United States at (317) 572-3993 or fax (317) 572-4002.

Wiley also publishes its books in a variety of electronic formats. Some content that appears in print may not be available in electronic books. For more information about Wiley products, visit our website at www.wiley.com.

Library of Congress Cataloging-in-Publication Data:

Dumont, Ron.
    Essentials of DAS-II assessment / by Ron Dumont, John Willis, Colin Elliott.
        p. cm; — (Essentials of psychological assessment series)
    Includes bibliographical references and index.
    ISBN: 978-0470-22520-2 (pbk. : alk. paper)
    1. Differential Ability Scales. I. Willis, John Osgood. II. Elliott, Colin D. III. Title.
    BF432.5.D49D86 2009
    153.9'3—dc22

                                                                        2008016818

Printed in the United States of America

10 9 8 7 6 5 4 3 2 1

To Marybeth and Kate,
Thank you both for always being supportive of my projects.
I couldn't, and wouldn't be able to do any of them without you.
Ron

To Ursula,
with all my love for all time and with deep gratitude, appreciation,
and admiration. You make everything possible and worthwhile.
John

To Marian,
With love and thanks for your unfailing and loving encouragement over
many years, and for your support once more during this project.
Colin

CONTENTS

SERIES PREFACE

n the *Essentials of Psychological Assessment* series, we have attempted to provide the reader with books that will deliver key practical information in the most efficient and accessible style. The series features instruments in a variety of domains, such as cognition, personality, education, and neuropsychology. For the experienced clinician, books in the series will offer a concise yet thorough way to master utilization of the continuously evolving supply of new and revised instruments, as well as a convenient method for keeping up to date on the tried-and-true measures. The novice will find here a prioritized assembly of all the information and techniques that must be at one's fingertips to begin the complicated process of individual psychological diagnosis.

Wherever feasible, visual shortcuts to highlight key points are utilized alongside systematic, step-by-step guidelines. Chapters are focused and succinct. Topics are targeted for an easy understanding of the essentials of administration, scoring, interpretation, and clinical application. Theory and research are continually woven into the fabric of each book, but always to enhance clinical inference, never to sidetrack or overwhelm. We have long been advocates of what has been called *intelligent testing*—the notion that a profile of test scores is meaningless unless it is brought to life by the clinical observations and astute detective work of knowledgeable examiners. Test profiles must be used to make a difference in the child's or adult's life, or why bother to test? We want this series to help our readers become the best intelligent testers they can be.

The *Essentials of DAS-II Assessment* is designed to be a helpful reference to all examiners, whether they have prior experience with the DAS or are just learning the DAS-II. Weaving expert guidance throughout to help the reader avoid common examiner errors, the authors offer guidance on the test's administration, scoring, and interpretation to assist examiners in building their competency with the DAS-II. This volume is also packaged with an accompanying CD-ROM, which contains several Microsoft Word and Excel files along with several Adobe PDF files. Many of the Word files can be opened so the user can add DAS-II evaluation results to them. Other Word files can be printed out to use as appendices to evaluation reports. The CD-ROM also contains an Excel spreadsheet file (labeled "DAS-II Computer Assistant"), designed to facilitate and automate the analysis and interpretation of obtained data.

Alan S. Kaufman, PhD, and Nadeen L. Kaufman, EdD, Series Editors
Yale University School of Medicine

ACKNOWLEDGMENTS

Our families have been wonderfully patient and forgiving throughout the long process of producing this book. We give loving thanks to Marybeth, Kate, Ursula, Janet, Doug, Amy, Bernie, Anna, Bob, and Marian.

We are most grateful to Alan and Nadeen Kaufman for allowing us to contribute to the expanding shelf of justifiably popular and valuable *Essentials of Psychological Assessment* books. We owe a special debt of thanks to the staff at John Wiley & Sons. Isabel Pratt, Editor, has been incredibly patient, tolerant, supportive, and helpful throughout this arduous process. She and Sweta Gupta, Senior Editorial Assistant, now Publisher's Assistant, have mastered the skill of herding cats, so they were able to help, guide, and redirect us through every step in producing this book. If this actually looks like a book, credit goes to Kim Nir, Senior Production Editor, and Joanna Carabello, who copyedited every letter and digit with an eagle eye.

Jerome Sattler generously permitted Ron Dumont and John Willis to work with him on the DAS chapter in his 2001 *Assessment of Children: Cognitive Applications* (4th ed.) and the DAS-II chapter in his 2008 *Assessment of Children: Cognitive Foundations* (5th ed.). Jerry's encyclopedic knowledge, sharp insight, and relentless questioning and editing tremendously enhanced our knowledge and understanding of the *Differential Ability Scales*.

We thank Dr. Gloria Maccow, Clinical Measurement Consultant for The Psychological Corporation, for contributing one of the case studies in Chapter 8. Our present and past colleagues and graduate students have contributed greatly to our thinking and—such as they are—our explanatory powers. We sincerely thank them. One graduate student in particular, Joseph Salerno, must be acknowledged. His co-authorship of Chapter 4 in this book, along with his constant comments and questions about all the materials, has helped us to fine tune what is presented. Most of all, we are indebted to all the children and young adults whom we have evaluated and to their parents, teachers, and therapists, all of whom have taught us more than we can acknowledge.

One

OVERVIEW

The Differential Ability Scales–Second Edition (DAS-II; Elliott, 2007a), developed and standardized in the United States, is a modern psychological assessment instrument with a longer history than its publication date would suggest (see Rapid Reference 1.1). It is based upon its predecessor, the Differential Ability Scales (DAS; Elliott, 1990a, 1990b), which had as its origin the British Ability Scales (BAS; Elliott, 1983). As its name suggests, the DAS-II was developed with a primary focus on specific cognitive abilities rather than on general "intelligence."

STRUCTURE OF THE DAS

The DAS-II consists of a cognitive battery of 20 subtests, covering an age range of 2 years, 6 months through 17 years, 11 months (2:6 through 17:11). The battery is divided into two overlapping age levels: (1) The Early Years battery is normed from age 2:6 through 8:11, with a usual age range of 2:6 through 6:11; (2) The School-Age battery is normed from age 5:0 through 17:11, and has a usual age range of 7:0 through 17:11. With those overlaps between the Early Years and the School Age batteries, it will be seen that the DAS-II Early Years and School-Age batteries were conormed for children ages 5:0 through 8:11 and therefore have a four-year normative overlap. (See Rapid Reference 1.2 for a description of the DAS-II subtests.)

The Early Years battery is further divided into two levels, lower and upper. The Lower Early Years level is most appropriate for young children ages 2:6 through 3:5, although it may also be used with older children with special needs. The Upper Early Years level is suitable for children normally in the age range of 3:6–6:11, although it may also be used with children up to age 8:11 if they have difficulty with the materials in the School-Age battery.

The DAS-II battery yields a composite score called General Conceptual

≡ *Rapid Reference 1.1*

DAS-II Batteries

Author: Colin Elliott

Publication date: 2007

What the test measures: Verbal (*Gc*), Nonverbal Reasoning (*Gf*), Spatial (*Gv*), Working Memory (*Gsm*), Processing Speed (*Gs*), Phonological Processing (*Ga*), Recall of Objects (*Glr*), and General Conceptual Ability (GCA), which is a measure of the general factor *g*.

Age range: 2:6–17:11

Average Administration time: Six core subtests to obtain three clusters and GCA score = 31–40 minutes. Diagnostic subtests—School Readiness = 17 minutes, Working Memory = 12 minutes, Processing Speed = 9 minutes, Phonological Processing = 10 minutes.

Qualification of examiners: Graduate- or professional-level training in psychological assessment

Computer program: Scoring program included as well as a CD, which includes help in administering the Phonological Processing subtest and also useful demonstrations of administering the test using American Sign Language.

Publisher: The Psychological Corporation
A division of Pearson
555 Academic Court
San Antonio, TX 78204-2498
Ordering phone number: 800-211-8378
http://www.psychcorp.com
Web site: www.DAS-II.com

≡ *Rapid Reference 1.2*

DAS-II Subtests

Verbal Subtests

- *Verbal Comprehension:* following oral instructions to point to or move pictures and toys.
- *Naming Vocabulary:* naming pictures.
- *Word Definitions:* explaining the meaning of each word. Words are spoken by the evaluator.
- *Verbal Similarities:* explaining how three things or concepts go together, what they all are (e.g., house, tent, igloo; love, hate, fear)

Nonverbal Reasoning Subtests

- *Picture Similarities:* multiple-choice matching of pictures on the basis of re-lationships, both concrete (e.g., two round things among other shapes) and abstract (e.g., map with globe from among other round things). [Nonverbal Cluster in Lower Early Years battery]
- *Matrices:* solving visual puzzles by choosing the correct picture or design to complete a logical pattern.
- *Sequential and Quantitative Reasoning:* figuring out sequential patterns in pic-tures or geometric figures, or common rules in numerical relationships.

Spatial Subtests

- *Copying:* drawing pencil copies of abstract, geometric designs.
- *Recall of Designs:* drawing pencil copies of abstract, geometric designs from memory after a five-second view of each design.
- *Pattern Construction:* imitating constructions made by the examiner with wooden blocks, copying geometric designs with colored tiles or patterned cubes. There are time limits and bonus points for fast work. An alternative, "un-timed" procedure uses time limits but no speed bonuses. [Nonverbal Cluster in Lower Early Years battery]

Diagnostic Subtests

- *Early Number Concepts:* oral math questions with illustrations—counting, number concepts, and simple arithmetic.
- *Matching Letter-Like Forms:* multiple-choice matching of shapes that are similar to letters.
- *Recall of Digits Forward:* repeating increasingly long series of digits dictated at two digits per second.
- *Recall of Digits Backward:* repeating, in reverse order, increasingly long series of digits dictated at two digits per second.
- *Recognition of Pictures:* seeing one, two, or three pictures for five seconds or four pictures for ten seconds and then trying to find those pictures within a group of four to seven similar pictures.
- *Recall of Objects—Immediate:* viewing a page of 20 pictures, hearing them named by the evaluator, trying to name the pictures from memory, seeing them again, trying again to name all the pictures, and repeating the process once more. The score is the total of all the pictures recalled on each of the three trials, including pictures recalled two or three times.
- *Recall of Objects—Delayed:* trying to recall the pictures again on a surprise retest 15 to 20 minutes later.
- *Speed of Information Processing:* the student scans rows of figures or numbers and marks the figure with the most parts or the greatest number in each row. The score is based on speed. Accuracy does not count unless it is very poor.
- *Phonological Processing:* rhyming, blending sounds, deleting sounds, and identi-fying the individual sounds in words.
- *Rapid Naming:* naming colors or pictures as quickly as possible without making mistakes. The score is based on speed and accuracy
- *Recall of Sequential Order:* sequencing, from highest to lowest, increasingly long series of words that include body parts, and for more difficult items, non-body parts.

Ability (GCA), which provides an estimate of overall reasoning and conceptual abilities. In addition, for ages 3:6 to 17:11, a Special Nonverbal Composite (SNC) is available and derived from the nonverbal core subtests appropriate for each battery level. The DAS-II also provides lower-level composite scores called *cluster scores* that are derived from highly *g*-saturated core subtests. Finally, there are numerous diagnostic subtests and clusters that measure other specific abilities. These diagnostic subtests do not contribute to the GCA or SNC, but give additional information about cognitive strengths and weaknesses. The overall structure is summarized in Figure 1.1.

Battery	Usual Age Range	Full Normative Age Range

Lower Early Years
  Core Clusters
    GCA
    Verbal
    Nonverbal
	2:6 – 3:5	2:6 – 8:11

Upper Early Years
  Core Clusters
    GCA
    Special Nonverbal Composite
    Verbal
    Nonverbal Reasoning
    Spatial
  Diagnostic Clusters
    School Readiness
    Working Memory
    Processing Speed
	3:6 – 6:11	3:6 – 8:11

School Age
  Core Clusters
    GCA
    Special Nonverbal Composite
    Verbal
    Nonverbal Reasoning
    Spatial
  Diagnostic Clusters
    Working Memory
    Processing Speed
	7:0 – 17:11	5:0 – 17:11

Figure 1.1 DAS-II Clusters by Battery

THEORETICAL UNDERPINNINGS

The DAS-II was not developed solely to reflect a single model of cognitive abilities but was designed to address processes that often underlie children's difficulties in learning and what scientists know about neurological structures underlying these abilities. The selection of the abilities to be measured by the DAS-II was influenced by a variety of theoretical points of view, but the end result is consistent with *Gf-Gc* theory (now commonly referred to as the Cattell-Horn-Carroll theory, or simply CHC). This is probably the best known and most widely accepted theory of intellectual factors among practitioners of individual psychological assessment and is derived from the Horn-Cattell *Gf-Gc* model [e.g., Cattell (1941, 1971, 1987), Cattell & Horn (1978), Horn (1988, 1991), Horn & Noll (1997)]. *Gf* and *Gc* refer, respectively, to "fluid" and "crystallized" intelligence, but current versions of the theory recognize as many as seven different broad cognitive factors or abilities. See Carroll (1993); Flanagan and McGrew (1997); Flanagan, McGrew, and Ortiz (2000); Flanagan and Ortiz (2001); Flanagan, Ortiz, and Alfonso (2007); Flanagan, Ortiz, Alfonso, and Mascolo (2002); Horn (1985, 1988, 1991); Horn and Cattell (1966); Horn and Noll (1997); McGrew (1997); McGrew and Flanagan (1998); Woodcock (1990); and Woodcock and Mather (1989) for discussions of *Gf-Gc*, now usually called the Cattell-Horn-Carroll (CHC) theory. Carroll's monumental (1993) review and re-analysis of hundreds of factor analytic studies of many psychological tests provided a solid empirical foundation for CHC theory. The factor structure that Carroll devised on the basis of his research was remarkably congruent with the theoretical structure developed by Cattell and Horn (1978; Horn, 1988, 1991), which lent further credence to the amalgamated CHC theory as subsequently developed by Woodcock, McGrew, Flanagan, and others [e.g., Flanagan & McGrew (1997); Flanagan, McGrew, & Ortiz (2000); Flanagan & Ortiz (2001); Flanagan, Ortiz, & Alfonso (2007); Flanagan, Ortiz, Alfonso, & Mascolo (2002); Horn (1991); McGrew (1997); McGrew & Flanagan (1998); McGrew, Werder, & Woodcock (1991); Woodcock (1990, 1993); and Woodcock & Mather (1989)]. However, even with a growing consensus as to the nature and structure of human cognitive abilities, there remains substantive debate regarding the number of factors representing independent abilities in a cognitive model, the precise nature of each of those factors (Horn & Blankson, 2005; Carroll, 2005), and to what extent, if any, subtests from different test batteries that purport to measure a given factor actually do so (Alfonso, Flanagan, & Radwan, 2005).

Despite the fact that no single theory or model has universal acceptance, there is a common core of theory and research that supported the development of the

DAS-II. Such research indicates that human abilities are complex and often are not best explained solely in terms of a single cognitive factor (*g*), or even in terms of several lower-order factors. These abilities are presented as multiple dimensions on which individuals show reliably observable differences, and are related to how children learn, achieve, and solve problems. Although these abilities are interrelated, they do not completely overlap, thus making many of them distinct (Carroll, 1993). The wide range of human abilities represents a number of interlinked subsystems of information processing that have structural correlates in the central nervous system, in which some functions are distinct and others are integrated. Some formulations of CHC theory (e.g., Carroll, 1993, 2005) include an overarching, single factor, *g,* at the top of the hierarchy. Others (e.g., Horn, 1991; Horn & Blankson, 2005) dispute the importance, or even the existence, of a single, overall level of cognitive ability and emphasize the importance of the separate abilities. Yet others (e.g., Flanagan & McGrew, 1997; Flanagan, McGrew, & Ortiz, 2000) do not take a rigid stand on the question of an overall *g,* but operationalize the theory on the basis of the separate factors. All of these versions of CHC theory maintain at least two strata of abilities: several broad abilities each including several narrow abilities. In the three-stratum model (e.g., Carroll, 2005), the narrow abilities are called Stratum I, the broad abilities Stratum II, and *g,* at the top of the hierarchy, Stratum III.

Flanagan and McGrew (1997); Flanagan, McGrew, and Ortiz (2000); Flanagan and Ortiz (2001); Flanagan, Ortiz, and Alfonso (2007); Flanagan, Ortiz, Alfonso, and Mascolo (2002); Horn (1991); McGrew (1997); McGrew and Flanagan (1998); McGrew, Werder, and Woodcock (1991); Woodcock (1990, 1993); and Woodcock and Mather (1989) have adopted a notation system, largely based on that of Carroll (1993). Symbols for broad (Stratum II) abilities are written with a capital G and italicized, lowercase letters (e.g., *Ga* is auditory processing, and *Glr* is long-term storage and retrieval). Symbols for narrow (Stratum I) abilities within the various broad abilities are usually written with one or two capital letters or a capital letter and a digit (e.g., SR is spatial relations within *Gv,* I is induction within *Gf,* and K1 is general science information within *Gc*). Other notations are used occasionally (e.g., PC:A and PC:S are, respectively, phonetic coding: analysis and phonetic coding: synthesis). Several similar, but not identical, verbal labels are given to the abilities (e.g., *Gv* has been called "visual processing," "visual/spatial processing," and "visual/spatial thinking"), so the more-or-less agreed-upon symbols function as a valuable common notation with less risk of misunderstanding.

The following section outlines some links between the DAS-II ability constructs and neuropsychological structures in the areas of verbal and spatial abilities, fluid reasoning abilities, several aspects of memory, and processing speed.

Broad Verbal and Spatial Abilities

The DAS-II Verbal and Spatial ability clusters reflect major systems through which individuals receive, perceive, remember, and process information. Both systems are linked to auditory and visual modalities and factorially represent verbal [crystallized intelligence (Gc)] and visual [visual-spatial (Gv)] thinking. Neuropsychologically, there is strong evidence for the existence of these systems. They tend to be localized in the left and right cerebral hemispheres, respectively, although the localization is complicated (see, for example, Hale & Fiorello, 2004, pp. 67–78) and there are individual differences in areas of localization of function. Moreover, the systems are doubly dissociated—that is, they represent two distinct, independent systems of information processing (McCarthy & Warrington, 1990; Springer & Deutsch, 1989). The systems are independent insofar as each one may remain intact if the other is damaged. In the DAS-II, the two factors (verbal and spatial) are measured by the Verbal and Spatial clusters in both the Early Years and School-Age batteries.

Crystallized ability (Gc) refers to the application of acquired knowledge and learned skills to answering questions and solving problems presenting at least broadly familiar materials and processes. Virtually all tests of Gc are verbal, as that is the nature of many crystallized tasks: language is the primary means by which we express and use acquired knowledge. Most verbal subtests of intelligence scales primarily involve crystallized intelligence. Subtests of general knowledge and vocabulary are relatively pure measures of crystallized intelligence. The overlap between crystallized intelligence and verbal information processing is indeed so strong that we believe that the meaning of the factor and the test scores that measure it is best expressed as "Verbal," as in the DAS-II cluster score.

We note here that within the area of auditory-verbal processing there are distinctions that have to be made between different types of cognitive processes. Most of the tasks that are included under the Gc factor are concerned with verbal knowledge (including vocabulary), comprehension of single or multiple sentences, and verbal reasoning. All these are relatively high-level cognitive tasks, requiring complex processing, analysis of meaning, and retrieval of information that has been stored in long-term verbal memory. In contrast, there are other verbal factors that require immediate, less complex verbal processing. *Auditory short-term memory* (Gsm) is measured by tasks that entail repeating words that have been heard, with little or no processing of the meaning of the words themselves.

We can characterize this as relatively simple information processing. Similarly, *auditory processing ability* (*Ga*) is measured by tasks that require the individual to analyze the component sounds of words that are presented. Again, such tasks do not require the meaning of those words to be an important component of the task. Both *Gsm* and *Ga* will be discussed below.

Visual-spatial thinking (*Gv*) involves a range of visual processes, ranging from fairly simple visual perceptual tasks to higher level, visual, cognitive processes. Woodcock and Mather (1989) define *Gv* in part: "In Horn-Cattell theory, 'broad visualization' requires fluent thinking with stimuli that are visual in the mind's eye. . . ." Although *Gv* tasks are often complex and mentally challenging, *Gv* primarily relies on visual processing that involves the perception of and ability to visualize mental rotations and reversals of visual figures. It is not dependent on the ability of the individual to use internal verbal language to help solve problems.

Again, we note at this point that not all "nonverbal" tasks measure *Gv*. Because we have stipulated the condition (which is borne out by factor-analytic research) that *Gv* tasks are not dependent upon the ability of the individual to use internal language in solving a problem, it follows that tasks that require this are measuring a different cognitive process. *Gv* tasks do not include the aspect of dealing with novel stimuli or applying novel mental processes, or using internal language to reason out the solution to a visually-presented problem, all of which characterize *Gf* tasks. This will be discussed below in the section on Integration of Complex Information Processing.

Auditory Processing Ability: Is it a Component of Verbal Ability?

It should be noted that Horn and Carroll both accepted that there is a separate factor of auditory processing (*Ga*) that is distinct from the verbal or *Gc* information processing system. Auditory processing is concerned with the analysis of sound patterns such as in speech sounds, rhythm, and sequences of sounds (Carroll, 2005; Horn & Blankson, 2005). Auditory processing ability is certainly related to the development of complex higher-order language skills. It is necessary but not sufficient for language development. It seems reasonable to suppose that auditory processing is mediated by a separate processing system that handles the analysis of auditory sensory input, and because of this, children with hearing impairment are likely to have difficulties with *Ga* tasks.

In the DAS-II, auditory processing (*Ga*) is measured by the Phonological Processing subtest, comprising four distinct components: Rhyming, Blending, Deletion, and Phoneme Identification and Segmentation.

Integration of Complex Information Processing

For normal cognitive functioning, the verbal and visual-spatial abilities operate as an integrated information processing system that is necessary for complex mental activity. Factorially, this integrative system is represented by the *fluid reasoning (Gf)* ability. Fluid reasoning refers to inductive and deductive reasoning, presenting problems that are new to the person doing the reasoning. The vast majority of fluid reasoning tests use nonverbal (that is, visual) stimuli using pictures or figures. These require an integration of verbal and nonverbal thinking. Indeed, it seems likely that the best measures of *Gf* always require integrated analysis of both verbal and visual information. This is achieved through the presentation of visual problems that, for most efficient solution, require the individual (1) to encode the components of the visual stimulus, (2) to use internal language to generate hypotheses, (3) to test the hypotheses, and (4) to identify the correct solution.

Neuropsychologically, it seems that the integrative function of frontal lobe systems is central to executive function, which is involved in planning and other complex mental processes (Hale & Fiorello, 2004, pp. 64–67; Luria, 1973; discussed by McCarthy & Warrington, 1990, pp. 343–364), and it is therefore reasonable to hypothesize that it may provide a structural correlate for *Gf*. Similarly, it is clear that the corpus callosum has a major role in connecting the right and left cerebral hemispheres, and that limitations in callosal transmission may be implicated in cases of poor visual-verbal integration. Whatever the localization of specific mechanisms may be, the fact that our brains have an integrative function seems incontrovertible. The best tests of *Gf* require that integrative process.

In the DAS-II, the *Gf* factor is measured in the Upper Early Years and School-Age batteries by the Nonverbal Reasoning cluster.[1] The subtests measuring this ability require integrated analysis and complex transformation of both visual and verbal information, and verbal mediation is critical for the solution of these visually presented problems for most individuals.

---

[1]In the Lower Early Years battery (ages 2:6 through 3:5 only), fluid reasoning (*Gf*) and visual-spatial thinking (*Gv*) are measured by one subtest each. The Nonverbal cluster combines these two subtests. Therefore the factors are only differentiated at the subtest level and not at the cluster level.

Short-Term Memory (Verbal and Visual) Systems

Short-term memory (*Gsm*) refers to one's ability to apprehend and maintain awareness of elements of information for events that occurred in the last minute or so. *Gsm* refers to aspects of memory that have limited capacity and that lose information quickly unless an individual activates other cognitive resources to maintain the information in immediate awareness. CHC theory does not distinguish, at the second-order, group factor level, between separate, modality-related visual and verbal memory systems. At the broad factor level there is only a single short-term memory factor (*Gsm*) that should really be called *auditory* short-term memory.

Because of evidence from both cognitive psychology and neuropsychology that shows clearly that verbal and visual short-term memory systems are distinct and independent (Hitch, Halliday, Schaafstal, & Schraagen, 1988; McCarthy & Warrington, 1990, pp. 275–295), the DAS-II does not treat short-term memory as unitary but keeps auditory and visual short-term memory tasks as distinct measures. Additionally, several subtests combine to create a working memory (*Gsm* MW) factor that is separate from auditory short-term memory (*Gsm* MS), as measured by the Recall of Digits Forward subtest, *and* the visual short-term memory (*Gv* MV) abilities measured by the Recall of Designs and Recognition of Pictures subtests.

Integration of Verbal and Visual Memory Systems

The *long-term storage and retrieval* (*Glr*) factor in the CHC model is typically measured by tests that have both visual and verbal components. *Long-term storage and retrieval* ability involves memory storage and retrieval over longer periods of time than *Gsm*. How much longer varies from task to task, but it is typically of the order of 1 to 30 minutes.

McCarthy and Warrington (1990, p. 283) call this "visual–verbal" short-term memory and conclude that it is underpinned by another distinct and independent, dissociable information-processing system. While its relationship with other processes is relatively small, it may be an important type of "gateway" process underlying some types of working memory. Holding information in visual-verbal short-term memory may be necessary in order to solve problems that require the manipulation and transformation of visual information that can be labeled verbally.

In the DAS-II, the visual-verbal memory factor (*Glr*) is measured by the Recall of Objects subtest. In this task, an array of pictures is presented, but they have to be recalled verbally. Sequential order is not important, and the child is able to organize and associate pictures in any way that helps in remembering them.

Processing Speed

The DAS-II Processing Speed cluster measures the CHC *processing speed factor* (*Gs*). This factor refers to the ability to automatically and fluently perform relatively easy or over-learned cognitive tasks, especially when high mental efficiency (i.e., attention and focused concentration) is required. It is typically measured by tests that require relatively simple operations that must be performed quickly—speed of decision, speed of naming, clerical speed, and so on. These types of timed activities are more complex than those involved in simple reaction-time paradigms, which seem to form their own factor (*Gt*), a factor not assessed by the DAS-II, nor by most cognitive ability tests.

While individual differences in neural speed may be one of the determinants of performance on processing speed tasks, it is clear that other determinants are involved. Speed of response may reflect not only neural speed but also perhaps efficiency in accessing information, efficiency in holding information in short-term memory, efficiency in visual-verbal integration, and willingness to commit to a decision and threshold for doing so. Performance on *Gs* tasks is not easily improved with practice. Prior experience on similar tasks is unlikely to be helpful. Therefore, measures on such tasks do reflect some function of the underlying speed and efficiency of processing systems.

DESCRIPTION OF DAS-II

The Differential Ability Scales—Second Edition (DAS-II; Elliott, 2007a) is an individually administered battery of cognitive tests for children and adolescents aged 2 years, 6 months (2:6) through 17 years, 11 months (17:11). Because the DAS-II covers such a wide age range, it is divided into three levels: Lower Early Years (ages 2:6 through 3:5); Upper Early Years (normally covering ages 3:6 through 6:11, but normed through 8:11); and School-Age (normally covering ages 7:0 through 17:11, but also normed for ages 5:0 through 6:11). The three levels allow both items and clusters that are appropriate to the several age ranges. It was designed to measure specific, definable abilities and to provide reliable, interpretable profiles of strengths and weaknesses. These profiles may lead to individualized interventions or treatments for students with learning concerns or issues. The DAS-II is considered suitable for use in any setting in which the cognitive abilities of children and adolescents are to be evaluated, although sev-

CAUTION

Several of the DAS-II subtests may not be appropriate for students with severe sensory or motor disabilities.

eral of the DAS-II subtests may not be appropriate for students with severe sensory or motor disabilities. The DAS-II cognitive battery yields a composite score labeled *General Conceptual Ability* (GCA) that is a measure of psychometric *g,* defined as "the general ability of an individual to perform complex mental processing that involves conceptualization and transformation of information" (Elliott, 2007b, p. 17).

Organization of the DAS-II

The DAS-II contains a total of 20 subtests grouped into *Core* or *Diagnostic* subtests. The *Core* subtests are those used to compute the GCA and three cluster scores: Verbal Ability, Nonverbal Reasoning Ability, and Spatial Ability. The *Diagnostic* subtests measure aspects of memory, speed of processing and early concepts taught in schools. They yield three cluster scores: Processing Speed, Working Memory, and School Readiness. These diagnostic subtests are considered important and useful in the interpretation of an individual's strengths and weaknesses in information processing, but they do not contaminate the GCA with subtests that have low *g* loadings.

This separation of Core and Diagnostic subtests is one of the strengths of the DAS-II. For a point of comparison, the Wechsler Intelligence Scale for Children, 4th ed. (WISC-IV; Wechsler, 2003) excludes the Information, Word Reasoning, Arithmetic, Picture Completion, and Cancellation subtests from the FSIQ and Indices, but does include in the IQs subtests such as Coding and Symbol Search, which are not good measures of complex mental processing or intellectual ability

DON'T FORGET

The separation of the DAS-II into *Core* and *Diagnostic* subtests can be helpful in reducing the overall administration time and a student's fatigue since examiners can tailor their assessments, administering only those subtests that are relevant based on the specific and different referral questions.

(*g*). The Stanford-Binet Intelligence Scale, 5th ed. (SB5; Roid, 2003) includes all subtests in the total score. The Woodcock-Johnson III Cognitive battery (WJ III; Woodcock, McGrew, & Mather, 2001) includes low-*g*-loading tests, but only in proportion to their *g* loading

The Lower Early Years battery of the DAS-II consists of four core subtests that combine to yield the

GCA and three diagnostic subtests that may be administered. The Upper Early Years battery includes six core subtests and an additional 11 optional diagnostic subtests. The School-Age battery includes six core subtests and nine additional diagnostic subtests. Some of the Early Years subtests can also be used at the school-age level, especially at younger ages, for diagnostic purposes. For the Upper Early Years and the School-Age batteries, the subtests not only combine to produce the GCA but also yield five or six cluster scores. For Upper Early Years children, these cluster scores represent Verbal (Gc), Nonverbal Reasoning (Gf), and Spatial (Gv) abilities along with School Readiness, Working Memory (Gsm), and Processing Speed (Gs). For School-Age children, the cluster scores represent Verbal (Gc), Nonverbal Reasoning [(Gf) fluid reasoning (Keith, 1990)], and Spatial (Gv) abilities along with Working Memory (Gsm) and Processing Speed (Gs) (see Rapid Reference 1.2 and Figure 1.1). Although the "typical" Upper Early Years battery is given to children aged 3 years, 6 months through 6 years, 11 months and the "typical" School-Age battery to children 7 years, 0 months through 17 years, 11 months, the Upper Early Years and School-Age batteries were also normed for an overlapping age range (5 years, 0 months through 8 years, 11 months).

Normative Overlaps

Depending on the examinee's age, if an examinee of low ability has little success at the ages covered by the battery you initially selected, you may be able to administer subtests from a lower level of the test. Conversely, if an examinee has high ability and has few failures at the ages covered by the battery you initially selected, you can administer subtests from a higher level of the test. All subtests at the Upper Early Years and School-Age Level have overlapping normative data for children ages 5:0 to 8:11. This overlap provides the examiner flexibility when testing bright younger children or less able older children. In these cases, subtests appropriate for the individual's abilities are available. For example, the Upper Early Years subtests can be administered to children ages 6:0 to 8:11 for whom the School-Age Level is too difficult. Similarly, the School-Age subtests can be administered to children ages 5:0 to 6:11 for whom the Upper Early Years is insufficiently challenging. In such cases, the examinee's raw scores can be converted to ability scores and then to T scores in the normal way.

DON'T FORGET

If a student has little success at the ages covered by the battery you initially selected, you may be able to administer subtests from a lower level of the test.

For children in the overlapping age range, examiners may choose to give either battery or choose one battery and administer additional subtests from the other battery.

Changes from DAS to DAS-II

Several goals were accomplished with the revision of the DAS to the DAS-II. Rapid Reference 1.3 lists the key features that were accomplished and changes made for this second edition.

In the DAS-II, many of the core subtests will be recognizable to DAS examiners, but there have been significant changes and modifications to some. For example, Block Building and Pattern Construction have been combined into one subtest; Recall of Digits has been expanded to two subtests: Recall of Digits–Forward and Recall of Digits–Backward; and Early Number Concepts has been

≡ *Rapid Reference 1.3*

DAS-II Key Revisions

- Updating of norms
- CHC interpretative basis now noted explicitly in manual and record form
- Development of three new Diagnostic Clusters (Working Memory, Processing Speed, School Readiness)
- Addition of four new subtests (Phonological Processing, Recall of Digits Backward, Recall of Sequential Order, Rapid Naming)
- Downward extension of Matrices subtest to age 3 years, 6 months, enabling the Nonverbal Reasoning cluster to be measured at the Early Years level.
- Core cluster scores (Verbal, Nonverbal Reasoning, Spatial) are now the same throughout the age range from 3:6 through 17:11
- Block Building and Pattern Construction combined into one subtest
- Revising content of 13 subtests
- Updating artwork
- Eliminating three achievement tests
- Linking DAS-II to the WIAT-II and providing correlational data also for the K-TEA-II and the WJ-III Achievement batteries
- Providing Spanish translation for nonverbal subtests
- Providing American Sign Language translation for nonverbal subtests in every kit for use by, and the training of, interpreters
- Publishing with Scoring Assistant computer software

removed from the GCA and is now included in the School Readiness cluster. There are four new diagnostic subtests (Phonological Processing, Recall of Digits—Backward, Recall of Sequential Order, Rapid Naming). The major structural changes in the DAS-II are the inclusion of separate Nonverbal Reasoning and Spatial Ability clusters at the Upper Early Years and the creation of three new clusters (Working Memory, Processing Speed, School Readiness), developed to help examiners assess the skills of the child.

Rapid Reference 1.4 compares the number of items on the DAS and DAS-II and the number of items retained and added. The DAS-II has increased the

≡ Rapid Reference 1.4

DAS to DAS-II Changes

Subtest	Number of Items on DAS	Number of Items on DAS-II	Number of DAS Items Retained on DAS-II	Number of New Items Written or Reworded for DAS-II
Core Cognitive Subtests				
Verbal Comprehension	36	42	28	14
Picture Similarities	32	32	14	18
Naming Vocabulary	26	34	21	13
Block Building*	12	12	8	4
Pattern Construction*	26	26	26	0
Copying	20	20	19	1
Matrices	35	56	25	31
Recall of Designs	21	22	21	1
Word Definitions	42	35	29	6
Verbal Similarities**	34	33	23	10
Seq. & Quantitative Reasoning	39	50	20	30
Diagnostic Cognitive Subtests				
Recall of Digits Forward**	36	38	36	2
Recognition of Pictures	20	20	20	0
Early Number Concepts	26	33	14	19
Recall of Objects	20	20	20	0
Matching Letter-Like Forms	27	27	27	0
Phonological Processing		53		53
Recall of Sequential Order		32		32
Recall of Digits Backward		30		30
Speed of Information Processing	6	6	6	0
Rapid Naming		105		105

(continued)

Subtest	Number of Items on DAS	Number of Items on DAS-II	Number of DAS Items Retained on DAS-II	Number of New Items Written or Reworded for DAS-II
Lower Early Years				
Verbal	62	76	49	27
Nonverbal	44	58	22	18
GCA	132	146	97	49
Upper Early Years				
Verbal	62	76	49	27
Nonverbal	78	88	59	49
Spatial		46		1
GCA	166	210	122	77
School-age				
Verbal	76	68	52	16
Nonverbal Reasoning	74	106	45	61
Spatial	47	48	47	1
GCA	197	222	144	78

Note: Subtests in Italics are new to the DAS-II.

* Block Building and Pattern Construction have been combined into one subtest.

** Similarities was renamed Verbal Similarities, and Recall of Digits was renamed Recall of Digits Forward.

number of items on five of the core tests, and two of the diagnostic tests and decreased the number on two subtests. The greatest increase in items came on the Matrices subtest (35 items to 56 items, a 60 percent increase) while the largest decrease came on Word Definitions (42 items decreased to 35, a 17 percent decrease). The regionally problematic word "wicked" was removed from Word Definitions. Four subtests (Recognition of Pictures, Recall of Objects, Matching Letter-Like Forms, and Speed of Information Processing) remain exactly the same on the DAS-II.

All DAS-II subtests have also been aligned with Cattell-Horn-Carroll (CHC) abilities (see Rapid Reference 1.5). This allows the examiner to use commonly understood and agreed-upon terminology when interpreting what the DAS-II is measuring. CHC theory provides for the interpretation of both Broad and Narrow abilities. The DAS-II provides measures of each of the seven most robust and replicable factors derived from research.

≡ *Rapid Reference 1.5*

DAS-II Subtests by CHC classification

	Broad Abilities	Narrow Abilities
Verbal Ability		
Verbal Comprehension	Gc	Listening Ability
Naming Vocabulary	Gc	Lexical Knowledge
Word Definitions	Gc	Language Development / Lexical Knowledge
Verbal Similarities	Gc	Language Development
Nonverbal Reasoning Ability		
Picture Similarities	Gf	Induction
Matrices	Gf	Induction
Sequential and Quantitative Reasoning	Gf	Induction / Quantitative Reasoning
Spatial Ability		
Pattern Construction	Gv	Spatial Relations
Pattern Construction–Alternative	Gv	Spatial Relations
Recall of Designs	Gv	Visual Memory
Copying	Gv	Visualization
Matching Letter-Like Forms	Gv	Visualization
Recognition of Pictures	Gv	Visual Memory
Retrieval		
Recall of Objects–Immediate	Glr	Free-recall Memory
Recall of Objects–Delayed	Glr	Free-recall Memory
Memory		
Recall of Digits Forward	Gsm	Memory Span
Recall of Digits Backward	Gsm	Working Memory
Recall of Sequential Order	Gsm	Working Memory
Processing Speed		
Speed of Information Processing	Gs	Perceptual Speed: Scanning
Rapid Naming	Gs	Perceptual Speed: Complex
Auditory Processing		
Phonological Processing	Ga	Phonetic Coding
Additional		
Early Number Concepts	Gc/Gf	Lexical Knowledge / General knowledge / Piagetian reasoning

Wider Score Ranges

The DAS-II has a wider range of possible T scores for the subtests and Standard Scores for the clusters in comparison with the DAS first edition. In the DAS, T scores ranged from 30 to 70 (that is, two standard deviations (SDs) on either side of the mean of 50), whereas in the DAS-II the range is 20 to 80 (three SDs on either side of the mean). Similarly, for the GCA, SNC and the cluster scores, the maximum DAS range was 45 to 165, whereas in the DAS-II the maximum range is 30 to 170 (that is, 4.67 SDs on either side of the mean).

RELATIONSHIPS BETWEEN THE DAS AND THE DAS-II

Rapid Reference 1.6 provides the results of comparisons of scores obtained on the first-edition DAS and the DAS-II. The major study presented in the DAS-II *Introductory and Technical Handbook* gave children the two batteries with a short interval between tests. We also present a clinical study carried out on children identified as ADHD in which the assessments were carried out over a period of years.

Over Short Periods of Time

The relationship between the DAS and the DAS-II was examined in a sample of 313 children aged 2:6 to 17:11 (Elliott, 2007b). Each test was administered in counterbalanced order with 6 to 68 days between testing. The overall correlation coefficients show that the Verbal Ability scores for the DAS and the DAS-II were the most highly related ($r = .84$) followed by the GCA ($r = .81$) and the Special Nonverbal composite ($r = .78$). As shown in Rapid Reference 1.6, the average DAS-II GCA is 2.7 points lower than the GCA of the DAS. The difference between the two tests is small for the Verbal Ability (0.1 points), while the Nonverbal Reasoning and Spatial abilities differ by 4 to 5 points. These differences, both in size and direction, are generally somewhat lower than expected according to the Flynn Effect (Flynn, 1984, 1987, 1998). The results indicate that if examinees continue to be assessed using the first edition of the DAS, their scores may be inflated by up to 4 or 5 standard score points in comparison with the DAS-II.

Over Long Periods of Time

In a small sample ($N = 26$) of children with ADHD who were administered the DAS first and then, after 3 to 6 years, were given the DAS-II, small changes in test

Rapid Reference 1.6

Comparison of Scores from DAS and DAS-II

	Standardization Sample					ADHD Sample				
	Time interval 6 to 68 days					Time interval 3 to 6 years				
	DAS		DAS-II			DAS		DAS-II		
	Mean	SD	Mean	SD	diff	Mean	SD	Mean	SD	diff
Word Definitions	51.5	9.6	51.4	8.5	−0.1	54.6	8.3	53.8	7.6	−0.8
Verbal Similarities	52.2	11.0	51.7	8.8	−0.5	54.8	10.9	50.0	7.6	−4.8
Matrices	54.9	10.3	51.4	8.5	−3.5	53.2	10.1	53.9	9.5	0.7
Seq. & Quantitative Reasoning	53.9	9.3	51.3	9.4	−2.6	53.8	9.8	53.2	7.2	−0.6
Recall of Designs	54.3	11.7	51.1	8.8	−3.2	54.2	10.0	50.4	11.7	−3.9
Pattern Construction	54.2	9.2	52.1	9.1	−2.1	53.7	10.3	52.7	9.2	−1.0
Recall of Objects–Immediate	53.4	10.6	53.3	11.6	−0.1	50.7	12.9	50.7	9.5	0.1
Recall of Objects–Delayed	52.0	10.6	53.4	10.5	1.4	50.5	13.7	49.8	8.4	−0.6
Recall of Digits Forward	49.8	9.9	51.0	10.2	1.2	50.4	9.8	48.8	10.2	−1.6
Speed of Information Processing	52.7	10.1	50.9	9.0	−1.8	54.2	9.7	52.9	10.1	−1.3
Verbal	102.5	15.0	102.4	12.8	−0.1	105.5	17.8	102.7	10.8	−2.8
Nonverbal Reasoning	107.2	15.0	101.9	13.4	−5.3	107.1	14.1	105.2	11.1	−1.8
Spatial	106.8	14.8	102.5	12.6	−4.3	104.8	15.3	102.3	16.0	−2.4
School-Age GCA	105.4	15.0	102.7	12.6	−2.7	108.0	14.2	104.0	12.6	−3.9

N for Standardization Sampling ranged from 209 to 313; N for ADHD Sampling = 26

Time between testing: Standardization Sampling = 6 to 68 days; ADHD Sampling: 3.4 to 6.8 years scores were observed (Schlachter, Dumont, & Willis, unpublished manuscript). In almost all cases, the test scores on the DAS-II were lower than their earlier scores on the original DAS. Only Matrices and Recall of Objects–Immediate were higher on the DAS-II, and in each case by less than 1 point. The smallest mean difference in composite scores was shown by the Nonverbal Reasoning cluster, with a mean score on the DAS-II 1.8 points lower than that on the DAS. The greatest difference in composite scores was shown by the GCA, with the mean score on the DAS-II being 3.9 points lower than that on the DAS. For individual subtests, the largest change between the DAS and the DAS-II was on Verbal Similarities and Recall of Designs (–4.8 and –3.9 points, respectively).

STANDARDIZATION AND PSYCHOMETRIC PROPERTIES

The DAS-II was standardized and normed on 3,480 children selected to be representative of non-institutionalized, English-proficient children aged 2 years 6 months through 17 years 11 months living in the United States during the period of data collection (2005). Although the DAS-II standardization excluded those children with severe disabilities (since for these children the DAS-II would be inappropriate), it did include children with mild perceptual, speech, and motor impairments, if the examiner judged that the impairments did not prevent the valid administration of the test. The demographic characteristics used to obtain a stratified sample were age, sex, race/ethnicity, parental educational level, and geographic region.

Additional samples of children, ranging in size from 54 to 313, were tested during standardization with three additional cognitive measures, three achievement measures, and two measures of school readiness, to provide evidence of validity. These additional children were not included in the norms calculation.

For the category of race/ethnicity, individuals were classified as White (N = 2,176), African American (N = 538), Hispanic American (N = 595), Asian (N = 137) and Other (N = 34). The five parental education categories ranged from one to eight years of education to 16 or more years of education. The four geographic regions sampled were Northeast, Midwest, South, and West. Demographic characteristics were compared to the October 2005 U.S. Census populations and were matched in three-way tables across categories and not just within single categories (i.e., age × race × parent education; age × sex × parent education; age × sex × race; and age × race × region). Total sample percentages of these categories and subcategories were very close to the Bureau of the Census data and seldom different by more than 1 percentage point.

In the standardization sample, there were 18 age groups: 2:6–2:11, 3:0–3:5,

3:6–3:11, 4:0–4:5, 4:6–4:11, 5, 6, 7, 8, 9, 10, 11, 12, 13, 14, 15, 16, and 17 years. In each six-month age group between 2 years 6 months and 4 years 11 months, there was a total of 176 children, while from ages 5 through 17 there were 200 children in each one-year age group. In each six-month age group between 2 years 6 months and 4 years 11 months, there were approximately equal numbers of males and females, while for all remaining age groups there were 100 males and 100 females per group. In our opinion, this sampling methodology was excellent.

RELIABILITY OF THE DAS-II

The DAS-II has excellent reliability (see Rapid Reference 1.7 for the average internal consistency reliability and standard error of measurement (SEm) for each Composite and Cluster). Average internal consistency reliability coefficients for the GCA and the Special Nonverbal Composites are above .90 for the Lower Early Years, Upper Early Years, and School-Age level. For the clusters, average internal consistency reliability coefficients for the Lower Early Years, Upper Early Years, and School-Age level are (a) .93, .89, and .89 for Verbal Ability (b) .87, .89,

≡ Rapid Reference 1.7

Average DAS-II Cluster Reliabilities

Composites / Cluster	Average internal consistency r_{xx}	SEm
GCA (Early Years, Lower)	.94	3.82
GCA (Early Years, Upper)	.96	3.10
GCA (School-Age)	.96	2.91
SNC (Early Years, Upper)	.95	3.45
SNC (School-Age)	.96	3.00
Verbal Ability (Early Years, Lower)	.93	4.11
Verbal Ability (Early Years, Upper)	.89	4.94
Verbal Ability (School-Age)	.89	5.04
Nonverbal Ability (Early Years, Lower)	.87	5.41
Nonverbal Reasoning Ability (Early Years, Upper)	.89	5.07
Nonverbal Reasoning Ability	.92	4.22
Spatial Ability (Early Years, Upper)	.95	3.40
Spatial Ability (School-Age)	.95	3.45
Working Memory (5–0 to 17–11)	.95	3.53
Processing Speed (5–0 to 17–11)	.90	4.80
School Readiness (5–0 to 8–11)	.90	5.09

and .92 for Nonverbal Reasoning Ability, (c) .95 for Spatial Ability, (d) .95 for Working Memory, (e) .90 for Processing Speed, and (f) .90 for School Readiness. These numbers indicate that all of these overall cluster scores are "reliable," the term "reliable" being defined by Sattler (2008) as a reliability coefficient with a value between .80 and .99.

Subtest Reliabilities

The internal consistency reliabilities for the subtests are lower than those for the GCA and the clusters, as would be expected (see Rapid Reference 1.8 for the average internal consistency reliability and SEm for each DAS-II subtest). Across all ages, the average internal consistency reliabilities range from a low of .77 for Picture Recognition to a high of .95 for Pattern Construction. Core

≡ Rapid Reference 1.8

Average DAS-II Subtest Reliabilities

Subtest, cluster, and GCA	Average internal consistency r_{xx}	Average SEm
Core		
Verbal Comprehension	.86	3.57
Picture Similarities	.83	4.25
Naming Vocabulary	.81	4.44
Pattern Construction	.95	2.38
Pattern Construction–Alternative	.94	2.63
Matrices	.84	4.09
Copying	.89	3.34
Recall of Designs	.86	3.79
Word Definitions	.81	4.44
Verbal Similarities	.81	4.36
Sequential and Quantitative Reasoning	.92	2.97
Diagnostic		
Recall of Objects–Immediate	.82	4.34
Recall of Digits Forward	.92	2.98
Recognition of Pictures	.77	4.84
Early Number Concepts	.88	3.49
Matching Letter-Like Forms	.87	3.68
Recall of Sequential Order	.92	2.86
Speed of Information Processing	.91	3.05
Recall of Digits Backward	.90	3.20
Phonological Processing	.91	2.82
Rapid Naming	.81	4.38

subtests ranged from .81 (Naming Vocabulary, Word Definitions and Verbal Similarities) to .95 (Pattern Construction). Reliability of the Diagnostic subtests was also generally high, ranging from a low of .77 for Recognition of Pictures to a high of .92 for Recall of Digits Forward. Subtest reliabilities therefore range from "relatively reliable" (that is, between .70 and .79) to "reliable" (over .80; Sattler, 2008).

Standard Errors of Measurement

The average standard errors of measurement (SEm) in standard score points (that is, with a mean of 100 and standard deviation (SD) of 15) for the Early Years and School-Age batteries (respectively) were 3.82 and 2.91 for the GCA, 3.45 and 3.00 for the SNC, 5.04 and 4.11 for the Verbal clusters, 5.41 and 4.22 for the Nonverbal clusters, and 3.53 and 3.45 for the Spatial clusters. Diagnostic clusters had SEms that ranged from 3.53 (Working Memory) to 5.09 (School Readiness).

Across the 13 whole-age groups (5 to 17), the average standard errors of measurement for the subtests in *T* score units (that is, with a mean of 50 and a SD of 10) range from 2.38 (Pattern Construction) to 4.84 (Recognition of Pictures).

Test-Retest Reliability

In the standardization sample, the stability of the DAS-II was assessed by having 369 individuals retested after an interval ranging from 1 to 9 weeks. The results of the test-retest study showed that for the age groups (3:6–4:11, 5:0–8:11, 10:0–10:11, 11:0–11:11, 14:0–14:11, and 15:0–15:11), reliability coefficients ranged from .92 for the GCA; .89 for the Verbal and Spatial Clusters; .88 for the School Readiness Cluster; .87 for Working Memory Cluster .83 for Processing Speed; and .81 for the Nonverbal Reasoning Cluster. Thus, the DAS-II provides reliable GCA and Cluster scores.

Stability coefficients for the DAS-II subtests ranged from a low of .63 for Matching Letter-Like Forms and Recognition of to a high of .91 for Naming Vocabulary. Subtest stability coefficients are therefore classified according to Sattler's (2008) system as ranging from "marginally reliable" (that is, between .60 and .69) to "reliable."

Changes in Composite and Subtest Scores

An examination of the mean test-retest scores and standard deviations for the Verbal, Nonverbal, Spatial, and GCA for the age groups found the following.

> ## CAUTION
> ....
> It would generally not be good practice to re-administer the DAS-II to a child after a short period of time.

On average, from the first to the second testing, the GCA increased by 5.1 points, the Verbal cluster by 3.7 points, the Nonverbal Reasoning 5.8 points, and the Spatial 3.3 points. Working Memory and Processing Speed had the lowest test-retest score gains of all the composites (2.4 and 2.1 respectively) while the School Readiness cluster showed the greatest increase of 5.2 points.

As with the Composite and cluster scores, each of the DAS-II subtests showed modest gains on retest, ranging from a low of .5 (Rapid Naming) to 6.8 (Recall of Objects-Immediate) T score points. In general, test-retest gains are smallest for the subtests that contribute to the Working Memory and Processing Speed clusters.

When the DAS-II is administered a second time, within 1 to 9 weeks, children are likely to have greater gains on the Nonverbal Reasoning Ability subtests than on the Verbal or Spatial subtests. The magnitude of the gains from first testing to second testing appears to account for the relative instability of the scores as well as the fact that children may be able to recall the types of items they were administered the first time and the strategies they used to solve the problems. Unless there was an imperative reason for doing so, it would generally not be good practice to re-administer the DAS-II to a child after a short period of time. If such re-administration were needed for some reason, the examiner should take into account the average gains cited above.

VALIDITY OF THE DAS-II

Criterion Validity

The degree to which a test is related to an established criterion measure, when both instruments are administered at approximately the same time, reflects concurrent validity. The DAS-II *Introductory and Technical Handbook* (Elliott, 2007b), pp. 163–207, reports the findings of a series of studies in which the DAS-II was given along with the original DAS, the Wechsler Preschool and Primary Scale of Intelligence–Third Edition (WPPSI-III; Wechsler, 2002), Wechsler Intelligence Scale for Children–Fourth Edition (WISC-IV; Wechsler, 2003), and the Bayley Scales of Infant and Toddler Development–Third Edition (Bayley-III; Bayley, 2006). The validity studies in these tables are based on samples that ranged in size from 42 to 313 and included samples of both nonclinical and clinical populations. Below is a summary of some of those studies.

Rapid References 1.9 and 1.10 indicate that the DAS-II has satisfactory concurrent validity. The GCA correlates with other global measures of intelligence developed and published by PsychCorp, ranging from moderate (.59 with the Bayley-III) to high (.88 with the original DAS). Overall, the mean correlation was high (Mr = .80).

For measures of academic achievement, the DAS-II GCA correlated well with the Total scores of tests of academic achievement, ranging from

≣ *Rapid Reference 1.9*

Summary of DAS-II Correlations With Other Measures of Intelligence

Criterion		GCA
DAS		
	GCA	.88
WPPSI–III		
	Full Scale	.87
WISC–IV		
	Full Scale	.84
Bayley–III		
	Cognitive	.59

.79 with the Wechsler Individual Achievement Test, 2nd ed. (WIAT-II; Psychological Corporation, 2001) for a sample of children identified with ADHD and LD, to .82 with the WIAT-II for a non-clinical sample.

Special Groups

The DAS-II *Introductory and Technical Handbook* presents 12 special group studies, summarized in Rapid Reference 1.11. Following are highlights of those tables:

≣ *Rapid Reference 1.10*

Summary of DAS-II GCA Correlations with Measures of Achievement

	Reading	Math	Written Language	Total Achievement
WIAT-II (Nonclinical)	.72	.77	.66	.82
WIAT-II (ADHD-LD)	.62	.84	.30	.79
WIAT-II (LD-R)	.67			
WIAT-II (LD-M)		.73		
KTEA-II	.67	.74	.65	.81
WJ III	.70	.82	.71	.80

≡ *Rapid Reference 1.11*

DAS-II Special Group Study Results

Special group	Verbal	Nonverbal Reasoning	Spatial	Working Memory	Processing Speed	School Readiness	GCA
Intellectually gifted	125.4	121.4	117.8	116.7	112.0	114.6	125.4
Mental retardation	54.1	60.7	58.8	57.3	67.8	49.9	51.0
Reading disorder	92.1	91.2	93.0	91.4	89.8	92.9	90.6
Reading and written expression dis.	93.1	90.4	89.6	90.2	87.7	87.8	89.5
Mathematics disorder	95.5	87.8	90.2	89.5	85.5	87.0	89.3
Learning disorder & ADHD	94.2	93.9	92.7	88.5	90.3	90.7	92.5
Attention-deficit/hyperactivity dis.	102.1	99.7	98.9	98.1	95.5	97.9	100.2
Expressive language disorder	85.7	91.3	85.9	85.7	89.3	83.8	85.7
Mixed receptive-expressive lan. dis.	80.8	81.7	81.4	76.2	86.2	79.2	78.5
Deaf/Hard of Hearing		98.5	101.3				100.0*
Limited English Proficiency	85.6	97.6	104.8	91.2	93.2	95.4	94.8
Developmental Disorder	94.0	92.8	95.8				92.5

*For the Deaf/Hard of Hearing, the SNC is used.

- Intellectually gifted: The sample obtained a mean GCA score of 125.4. The individual Cluster scores ranged from 112.0 (Processing Speed) to 125.4 (Verbal).

- Mental retardation—mild or moderate: The sample obtained a General Conceptual Ability score of 51.0. The individual Cluster scores ranged from 49.9 (School Readiness) to 67.8 (Processing Speed).

- Reading disorder: The sample obtained a mean General Conceptual Ability score of 90.6. The individual mean Cluster scores ranged from 89.8 (Processing Speed) to 93.0 (Spatial).

- Reading and written expression disorders: The sample obtained a mean General Conceptual Ability score of 89.5. The individual mean Cluster scores ranged from 87.7 (Processing Speed) to 93.1 (Verbal).

- Mathematics disorder: The sample obtained a mean General Conceptual Ability score of 89.3. The individual mean Cluster scores ranged from 85.5 (Processing Speed) to 95.5 (Verbal).

- Attention-deficit/hyperactivity disorder: The sample obtained a mean General Conceptual Ability score of 100.2. The individual mean Cluster scores ranged from 97.5 (Processing Speed) to 102.1 (Verbal).

- Attention-deficit/hyperactivity disorder and Learning disorder: The sample obtained a mean General Conceptual Ability score of 92.5. The individual mean Cluster scores ranged from 88.5 (Working Memory) to 94.2 (Verbal).

- Expressive language disorder: The sample obtained a mean General Conceptual Ability score of 85.7. The individual mean Cluster scores ranged from 83.8 (School Readiness) to 91.3 (Nonverbal Reasoning).

- Mixed receptive-expressive language disorder: The sample obtained a mean General Conceptual Ability score of 78.5. The individual mean Cluster scores ranged from 76.2 (Working Memory) to 86.2 (Processing Speed).

- Limited English Proficiency: The sample obtained a mean General Conceptual Ability score of 94.8. The individual mean Cluster scores ranged from 85.6 (Verbal) to 104.8 (Spatial).

- Developmentally At Risk: The sample obtained a mean General Conceptual Ability score of 92.5. The individual mean Cluster scores ranged from 92.8 (Nonverbal Reasoning) to 95.8 (Spatial).

- Deaf/Hard of Hearing: The sample obtained a mean Special Nonverbal Composite score of 100.0. The individual mean Cluster scores ranged from 98.5 (Nonverbal Reasoning) to 101.3 (Spatial).

DAS-II SUBTESTS AS MEASURE OF g

Examination of the loadings of subtests on the general factor allows one to determine the extent to which the DAS-II subtests measure this general factor, which is often referred to as psychometric g. The factor is also often—and misleadingly—referred to as general, global, or overall intelligence. As long ago as 1927, Charles Spearman, one of the great pioneers of the study and measurement of human abilities, observed that "in truth, 'intelligence' has become a mere vocal sound, a word with so many meanings that finally it has none" (p. 14). He went on, "For scientific purposes, then, 'intelligence' can best be thrown out altogether" (p. 196).

So what is the nature of psychometric g? Elliott (2007b, p. 17) states, "Psychometric g is the general ability of an individual to perform complex mental processing that involves conceptualization and the transformation of information."

The DAS-II *Introductory and Technical Handbook* provides g loadings for all subtests for four age groups. These are derived from the confirmatory factor analyses that were conducted on the DAS-II standardization data, and are arguably the best method of estimating g loadings. The traditional way of doing this has been by taking the first unrotated loadings from either a principal components analysis or a factor analysis. This is the method favored by Sattler, and estimates using this method may be found in Sattler, Dumont, Willis, and Salerno (2008).

Across all ages for which each subtest is normed, the 20 DAS-II subtests had g loadings ranging from a low of .38 (Speed of Information Processing) to a high of .81 (Early Number Concepts). The best measures of g includes five Core (Naming Vocabulary, Sequential and Quantitative Reasoning, Verbal Comprehension, Pattern Construction, and Matrices) and two Diagnostic (Early Number Concepts and Recall of Sequential Order) subtests. The poorest measures of g are Recall of Objects, Rapid Naming, and Speed of Information Processing, each a Diagnostic subtest (see Figure 1.2).

SUBTEST SPECIFICITY

Subtest specificity refers to the proportion of a subtest's variance that is both reliable (that is, not due to errors of measurement) and distinct to the subtest (that is, not overlapping with other subtests). Although individual subtests on the DAS-II overlap in their measurement properties (that is, one of the components of the reliable variance for most subtests is common factor variance), all

Good measure of g		Fair measure of g		Poor measure of g	
Subtest	Average loading of g	Subtest	Average loading of g	Subtest	Average loading of g
ENC [a]	.81	PC [d]	.70	RObjI [c]	.51
NVoc [a]	.81	PhP [c]	.70	RObjI [d]	.49
SQR [d]	.78	PSim [b]	.68	RObjI [b]	.44
ENC [b]	.76	VSim [d]	.68	RN [c, d]	.43
SQR [c]	.76	RDigB [c]	.68	RPic [b]	.42
VComp [a]	.75	PC [b]	.67	SIP [c]	.41
PC [c]	.72	WD [c, d]	.67	SIP [d]	.38
Mat [c, d]	.72	VSim [c]	.67		
RSO [c]	.72	RDes [c]	.66		
		RDigB [d]	.66		
		RSO [d]	.66		
		NVoc [b]	.65		
		RDes [d]	.65		
		MLLF [b]	.64		
		Copying [b]	.62		
		RDigF [b]	.62		
		VComp [b]	.61		
		PSim [a]	.60		
		RDigF [a, c]	.60		
		PC [a]	.59		
		RPic [a]	.59		
		RPic [b]	.57		
		Mat [b]	.57		
		RDigF [d]	.57		
		RPic [c]	.53		
		PSim [a]	.53		

[a] Ages 2:6 to 3:5.

[b] Ages 4:0 to 5:11.

[c] Ages 6:0 to 12:11.

[d] Ages 6:0 to 17:11.

ENC = Early Number Concepts; MLLF = Matching Letter-Like Forms; NVoc = Naming Vocabulary; PC = Pattern Construction; PhP = Phonological Processing; PSim = Picture Similarities; RDes = Recall of Designs; RDigB = Recall of Digits Backward; RDigF = Recall of Digits Forward; RN = Rapid Naming; RObjI = Recall of Objects-Immediate; RPic = Recognition of Pictures; RSO = Re call of Sequential Order; SIP = Speed of Information Processing; SQR = Sequential & Quantitative Reasoning; VComp. = Verbal Comprehension; VSim = Verbal Similarities; WD = Word Definitions

Figure 1.2 DAS-II Subtests as Measures of g at the Early Years and School-Age Levels

Source: Adapted from Elliott (2007b, p. 162). Differential Ability Scales–Second Edition. Adapted by permission. Reproduced by permission of the Publisher, The Psychological Corporation. All rights reserved. "Differential Ability Scales–Second Edition" and "DAS-II" are trademarks of The Psychological Corporation.

Battery	Mean s	Range of s
DAS-II Early Years	.43	.25 to .68
DAS-II School-Age	.41	.17 to .75
WPPSI-III	.34	.16 to .51
WISC-IV	.38	.18 to .60
KABC-II	.41	.11 to .70
SB5 (ages 3-5)	.28	.14 to .47
SB5 (ages 6-10)	.24	.09 to .37
SB5 (ages 11-16)	.25	.11 to .41
WJ III COG (ages 6-13)	.43	.11 to .63
WJ III COG (ages 4-5)	.44	.00 to.76

Figure 1.3 Specificity of Various Cognitive Batteries

Note: s, specificity (proportion of reliable specific variance)

These figures are adapted from Table 18.5 in Contemporary Intellectual Assessment, Flanagan and Harrison (2005)

DAS-II subtests possess sufficient (ample or adequate) specificity to justify the interpretation of specific subtest functions. This important characteristic is not true of all tests of cognitive ability. In many tests of cognitive abilities, some or all of the subtests lack sufficient specificity to be interpreted individually. Those subtests do not stand alone, but only contribute to their scale or factor within the test or only to the total test score. Figure 1.3 shows the mean specificity and ranges for various cognitive batteries. As noted, the DAS-II mean specificities of .43 for the Early Years battery and .41 for the School-Age battery are high. These mean specificities are similar to those of the KABC-II and the WJ III COG, but greater than those of the Wechsler scales or the Stanford-Binet 5.

RANGE OF GCAs, SNCs, CLUSTER STANDARD SCORES

The GCAs and SNCs can range from 30 to 170. Although this range is not available at all ages (Sattler, Dumont, Willis, & Salerno, 2008, pp. 623–624), the DAS-II does provide, at all ages, GCA and SNC scores that are between 48 and 170. For the Verbal, Nonverbal, Nonverbal Reasoning, and Spatial Clusters, at all ages the scores fall between 52 and 157. Across all ages, the Working Memory Composite scores ranges from 69 to 150; the Processing Speed Composite from 57 to 170; and the School Readiness Composite from 42 to 108. Although there appears to be some ceiling effect on the School Readiness Composite, this restriction is mainly at the upper ages for which the composite can be administered. As you would expect, the School Readiness Composite was designed primarily for use with children between the ages of five and six, and at these ages the Composite scores range from 42 to 138. As far as the other composite scores are concerned, the restriction of range that is found is always at the extremes of the age range for the composite. For most ages, the full range of standard scores is available.

RANGE OF SUBTEST *T* SCORES

The DAS-II provides *T* scores that can range from 10 to 90 (−4 to +4 standard deviations from the mean, percentile ranks 0.01 to 99.99), but this range is not available for all subtests at all ages of the test (Sattler, Dumont, Willis, & Salerno, 2008, pp. 623–624). None of the 20 cognitive subtests provides a *T* score of 10 at the lowest ages administered, and only seven of the 20 cognitive subtests provide a *T* score of 90 at the highest ages administered. Although the score range limitations must be viewed carefully, you should remember that many subtests can be administered at either a typical age, an extended age, or at an out-of-level age. Examination of Core and Diagnostic subtest score range finds that when subtests are administered at the ages for which they are primarily intended, adequate floor and ceiling exists. Only a few Diagnostic subtests have range restrictions that must be viewed carefully. See Rapid Reference 1.12 and 1.13 for details of the range of subtest *T* scores by age.

On the Core subtests at the lower Early Years (Verbal Comprehension, Picture Similarities, Naming Vocabulary, and Pattern Construction), all have adequate ceiling. Each has some minor limits to their lowest *T* score (19 to 23, percentile ranks 0.1 to 0.3). On the Core subtests at the Upper Early Years (Verbal Comprehension, Picture Similarities, Naming Vocabulary, Copying, Matrices, and Pattern Construction), all have adequate ceiling. All but Verbal Comprehension have some minor limits to their lowest *T* score (11 to 23, percentile ranks 0.01 to 0.3).

On the Core subtests of the School-Age level, four subtests (Pattern Construction, Matrices, Recall of Designs, and Verbal Similarities) provide the full range of subtest *T* scores at all ages. Word Definitions has some minor limitation of floor (minimum *T* score of 17, percentile rank 0.06 at age 7:0) and Sequential and Quantitative Reasoning has minor limitations to its floor and ceiling *T* scores (minimum and maximum *T* scores 18 to 81, percentile ranks 0.07 to 99.9).

Rapid Reference 1.12

Range of Lower and Upper Early Years Subtest T Scores by Age

Ages by Year and Month

Subtest	2 — 6	2 — 9	3 — 0	3 — 3	3 — 6	3 — 9	4 — 0	4 — 3	4 — 6	4 — 9	5 — 0	5 — 3	5 — 6	5 — 9	6 — 0	6 — 3	6 — 6	6 — 9
VComp	19	17	15	12								10-90						
PSim	23	21	19	17	15	11					10-90							
NVoc	19	17	15	13	11						10-90							
PC	20	18	16	14	12						10-90							
Copy					23	20	17	14	11				10-90					
Mat					23	21	19	17	16	15	14	13	11		10-90			
RDf	30	27	24	22	19	17	15	13					10-90					
RPic	30	27	25	23	21	19	17	15	13	11				10-90				
ENC	22	21	20	19	18	17	16	15	13	11		10-90						
ROi							20	18	14	12	11				10-90			
MLLF							32	28	25-89	22-88	18-85	15-82	13-79	11-76	10-74	10-72	10-70	10-67
PhP											16	11	10-89	87	86	84	82	81
RSO											26	25	24	23	22	21	20	19
RDb											34	31	29	26	24	22	20	18
SIP											37	35	33	31	29	27	26	24
RN											14	12	11		10-90			

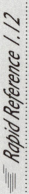

Note: Cells marked 10-90 show ages at which full range of scores is available. Cells with T scores less than 50 show lowest score available at that age. Cells with T scores greater than 50 show highest score available at that age.

VComp = Verbal Comprehension; PSim = Picture Similarities; NVoc = Naming Vocabulary; PC = Pattern Construction; Copy = Copying; Mat = Matrices; RDf = Recall of Digits–Forward; RPic = Recognition of Pictures; ENC = Early Number Concepts; ROi = Recall of Objects–Immediate; MLLF = Matching Letter-Like Forms; PhP = Phonological Processing; RSO = Recall of Seq. Order; RDb = Recall of Digits–Backward; SIP = Speed of Information Processing; RN = Rapid Naming

Rapid Reference 1.13

Range of School-age Subtest T Scores by Age

Ages by Year and Month

	7 (0)	7 (3)	7 (6)	7 (9)	8 (0)	8 (3)	8 (6)	8 (9)	9 (0)	9 (3)	9 (6)	9 (9)	10 (0)	10 (6)	11 (0)	11 (6)	12 (0)	12 (6)	13 (0)	13 (6)	14 (0)	14 (6)	15 (0)	15 (6)	16 (0)	16 (6)	17 (0)	17 (6)
PC									10-90																			
Mat									10-90																			
RDes									10-90																			
WDef	17	15	14	13	11										10-90													
VSim																10-90												
SQR	18	17	16	15	14	13	12		11								10-90								87	84	81	
RDf													10-90										89		88		87	
RPic	88		86		84		82		80		78				74		72	70	68	66	64		62		61		60	
ROi														10-90														
PhP	80		79		78		77		76				75		74		73		10-90									
RSO	18	17	16	15	14	13	12		11								10-90								86	83	81	
RDb	17		15		14		12		11						89		88		87	86	85	84	83	82	81	80	79	78
SIP	23	22	21	20	18	17	16	15	14	13	12						10-90				90	87	86		85		84	
RN														10-90														

Note: Cells marked 10-90 show ages at which full range of scores is available. Cells with T scores greater than 50 show highest score available at that age. Cells with T scores less than 50 show lowest score available at that age.

PC = Pattern Construction; Mat = Matrices; RDes = Recall of Designs; WDef = Word Definitions; VSim = Verbal Similarities; SQR = Sequential & Quantitative Reasoning; RDf = Recall of Digits Forward; RPic = Recognition of Pictures; ROi = Recall of Objects–Immediate; PhP = Phonological Processing; RSO = Recall of Seq. Order; RDb = Recall of Digits Backward; SIP = Speed of Information Processing; RN = Rapid Naming

The range limitations at each level are, as you would expect, usually associated with the youngest and/or the oldest ages at which the subtests are administered.

Diagnostic subtests generally have more restriction in T score range than do the Core battery subtests. On the three Diagnostic subtests at the Lower Early Years level, each has a maximum T score of 90 and they have minimum T scores that range from 22 to 30 (percentile ranks 0.3 to 2). Of the 10 Diagnostic subtests at the Upper Early Years level, seven have a maximum T score of 90 (Early Number Concepts, Matching Letter-Like Forms, and Phonological Processing have maximum T scores of 70, 67, and 81, percentile ranks 98, 96, and 99.9, respectively, at the upper age of the battery), and none has a minimum T score of 10, although the minimum T score for each does range from 14 to 37 (percentile ranks 0.02 to 10). Of the eight Diagnostic subtests at the School-Age level, two (Recall of Objects and Rapid Naming) have a full range of subtest T scores. Of the remaining six subtests, three have a minimum T score of 10, while three have a minimum T score range of 17 to 23 (percentile ranks 0.06 to 0.3). These six subtests also have maximum T scores that range from 60 (percentile rank 84; Recognition of Pictures) to 87 (percentile rank 99.98; Recall of Digits–Forward).

 TEST YOURSELF

1. **Which of the following clusters are included in the computation of the GCA for an 8-year-old child?**
   (a) Working Memory
   (b) Processing Speed
   (c) Spatial Ability
   (d) Verbal Ability
   (e) School Readiness
   (f) Nonverbal Reasoning Ability

2. **If you had to re-administer the DAS-II to the same child over a short period of time, on which Cluster would you expect the least amount of change to occur?**
   (a) Working Memory
   (b) Processing Speed
   (c) Spatial Ability
   (d) Verbal Ability
   (e) School Readiness
   (f) Nonverbal Reasoning Ability

3. **The proportion of a subtest's variance that is both reliable and distinct to the subtest is known as:**

   (a) Reliability

   (b) Specificity

   (c) g loading

   (d) Standard Error of Measurement

4. **You are testing a 7-year-old child believed to have below average intelligence, who is also suspected of having a language disorder. As you test, the child is having little success on the subtests and tasks you are administering. Is it acceptable to administer the battery or subtests from a lower level of the test?** Yes or No?

5. **What is the typical age range for the DAS-II School-Age battery?**

Answers: 1. c, d, and f; 2. b; 3. b; 4. Yes; 5. Ages 7 years 0 months to 17 years 11 months

Two

HOW TO ADMINISTER THE DAS-II

INTRODUCTION

When administering a comprehensive measure of cognitive abilities such as the Differential Ability Scales–Second Edition (DAS-II), it is necessary to use both standardized and nonstandardized procedures. Because a child's scores are derived from comparison to a large sample of children that was administered the same subtests in the same order, it is necessary to follow the standardized procedures to make a fair comparison of the examinee to others who are represented by the normative group. Nonstandardized procedures, which can be just as important, include monitoring examinee behaviors during testing, observations conducted outside of the individual assessment in multiple environments, interviews of the student and informants familiar with him or her, and the administration of informal and nonstandardized measures. The combination of information from all of these sources should be interpreted by a skilled clinician to determine a child's cognitive strengths and weaknesses and, importantly, to understand them. In understanding them, targeted and individualized interventions can be applied in an efficient manner when learning difficulties exist.

Practice Administrations

Prior to the first practice administration with a non-referred examinee, the examiner should carefully read the *Administration and Scoring Manual* (Elliott, 2007a) and, at a minimum, the first four chapters in the *Introductory and Technical Manual* (Elliott, 2007b), and familiarize herself or himself with the *DAS-II Normative Data Tables Manual* (Elliott, 2007c). Familiarity with the test materials will also assist the examiner in test administration. The more times the examiner gives the test, the more familiar he or she will be with the test instructions and procedures. For this reason, we recommend that examiners take the following steps before attempting to administer the DAS-II to a referred child. First, take all items of the test yourself. If you are an experienced examiner, you can manage to administer some of the test to yourself independently, such as by writing your answers to the Word Definitions items. Even experienced examiners will need to recruit a helper to administer some subtests, such as Recall of Digits. This process of taking the test yourself will help you become familiar with the test materials and items. Do not assume that, by itself, your prior experience with the DAS is enough to allow you to administer and interpret the DAS-II. Also, introspection (Wundt, 1858–1862) while you are attempting the tasks may give you some insight into the mental processes involved. Of course, your particular cognitive style and strengths and weaknesses may lead you to approach a task in an idiosyncratic manner, and your approach to the Early Years subtests will almost certainly differ from the methods of most preschool children, but you may still gather some useful insights.

Second, study the *Administration and Scoring Manual* (Elliott, 2007a), the first four chapters in the *Introductory and Technical Handbook* (Elliott, 2007b), the *Normative Data Tables Manual* (Elliott, 2007c), and all the test materials. Use a pencil and a highlighter to make notes in the Manual and Handbook. Start attaching index tabs to the books. Read instructions aloud and practice manipulating blocks, toys, and picture books. Pretend to administer the entire test to a doll or Teddy bear.

Third, with parental consent, it is desirable to observe an administration of the DAS-II by a skilled and experienced DAS-II examiner. You may do this through a one-way mirror, by video, or in person. Afterwards, discuss with the examiner anything you did not fully understand.

Fourth, if possible, it is desirable to practice administering the different levels of the DAS-II to a "tame" adult. Ask them to imagine that they are a child of a given age

Fifth, with parental permission, conduct several practice assessments with children who are not referred for testing. Have a skilled, experienced examiner review your test administration and your Record Form.

Sixth, administer the test to a referred child whose results will have to be reported. Again have a skilled colleague review your work and independently score the child's item responses on Word Definitions, Verbal Similarities, Copying, or Recall of Designs. Discuss any discrepancies with your colleague and resolve them. If you or your peer supervisor suspect any significant anomalies, be prepared to administer to the child another test of cognitive ability with which you are more familiar and base your report on that testing.

≡ Rapid Reference 2.1

Learning the DAS-II

1. Take all items of the test yourself with assistance as needed (e.g., Recall of Digits). Pay attention to how you solve the problems.
2. Study the Manual and Handbook and all the test materials. Highlight, take notes, and attach index tabs. Practice reading aloud the items and following the instructions. Pretend to administer the test to a doll or Teddy bear.
3. With parental consent, observe an administration of the DAS-II by a skilled and experienced DAS examiner.
4. Practice administering the different levels of the DAS-II to adults pretending to be children of different ages.
5. With parental permission, conduct several practice assessments with children who are not referred for testing. Have a skilled, experienced examiner review your test administration and your Record Form.
6. Administer the test to a referred child whose results will have to be reported. Again have a skilled colleague review your work. Be prepared, if necessary, to administer another test of cognitive ability.
7. Periodically review the Manual and Handbook thoroughly and carefully and ask skilled, experienced colleagues to observe you and check your Record Forms occasionally.

Seventh, and last, periodically review the Manual and Handbook thoroughly and carefully and ask skilled, experienced colleagues to observe you and check your Record Forms occasionally. By now you are prepared to do the same for them. (See Rapid Reference 2.1.)

TEST PREPARATION

Testing Environment

The ideal testing room would be a quiet, well-lit, and ventilated room that is free from interruptions and distractions and in which the temperature is comfortable. The examinee should be positioned to face away from any windows and his or her attention should be on the tasks presented, not on other stimuli or test materials not in use. There should not be distracting stimuli on the walls or an abundance of toys in the testing room. It is prudent to work only in rooms with windows that allow passers-by a clear view of you, but not of the child. The child should not have access to the test materials when they are not in use and should not be allowed to play with them as if they were toys. Bring toys if you think play time might be needed. The furniture should be comfortable and sized appropriately for the child so that his or her feet will touch the floor when sitting in a chair. You should also use a low chair to avoid towering over the child. In a school or clinic, you

CAUTION

Any less than minimal standards for the room or use or presence of another person should always be documented in the assessment report

should be able to arrange in advance to borrow a table and chairs, but you may need to purchase a set of portable table and chairs to carry with you. You should have room to write comfortably on the Record Form without the child being able to observe your writing.

Obtaining adequate testing rooms in schools, clinics, and hospitals can be challenging. You may need to write a rough draft of an actual evaluation report excerpt describing test conditions and share that draft with administrators. It helps to develop warm, collegial relationships with secretaries and custodians. Explaining the importance of good testing conditions and the probable consequences of bad testing conditions may help to inspire a collaborative effort by secretaries, custodians, and administrators. If all else fails, you can write honest, accurate, and detailed descriptions of test conditions in your reports.

As discussed below, a special consideration is the presence of another adult in the room. There may be times when an interpreter, parent, or other person may need to be present.

Testing Materials

The examiner and examinee should sit at the corner of a table or desk so that they are at a 90-degree angle to each other. This position is preferred so that the child can look forward without engaging the examiner's gaze, and the examiner can control the child's movement and can see the child's responses from the child's viewpoint. If the examiner is right-handed, the child should be seated on the examiner's left so that the examiner's right hand can be used to write on the Record Form, operate the stopwatch, or gather materials from the test kit. If the examiner is left-handed, the child should be seated on the examiner's right. It is very helpful to have a sufficiently long table to accommodate the *Manual,* the Record Form on

CAUTION

On the CD provided with the DAS-II test kit, the seating arrangement shown in the American Sign Language demonstration video was done only for the purposes of filming and should not be used as a model for the proper seating arrangement.

a clipboard, the stopwatch, pencils, and the materials needed for the current subtest. Holding materials in your lap does not work well.

It is essential that the child not be able to see the Record Form. If the child can see the eraser end of your pencil, you must learn to make 0 and 1 with similar pencil strokes. Children can and will learn to distinguish between the sounds and eraser-end movements of 0s and 1s. An example of making a 1 and a 0 with similar strokes is shown in Figure 2.1.

Only the testing materials that are in immediate use should be visible to the examinee. Stimulus materials can distract young children easily if they are left in view. For this reason they should be kept in the testing kit on the floor or on a chair beside the examiner when they are not in use. Even test materials that are in use should be kept out of reach of children who tend to grab things.

The DAS-II contains a great many stimulus materials—not all of these materials are needed in every administration. The Psychological Corporation (Harcourt Assessment, 2007a) recommends that examiners pack only the components needed to administer the test in the rolling bag and leave the *Introductory and Technical Handbook* and any protocols not needed in the examiner's office. At the same time, this advice must be tempered—the examiner may need the flexibility to pursue clinical hypotheses with diagnostic and out-of-level subtests when needed. The use of varied materials and manipulatives allows the DAS-II to work well with a wide range of examinees ages 2:6 to 17:11. The ultimate goal of the design of the testing materials was for the examiner to be able to spend most of his or her time observing the child rather than arranging the materials. The rolling bag is larger than necessary. Unless you pack additional materials, such as achievement tests and the record folders of the examinees, in the bag, you may wish to visit yard (tag) sales to obtain inexpensively a smaller piece of rolling luggage. You may find that plastic food containers with snap-on lids will help you organize test materials for easier retrieval and protect them from wear and tear. Whenever you find yourself in an office or teachers' workroom with a big paper

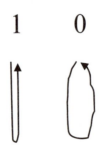

Figure 2.1 Deceiving the Child (!): Making 1s and 0s with Similar Strokes

cutter, take time to make lots of 4" x 5" squares of paper. You can never have too many for the Copying and Recall of Designs subtests.

Manuals, Handbook, and Stimulus Books 1–4

The DAS-II kit includes an *Introductory and Technical Handbook,* which contains background information about the test, its interpretation, and its technical properties. While reading this manual before administration is necessary, and use of it in writing reports is helpful, it is not needed during test administration. A *Normative Data Tables Manual* which is also included in the kit, contains the necessary tables to score the test following administration. Again, this manual is not needed if you use a computer with the Scoring Assistant software that comes with the DAS-II kit.

The *Administration and Scoring Manual* is needed during administration to properly administer the test. It contains all the standardized instructions for administering the DAS-II. It has a sturdy back which has a crease in the middle, enabling the lower half to be folded backwards so that it can stand upright during test administration. The *Administration Manual* of the DAS-II, unlike those for the WISC-IV (Wechsler, 2003), does not reproduce the question or answer for every item in the test, and those can be found only on the Record Form. However, it is nonetheless necessary for the examiner to have both the *Administration Manual* and appropriate Record Form open during every test administration. The *Administration Manual,* for example, provides essential guidelines for querying specific responses to verbal test items.

Stimulus Books 1–4 contain materials that are necessary for proper administration of various DAS-II subtests. When a Stimulus Book is required, it should first be placed flat and closed on the table, within reach of the child, with the coil-bound edge facing away from the child.

C A U T I O N

When first learning the DAS-II, it is very helpful to hand score the Record Form and use the *Normative Data Tables Manual* rather then the DAS-II Computer Scoring Assistant. Once you are fully familiar with how to convert raw scores to ability scores, ability scores to *T* scores, Sums of *T* scores to Standard scores, and so on, you can rely more on the computer program. It is extremely important that you are able to completely and competently score the test without the use of the Scoring Assistant. All the materials needed to do so are provided in the test kit.

DON'T FORGET

The *Administration and Scoring Manual* contains all the standardized instructions for administering the DAS-II.

Correction of Errata

The first printing of the DAS-II *Administration and Scoring Manual* and Record Forms included a few relatively minor errors that were corrected in later printings. If in doubt about your version, you can check this on the DAS-II website (www.DAS-II.com). Click on the "Research and Resources" tab, and then click on "Reference Materials." Details of these changes are also given below in the next two paragraphs.

The first printing of the *Introductory and Technical Handbook* included an error in the Raw Score to Ability Score table for the Matrices subtest. For Item Set 35–36, the Ability Score that corresponds to a Raw Score of 22 should be 155, not 145. This error appeared on page 237. According to the Psychological Corporation, if left unchecked, this error would result in scores that slightly underestimate the ability of very bright children in the 10:6 to 17:11 age range (Harcourt Assessment, 2007b). This error also appeared on the first printings of the Record Forms (Early Years, page 12; School Age, page 11).

Additionally, a set of alternative instructions for the Pattern Construction subtest was omitted from the first printing of the *Administration and Scoring Manual*. This error occurred on page 219 of that *Manual*. Further discussion of this error can be found under that subtest in this chapter. For both of these errors, the Customer Service at the Psychological Corporation (Harcourt Assessment, 2007b) can provide updated pages with adhesive backing that can be applied to the existing pages.

An error that has not yet been corrected (Pamela Trainor, personal communication, April 19, 2008) appears on page 246 of the *Administration and Scoring Manual* on the Sequential and Quantitative Reasoning subtest. The error concerns an instruction that appears to require a positive acknowledgement for a correct response on Items 41–48. This is incorrect. The method of administration should be the same as that for Items 24–31, given on page 244 of the DAS-II *Administration and Scoring Manual*. The revised instructions for Items 41–48 should read as follows:

Items 41–42
Turn to the appropriate page of Stimulus Book 1, point to the blank space, and ask: What number should go here?

If the child passes, acknowledge the response by saying: That's right.

◆ If the child fails, provide the following teaching. Ask the child to tell you how the numbers in the first two boxes go together (or what the rule is). Provide help if necessary. Then ask the child to tell you what number should go in the blank space. Again, help if necessary.

Items 43–48

Items 43–48 are all administered in the same way. Turn to the appropriate page of Stimulus Book 1, point to the blank space, and ask: What number should go here?

After the first few items, repeating the question should be unnecessary.

Record Form

The DAS-II has two record forms: the Early Years Record Form (normally for ages 2:6 to 6:11, but with norms that extend up to 8:11), which has green print, and the School-Age Record Form (normally for ages 7:0 to 17:11, but with norms that extend downward to 5:0), which is printed in blue. Each Record Form includes a table of all the core and diagnostic subtests, showing the ages at which each subtest is normed; a table of abilities measured by the subtests; a normal curve; summary pages showing scores for each subtest; and analysis pages, where scores can be compared. There is space to record behavioral observations on the back of the record form. The green Early Years Record Form contains administration information, forms for recording responses, and ability-score tables for all of the core Early Years subtests and all of the DAS-II diagnostic subtests. The blue School-Age Record Form includes the core School-Age subtests and all of the diagnostic subtests except for Matching Letter-Like Forms and Early Number Concepts.

In addition to the Record Form, the Speed of Information Processing subtests use their own Response Booklets labeled A, B, and C, which must be used for the administration of this subtest. Be sure to keep Response Booklets and Record Forms in stock.

Manipulatives

Manipulatives included in the DAS-II kit include 10 plastic green squares, nine black-and-yellow plastic blocks, six black-and-yellow crepe foam squares, eight natural-finish wooden blocks, a deck of 32 Picture Similarities cards, nine colored chips, an inset tray of wooden figures, a primary thickness pencil without an eraser, a box of toys for Verbal Comprehension (including a car, horse, dog, cat, watch, and pencil), a photograph of a Teddy bear, and a Recall of Objects card. The photograph of the Teddy bear and the Recall of Objects card may usefully be laminated using hard plastic to prevent them from bending or being torn. Always check for glare and reflections while you sit in the child's seat before beginning the evaluation. All of the non-paper test materials provided in the test kit can be hand washed with application of a gentle cloth.

In addition to these materials, the *Administration and Scoring Manual* lists several materials that the examiner must provide. These include a stopwatch (one that operates quietly), two pencils without erasers, one pencil with an eraser (which can be a primary pencil or have a pencil grip), and a plentiful supply of blank, unlined sheets of white paper (approximately 4" × 5").

The *Administration and Scoring Manual* (pp. 105, 149) calls for the Copying and Recall of Designs subtests to be administered with the 4" × 5" sheets of paper and suggests making them by cutting 8½" × 11" paper in quarters. Be sure to present the paper to the child with the longer edge as the base and to number each picture, always in the same corner.

Another item that you may want to provide is a bluntly pointed wooden dowel. Unlike the comparable Wechsler tests, the DAS-II Verbal Comprehension, Early Number Concepts, Matrices, and Sequential and Quantitative Reasoning subtests of the DAS-II have no number or picture labels under the pictures in the stimulus book that the examinee must point to indicate a selection. It may be advisable for the examiner to provide the dowel as a pointing instrument so that the examinee's finger will not smudge the page and thereby provide a prompt to later examinees.

In addition to these materials, we have learned from experience that every test kit should include a hand-held pencil sharpener with standard and primary holes; a spare stopwatch; small, sealed packets of tissues; alcohol wipes for pencils, blocks, and toys; and a little bottle of hand-cleaning solution. Blank paper is also a good thing to have to obtain writing samples and drawings. (See Rapid Reference 2.2.)

ESTABLISHING AND MAINTAINING RAPPORT

Rapport with Children

Much has been written about this topic in other texts. Good advice is given on page 20 of the DAS-II *Administration and Scoring Manual*. For a more amplified account of the development of rapport with preschool children, see Bracken (2007) and also Chapter 6 in Sattler (2008).

≡ *Rapid Reference 2.2*

Items Needed and Recommended Additions for the Test Kit

Needed but not included in the test kit

- a plentiful supply of blank, unlined sheets of white paper (approximately 4" × 5")
- a stopwatch (one that operates quietly)
- two pencils without erasers
- one pencil with an eraser (either a primary pencil or have a pencil grip)

Recommended additions

- a hand-held pencil sharpener
- a spare stopwatch
- small, sealed packets of tissues
- alcohol wipes for pencils
- a little bottle of hand-cleaning solution
- bluntly pointed wooden dowel
- large paper clips or a stapler for saving the Copying and/or Recall of Designs pages
- laminate the Recall of Designs and Teddy bear cards in low-glare hard plastic to protect them

Positive Feedback

It is important for the examiner to use positive feedback to encourage the child's hard work rather than to indicate performance on specific items unless specifically indicated to do so by the directions for that item. The examiner should work at a steady pace and demonstrate enthusiasm and interest by praising the child's work. The *Administration and Scoring Manual* indicates that statements such as "You are working hard!" and "Way to work!" are acceptable. Note that verbal reinforcers that indicate correct answers or satisfactory performance such as "Good" or "Right" are only allowed on teaching items.

If a child performs poorly on an entire subtest and is clearly aware of it, the examiner should say, "That was a hard one. Let's try another one and see if it's easier." Be careful to respond to the child's perception, not to the Ability Score on your record form.

"I Don't Know" Responses

If a child says that he or she cannot answer a question or perform a task, the examiner should encourage the child by saying, "Give it a try" or "Take a guess." Some children will not take a guess, but are willing to take a "wild" guess. It is important that the examiner provide this prompt but also avoid turning these simple urgings into badgering, which can frustrate the child.

If a child asks for help or asks for the examiner to do it, the examiner should respond by saying, "My job is to see how you do it." If on the Word Definitions subtest, the child asks for the examiner to use the word in a sentence, the examiner should respond that he or she is not allowed to do so.

Limit Setting

The examiner should expect age-appropriate behavior of the examinee; to elicit this behavior, the examiner should be polite and respectful but also firm. If an examinee is not exhibiting appropriate behavior during testing, the examiner should evaluate whether the child's behavior is interfering with test administration or the child's performance. If it is not, then either prompts or a break might be appropriate along with a clear review of appropriate behavior.

Breaks

If a child begins to get fidgety or fatigued, the child should be allowed to walk about the room, stretch, or take a short break. Very young children are not as used to sitting for long periods of time in a structured setting. For that reason more than one break may be necessary when testing them.

If a child feels the need to finish at a given time (for recess or for a special event), you should allow for that if at all possible.

Related to breaks is the issue of testing pace. The briskness with which you move from item to item and from subtest to subtest should be dictated by your observations of the child's comfort level, not by your own preferences. Some children's attention cannot be held during even brief pauses in examiner-directed activity, but other children feel pressured by too fast a pace and may begin to respond impulsively or to shut down. Be prepared to administer items and subtests smoothly and seamlessly, without breaks, but be flexible enough to allow them if necessary.

It is important the examiner keep in mind the need to administer Recall of Objects—Delayed at least 10 minutes but not more than 30 minutes after the last

Recall of Objects–Immediate trial. The usual period of time between these two subtests is 15 to 20 minutes and Recall of Objects–Delayed should not be administered more than 30 minutes after the final Recall of Objects–Immediate trial.

> **CAUTION**
> ....
> The briskness with which you move from item to item and from subtest to subtest should be dictated by your observations of the child's comfort level, not by your own preferences.

TESTING INDIVIDUALS WITH SPECIAL NEEDS

Sometimes children with specific motor, sensory, or behavioral problems will require particular adaptations to the test materials and instructions. Some medications or brain injuries will cause fatigue and these children will require frequent breaks. Children with low frustration tolerance will need encouragement. The DAS-II also has specific instructions and procedures for testing children who understand Spanish or American Sign Language (ASL): Appendix B in the DAS-II *Administration and Scoring Manual* (Elliott, 2007a) gives Spanish standard sentences that are used in administering subtests that do not require a verbal response; and ASL signed standard sentences are demonstrated on a video on the CD that accompanies the DAS-II test kit. The DAS-II *Introductory and Technical Handbook* (Elliott, 2007b, Chapter 9, pp. 209–218) also considers accommodations for children with a wide range of special needs.

All adaptations should be planned in advance, possibly by conversing with the parents, teachers, therapists, and specialists, such as teachers of the deaf or teachers of the blind and visually impaired. These individuals can tell you what changes have already been made in the classroom and in other settings. Changes in testing procedures to accommodate children with special needs (e.g., use of interpreters, adaptive equipment) should be noted on the record form and in both the text and the score tables of the resulting psychological report. When these adaptations are provided, the resulting performance may differ so fundamentally from that which was performed by the standardization sample that it would be unfair to calculate a score for the child being tested. Clinical judgment should determine whether a score should or should not be reported.

You must be *very* sure to learn in advance about adaptive and prosthetic devices routinely used by the child. You do not want to complete two long days of cognitive and academic testing before discovering that the child should have been wearing his glasses or that the batteries in her hearing aids or auditory trainer were dead. If a child customarily does all paperwork on a slant board, there is no reason not to, and every reason to allow the child to use the slant board for

Speed of Information Processing, Copying, and Recall of Designs. Special pencils or pencil grips, fidget toys or putty to occupy the non-dominant hand, special seat cushions or adaptive chairs, large rubber bands on chair legs, weighted vests, and brief sensory stimulation breaks are examples of adaptations that should be reported, but would not necessarily invalidate the test scores. In fact, if the child were accustomed to or dependent on such adaptations, denying them might be more likely to invalidate test scores.

GENERAL TESTING PROCEDURES

The following sections cover a number of test administration points that occur across many subtests.

Use of Sample and Teaching Items

Sample Items

Sample items should be completed by the child before the scored items. The purpose of sample items is to clarify the task before proceeding to scored items, so the examiner should repeat or rephrase instructions until the child understands the task. Sample items are always denoted by letters in the *Administration Manual* and on the Record Forms, while scored items are always denoted by numbers. Sample items should never be scored or counted toward the Raw Score—therefore the box next to them on the protocol is shaded.

Not all subtests include sample items. Those that do are Pattern Construction, Matrices, Recognition of Pictures, Matching Letter-Like Forms, Recall of Sequential Order, Speed of Information Processing, Recall of Digits Backward, Phonological Processing, Rapid Naming, and Recall of Designs.

Two subtests have pretest items: Verbal Comprehension Chips and Recall of Sequential Order. Sample items can also serve as pretest items for Speed of Information Processing and Rapid Naming. Pretests are used to determine whether to drop back to a different test booklet on Speed of Information Processing or to discontinue the subtest or section altogether (Verbal Comprehension, Recall of Sequential Order, Speed of Information Processing, and Rapid Naming).

Teaching Items

Regardless of the presence or absence of sample items, the first scored items on each subtest of the DAS-II are very easy for most children of the appropriate ages; therefore failure of one of them can sometimes indicate a misunderstanding of the instructions. The purpose of teaching items is to provide additional instruction *after* a child has failed a teaching item so that he or she can do better on subsequent items. As much as possible, we wish to distinguish between misunderstanding of the task and inability to perform the task.

Teaching can include repeating and rephrasing the question or instruction and providing clues, and if those procedures do not result in the child finding the correct answer, the examiner should demonstrate or say the correct response. The *Administration Manual* contains a paragraph on specific teaching instructions for each subtest in the administrative directions. After a child fails an item on which teaching is permitted, the examiner should score the item as a failure and then teach the item, first by providing clues or rephrasing the question or instruction. Even if the child improves after this initial teaching, the original score of a failure on that item should stand. If he or she does not improve, the correct answer should be provided by the examiner (and, of course, the original failure score should still stand).

If a child passes a teaching item on the first attempt, this child should also receive positive feedback so he or she will be reassured that his or her understanding of the task was correct. If a child passes a teaching item, the examiner should acknowledge the correct response by saying something like: "That's right; now let's try another one." Such feedback should only be given on designated teaching items.

Teaching items are indicated in the *Administration Manual* and on the Record Form with an apple icon (see examples below in Figure 2.2). The subtests of Recall of Objects–Immediate, Pattern Construction, Recall of Objects–Delayed, Recall of Digits Forward, Speed of Information Processing, Recall of Digits Backward, Verbal Comprehension, and Copying have no teaching items.

Teaching should only be done on teaching items if they are among the first items administered or if the child has failed the first items administered for his or her age and has dropped back to an earlier start point that has teaching items. If additional teaching items are encountered as the child passes the start point for an older age group, teaching should not be provided on these teaching items. Figure 2.2 shows an example of this rule

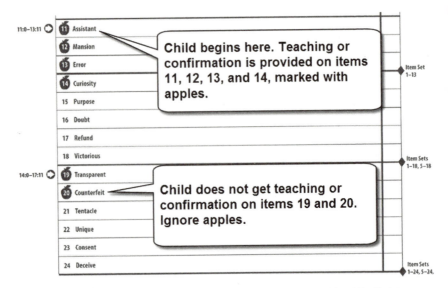

Figure 2.2 An Example of the Use of Teaching Items in Word Definitions

for the Word Definitions subtest. For a child who begins with Item 11, teaching and confirmation would be given for Items 11 through 14 (each is marked with an apple icon). However, no teaching or confirmation is given for Items 19 or 20 because these Items are teaching items only for those children starting the subtest at Item 19.

There are several exceptions to this rule that are noted in the subtest directions and on the Record Forms. First, if the nature of the task shifts within the subtest, teaching is provided on any new post-shift sample items and on the one or two teaching items immediately after the shift. This can happen in the subtests of Matrices, Sequential and Quantitative Reasoning, and Recall of Sequential Order. In Pattern Construction, there are several items with second trials that function essentially as teaching items: 1, 13, 14, 16, 20, 21, 26, and 27. Second, sample items that occur well after the start point are always taught regardless of where the child started. This can happen with Samples D and E in Sequential and Quantitative Reasoning, Sample D in Matrices, Sample F in Recall of Sequential Order, and the sample items in Rapid Naming. Third, the Picture Similarities subtest has specific teaching instructions that are given *regardless* of whether the child passes or fails the item.

The purpose of teaching items and sample items is help the child do as well as possible on subsequent items while preserving the standardization rules. It is this flexibility in the DAS-II's design that has contributed to its popularity as an instrument with children and examiners.

Questioning

Questioning is a useful way to elicit elaborated information or further explanation when a child's response is incomplete, vague, or unclear or if the response is of a borderline quality or is too brief to evaluate with confidence. The examiner should question in such a manner as to not suggest that the first response was entirely wrong and should refrain from giving hints or clues to direct the child toward the correct answer. It should be simply indicated to the child that his or her response should be either clarified or expanded. Some children respond to questioning of a promising but incomplete answer by recanting what they had said and trying an entirely new (and incorrect) response. Try, by your tone of voice, your posture, your facial expression, and perhaps even an approving "Um hm" at the beginning of your question to induce the child to elaborate or clarify, not to recant and start over. Questioning should be indicated on the Record Form with a "Q" after the child's prior incomplete response followed by the child's elaborated response.

Repeating Directions and Items

Repeating directions is another method to ensure the child understands the task. The general instructions that are part of the subtest can be repeated when the child asks for it to be repeated or does not seem to understand the task. The examiner can rephrase these directions as long as no additional information about how to complete the task is provided.

As for the specific individual items of the test, most items can be repeated. The exception to this rule is items of the short-term/working memory subtests (which include Recall of Sequential Order, Recall of Digits Backward, and Recall of Digits Forward). Additionally, Recall of Designs and Recognition of Pictures, both tests of visual memory, also prohibit repetition of items. Repetition of items of these subtests might confer an unfair advantage; therefore it is important that the examiner capture the child's full attention before administering these items. It is also important for the examiner to recognize when these subtests are spoiled by unavoidable interruptions of items. If you are testing in a school, it is prudent to build a good relationship with the person in charge of scheduling fire drills, so you can arrange not to have fire drills while you are administering timed tests. You also need a Do Not Disturb sign that will really get people's attention.

Order of Administration of Subtests

The core subtests of the DAS-II should be administered in a sequence prescribed by the layout of the Record Form and *Administration and Scoring Manual* and before most of the diagnostic subtests. This order of core subtests was designed to maintain the child's interest and elicit optimal performance by starting the test session with relatively nonthreatening subtests that do not require verbal responses and placing demanding subtests in the middle of the administration to avoid start-up and fatigue effects. This order is strongly recommended, but it may be modified under special circumstances. When a child refuses to work on a particular subtest the examiner may temporarily suspend that subtest and administer the next one and return to the suspended subtest when the child appears to be more engaged. For example, Recall of Designs might not be the best starting test for a child with fine-motor difficulties who strongly dislikes drawing tasks. Any alteration should be made based on situational factors particular to one testing situation with one child and not based on examiner preference across testing situations regardless of clinical need. Modified administration order should be noted on the Record Form and in psychological reports based on the testing.

According to the test developers, the diagnostic subtests may be administered in any order, although the order in Chapter 6 of the *Administration and Scoring Manual* follows the order used by the standardization sample. One exception is that the diagnostic subtest, Recall of Objects, has immediate and delayed recall conditions that should be administered with a 20- to 30-minute delay between them with no verbal subtests given during this delay. To control for interference, Recall of Objects is placed among the core subtests, even though it is a diagnostic subtest that does not contribute to the GCA. If you elect not to administer Recall of Objects, simply skip both the immediate and delayed recall tasks when you reach them in the Record Form.

Extended Age Ranges and Out-of-Level Norms

Under most circumstances, examiners will give children the usual age-range subtests for that child's age (Early Years or School-Age). However, the DAS-II was constructed and normative data were collected to give the examiner considerable flexibility to examine clinical hypotheses by providing scores for subtests outside their usual age ranges that may be more appropriate in level of difficulty or type of task for the referred child's ability level. In fact, for children ages 5:0 to 8:11 scores are available for all Early Years and School-Age subtests.

Several core subtests have extended age ranges. Recall of Designs, Word Definitions, Verbal Similarities, and Sequential and Quantitative Reasoning can be given to children ages 5:0 to 6:11 as well as to School-Age children. This extension means that bright children ages 5:0 to 6:11 can be given the School-Age Battery or the examiner can give children these ages the Early Years battery and make diagnostic additions by using the School-Age Record Form to administer one or more of subtests with extended age ranges in addition to the Early Years Battery. Similarly, children ages 7:0 to 8:11 can be given Verbal Comprehension, Picture Similarities, Naming Vocabulary, and Copying as extended age range diagnostic subtests, or children ages 7 or 8 who are less able can be given the Early Years Battery.

By having two subtests that function somewhat similarly with extended age ranges, the DAS-II can allow the examiner to either compare performance on higher- versus lower-order tasks or give more options about what information can be gathered. For example, comparing Visualization ability in the Copying subtest versus Visual Memory ability on the Recall of Designs subtest for a child who is about to enter first grade can provide different information. The Copying subtest can provide information about perceptual and fine-motor skills without having visual memory as a confounding variable as it would be in the Recall of Designs subtest. Other possibilities are evident. For some 7- and 8-year-olds, Naming Vocabulary can provide a more appropriate measure of a child's expressive language and knowledge of names and words (lexical knowledge) than Word Definitions, because it is less dependent on the child having spoken language skills to demonstrate the meaning of words through the longer composed responses needed in Word Definitions. Conversely for an advanced five-year-old child, Word Definitions may provide a better measure of expressive language development. Comparing the two subtests can help pinpoint the cause of a low score on Word Definitions.

Some subtests have had normative information collected for out-of-level testing. These are indicated on Figure 2.2 in the *Administration and Scoring Manual,* on page 30 in the School-Age Record Form, and on page 31 of the Early Years Record Form with an H or L. At these ages the subtest should only be used to measure average-to-high (H) or low-to-average (L) levels of ability. Subtests designed with an H are too difficult to make reliable discriminations among children who are low in ability. But for children who are average-to-high in ability, the subtests are appropriately difficult and can provide reliable information. Out-of-level average-to-high subtests include the diagnostic subtests of Recall of Sequential Order and Recall of Digits Backward at ages 5:0 to 5:5 and Speed of Information Processing at ages 5:0 to 5:11. Similarly, subtests designed as low-to-average are too easy for children of high ability but are appropriate and reliable for children of low or average levels of ability. These subtests include the Alternative (untimed) Pattern Construction subtest at ages 13:0 to 17:11 and the diagnostic subtests of Recognition of Pictures at ages 13:6 to 17:11 and the subtests of Early Number Concepts and Matching Letter-Like Forms at ages 7:0 to 8:11.

The shaded portions of the subtest norms tables in the *Normative Data Tables Manual* indicate those ability levels within an age for which the subtest reliability is relatively low because the subtest is either too easy or too difficult. Scores that fall within the shaded areas should be regarded by the examiner as relatively inaccurate and therefore should be interpreted with caution. However, the Pattern Construction (Alt.) ability scores in these tables are shaded a light gray to help differentiate it from the Pattern Construction score that is located next to it and not to indicate low subtest reliability. The darker shading that is applied to Pattern Construction (Alt.) ability scores at ages 13:0 to 17:11 indicates low reliability levels.

Selection of Subtests

It is expected that normally either the Early Years or the School-Age Core subtests will be selected for administration to a child. Sometimes, if a child is 7 or 8 years old, you will find that he or she hits difficulties with the School-Age Core battery and you need to switch to the Early Years core battery, which is more developmentally appropriate for the child in question. However, it is perfectly permissible to make an *a priori* decision, and choose the Early Years battery as the most appropriate for a 7- or 8-year-old before the session starts.

Diagnostic subtest selection should be guided by referral information and concern. If the concern is reading achievement, then diagnostic subtests such as Early Number Concepts, Recall of Digits Forward, Recall of Digits Backward, Recall of Sequential Order, Phonological Processing, and Rapid Naming are particularly important selections among the diagnostic subtests. If there is a referral concern about letter reversals (or you observe evidence of them), Matching Letter-Like Forms might also be important, although letter reversals are more often a symptom than a cause of reading weakness. If the referral relates to math achievement, then the diagnostic subtests that would relate most significantly include Early Number Concepts, Recall of Digits Forward, Recall of Digits Backward, and Recall of Sequential Order. Diagnostic subtests that relate to writing achievement include Early Number Concepts, Recall of Digits Forward, Phonological Processing, and Rapid Naming. Experts in the field of Cross-Battery assessment have identified the DAS-II as a particularly useful cross-battery instrument to use with the WPPSI-III. In particular *Gsm,* an ability not measured by the WPPSI-III, can be measured using the DAS-II subtests of Recall of Digits Forward and Recall of Digits Backward and *Glr* can be measured using Recall of Objects–Immediate and Rapid Naming (Flanagan, Ortiz, & Alfonso, 2007).

Although we urge persistent efforts to collect referral questions from all interested parties, and we strongly recommend paying close attention to and responding explicitly to those questions, it is also important for evaluators to ask and answer their own questions. Almost all concerns about poor academic achievement, for example, really include a referral question about memory. The question almost always includes at least a component of, "I try to teach the child something, and the child does not remember what I have taught." It is often helpful to give all of the memory and processing speed tests. Memory and processing speed tend to interact. The faster one processes, the less demand there is on memory. If one's memory is very powerful, there's no real hurry in completing tasks—all the components and steps will be recalled as long as necessary. Concurrent weaknesses in both memory and processing speed can, however, severely impair performance on many tasks, such as sounding out words or solving math problems.

Subtest Substitution

Like other cognitive tests, the DAS-II allows for subtest substitution when necessary. Subtests should be substituted only for clinical reasons and never as a matter of individual examiner preference. For example, it is acceptable to substitute when a core subtest is invalidated or a child needs an easier or more difficult subtest to adequately assess ability levels. Unacceptable examples of subtest substitution include situations in which the examiner simply prefers to always use one subtest instead of another in all cases or when the examiner substitutes

DON'T FORGET

Acceptable DAS-II Core Subtest Substitutions at ages 5:0–8:11

Early Years Subtest		School-Age Subtest
Verbal Comprehension	↔	Verbal Similarities
Naming Vocabulary	↔	Word Definitions
Picture Similarities	↔	Sequential and Quantitative Reasoning
Copying	↔	Recall of Designs

a subtest for another after administrating both and finding with the substituted subtest a higher composite score can be obtained. It is important that only one substitution is allowed across the core subtests and that substitution in the DAS-II is possible only between ages 5:0 and 8:11. When substituting one subtest for another, the examiner should always write "(Est.)" for "estimated" next to the index on the Record Form and in any resulting psychological report. The psychological report should also clearly document what exact substitution was used. Table 2.2 in the *Administration and Scoring Manual* indicates acceptable substitutions for core subtests.

Timing

There are several subtests that require timing on the DAS-II. Some subtests incorporate response time as a required part of scoring (Rapid Naming, Speed of Information Processing, and the Standard administration of Pattern Construction). Six other subtests require the examiner to use timing to control the exposure of each stimulus (Recall of Digits Forward, Recall of Digits Backward, Recall of Sequential Order, Recall of Objects, Recall of Designs, and Recognition of Pictures). Recall of Objects also requires timing of the responses and the period between the end of the Immediate subtest and the beginning of the Delayed subtest. A stopwatch icon is used to indicate subtests that require timing. Times are not rounded. For example, 19.99 seconds is still 19 seconds, not 20.

Timing should begin at the precise point indicated in the *Administration and Scoring Manual* for each subtest. The examiner should not pause the timing while clarifying or repeating for those subtests that allow for repetition of instructions or items. The stopwatch should be kept in view, but the child should not be allowed to see the face of the watch. If the stopwatch upsets or distracts the child, it should be taken out of sight. As noted above, it is important to use a silent stopwatch. If the watch you want to buy beeps on stopping or starting, tell the salesperson you will buy the watch if the salesperson will first disable the beeper. Young children may be curious about a stopwatch, and taking a minute or two to show and demonstrate the watch to them before the testing begins may help satisfy their curiosity and foster better rapport with the student.

For the other subtests that do not incorporate formal timing with a stopwatch, there are no strict time limits as to how long the child should be given to respond to a question or complete an item. Therefore the examiner must use professional judgment to decide when the child is going to not respond after a protracted interval. If the child does not respond within an appropriate period of time, the examiner should repeat the item, if allowed for that subtest. If the child still does not respond or repetition is not allowed, the examiner should score that item as a failure and move on by saying, "Let's try another one." It is important that the examiner moves briskly, but also allows for sufficient time for the child to think and respond. Striking this balance can be a challenge. You need to pay close attention to the child's verbal and nonverbal cues. There is a risk of significantly underestimating the ability of a shy, hesitant child who is reluctant to guess in the face of even the slightest uncertainty. However, an excessively cautious examiner with a child who never says, "I don't know," but just sits silently could prolong a test session beyond all reason.

Administering Multiple Choice Subtests

A number of subtests are in a multiple-choice format: Matrices, Sequential and Quantitative Reasoning, Picture Similarities, and Matching Letter-Like Forms. Additionally, one item set (Items 24 to 36) in Verbal Comprehension is also multiple-choice.

With all of the multiple-choice subtests, it is important (as far as the subtest instructions allow) to ensure that the child does not respond impulsively without considering all of the choices. Once the choice has been made it is too late. All you can do then is note in your report that the score might be depressed by one or more impulsive responses that you had failed to forestall. You can reduce impulsive responses by the pace at which you administer the items. Be sure to place the booklet in a position that best allows the child to view all the choices.

One possible strategy to reduce impulsive responding is to admonish the child to "be sure to look at all the choices" or "all the pictures" and demonstrate by sweeping your hand across all the choices. However, if you insert this non-standardized admonition, you MUST NOT do so only after errors and your tone should suggest it is a normal instruction. It must be done every time or in a fixed ratio. Otherwise the child will take the admonition as an indication that the previous response was incorrect. This assumption by the child can distort the child's performance regardless of whether the assumption is correct. Similarly, you MUST NOT let your hand sweep (or your gaze) suggest in any way a possibly favored choice. Always sweep the same way if you need to sweep. Although, if done properly, this intervention should be benign; it is not part of the standardization procedure and must be mentioned in the report.

Prior knowledge of the child's hearing and near vision status is also essential. If the child has a vision problem, you would do well to review the latest Functional Vision Assessment. If a child with a vision problem has not had a Functional Vision Assessment, you might solicit one before your evaluation. More information on testing children with vision and hearing limitations can be found in Sattler and Evans (2006) and Sattler, Hardy-Braz, and Willis (2006).

Recording Responses

It is advisable to record verbatim all verbal and nonverbal responses given by the child. The primary purpose of verbatim recording is to provide a complete record of the child's response to allow clear examination of performance later in scoring. The examiner should be prepared to write down on the Record Form not only the child's incorrect response but also correct responses. These can include not only the verbal responses in Word Definitions or Verbal Similarities but also drawings of designs attempted in Pattern Construction, listings of items recalled and in what order in the Recall of Objects subtests, and any names of items given by the child that were not initially presented, and the exact sequence of numbers given on the Recall of Digits subtests. At the same time, the examiner should strive to be efficient—this balance can be accomplished by liberal use of abbreviations that the examiner would understand later when scoring. Time can be saved by omitting all but initial vowels. Consistent abbreviations are important in case you need to translate your notes for another professional or an attorney or judge.

Useful abbreviations for recording responses

@	at	PI or PX	points incorrectly
↓	decrease	PPL	people
↑	increase	Prmt	prompt
B	both	Q	question/query
DK	don't know	R	reflects before responding
EO	everyone	Rpt	repeat instruction
F	fail	SC	self-corrects
IMP	impulsive	Shd	should
INC	incomplete	SO	someone
LL	looks like	Smtg	something
LP	long pause	U	you
NR	no response	V	verbalizes
OT	overtime	Wld or w/d	would
P	prompt/pass	w/o	without
PC	points correctly	w/	with

SUBTEST-BY-SUBTEST ADMINISTRATION

The specific rules for administering the DAS-II are presented in the *Administration and Scoring Manual,* which should be used during test administration, and which you should have open and ready to refer to while reading this section. The Record Form provides enough information to tempt you to ignore the *Administration and Scoring Manual* while testing. Resist this temptation!

In this section, important reminders for competent administration are discussed, subtest by subtest.

Copying and Recall of Designs

These drawing subtests have a number of features in common. For each subtest you should provide a choice of standard and primary pencils with erasers and with and without rubber grippers, and you should have a back-up pencil of each kind in reserve, along with a sharpener, in case of breakage. The *Manual* calls for sheets of paper approximately 4" × 5," which you can easily create by cutting 8½" × 11" paper in quarters. *Do not* allow the child to put all the drawings on a single sheet, or to see previous drawings, as in the Bender-Gestalt test.

When making 4" × 5" sheets, an office paper-cutting board works much better than scissors. It is prudent to include in your test kit a stapler capable of stapling all the sheets you would use with one child.

The general procedure for each subtest is to provide the child a fresh 4" × 5" sheet of paper for each item. You should number the sheets or quarters with item numbers always in the same corner. This coding allows you to know the orientation of the child's drawing, so you should, after collecting the paper, write "top" at the new top edge of the paper if the child rotates the paper before or while drawing. The word "top" is safer than an arrow, which might later be confused with the child's drawing. You remove the previous drawing and provide the fresh sheet before you present the next item.

The child is allowed to erase drawings and to make a second attempt, but you must not suggest erasing or making a second try. If the child asks or begins to make a second try, immediately provide a fresh sheet of paper (not the back of the original sheet), which you will then mark with the item number and a notation to indicate it is a second attempt (e.g., 7-2). When the subtest is finished, either you or the child should write the child's name and the date on the back of the last sheet used, and you should staple the sheets together. A paper clip is risky.

The Manual requires you to tentatively score the drawings as the subtest progresses. It is generally quite easy to decide if the child's drawing is an excellent copy (Score P+), or if it bears little or no resemblance to the target figure (Score F), or if it's somewhere in between (Score P). This is all you need to decide when carrying out the initial, tentative scoring.

If, at the Decision Point, the child appears to have earned the maximum possible score (marked with P+ in the P/F column in the Record Form) on all or all but one or two items, you should keep going to the next Decision Point. If the child appears not to have passed (at least one point, marked with P in the P/F column) at least three items, you should go back to the previous Start Point unless you have already administered item 1. In most cases, the items between a Start Point and a Decision Point will provide a sufficient number of passing and failing items for a valid score. However, when in doubt, it is better to administer extra items than not to administer enough. You may cease offering more difficult items if you are sure the child has reached the Alternative Stop Point of five consecutive zero scores (F in the P/F column). If the child has not been scored with a P on at least three items up to that point, you should go back to the previous Start Point unless you have already administered Item 1. If the child is not frustrated, and is not failing the items too badly, you may ignore the Alternative Stop Point and continue to the next Decision Point.

The Copying and Recall of Designs subtests take some practice before you can administer them smoothly. You should number the sheets of paper or quarters of full-sized sheets in advance (with some blank extras). Then you need to provide the paper, turn the page in Stimulus Book 1, give the instruction, keep an eye on the child's work on the current item, record a tentative score for the previous item in preparation for the upcoming Decision Point, and turn the page in the *Administration and Scoring Manual* to be ready to assign the tentative score to the item the child is currently drawing. You MUST practice as often as necessary before administering this subtest in a real evaluation.

Final scoring requires careful study of the item instructions. These are on pages 108–147 for Copying and on pages 152–195 for Recall of Designs. Familiarize yourself, too, with Appendix A on pages 279–289 of the *Administration and Scoring Manual* and with correct, careful use of the Scoring Templates. Note that Template A is for evaluating the straightness of lines and for measuring gaps and extensions in lines. Template B is for assessing vertical or horizontal orientation and angles. Once you have administered the subtests a few times you will not often need to use the templates, but be sure to use them whenever there is any doubt.

Finally, if you have difficulty with any aspect of these subtests, consult with an experienced DAS examiner.

Timing Item Exposure for Recall of Designs

After administering the samples, according to the rules on page 151, for each actual test item, you expose the relevant item page from Stimulus Book 1 and say, "Now look at this one." Then expose the item page for *exactly* five seconds. To do this, it may be easiest simply to leave the stopwatch running so you can precisely count five seconds. However you do it, you must expose each picture for no more and no less than five seconds. Be certain to maintain the child's full attention while the picture is being exposed. If necessary, quickly say "Keep looking" if the child looks away before the time is up. Make a note on the Record Form if the child persists in not using the entire five seconds to study the stimulus pictures, especially if the child is aware of making mistakes. If, after removing the Stimulus Book, you prop the partially closed Stimulus Book on its side with the covers facing the child, the stimulus pictures will remain out of view.

Early Number Concepts

For the first two items, all of the squares should be laid out in a horizontal row before the child with about 1/2" to 3/4" between them. The examiner should provide the instructions and repeat those instructions exactly or encourage as necessary. If on the second item, the child has given an initial response as noted on page 253 of the *Administration and Scoring Manual* and is looking expectant or uncertain, the instructions should not be repeated at that point but rather the square should be placed back with the others and the instructions for Item 2 should be repeated from the start. When a child is asked to give you a certain number of objects and cannot count out the number in question, the child is likely to keep tentatively proffering objects until you stop looking expectant (Pfungst, 1911).

The administration and scoring of Item 3 is unique. You should read the detailed special instructions on pages 252 and 253 of the *Administration and Scoring Manual*. Read these instructions very carefully and, as the instructions recommend, practice administering and scoring this item several times. The examiner should give the initial instructions, point to the first piece on the child's left, and continue with the next sentence of the instructions. (If a child with even slightly limited hearing acuity or auditory perception is watching your face for cues, be sure never to talk and point at the same time. Say something, point, give the child time to look, stop pointing, and resume talking.) The child should be encouraged and may be prompted by the examiner saying the first two numbers. But the examiner must *not* count to more than two.

The scoring for this item is based on two different aspects of the child's response. The first reflects the highest number to which the child can recite in the correct sequence. The examiner should circle on the Record Form the highest number the child could correctly count up to and then determine the score corresponding to that number. The second part of the item is the highest number the child points to correctly while reciting. The examiner should once again circle the number on the Record Form that is appropriate and determine the associated score. If the child obtains a score of less than 6, this item should be given a second trial. Scoring is based on the addition of the higher scores from the two trials for each part of the item, so scores of 0 to 6 are possible for the item.

The rest of the subtest uses the Stimulus Book. Item responses on the Record Form are presented from the child's view. Therefore, if the examiner is sitting at a table directly facing the child (which we do not recommend—see page 39), the examiner may find it convenient to rotate the Record Form 180 degrees to more easily score the items. Items may be repeated as necessary as long as the wording is not changed, and questioning may be used if the child's response is incomplete or unclear. On Items 24 and 26, if the child's response is incomplete, the examiner should ask, "Are there any more?" once for each item. If the child fails the teaching items, the examiner should provide teaching, and if the child passes such items, the examiner should acknowledge the correct response by saying, "Yes, that's correct."

Matching Letter-Like Forms

The Stimulus Book should be placed in front of the child and opened so that the single figure is on the top, away from the child. The child is then asked to point to the identical abstract figure from the selection of six choices, five of which are rotations or reversals of the original figure. The examiner should circle the number corresponding to the figure chosen for each item on the Record Form.

The Record Form is constructed so that the numbers on the form correspond to figures in the Stimulus Book beginning from the child's left. Again, if the examiner is sitting directly opposite the child (which is not the recommended arrangement), it may be helpful, during administration, for the examiner to rotate the Record Form upside down.

This is one of the subtests for which the examiner should give the child a bluntly pointed wooden dowel so that he or she can point to his or her response without leaving a smudge mark on the page on the Stimulus Book. Do not stare intently at the child or the stimulus book while the child studies the choices, but remain alert and let your body language convey your belief that, even though you are not participating directly, as you do with most subtests, this subtest is also important. Do not spend the time scoring other subtests.

Matrices

As the child must indicate a choice by pointing to the response, and verbal responses such as naming the picture should be responded to with the examiner saying, "Show me which one," we recommend that the examiner provide the child with the bluntly pointed wooden dowel to allow a pointing response without leaving a smudge mark on the page of the Stimulus Book.

The Record Form is constructed so that the numbers on the form correspond to figures in the Stimulus Book beginning from the child's left. Additionally, directional words in the *Administration and Scoring Manual* refer to the child's point of view. Therefore the examiner should be careful to point to the appropriate part of the matrix when giving instructions and, if sitting opposite the child instead of in the recommended position, may want to rotate the Record Form upside down to make it easier to record in the Response column in the Record Form which item the child selected.

Directions for this subtest may be repeated as often as necessary, but should be repeated as they are presented in the *Administration and Scoring Manual*. If the child passes a teaching item, the examiner should acknowledge the correct response by saying, "Yes, that's correct." If the child fails a teaching item, the specific teaching instructions given in the *Administration and Scoring Manual* should be given. Because of the shift in the nature of the task, teaching should be provided to all children on Sample D regardless of whether they pass or fail this item.

As with other multiple-choice subtests discussed earlier, you may need to retrain impulsive responses and encourage careful consideration of all choices before the child selects one.

You should not increase the child's anxiety by staring fixedly at the child or the stimulus book (especially the right choice) while the child tries to think. However, you should also remain alert and attentive. This is not the time to start trying to score Copying or Recall of Designs! The child must realize that, even though your participation is limited, your interest in this subtest is just as keen as your interest in the more interactive ones.

Naming Vocabulary

For all items in this subtest, the examiner should point to the whole object, using a sweeping motion or several fingers to clearly indicate the whole object, and ask, "What is this?" When the child's response is unclear, the examiner should question to elicit a more detailed response. The examiner should record a Q on the item line in the Record Form to indicate that he or she questioned the child. If the child does not respond, the examiner should encourage the child by saying, "What is this called?" or "Tell me what this thing is." Use the "Tell me what this thing is" version if the picture is of something likely to have a personal name for the child, such as the picture of the kitten (e.g., "Fluffy"). If the child responds with a description of function, materials, or parts, the examiner should point again to the whole picture and say, "Yes, but what is it called?" or "Tell me its name." Again, do not use "Tell me its name" if the picture is of something likely to have a personal name, such as the picture of the kitten or the fish. If the child's response is too general, the examiner should ask for a specific response by saying, "Yes, what kind of . . . ?" And if the child provides a name of a related object, the examiner should ask, "What else could you call it?" If the child responds correctly after questioning, the examiner should give credit for the response. Item instructions may be repeated as necessary, but when repeating instructions, the examiner should carefully adhere to the wording provided. If the child passes a teaching item, the examiner should acknowledge the correct response by saying, "Yes, that's correct." If a teaching item is failed, the examiner should provide teaching by rephrasing the question or providing cues. If necessary, provide the correct response and ask the child to repeat it.

Pattern Construction

In addition to the Record Form, administration of this subtest requires, for Set A, the eight natural-finish wooden blocks, for Set B, Stimulus Book 2 and the six black-and-yellow crepe foam squares, and for Set C, Stimulus Book 1 and the nine black-and-yellow plastic blocks. Sets B and C will both require the use of a stopwatch to keep accurate timing.

For Set A, all items on the Record Form are presented from the child's point of view. The small arrow pointing to CH indicates the child's position relative to the constructed item. The examiner should build his or her own model and leave sufficient space between the model and the table edge for the child to build his or her own structure. For Items 1 and 2, the examiner should build his or her model, leave it standing for a few seconds while the child examines it and then disassemble the model and provide the same blocks to the child for him or her to construct the response. *For Items 3 through 12, the examiner should leave his or her model standing.*

Phonological Processing

"Phonological processing," "phonological awareness," and "phonemic awareness" refer to the ability to correctly perceive, remember, keep in sequence, and mentally manipulate the sounds in *spoken* words. This auditory and cognitive skill is a precursor to and foundation for "phonics," or "phonetic encoding and decoding," or "phonetic analysis and synthesis." Phonics involves relating the sounds in spoken words to written symbols.

This subtest consists of four different phonological tasks in which the child must rhyme, blend, delete, segment, and identify phonemes, sounds, and syllables in words.

The examiner should first listen to the Phonological Processing CD provided in the test kit. This contains administration demonstrations and sample responses for common scoring dilemmas. This CD can be played in any standard CD player, and *the examiner should become familiar with its contents before administering this subtest.* Importantly, this CD is to be used to train the examiner, and *should not be played to the child.* Important points to remember during sound presentation are that all sounds should be produced in isolation and that the letter should not be named when presenting the sound (the difference between saying the sound for the letter "m" and saying the letter "m"). The examiner should not present the sounds in an exaggerated manner nor add vowel sounds at the end of a sound. For example, you should make the crisp sound /m/, not "muh" with a schwa [ə] or "uh" sound added, nor "mmmmm" with the sound exaggerated and prolonged. If these instructions are not absolutely clear, consult with a speech pathologist or a teacher of phonology and phonics.

If the child adds a schwa ([ə] or "uh") at the end of the target sound, do not penalize the child—as this, unfortunately, is the way phonological awareness and phonics are taught in some classrooms. However, you should note the frequent addition of schwa sounds and comment on them in the report. The addition of schwa sounds interferes badly with blending. The /k/, /ă/, and /t/ sounds can readily be blended into the spoken word "cat." However, "kuh," "ah," and "tuh" cannot. They would make something like "kuhahtuh." In your report, you might even commend the child's teacher if the child produces crisp, isolated sounds without schwas.

The addition of some other vowel sounds at the end of the target sound can render the entire response incorrect, so consult the *Administration and Scoring Manual* and CD for specific instructions. All children who are administered this subtest should be administered all four tasks, and each task should begin with the sample item. Instructions and sample items may be repeated but scored items should not be repeated.

For the Rhyming task, nonword (nonsense words, made-up words) rhymes are considered correct.

For the Blending task, a red divider tab is presented in the Stimulus Book as a place holder, as there is no visual stimulus for this task. The examiner should present a brief but distinct silence between sounds for items for this task.

Examiners should be aware of the following error on the Record Forms: Item 52 should be segmented as "$k - r - u - ch$," as there is no /t/ sound in that word. The child should be given credit for either "$k - r - u - ch$" or "$k - r - u - t - ch$."

Phonological Processing is constructed in such a way that you can identify whether the child has a specific strength or weakness in one of the four tasks. The easiest way to evaluate this is by using the Scoring Assistant computer software.

Nevertheless, although scoring Phonological Processing by hand appears, at first glance, to be complicated, it is simpler than it seems. Please turn to the Phonological Processing pages on one of the Record Forms before continuing to read the next paragraphs. The procedure is as follows. First, administer each of the four tasks and stop each task after four consecutive failures on that task. Then count the number of correct responses for each task (ignoring the sample items in colored boxes). On pages 26 and 27 of the Early Years or pages 25 and 26 of the School-Age Record Form, you record the child's responses in the Task 1: Rhyming, Task 2: Blending, Task 3: Deletion, and Task 4: Phoneme Identification and Segmentation boxes. The boxes are labeled Task X Raw Score and have the task number in both the label and in the blue box next to the empty box in which you write the raw score. If you write a raw score of, say, 6 in the Task 2 Raw Score box with the white "2," then be sure to write the same number, 6, in all other boxes with white "2" labels. When you have finished the scoring, all boxes with the same white number or same white letter label should contain the same number written in by you.

At the top of the third page, there are boxes labeled "1," "2," "3," and "4" for the raw scores from the previous two pages. As noted above, the third-page box "1" should receive the same raw score you wrote in box "1" two pages earlier and so on. The Ability Scores (boxes "A," "B," "C," and "D") and Standard Errors (boxes without letter or number labels) are filled in with Ability Scores and

Standard Errors (in parentheses) from the Phonological Processing Raw Score to Ability Score table on the right side of the third page. The columns are Item Sets. Task 1 = 1–11, Task 2 = 12–26, Task 3 = 27–41, and Task 4 = 42–53. The rows are numbers correct in each separate Item Set (Task). Entering the table with the number correct in the first, shaded column ("Raw Score"), you find an Ability Score and a Standard Error (in parentheses) by drawing a horizontal line straight across from the raw score to the Ability Score (and Standard Error) in the correct column for the particular task.

Finding the Differences Between Ability Scores for Task Pairs Required for Statistical Significance is easier than it looks. Go to the table with that title in the middle of the third page of the Phonological Processing subtest in the Record Form. To compare, for instance, Task 3 and Task 4, circle the Standard Error number for the first task (in this example, Task 3) from the Task 3 Standard Error box at the top of the page. Go down to the Differences Between Ability Scores for Task Pairs Required for Statistical Significance. In the shaded column labeled "Standard Error of Ability Score on First Ability Score," circle the number (6, 7, 8, 9, etc.) representing the Standard Error for the first Ability Score (in this case Task 3). Now, go back up and find the Standard Error for the Second Task (in this case, Task 4). Circle that number (the Standard Error) in the row (6, 7, 8, 9, etc.) under the label "Standard Error of Ability Score on Second Ability Score." A horizontal line across from the first score will intersect with a vertical line down from the second score in the box showing the difference between the ability scores required for statistical significance at the .10 level, two-tailed (see Figure 2.3).

Below that table are rows of boxes for computations. In each row, you enter the appropriate ability scores in the first two boxes, subtract, and enter the difference in the third box ("Observed Difference"). The "Critical Value" in the fourth box is the difference between the ability scores required for statistical significance that you looked up for that pair of tasks. If the observed difference is smaller than the critical value for the difference between the ability scores required for statistical significance, the scores on the two tasks are not significantly different from one another and should not be interpreted separately. The difference between the two scores could easily have occurred just by chance even if the underlying skills were the same. If the observed difference is at least as large as the critical value, then the difference is significant at the .10 level, two-tailed. That is, a difference that large would occur simply by chance less than 10 times in 100, so we suspect there may be a genuine difference between the two measured skills.

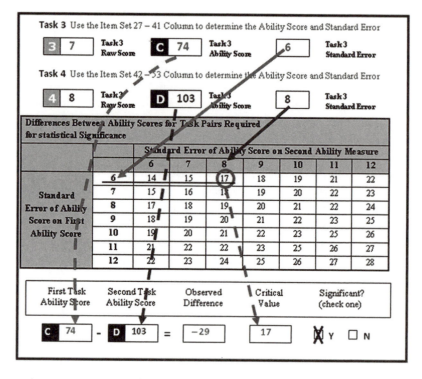

Figure 2.3 Scoring the Phonological Processing Subtest

Picture Similarities

Before administering this subtest, the examiner should arrange the picture cards face down, with the first item card on top. Keep the cards well out of the child's reach. In the Stimulus Book, the vertical lines between the pictures are intended to help the examiner determine the picture under which the child places the card. If the child's choice is unclear, the examiner should ask the child, "Which picture do you mean?" Item instructions may be repeated as many times as necessary, *without modification of the wording.* If a teaching item is passed, acknowledge the correct response using the specific teaching statement provided in the instructions and on the Record Form. If a teaching item is failed, the appropriate specific teaching statement should also be provided, but without the indication that the child's response was correct. The Record Form is constructed so that the numbers on the form correspond to figures in the Stimulus Book beginning from the child's left. Therefore the examiner may want to rotate the Record

Form upside down to make it easier to record which item the child selected in the Response column in the Record Form.

This is another multiple-choice test, so you may need to be careful to ensure thoughtful consideration of all the choices by the child. Do not allow the child to lead you into an excessively rapid administration of this subtest and do not stare at the correct choice.

> **DON'T FORGET**
>
> **Picture Similarities:**
> Be sure to check that the cards are in the correct sequence before putting them away.

As soon as possible after the evaluation, make sure the cards are in the correct sequence. You don't want to waste time or attention on carefully maintaining the card sequence while administering the test, so one or more cards may be out of order. If you do not check them soon after an evaluation, you are not likely to remember to check them before the next evaluation.

Rapid Naming

The examiner will need a stopwatch in addition to the Record Form and Stimulus Book 4 to administer this subtest. The examiner should become *thoroughly* familiar with the instructions in the *Manual* due to the rapid pacing of this subtest. It is important that the child being tested understands that this is a timed task, and so, if the child appears to be moving slowly or does not continue to the next row automatically, there are specific prompts in the *Administration and Scoring Manual*. In addition, if the child loses his or her place while being timed, the examiner should point to the first skipped color or picture and say, "Start again from here." If the child loses his or her place three times in an item, then the examiner should discontinue that item.

The first two items (Colors and Pictures) are characterized as Simple Naming. The third item (Color-Picture Naming) is more complex. The subtest is designed to enable an examiner to determine whether the child has a specific strength or weakness in Complex Naming in comparison with Simple Naming. As in the case of Phonological Processing, this comparison is quickly done using the Scoring Assistant computer software.

Nevertheless, although scoring Rapid Naming by hand appears at first glance to be complicated, it is simpler than it seems. Once again, before reading the following paragraphs, please turn to the Rapid Naming section on one of the Record Forms. On page 29 of the Early Years or page 28 of the School-Age Record Form, you record the child's responses in the A Color Naming, Item 1, B

Picture Naming, Item 2, C Color-Picture Naming, and Item 3 boxes. You draw a slash through any word (color or picture) that is omitted and circle any word that is named incorrectly, writing the substituted word next to or above the circled word. Write "SC" above any self-corrections. Write "Q" wherever you direct the child to "Start again from here." Make an X after the last word named at 120 seconds. Record the ending time (120 seconds or less). Count the number of stimuli named correctly within the 120-second time limit for each item. Do *not* count the six sample stimuli in each of the A, B, and C teaching item boxes, only the 35 stimuli in each of the Item 1, Item 2, and Item 3 boxes (see Figure 2.4).

For each of the three items (Colors, Pictures, and Color-Pictures), record the completion time (120 seconds or fewer) and number correct (35 or fewer). Note that for Color-Picture Naming both the color and the picture name must be correct for credit, so the maximum score is again 35, not 70. Then for each item, go to the Raw Score Conversions table at the top of the next page. The columns are completion times. The rows are numbers correct. Entering the table with the completion time and number correct, you find a Converted Raw Score for each item. The appropriate Converted Raw Score goes into Box 1 (for Color Naming), Box 2 (for Picture Naming), and Box 3 (for Color-Picture Naming).

On the second page, under the Raw Score Conversions table, you will find boxes labeled 1 and 2 for Simple Naming and 3 for Complex Naming. Simply enter the same Converted Raw Scores for Boxes 1, 2, and 3 on the first page to

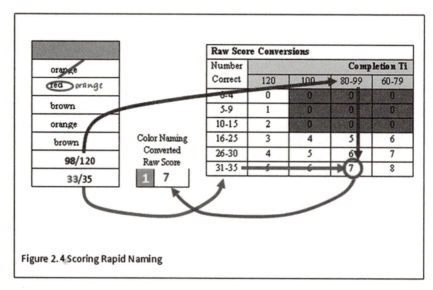

Figure 2.4 Scoring Rapid Naming

Figure 2.4 Scoring for the Rapid Naming Subtest

these boxes 1, 2, and 3 on the second page. At the very bottom of the second page, you will find three more boxes labeled 1, 2, and 3. The same numbers go in those boxes. All "1" boxes on both pages should have the same number in them. All "2" boxes should have the same number. All "3" boxes should have the same number. The Simple Naming Converted Raw Score is the sum of Box 1 and Box 2. In the Rapid Naming Raw Score to Ability Score table on the right edge of the second page, finding the combined raw score (Box 1 + Box 2) in the Raw Score column and draw a horizontal line straight across to obtain the Simple Naming Ability Score to put in Box A and the Simple Naming Standard Error (the number in parentheses) to put in Box B.

The Complex Naming (Color-Picture) Converted Raw Score is copied from Box 3 to the box on the other side of the = sign. Find that raw score in the Raw Score column of the Rapid Naming Raw Score to Ability Score table and draw a horizontal line straight across to the Item 3 column (which is half as long as the Items 1 and 2 column you used before). The Ability Score you obtain goes into Box C and the parenthetical Standard Error goes in Box D.

Finding the Differences Between Ability Scores for Simple versus Complex Naming Required for Statistical Significance is very easy. Go to the table with that title in the bottom half of the second page. Put the number from Box D above in Box D in this table. Put the number from Box B above in Box B in this table. D and B tell you the column and row whose intersection gives you F: the minimum difference between Ability scores required for statistical significance at the .10 level, two-tailed. The Observed Difference between Ability Scores is the Difference (E) between A and C. If the Observed (actual) difference between the Simple and Complex Ability Scores (A − C = E) is as great as the required difference (F) or greater, then there are only 10 chances in 100 (.10) that such a large difference (in either direction) would occur by chance unless the student really was faster with simple or faster with complex naming. That would be a "significant difference" that you might wish to interpret. If the actual, observed difference (E) is less than the needed difference (F), there are more than 10 chances in 100 of the difference occurring simply by chance, and you should treat the simple and complex naming scores as being the same.

Finally, at the very bottom of the page, you add the 1, 2, and 3 score boxes for a Total Converted Raw Score for Items 1 + 2 + 3. Find that Total Converted Raw Score in the Raw Score column of the Rapid Naming Raw Score to Ability Score table on the right edge of the second page and draw a horizontal, straight line all the way across to the third column, which is longer than both the Items 1 and 2 and the Item 3 columns and is not shaded. There you find the Ability Score (and

Standard Error in parentheses) for the total Rapid Naming subtest. The Ability Score goes in the box in the middle of the bottom edge of the second page.

Recall of Digits Forward

An experienced user of the DAS-II could administer this subtest using only the Record Form. However, detailed instructions can be found in the *Administration and Scoring Manual* and examiners should keep the manual open to this page during administration, if only not to lose their place in the *Manual*. The examiner should simply say, "Now get ready to listen. Say these numbers after me"; and then read the numbers at a steady rate of two digits per second.

Examiners who are familiar with other batteries should note that this is a faster rate of saying the numbers than is used on comparable tasks in the WISC-IV and KABC-II. You need to practice with a clock or metronome. If you have a sense of rhythm, we recommend that you do the following: (1) Look at the stopwatch and gently (and inaudibly) start tapping your foot under the table at the rate of 2 taps per second; (2) Maintain this tapping speed as you talk to the child and introduce the items; (3) Then administer the items at the speed of your taps. Don't start administering the items until you are tapping continuously at the correct speed. You may be surprised at how easy it is to maintain the taps even when you are talking to the child!

Also unlike the KABC-II, the examiner should drop his or her voice on the last digit in Recall of Digits Forward (and Recall of Digits Backward) in the DAS-II. But as with other tests, it is very important that the examiner not repeat the number sequences. If necessary, the examiner should prompt the child to listen carefully prior to beginning a sequence and wait to be sure of the child's full attention. If you are testing in a school, try to make sure there will not be a fire drill or other likely disturbance during this part of the assessment. Be sure not to administer this and similar subtests near the end of a class period when bells and announcements over the public address system are likely to be heard. If the child asks for a number sequence to be repeated, the examiner should say, "I can't say them again. Give it a try." After the child's response, the examiner should say, "Listen carefully. I won't be able to repeat the numbers."

If an item is spoiled due to an interruption, the examiner should refrain from repeating the sequence and instead use clinical judgment to decide how to proceed or if the subtest is spoiled. In such a case, it may be best to switch to another subtest and to return to this subtest later.

If the child repeats the digits in a different manner than they were given (says "twelve" instead of "one-two") give credit but then say, "Try to say them just like

I do." If the child starts repeating the numbers before you finish reading them, we recommend that you hold up your hand, palm toward the child, in a "stop" gesture.

Recall of Digits Forward is one of the three subtests (along with Recall of Digits Backward and Recall of Sequential Order) that use a more traditional basal and ceiling procedure

and that give credit for unadministered items before the lowest item administered. Procedures for using basal and ceiling rules are described in detail in Chapter 3.

Recall of Digits Backward

The examiner will again require the Record Form, and it is important that the examiner provides the directions included in the *Administration and Scoring Manual*.

Except for the Sample, and of course the requirement that the child repeat the numbers backwards, administration of this subtest is roughly analogous to the Recall of Digits Forward subtest.

Recall of Objects

The subtest Recall of Objects is actually administered in two different parts— Immediate and Delayed. Both parts require a stopwatch as well as the Recall of Objects card and the Record Form. Representatives from the publisher have suggested that examiners laminate the Recall of Objects card to prevent it from becoming dirty or torn during regular practice with the kit. If you do this, be sure to check for glare from the examinee's viewpoint in the room you are using for testing. The laminate may be more reflective than the original surface of the card. Note that both parts of this subtest are considered Diagnostic subtests because neither one contributes to the GCA. However both parts are administered among the Core subtests, and the administration instructions are included among the Early Years battery and School-Aged battery sections of the *Administration and Scoring Manual*. The reason for this is to control for what happens in the interval between the Immediate and the Delayed trials.

For Recall of Objects–Immediate, it is important that the examiner allow precisely the full time allocated for each exposure. In the Recall time period, the examiner should encourage the child to give as many responses as possible, by prompting the child if no response is produced during a period of ten seconds. If the child indicates that he or she cannot remember any more before the time allowed for recall has expired, the examiner should again prompt as described in the *Administration and Scoring Manual.*

The record form provides the names and picture for each item in alphabetical order to aid you. Don't be confused by this aspect of the record form—the child can recall items in *any order.* When recording the child's response, the *Administration and Scoring Manual* recommends that you place a checkmark on the record form next to the item correctly recalled. This recording procedure may be difficult until you become fluent with this type of recording, since you must search the alphabetized list for the correct item, place the checkmark, and then search again for each recalled item. You may find it more efficient merely to record each item recalled in order in the response column (see the example in Figure 2.5). Another approach is to use the minimum number of letters needed to distinguish pictures (e.g., bl, bsk, bc, brd, boat, bttl, bwl, bs, etc.) Such methods will allow you to record the child's responses more quickly than rewriting the word for each item and will also allow you to record the order in which the items were recalled. At the end of Recall of Objects–Immediate, the examiner should record the clock time (e.g., 10:37) that this part of Recall of Objects ended.

If the child continues recalling pictures fairly steadily after the time limit (45 or 40 seconds) has expired, you may want to allow a few extra seconds, but you must not give credit for any responses beyond the time limit. As a testing-of-limits procedure for a very slowly responding child (perhaps one with a speech articulation disorder or word-finding weakness), you might wish to record responses beyond the time limit until the child is clearly done. You could then comment in the report that the child added more words than the child named during the time limit. However, not only are those additional items not countable, but you have given the child more thinking time, which might be an advantage, and delayed the subsequent trials and failed to signal the importance of quick responses, which might be disadvantages. You would need to describe and explain this adaptive procedure in detail in your report and acknowledge that the scores from Recall of Objects might not be valid. Extra time (without credit for additional responses) for responding on the Delayed trial would not present these problems, but would still require careful explanation.

In both the Early Years and the School-Age batteries, the subtests of Pattern Construction and Matrices come between Recall of Objects–Immediate and Recall of Objects–Delayed. The *Administration and Scoring Manual* states that these

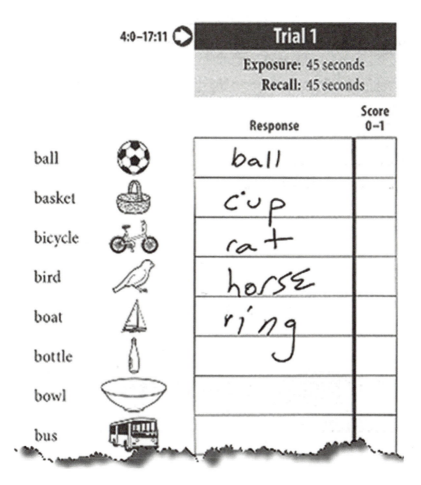

Figure 2.5 Example of Recording a Child's Responses on the Recall of Objects Subtest

intervening subtests were selected to avoid interference with the content of the Recall of Objects subtest. The usual time span between the end of the Immediate and the beginning of the Delayed trials is 15 to 20 minutes. It should not be less than 10 nor more than 30 minutes. For the Delayed trial, the examiner should cautiously present the Recall of Objects card face down on the table without allowing the child to see the side with the objects on it or flip the card over.

For all parts of this subtest, precise timing with a stopwatch is essential. The

Record Form must be kept out of view with even more than the usual care, because the pictures are so clearly printed on the Record Form. Similarly, be very careful to set aside the picture card face down and out of reach at all times.

Recall of Sequential Order

The examiner will require the Record Form and Stimulus Book 2 to administer this subtest in which the child hears a list of the parts of the body in random sequence and is asked to order the list from highest to lowest (head to toe). The most difficult items also require the child to remember one or two additional words that are not parts of the body.

The purpose of Sample Items A, B, and C is to test whether the child understands the concepts of "highest" and "lowest," so if the child fails all of these items or both Sample Items D and E, the examiner should not administer this subtest and should not record a score for it.

The first 12 items are administered with the stimulus picture in front of the child but the examiner should not allow the child to touch the picture. The picture should be removed from the child's view starting with Item 13. Sometimes, the process of obtaining a basal and a ceiling will require you to move forward and back past Item 13, removing and replacing the stimulus picture two or more times.

For each item, the stimulus words should be said at a rate of approximately one word per second (not two) and the examiner should drop his or her voice on the last word. Sequences should *not* be repeated even if the child requests a repetition. The specific teaching statements listed in the Item Administration instructions should be provided for all children on Samples A to F. For Items 1, 2, 3, 5, and 21 the teaching statements should be provided if the child fails an item. As with all DAS-II teaching items, if a child passes a teaching item, you give positive feedback, such as "Good. Hair is higher than mouth," or, "Good. That's right."

There are special instructions on page 260 of the *Administration and Scoring Manual* and page 21 of the School-Age Record Form for deciding whether to continue on to Items 21–32. Study these rules carefully before administering the subtest.

The process of obtaining a basal and ceiling and scoring the subtest is otherwise similar to those for Recall of Digits Forward and Recall of Digits Backward.

Recognition of Pictures

In addition to the Record Form, the examiner will need Stimulus Book 4 and a stopwatch to administer this subtest. For Sample B and each scored item, the examiner should provide the direction, "Look at this (or these)" before turning to the first page of each item and then exposing the first page for 5 seconds. Then the examiner should turn to the next page of the item and say, "Find it (or them) here." This procedure allows the examiner to make sure that the child is looking at the first page before proceeding with the item. You should make sure the child is not distracted before exposing each stimulus page. The examiner should keep the stopwatch running for the duration of the subtest and be careful to expose the item for *exactly* 5 seconds before turning to the second page of each item.

The examiner should practice turning the pages while using the stopwatch to become fluent with this procedure. Rubber covers for fingertips, which can be purchased in stationery stores, facilitate turning pages. We recommend that you lift *two* pages in preparation for each item. Turn over the first page to show the stimulus page, while keeping a finger under the second page. Then after *exactly* 5 seconds, flip over the second page with the finger that was underneath it.

The examiner should not name the objects in any picture but should encourage the child to look at the first page of each item for the full 5 seconds by also looking in an obvious manner at the first page during the exposure time. If the child points to only one object when two or more are required for the item to be marked correct, the examiner should ask, "Are there any more that were in the other picture?" This may be asked only once on each item. If the child then points to the remaining correct pictures and the overall response is correct, the item should be scored as correct. If the child points to all of the objects in turn, the examiner should say, "No not all of them. Just show me the ones that were in the other picture." Sample Items A and B are teaching items, so if the child fails those items, the examiner should use the specific teaching instructions included with these items. If the child passes these teaching items, the examiner should say, "Yes, that's correct."

The Record Form presents the scoring key in two ways. The first column shows the answers from the child's point of view and the second column shows the items from the opposite point of view. The examiner should use the column that is most convenient and draw a line through the column that will not be used. The correct responses are in color, so again be sure the child cannot see the Record Form. To record the child's response, circle the objects that the child points to. Items should be scored correct if the child correctly points to all correct objects and incorrect if the child omits any correct objects or points to any incorrect objects.

The examiner should not allow the child to turn the pages and should not repeat exposure even if the child asks for another look. The child should be discouraged from looking away during the exposure time, and this behavior should be noted on the Record Form. Some children impatiently look away and ask to have the page turned immediately. After realizing they had forgotten some or all of the pictures, some children will spontaneously begin paying more attention during the five-second exposure. Others will continue to rush and continue to fail without apparently understanding why they cannot remember. Be sure to note these and other behaviors.

Sequential and Quantitative Reasoning

The examiner will require a bluntly pointed wooden dowel to administer items in Set A located in Stimulus Book 4, and will need Stimulus Book 1 to administer the items in Set B. In Set A, the child must respond by pointing (preferably using the blunt-ended wooden dowel provided by the examiner to prevent smudge marks from appearing on the page of the Stimulus Book). If the child responds verbally, by naming the picture, the examiner should say, "*Show* me which one." Item instructions may be repeated as many times as necessary, but the examiner should not modify or omit wording when repeating the instructions. Items in Set B require short oral responses. For children who have trouble verbalizing a response, the examiner can let the child write the response on a slip of paper. But the child must not be allowed to use the paper to calculate a response.

If the child passes a teaching item, the examiner should acknowledge the correct response by saying, "That's right." If the child fails a teaching item, the examiner should provide the specific teaching instruction provided in the Item Administration instructions on pages 242–246 in the *Administration and Scoring Manual*. Item instructions may be repeated but not altered.

For Set A, the Record Form is constructed so that the numbers on the form correspond to figures in the Stimulus Book beginning from the child's left. Additionally, directional words in the *Administration and Scoring Manual* refer to the child's point of view. Therefore the examiner should be careful to point to the appropriate part of the page when giving instructions. If sitting opposite the child, which is not recommended, the examiner may want to rotate the Record Form upside down to make it easier to record which item the child selected in the Response column in the Record Form.

Because the nature of the task shifts in Set B of Sequential and Quantitative

Reasoning, it is necessary to treat items marked with an apple as teaching items even if they are not among the first items presented to the child. Specifically for children ages 11:0 to 14:11, Items 24, 25, 32, 33, 41, and 42 should all be treated as teaching items, and if a child of those ages fails any of these items, teaching should be provided. This rule allows the child to be instructed that the possible rules invoked by the items have changed from addition and subtraction to include multiplication and division and from one-step to two-step operations. For children ages 15:0 to 17:11, Items 36, 37, 41, and 42 are teaching items, and again teaching should be provided if the child fails these items.

There is an error (Pamela Trainor, personal communication, April 19, 2008) on p. 246 of the *Administration and Scoring Manual* (Elliott 2007a). This is explained under "Correction of Errata" earlier in this chapter.

Also, for Set B, the examiner should give the full item administration instructions for all of the Sample Items (A through E) regardless of whether the child passes or fails these items and regardless of the point at which the child encounters these items in the administration sequence.

The provision of extensive teaching allows the directions and nature of the task demands to be clear to the examinee.

Speed of Information Processing

For this subtest, it is important that the examiner pay close attention to whether the child makes errors or demonstrates hesitation on the first sample item of Booklets B or C, or alternatively does well on the first sample of these booklets but then makes many uncorrected errors on the second sample. In either of these cases, the examiner should administer the next easier response booklet.

The child responds to the first sample with pointing rather than with a pencil; this way, if the task is too difficult, the examiner can move back to an earlier booklet and the booklet will not be spoiled. In most cases, the examiner should administer all items in the selected booklet, but for Booklets B or C, if the child makes two or more uncorrected errors per page on the first two scored pages, the examiner should discontinue that booklet and drop back to an easier booklet and then administer all of the items in that booklet. In that case, an extra Response Booklet must be sacrificed.

This is a test of speed of processing of simple mental operations. It is therefore essential that timing be accurate and that the task is easy for the child so that the measurement of speed will be accurate. The examiner should *begin* timing when the child makes a mark on the first row and *stop* timing when the child makes a mark on the last row.

The examiner should present Booklet A with the long side down toward the child and Booklets B and C with the short side toward the child. The first page should be folded back so that the child sees only one page at a time. The examiner and not the child should turn the pages of the booklet. There are specific instructions in the *Administration and Scoring Manual* that the examiner should use to encourage the child to work as fast as he or she can, make small marks quickly, and explain what the "biggest number" means.

On all items, the examiner should praise the child for speed and accuracy. The examiner should be obvious in checking the choices after each page is completed. Any errors should be pointed out at the end of each item by pointing to the row in which the error occurs and saying, "There's a mistake on this row." Then, pointing appropriately, the examiner should say, "You should have marked this one because it has the most squares (or it's the biggest number)." Repeat the procedure for any other errors on the page, and then say, "Remember, do your best." The examiner should not mark the booklet. The Speed of Information Processing subtest will not accurately assess processing speed if the child is making marks carelessly or randomly. The correction procedure for each page is intended to make the child pay conscious attention to her or his choices, even if they are wrong.

As illustrated in Figure 2.6, the Record Form provides space to record the completion time (examinee's first mark to examinee's last mark on each page) and the number of errors that the examinee does not correct spontaneously while working on the page or immediately upon completion of the bottom line of the page. Errors do not affect the score unless there are three or more uncorrected errors, in which case the score for the item is 0. The point value for a particular time varies from item to item within the same booklet, so check them carefully as shown in Figure 2.6.

Verbal Comprehension

There are various materials used in this subtest: Stimulus Book 3, the box of toys, the primary grip pencil, the inset tray of wooden figures, the set of nine colored chips, and the Teddy bear photo. Representatives from the Psychological Corporation recommend that the examiner laminate the Teddy bear photo in hard plastic to prevent it from being damaged or dirtied during use. If you do this, be sure to check for glare from the examinee's viewpoint in the room you are using for testing. The laminate may be more reflective than the original surface of the card. To facilitate testing, the words that should be spoken by the examiner are printed on the Early Years Record Form in addition to being in the Item Administration section on pages 72–74 of the *Administration and Scoring Manual*.

Response Booklet B

Item	Time	Errors*	Score Circle appropriate time band. Score 0 if 3 or more errors.							Score
C			6	5	4	3	2	1	0	Score
D	16	0	6	5	4	3	2	1	0	0-6
7	9	1	1-11	12-13	14-16	17-19	20-24	25-29	30+	6
8	9	0	1-11	12-13	14-16	17-19	20-24	25-29	30+	6
9	9	0	1-7	8-9	10-11	12-13	14-16	17-21	22+	5
10	9	3	1-8	9-10	11-12	13-14	15-17	18-23	24+	0
11	9	0	1-6	7-8	9-10	11-12	13-14	15-19	20+	4
12	9	0	1-6	7-8	9-10	11-12	13-14	15-19	20+	4

Raw Score (Items (7-12))   25

* Number of uncorrected errors.

With unusual consistency, this examinee took precisely 9 seconds to complete each page. However, the scores varied from 4 to 6 because point values differ from page to page. Item 10 included 3 errors that the examinee did not correct spontaneously while completing the page, so that item was scored 0. If the examinee corrects her or his own error while working on the item (page) or immediately after completing the bottom row while you continue timing, the error does not count. Errors pointed out by the examiner after the item (page) is completed do, of course, count.

Figure 2.6 Example of Scoring the Speed of Information Processing Subtest

However, it is recommended that the examiner have the *Administration and Scoring Manual* open during administration to facilitate proper use of the starting and stop points.

The examiner should check that the child is paying attention before speaking the instructions in an engaging manner with appropriate vocal inflections and facial expressions. For items that begin with the words, "Give me," the examiner should hold out his or her hand so that the child can place the object in the examiner's hand. However, if the child pushes the object toward the examiner, that should be regarded as a correct response. Items may be repeated once if the child does not respond, does not appear to understand, or asks for a repetition. After the child has responded, the instructions may not be repeated again unless the child asks. The examiner must not repeat the instructions just because the child responds incorrectly.

The child must pass the "Chips Pretest" before Item 37. If the child does not know all the colors and shapes, do not administer Items 37 to 42.

Verbal Similarities

Complete administration and scoring instructions are provided in the *Administration and Scoring Manual*, and this book should be propped open for the examiner during test administration. For this subtest, the examiner should start every item with the words, "Listen carefully: ___, ___, ___" (inserting the three stimulus words in the blanks). Then the examiner should ask one of the three questions listed at the top of the Item Administration pages. Once the child understands the task the examiner can simply say the three stimulus words. If the child asks the examiner to repeat the words or appears to have misheard, the examiner should repeat them no more than three times.

Items similar to those in DAS-II Verbal Similarities have long been used in individually administered tests of cognitive ability. The difference between this subtest and those in tests such as the WISC-IV is the use of three stimulus words instead of only two. Since there are three words, it is possible that a child could not know one of the three words and still be able to answer the question based on his or her knowledge of the other two words. This construction methodology influences the nature of the subtest to be much less a vocabulary or lexical knowledge subtest and more one that taps more inductive skills and language development. It is worthwhile to observe and record whether a child who knows only two of the words is willing and able to guess the answer on the basis of those two words or simply gives up. However, you must not suggest this strategy to the child.

Using the phrase, "Yes. Now tell me another way of saying what they all are," question responses that are incorrect but indicate some understanding, responses that are either too general or too specific, or other incorrect responses marked with a (Q) in the *Administration and Scoring Manual*. On Items 1–9 all 0-point responses should be questioned and on all 2-point items (Items 27, 28, 29, 32) all 1-point responses should be questioned, using the above phrase.

If a child passes a teaching item, the examiner should say, "Yes, that's correct." If the child fails a teaching item the examiner should say, "___, ___, and (stimulus words) are all ___ (correct response). The best way of saying how they go together is to say they are all ___ (correct response)."

Word Definitions

Complete administration and scoring instructions are included in the *Administration and Scoring Manual*, which should be open during test administration. The examiner should begin the subtest by saying, "I will say a word, and you tell me what it means." For early items in the subtest, the examiner should present the word in one of the three phrases listed on page 198. All three of these phrases begin with the word and then a standard interrogatory phrase. For example, "Run. What does run mean?" or "Lamppost. What is a lamppost?" When the child is used to the format of the test, new words may be presented in isolation.

In the Incorrect Responses column in the Item Administration section of the *Administration and Scoring Manual,* responses marked (Q) are borderline or incomplete quality. These responses should be queried, as should other responses similar to those marked (Q). Specific questions are listed on pages 197–198.

Items marked with an apple are teaching items; if these items are failed, the examiner should provide teaching by repeating the word and explaining the correct response using the teaching statement provided in the item instructions. If a child passes a teaching item, the examiner should say, "Yes, that's correct."

To ensure accurate scoring the examiner should record the child's response verbatim. A Q should be recorded on the Record Form to indicate that a question has been asked. During administration, the examiner should assign tentative scores and use these scores for the Decision Points and Alternative Stop Point rules. When making sure you have at least three wrong, assume all questionable items are correct. When making sure you have at least three correct, assume all questionable items are wrong. You don't want to go back another day to finish this subtest! After testing, the detailed scoring rules in the *Administration and Scoring Manual* should be consulted and scores for all items should be checked and tallied. Incorrect responses should be scored 0 points and correct responses—even if the response is given after questioning—should be scored 1 point.

Generally, a correct response is a definition that includes one or more key concepts that are central to the word's meaning. Key concepts are listed immediately below each item in the Item/Key Concept column. Expressive quality of response (use of correct grammar or pronunciation) should *not* affect scoring. Usually correct responses do not include the item word, but a correct response can include the item word (referred to in the *Administration and Scoring Manual* as the target word) if the response would still be correct after that word was deleted from the response.

If the child is less than nine years old and appears to have severe difficulty with this subtest, administer Naming Vocabulary from the Early Years battery.

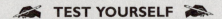

TEST YOURSELF

1. Which of the following is NOT appropriate when testing children using the DAS-II?

(a) The child should be positioned to face away from any windows and his or her attention should be on the tasks presented, not on other stimuli or test materials not in use.

(b) To aid in maintaining the child's interest, the child should be allowed to play with the test materials as if they were toys.

(c) The furniture should be comfortable and sized appropriately for the child so that his or her feet will touch the floor when sitting in a chair.

(d) You should have room to write comfortably on the Record Form without the child being able to observe your writing.

2. Regarding *teaching items* on the DAS-II, which of the following is not true:

(a) Teaching items provide additional instruction *before* a child has failed a teaching item so that he or she can do better on subsequent items.

(b) Teaching can include repeating and rephrasing the question or instruction and demonstrating or saying the correct response.

(c) If a child passes a teaching item on the first attempt, this child should also receive positive feedback.

(d) Teaching should only be done on teaching items if they are among the first items administered or if the child has failed the first items administered for his or her age and has dropped back to an earlier start point which has teaching items.

3. If a child stops during the middle of a timed test to ask you a question, it is important to immediately stop timing and resume the timing only when the child's question has been answered. True or False?

4. You can query virtually any verbal response that the child gives if you feel that it is vague, incomplete, or ambiguous. True or False?

5. Which of the following is an unacceptable reason for substituting a subtest:

(a) Subtests can be substituted when a core subtest is invalidated.

(b) Subtests can be substituted when a child needs an easier or more difficult subtest to adequately assess ability levels.

(c) Subtests can be substituted when the examiner finds that a higher composite score can be obtained by using the substituted subtest.

6. The core subtests of the DAS-II should be administered in a sequence prescribed by the layout of the Record Form and *Administration and Scoring Manual* and before most of the diagnostic subtests. However, describe a situation in which you might choose to change the order of the core subtests.

Answers: 1. b; 2. a; 3. False; 4. True; 5. c; 6. When a child refuses to work on a particular subtest the examiner may temporarily suspend that subtest and administer the next one and return to the suspended subtest when the child appears to be more engaged.

Three

S ince the publication of the first edition of the DAS (Elliott, 1992), other batteries have included item sets. These are found in several subtests of the Kaufman Test of Educational Achievement, 2nd ed., (K-TEA-II; Kaufman & Kaufman, 2004b), Writing Samples on the Woodcock-Johnson III Achievement (WJ-III Ach; Woodcock, McGrew, & Mather, 2001), and Reading Comprehension on the Wechsler Individual Achievement Test, 2nd ed. Update (WIAT-II; Psychological Corporation, 2001). However, it *is most important to use the precise methods outlined in this chapter, and in the DAS-II* Administration and Scoring Manual, *for administering and scoring item sets in the DAS-II.*

USING ITEM SETS

Most DAS-II subtests divide items into *item sets.* This is a unique feature of the DAS-II that has two major benefits. First, the use of item sets leads to time-efficiency—the DAS-II is quick to administer and arguably yields more reliable information in a shorter time than competing batteries. Second, the use of item sets minimizes children's experience of failure and maximizes their experience of success. When we consider that probably the majority of children referred for assessment have a history of failure to learn, the use of item sets leads to a more enjoyable experience for them, which in turn leads to higher motivation and to the child being more likely to function at an optimal level during the assessment.

Item sets are characterized by three rules relating to Suggested Start Points, Decision Points, and Alternative Stop Points.

Suggested Start Points

Suggested Start Points are noted on the Record Form and in the subtest directions with an arrow icon ◖. These points have been chosen so that most children of the specified age will find the initial items of the subtest either fairly easy or only moderately difficult and will pass several of them. If the examiner strongly suspects that the child will have difficulty with the initial items at the suggested Start Point for the child's age, an earlier Start Point in the subtest should be used. Under these conditions, starting at an earlier Start Point will reduce the total number of items to be administered and avoid the frustration of having to go back to easier items after failure. However, starting at an unnecessarily low point will increase the number of items to be administered. Children who are suspected to be above average should start at a Start Point recommended for older children. This will again reduce the total number of items to be administered. In general, the examiner should not hesitate to use an earlier Start Point if genuinely in doubt and should keep in mind that the most important factor in obtaining an accurate score is the administration of items that are of an appropriate level of difficulty for the child being tested.

Decision Points

In the DAS-II, the usual place to stop a subtest is at one of the Decision Points, which are designated with a diamond icon (♦) on the Record Form. The examiner administers items up to one of these Decision Points and then makes one of three choices:

Continue with the subtest
Go back to an earlier Start Point
Stop the subtest

To decide which of these three choices to make, use the "3 by 3 rule" (see Rapid Reference 3.1). A child should pass three items and should also "fail" three items in an item set. The rationale is that if a child has passed *any* three items within an item set, the child has demonstrated enough of the required skill for you to feel confident in the resulting score. Similarly, if the child has also failed any three items in the item set, you can feel confident that you don't need to go to more "difficult" items.

Let us spell out the decision process in some more detail. The three choices we need to make are as follows:

1. *Continue with the subtest.* If the child has not failed at least three items upon reaching the Decision Point, administer all the items up to the next Decision Point. When this next Decision Point is reached, the examiner should again make a decision about whether to continue.

If the child has failed at least three items out of *all* the items administered in the entire subtest, no higher items should be administered. If the child still has not failed at least three items in the *entire* subtest, administration should continue to the next Decision Point.

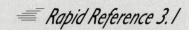

Rapid Reference 3.1

3 by 3 Rule for Item Sets

A child should pass at least 3 items *and* fail at least 3 items in an item set.

2. *Go back to an earlier Start Point.* If the child has not passed at least three items in the item set at the Decision Point, the examiner should go back to an earlier Start Point and administer those easier items in forward sequence. When the Decision Point for those items or the child's original Start Point is reached, the examiner should check if the child has now passed at least three items out of *all* items given in the expanded item set (that is, the first item set selected, with the addition of the earlier items up to the start of that item set).

3. *Stop the subtest.* If the child has failed at least three items and passed three items out of all of the items administered in the item set(s), the examiner should stop the subtest. However, we must emphasize that this rule does *not* imply that you stop as soon as the first three items are failed. Stopping as soon as the third item is failed will produce an underestimate of the child's ability. Scores should be based on complete sets of items. You must not deny the child the opportunity to attempt and possibly to pass items up to the next Decision Point.

Following the Decision Point rules as described above will efficiently allow the examiner to obtain an accurate estimate of ability. But the DAS-II allows for the examiner to administer an additional block of items if he or she suspects that the child has failed an item due to invalid reasons (temporary inattention or misunderstanding the task). Also if the examiner suspects that the child has passed three items in a set through chance, he or she can go back to an earlier Start Point and administer easier items that would give better information about the child's ability. The child is likely to pass additional

DON'T FORGET

For veteran DAS examiners: The Decision Points are no longer based on the child's age. *On the DAS-II, Decision Points are based on item sets, regardless of the child's age.*

items and obtain a higher raw score, and if so, that score will be weighted appropriately in the raw score to ability score table for that item set.

Alternative Stop Point

As noted above, the usual rule is for the examiner to administer all items up to the Decision Point, but there are occasions when the child fails so many items in succession that it is useless and harmful to rapport to continue to administer items up to the Decision Point. This is the exception to which we referred earlier. To control for this potential problem, the DAS-II includes an *Alternative Stop Point rule* for most subtests. This rule states that upon failure of a specified number of consecutive items or proportion of consecutive items (the exact numbers vary for each subtest) items after that point need not be administered.

If the child fails the specified number of consecutive items in a row (Alternative Stop Point rule) but has *not* passed three items (Start Point rule), then the examiner should drop back to an earlier Start Point and administer items in a forward sequence. If the child has passed three items in a subtest but then the child fails the specified number of items under the Alternative Stop Point rule, testing on that subtest can stop.

Be sure that, if you consider using the Alternative Stop Point rule, you evaluate the entire item set when deciding whether or not to administer an earlier item set. Look at the following example from the Sequential and Quantitative Reasoning subtest, shown in Figure 3.1. To follow this, it may also be helpful to have a Record Form open in front of you (School-Age, page 15). In this example, the Sequential and Quantitative Reasoning subtest Set A has an Alternative Stop Point of "3 failures in 4 consecutive items." The child was started at Item 9 with the expectation that the first Decision Point would be after administering the Item Set 9–23. However, the examiner administered only Items 9 through 15 because the Alternative Stop Point was met by the time the child had taken Item 15. Although the entire Item Set 9–23 was not completely administered, you would evaluate the 3 by 3 rule for this child for Item Set 9–23. If the child had passed at least three items, as in this example, you could discontinue the subtest, but if the child had not passed at least three items you would have needed to administer the earlier item set, 1–8 (unless you had already done so). If you choose to use the Alternative Stop Point rule, consider any unadministered items up to the item set Decision Point to be failed.

Another example is shown in Figure 3.2, which was taken from the Picture Similarities subtest. Once again, the Alternative Stop Point rule is 3 failures in 4 consecutive items. In the example, a child starts at Item 18, and gets the first three

Set A (Stimulus Book 4)

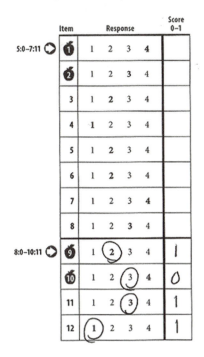

Item		Response				Score 0–1		Item		Response				Score 0–1
5:0–7:11 ⟶	**①**	1	2	3	**4**			13	1	②	3	4		0
	②	1	2	3	4			14	1	2	3	④		0
	3	1	2	3	4			15	①	2	3	4		0
	4	1	2	3	4			16	1	2	3	4		
	5	1	2	3	4			17	1	2	3	4		
	6	1	2	3	4			18	1	2	3	4		
	7	1	2	3	4			19	1	2	3	4		
	8	1	2	3	4			20	1	2	3	4		
8:0–10:11 ⟶	**⑨**	1	②	3	4		1	21	1	2	3	4		
	⑩	1	2	③	4		0	22	1	2	3	4		
	11	1	2	③	4		1	23	1	2	3	4		
	12	①	2	3	4		1							

Item Sets
1–23,
(Continues on next page.)   9–23

Figure 3.1 Example of Alternative Stop Point in the Sequential and Quantitative Reasoning Subtest

right and the next three or four wrong. The examiner would therefore stop; the 3 by 3 rule has been met along with the Alternative Stop Point rule. Note that there is no Item Set 18–24. The correct scoring block would be 18–32, despite the fact the child never completed the block.

Important Note

If the child does not seem to be distressed or discouraged and there seems to be some chance of the child passing additional items, you may be tempted to administer some additional items in the hope that the child would get one or two more correct. *Do not do so!* The reason for this is that, on a subtest with multiple-choice items such as Matrices, if the child has reached the criterion of 3 failures in 4 consecutive items, he or she is responding at a chance level. With only 4 choices of response available for each item, a child with no understanding whatsoever of

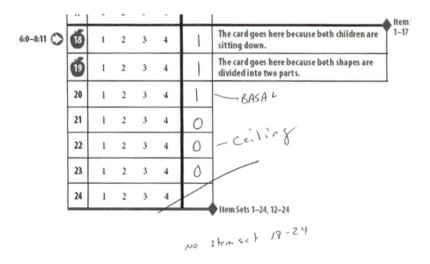

Figure 3.2 Example of Alternative Stop Point in the Picture Similarities Subtest

the test would still on average get one item in four correct. For this reason, the norms were constructed with the Alternative Stop rule applied. All items passed after the child had reached the Alternative Stop Point were not counted in the estimation of the norms.

SUBTESTS WITH DIFFERENT ALTERNATIVE STOP POINT RULES WITHIN THE SUBTEST

Four subtests—Matrices, Pattern Construction, Sequential and Quantitative Reasoning, and Verbal Comprehension—have different Alternative Stop Point rules *within* the subtest. For the first three of these subtests the different rule occurs within at the transition between Sets A and B. For Verbal Comprehension, there are three different Alternative Stop Point rules that are applied to three different sets of items.

For these subtests, any failures accumulated in an earlier set of items should *not* be carried through to the later set for the Decision Point rule, the Alternative Stop Point rule, or both. When the next set of items is started, you should apply the next appropriate Alternative Stop Point rule from the starting point of the next set. For example, if the child fails three consecutive items in Set A of Pattern Construction and after moving to Set B fails the first item, the examiner should continue with Set B and use the Decision Point and Alternative Stop Point rules that apply to Set B.

Summary of Rules for Item Sets

The rules that have been outlined above for using item sets in most subtests are summarized in Rapid Reference 3.2. Exceptions to these standard 3 by 3 rules are discussed below.

Most, but not all, subtests have item sets using the standard 3 by 3 rule. These are shown in Rapid Reference 3.3. A few subtests do not use the standard 3 by 3 rule for item sets and have different administration procedures; these are listed in Rapid Reference 3.4.

Examples of Using Standard Item Set Rules

In order to follow the example given below, it would be helpful for you to have the green Early Years Record Form open at page 4 (Naming Vocabulary). Note, however, that the rules illustrated below apply to all subtests listed in the first part of Rapid Reference 3.3.

≣ *Rapid Reference 3.2*

Summary of Rules

- Most children will begin at the suggested start points and end at the designated decision points.
- A child should take a continuous set of items from the start point to the decision point (unless ending at an alternative stop point or the end of the subtest).
- You may start a child suspected of having low ability at a lower start point or a child suspected of having high ability at a higher start point.
- If a child reaches a decision point (or an alternative stop point) and has not passed at least three items, you must administer a lower, easier set of items.
- If a child reaches a decision point and has not "failed" at least three items, you must continue testing through the next item set, if available.
- Passed or failed items need not be consecutive items.
- Remember to administer the entire item set. You don't stop as soon as the child has had three (or even more) failures unless the examinee's errors reach the "Alternate Stop Point" criterion for the subtest.

≡ Rapid Reference 3.3

Subtests Using Standard 3 by 3 Rules for Item Sets

The following subtests require administration of one or more complete item sets in which the examinee passes at least three items and fails at least three items

- *Verbal Comprehension*
- *Picture Similarities*
- *Naming Vocabulary*
- *Matrices*
- *Recognition of Pictures*
- *Early Number Concepts*
- *Matching Letter-Like Forms*
- *Word Definitions*
- *Verbal Similarities*
- *Sequential and Quantitative Reasoning*

Pattern Construction: A special case of the 3 by 3 rule

- *Pattern Construction* requires the administered item set(s) to include (1) at least three items that were passed on the first trial (some items have two possible trials); and (2) at least three items on which the examinee did not earn the maximum possible score. For example, on Item 17, the range of possible scores (including bonus points for speed) is 4, 3, 2, 1, and 0. Thus, a score of 3 would count as "less than maximum score" for this purpose, even though the student passed the item and obtained bonus points.

Subtests Using 3 by 3 Rules for Item Sets

Two subtests have special rules based on estimating passed and failed items.

- *Copying* awards 0, 1, or 2 points for each drawing. When you reach a Decision Point, you continue to another Decision Point if only 1 or 2 items *apparently* earn less than maximum possible scores. You go back to an earlier item set if there are fewer than 3 apparent passes (at least one point) throughout the set(s) administered so far.
- *Recall of Designs* awards 0, 1, 2, or 3 points for each drawing. Rules for Decision Points are the same as those for Copying.

One subtest has separate booklets for three item sets

- *Speed of Information Processing* requires you to select one of three item set booklets and administer all six items in the chosen booklet. Selection is based on the child's age, but can be revised on the basis of the child's performance on sample items.

☰ *Rapid Reference 3.4*

Subtests NOT Using 3 by 3 Rules for Item Sets

Two subtests have separate "tasks" with special administration rules.

- *Phonological Processing* has 4 tasks with no decision points and a discontinue rule for each, separate task of 4 consecutive failures within that task. All tasks are administered.
- *Rapid Naming* has 3 tasks, each with a time limit. All tasks are administered.

Recall of Objects has a single item set

- The single item set of *Recall of Objects* usually includes all three trials. *Recall of Objects—Delayed* gives only a raw score, which is converted to a *T* score.

Three subtests are administered using "basal" and "ceiling" rules

- *Recall of Digits Forward* is organized into blocks of increasingly long series of digits. You administer the first item of each successive block until the examinee fails an item. Then you drop back, one block at a time, administering all items in each block until the examinee passes all or all but one of the items in a block (basal). Then you return to the failed item and administer more difficult items until the student fails all or all but one of the items in a block (ceiling). The raw score is the total number of items passed, PLUS items not administered below the basal.
- *Recall of Digits Backward* follows the same rules.
- *Recall of Sequential Order* follows the same rules with a special rule for deciding whether to move to the second set of items. If, after you have followed the above rules, the examinee has failed at least three items among Items 1 through 20, you discontinue testing. Otherwise, you continue with Item 21, but administer all items in order to the end unless the examinee fails all or all but one of the items in a block. Recall of Sequential Order has two different item sets for scoring (1–20 and 1–32), but you DO give credit for easier items not administered before the basal.

In Figure 3.3, an example from the Naming Vocabulary subtest, the child was administered the Item Set 8–22 and passed 11 items and failed 4. Using the 3 by 3 rule (passing at least 3 items and failing at least 3 items) at the Decision Point after Item 22, you would know to discontinue testing this subtest. The child would obtain a raw score of 11 for the subtest. Remember, on most subtests children obtain credit only for items they are actually administered. Since Items 1–7 were not administered, the child receives no credit for them.

What if the child passes only two items in a specified block? In that case, you have not met the "3 by 3 rule" and you need to administer an earlier ("easier") block of items because the child has not been able to demonstrate his or her

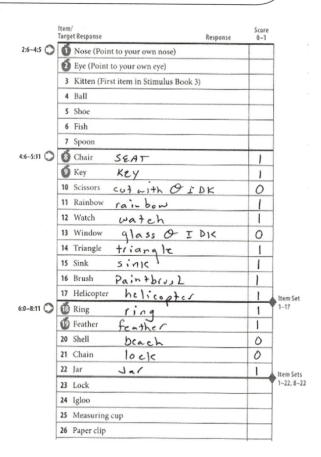

	Item/ Target Response	Response	Score 0–1	
2:6–4:5	1 Nose (Point to your own nose)			
	2 Eye (Point to your own eye)			
	3 Kitten (First item in Stimulus Book 3)			
	4 Ball			
	5 Shoe			
	6 Fish			
	7 Spoon			
4:6–5:11	8 Chair	SEAT	1	
	9 Key	KEY	1	
	10 Scissors	cut with O I DK	0	
	11 Rainbow	rainbow	1	
	12 Watch	watch	1	
	13 Window	glass O I DK	0	
	14 Triangle	triangle	1	
	15 Sink	sink	1	
	16 Brush	Paintbrush	1	
	17 Helicopter	helicopter	1	Item Set 1–17
6:0–8:11	18 Ring	ring	1	
	19 Feather	feather	1	
	20 Shell	beach	0	
	21 Chain	lock	0	
	22 Jar	Jar	1	Item Sets 1–22, 8–22
	23 Lock			
	24 Igloo			
	25 Measuring cup			
	26 Paper clip			

Figure 3.3 Naming Vocabulary 8–22; Testing Complete

ability on the tasks presented. The tasks presented were "too difficult" for the child.

This situation is illustrated in Figure 3.4 from the Naming Vocabulary subtest, in which the child was administered the Item Set 8–22 and passed only two items while failing all the others. In this case, when you make your decision at the decision point following Item 22, you see that the 3 by 3 rule has not been met. Although the child failed three or more items, only two items were passed. This set of items was too difficult for the child, and you would drop back to an earlier starting point, in this case Item 1, and test forward completing that item set.

Finally, what about the child who passes many items but who fails only one or two items in the block?

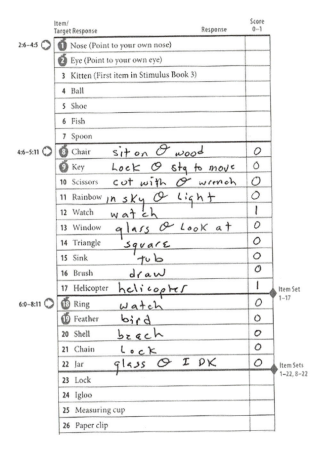

Item/Target Response	Response	Score 0–1	
2:6–4:5 ⊙ ❶ Nose (Point to your own nose)			
❷ Eye (Point to your own eye)			
3 Kitten (First item in Stimulus Book 3)			
4 Ball			
5 Shoe			
6 Fish			
7 Spoon			
4:6–5:11 ⊙ ❽ Chair	sit on & wood	0	
❾ Key	Lock & stq to move	0	
10 Scissors	cut with & wrench	0	
11 Rainbow	in sky & light	0	
12 Watch	watch	1	
13 Window	glass & Look at	0	
14 Triangle	square	0	
15 Sink	tub	0	
16 Brush	draw	0	
17 Helicopter	helicopter	1	Item Set 1–17
6:0–8:11 ⊙ ❶❽ Ring	watch	0	
❶❾ Feather	bird	0	
20 Shell	beech	0	
21 Chain	Lock	0	
22 Jar	glass & I DK	0	Item Sets 1–22, 8–22
23 Lock			
24 Igloo			
25 Measuring cup			
26 Paper clip			

Figure 3.4 Naming Vocabulary 8–22; Test Earlier (Item Set 1–7)

In the third example from the Naming Vocabulary subtest, Figure 3.5, the child was administered the Item Set 8–22 and passed almost all the items, failing only two of all administered. In this case, when you make your decision at the Decision Point following Item 22, you see that the 3 by 3 rule has not been met. In this case, although the child passed three or more items, only two items were failed. This set of items was too easy for the child and you must continue to test forward, completing that item set.

Since almost all items on all subtests are scored dichotomously (1 or 0), using the 3 by 3 rule at the decision points typically presents no problem. However, three subtests (Pattern Construction, Recall of Designs, and Copying) can have more item scores than just 1 and 0 (e.g., 0-1-2-3).

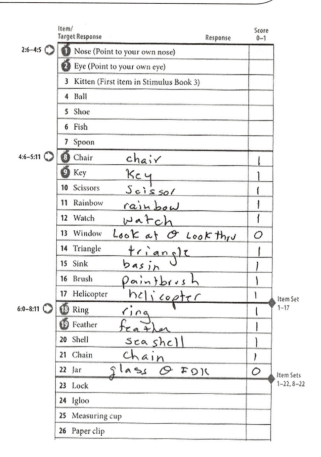

Item/Target Response	Response	Score 0–1
2:6–4:5 ① Nose (Point to your own nose)		
② Eye (Point to your own eye)		
3 Kitten (First item in Stimulus Book 3)		
4 Ball		
5 Shoe		
6 Fish		
7 Spoon		
4:6–5:11 ⑧ Chair	chair	1
⑨ Key	Key	1
10 Scissors	Scissol	1
11 Rainbow	rainbow	1
12 Watch	watch	1
13 Window	Look at O Look thru	0
14 Triangle	triangle	1
15 Sink	basin	1
16 Brush	paintbrush	1
17 Helicopter	helicopter	1
6:0–8:11 ⑱ Ring	ring	1
⑲ Feather	feather	1
20 Shell	sea shell	1
21 Chain	chain	1
22 Jar	glass O FOK	0
23 Lock		
24 Igloo		
25 Measuring cup		
26 Paper clip		

Item Set 1–17

Item Sets 1–22, 8–22

Figure 3.5 Naming Vocabulary 8–22; Test Forward, Next Item Set

Examples of Applying Item Set Rules in the Copying and Recall of Designs Subtests

For the Copying and Recall of Designs subtests, when applying the 3 by 3 rule, item scores are *estimated* after the child has drawn each figure. Final decisions on item scores are made after the conclusion of the test session. The estimated item scores are used in the decision-making process at the item set decision points.

In looking at the following specific examples of administering Recall of Designs and Copying, it would be helpful for you to have the blue Record Form open at page 1 and the green Record Form open at page 14 while reading this section. Because you cannot spend the time to fully score the individual draw-

≡ *Rapid Reference 3.5*

Quick Initial Estimates of Item Scores in Copying and Recall of Designs

Child's drawing good: Shows all major features of target figure— **Score P+**

Child's drawing bad: Bears little or no relation to target figure— **Score F**

Child's drawing not bad, not good: Shows some features or target figure— **Score P**

ings on these subtests after the child has completed each one, the Record Form has columns labeled P/F. The P/F is used to tentatively decide to stop, continue, or administer another, easier item set. You typically look to see if the individual drawing appears to be an apparent maximum pass (P+, usually 2 points but sometimes 3), a less than perfect pass (P, usually 1 point), or a fail (F, 0 points) and you mark the Record Form as P+, P, or F. Look at Rapid Reference 3.5 for brief guidelines on making quick tentative scores of each drawing.

Note that for the Copying and Recall of Designs subtests, a child does not need to actually fail any item (get a 0) to discontinue at a decision point; they need only get "less than perfect" scores on three items or more. This is one of the major advantages in using the item set approach to test administration.

Carefully work through the examples in Rapid Reference 3.6. We can summarize its contents as follows:

- In the item set administered, as long as the child has three passed items (P+ or P) AND has three items with P or F, you can stop and do not need to extend into another item set and administer more items.
- A child could in fact pass every item with less than maximum score (for example, 1 point each) and you could still stop (no "failure" needed).
- If all items are scored P+ (except for either one or two items scored P or F), you must administer the next block of items and at the next decision point reassess Ps and Fs.
- If you have fewer than three items scored P+ or P, you go back a block.

≡ Rapid Reference 3.6

Three Examples of Administration of Recall of Designs (page 1 of 3)

Example 1, for Recall of Designs (3 pass, 3 "fail"—no further testing)

In Example 1, the child was administered block 4–12. Since the tentative scoring showed at least 3 passes (P+ **OR** P), we know that the skill has been measured and we don't need to go back to an earlier item. We also see that not all were P+ (except 1 or 2 P or F's), so we know that we don't have to go forward another block.

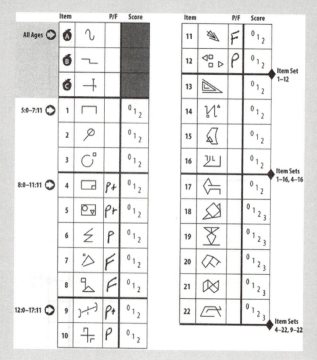

EXAMPLES OF APPLYING ITEM SET RULES IN THE PATTERN CONSTRUCTION SUBTEST

Because Pattern Construction can be scored as you go, it is much easier to make decisions at the decision points than it is for Copying and Recall of Designs. You can circle the numerical score for each item in the Score column as soon as the child has finished the item, and then, at the appropriate decision points, decide

☰ Rapid Reference 3.6

Three Examples of Administration of Recall of Designs (page 2 of 3)

Example 2, for Recall of Designs (2 pass, 3 "fail"—test earlier block)

In Example 2, a child was administered block 4–12. Since the tentative scoring showed only two passes (P+ **OR** P), we know that the skill has not been measured and we need to go back to an earlier item. We also see that because more than two items (in fact, six) have tentative scores less than P+, we know that we don't have to go forward another block.

	Item		P/F	Score		Item		P/F	Score	
All Ages	A	〰				11		F	$0\ 1\ 2$	
	B	⌐				12		F	$0\ 1\ 2$	Item Set 1–12
	C	┼				13			$0\ 1\ 2$	
5:0–7:11	1	⌐		$0\ 1\ 2$		14			$0\ 1\ 2$	
	2			$0\ 1\ 2$		15			$0\ 1\ 2$	
	3	C		$0\ 1\ 2$		16			$0\ 1\ 2$	Item Sets 1–16, 4–16
8:0–11:11	4		F	$0\ 1\ 2$		17			$0\ 1\ 2$	
	5		F	$0\ 1\ 2$		18			$0\ 1\ 2\ 3$	
	6		P+	$0\ 1\ 2$		19			$0\ 1\ 2\ 3$	
	7		F	$0\ 1\ 2$		20			$0\ 1\ 2\ 3$	
	8		P	$0\ 1\ 2$		21			$0\ 1\ 2\ 3$	
12:0–17:11	9		F	$0\ 1\ 2$		22			$0\ 1\ 2\ 3$	Item Sets 4–22, 9–22
	10		F	$0\ 1\ 2$						

what option to take. You might find it helpful to place a big minus sign (–) next to each item that is "less than perfect" and then, when you come to a decision point, look to see if you have three minus signs. (See the example in Rapid Reference 3.7.) If you do, you know you don't need to test further. If you see only one or two minus signs, you know that you must test further and administer the next item set. Conversely, if you see only one or two scores above 0, you know you need to go back to an earlier Start Point.

≡ *Rapid Reference 3.6*

Three Examples of Administration of Recall of Designs (page 3 of 3)

Example 3, for Recall of Designs (all P+ but two, 2 "fail"—test more)

In Example 3, a child was administered block 4–12. Since the tentative scoring showed at least three passes (P+ **OR** P), we know that we don't need to go back to an earlier start point. We also see that all except two items were tentatively scored P+, so we know that we have to go forward another block.

Age group	Item	P/F	Score		Item	P/F	Score	
All Ages	A				11	P+	0 1 2	
	B				12	P	0 1 2	Item Set 1–12
	C				13		0 1 2	
5:0–7:11	1		0 1 2		14		0 1 2	
	2		0 1 2		15		0 1 2	
	3		0 1 2		16		0 1 2	Item Sets 1–16, 4–16
8:0–11:11	4	P+	0 1 2		17		0 1 2	
	5	P+	0 1 2		18		0 1 2 3	
	6	P+	0 1 2		19		0 1 2 3	
	7	P+	0 1 2		20		0 1 2 3	
	8	F	0 1 2		21		0 1 2 3	
12:0–17:11	9	P+	0 1 2		22		0 1 2 3	Item Sets 4–22, 9–22
	10	P+	0 1 2					

≋ Rapid Reference 3.7

Administering Pattern Construction

Pattern Construction can be scored while you administer it. Circle the numerical score in the Score column and decide what option to take at each decision point. Place a big minus sign (–) next to each item that is "less than perfect" (lower than the maximum possible score). At each decision point, look for three minus signs (as shown at the left). If there are three *anywhere in the item set*, stop testing. If there are zero, one, or two minus signs, *administer the next item set*. If there are only one or two scores above zero, *go back to an earlier item set*.

(Continues on next page.)

HOW DO I APPLY THE 3 BY 3 RULE IF I NEED TO ADMINISTER EASIER OR HARDER ITEMS?

If, after reaching a decision point, you do go on to administer another item set (either an earlier or a later one) *the same 3 by 3 rule applies to the entire, combined item set.* For example, on the Word Definitions subtest, if you administer Items 5 to 18, your first decision point for applying the 3 by 3 rule will be for Item Set 5–18. If you need to keep going (fewer than three failures) and administer the next set of items (19 to 24), the next decision point would be for Item Set 5–24 and the 3 by 3 rule is again applied, but in this case the *total* pass and fail decision is made for the *entire* item set (5–24), not just the new item set administered. You don't restart counting passed or failed items only on the new item set.

THREE SUBTESTS THAT DO NOT HAVE STANDARD ITEM SET RULES

Three DAS-II subtests (Recall of Objects, Phonological Processing, and Rapid Naming) have fixed start points and discontinuation rules. All children start with Item 1 and proceed through the items until a specific criterion is met.

Recall of Objects consists of a card with 20 pictures that is shown to the child who tries to memorize each object. The card is given three successive presentations, or trials. The sum of objects correctly remembered by the child on all three trials is counted as a single item set. As well as having a single start point, there are no decision points and no alternative stop rule.

Phonological Processing consists of four separate tasks, each of which is administered separately, and children always start at the first item for each task. There are no decision points. Each task has a discontinue rule of four consecutive failures. After the child has discontinued a task, you proceed to the next task. The child's performance on each task may be compared. For reporting purposes, the four tasks are summed to provide a single item set for the whole subtest.

Similarly, Rapid Naming has three tasks that are presented to every child taking the subtest. There are no decision points and no alternative stop rule. The child's performance on the first two tasks may be compared with his or her performance on the third task. As with Phonological Processing, scores from each task are summed to yield a single item set for the whole subtest.

SOME FINAL THOUGHTS ON THE ITEM SET APPROACH TO TEST ADMINISTRATION

Unlike some other test batteries, the use of item sets in the DAS-II creates a different type of testing expectation for you. Item sets are designed to present a series of items that are appropriately challenging to a child, but without repeatedly exposing the child to relatively large numbers of items that are too difficult and on which the child fails to make correct responses. Thus, most of the DAS-II subtests do not use a "traditional" ceiling rule in which a child must fail a certain number of consecutive items in order for you to discontinue testing. Instead, many children will in fact be passing items near or at the end of an item set, and yet you will be able to stop and still have a reliable measure.

If you have not used tests with this structure before, you will probably feel uncomfortable. It just doesn't seem right to stop testing while the examinee is still passing some items nor not to test down to a level where the examinee is bored but 100 percent accurate. When you are practicing the DAS-II with your children, grandchildren, neighbors, or other victims, go ahead and administer additional item sets above (more difficult than) and below (easier than) the item sets defined by the 3 by 3 rule. Then score the subtest by all possible item sets and combinations of item sets. You will find that, almost always, the ability scores based on the raw scores for the several item sets will be very close to one another. For this purpose, you should only compare item sets that satisfy the 3 by 3 rule—ability scores from item sets with only one or two passes or with only one or two failures will be less accurate. Eventually, these experiences will help you become comfortable with the item set format on the DAS-II. If you persist, we are confident that you will come to welcome the loss of boring or insultingly easy items and frustrating and de-motivating difficult ones in your test sessions. No matter how much you explain the design of the test, some children will interpret too-easy items as evidence that you really consider them unintelligent, and they may decide to "live down" to your inferred assessment of them (Ursula Willis, personal communication, June 12, 2008).

BASAL AND CEILING RULES

Three subtests—Recall of Digits Forward, Recall of Digits Backward, and Recall of Sequential Order—use a basal and ceiling rule for administering items. These subtests are divided into blocks of four or five items each. The aim of administration is to establish a basal block and a ceiling block. A basal is defined

Rapid Reference 3.8

Basal and Ceiling Rules

Basal Level:

- No more than one failure in a block
- Give credit for all unadministered items before the basal block

Ceiling Level:

- No more than one pass in a block
- Give zero scores for all unadministered items after the ceiling block

as "No more than one failure in a block," while a ceiling is defined as "No more than one pass in a block" (see Rapid Reference 3.8).

On the Record Form, the first item in each block for these subtests is highlighted with an oval (⬭). On each of these subtests, all children start with Item 1. If the child passes, the examiner should proceed to the first highlighted item of the next block and continue with the first highlighted item of each successive block until an item is failed or until the first item in the last block is administered. Then, once an item has been failed, the examiner *first* establishes the basal block and *then* establishes the ceiling block.

If the child fails Item 1, continue testing forward, administering the other items in the first block. Since you have started with Item 1, there is no basal that needs to be established (there are no lower items to go back to). When you complete the block, evaluate whether or not a ceiling ("No more than one pass in a block") has been reached. If, in this first block, the child has passed at least two items, continue testing the second block. If the child cannot pass any item in this block *or* passes only one item in this block, you have reached the ceiling ("No more than one pass in a block") and should discontinue the subtest.

If the child fails the first item in any block, you should move back to the previous block and administer all remaining items in that block. If the child fails more than one item in that block (no basal established), immediately move back to previous blocks, one at a time, and continue until the basal level is established with no more than one failure in a block. Then go forward to the block in which the first item was failed and administer the remaining items in that block. If the child passes more than one item in that block, move forward one further block and administer those items. Continue in this way until the ceiling is established. If the child cannot pass any item in a block *or* passes only one item in a block, you have reached the ceiling ("No more than one pass in a block") and should discontinue the subtest.

If the child passes the first item of the last block, the examiner should administer all the remaining items in this last block and a basal would be established by no more than one failure in that block. If the child fails more than one item in that block, the examiner moves back to the previous block to establish a basal level, as described above.

Once the basal level has been established, *be sure to give credit for all items not administered below the basal block to obtain the raw score.* Unlike most DAS-II subtests that use item sets, these subtests with basal and ceiling rules allow the child to receive credit for the items not administered, since establishing a basal allows you to assume that the child would have passed any (easier) items below the basal. To recapitulate, the basal is the block with no more than one error, the ceiling is the block with no more than one pass, and credit is also given for unadministered items below the basal.

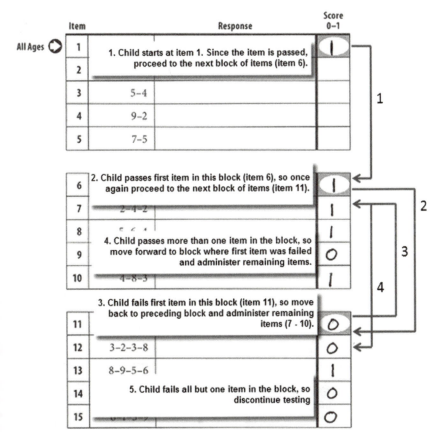

Figure 3.6 Basal and Ceiling Rules Applied in Recall of Digits Forward

The procedure is illustrated in Figure 3.6, taken from the Recall of Digits Forward subtest. Items are administered in the following sequence:

- Item 1 is passed, so the examiner proceeds to Item 6.
- Item 6 is also passed, so the examiner proceeds to Item 11 (the first item in the third block).
- The child fails Item 11, so the examiner moves back to the previous block and administers the remaining items in that block after Item 6.
- The child fails only one of those items, so this becomes the basal block. All items below Item 6 are credited as passed.
- The examiner then moves to the third block and administers the remaining items in that block (Items 12 through 15).
- Only one item is passed in that block. This establishes the ceiling. Testing is discontinued.

✎ TEST YOURSELF ✎

1. If an examiner strongly suspects that the child will have difficulty with the initial items at the suggested Start Point for the child's age, it is appropriate to start the child at an earlier Start Point. True or False?

2. When considering the Alternative Stop Points, if the child does not seem to be distressed or discouraged and there seems to be some chance of the child passing additional items, you may administer some additional items in the hope that the child would get one or two more correct. True or False?

3. If the child has not passed at least three items upon reaching the Decision Point, which of the following should you do?

    (a) Continue with the subtest to the next Decision Point

    (b) Go back to an earlier Start Point

    (c) Stop the subtest.

4. Four subtests—Matrices, Pattern Construction, Sequential and Quantitative Reasoning, and Verbal Comprehension—have different Alternative Stop Point rules *within* the subtest. For these subtests, any failures accumulated in an earlier set of items should be carried through to the later set for the Decision Point rule, the Alternative Stop Point rule, or both. True or False?

5. **When applying the 3 by 3 rule, if the child has passed three or more items, but only failed two items, which of the following should you do?**

   (a) Continue with the subtest to the next Decision Point

   (b) Go back to an earlier Start Point

   (c) Stop the subtest.

6. **On three DAS-II subtests, a child does not need to actually fail any item (get a 0) to discontinue at a decision point; they need only get "less than perfect" scores on three items or more. Name the three subtests.**

Answers: 1. True; 2. False. The norms were constructed with the Alternative Stop rule applied. All items passed after the child had reached the Alternative Stop Point were not counted in the estimation of the norms.; 3. b. The child has not been able to demonstrate his or her ability on the tasks presented.; 4. False, for these subtests, any failures accumulated in an earlier set of items should *not* be carried through to the later set for the Decision Point rule, the Alternative Stop Point rule, or both.; 5. a. This set of items was too easy for the child and you must continue to test forward.; 6. Pattern Construction, Copying, and Recall of Designs.

Four

HOW TO SCORE THE DAS-II*

TYPES OF SCORES

The DAS-II, like most other cognitive ability measures, uses several types of scores (raw scores, ability scores, T scores, and Standard scores, PR, AE). Base rates by overall sample and ability level can also be reported. The DAS-II uses normalized standard scores (M =100, SD = 15) for all Cluster scores (Verbal, Nonverbal, Nonverbal Reasoning, Spatial, Working Memory, Processing Speed, School Readiness) and for the Special Nonverbal and General Conceptual Ability composites. Normative scores for the twenty individual subtests are expressed as T scores (M = 50, SD = 10). (See Rapid Reference 4.1.)

Tables A.2 and A.3 (pp. 102–118) in the DAS-II *Normative Data Tables Manual* (Elliott, 2007c) are used to obtain Cluster and GCA scores based on the battery-appropriate standard subtests. It is essential to use the Cluster and GCA tables that correspond to the battery actually given. Examiners may find it useful to color code, green or blue, the table titles so that they match the record form used. For example, Table A.2 on page 102 is titled "Verbal: Lower Early Years." This table would be used for the green Early Years Record Form, and so, color coding the title in green will assist you in choosing this rather than the Verbal: School-Age table on page 107. Fredye Sherr (personal communication, July 18, 2006) recommends reading aloud the title of each table and the heading of each column and row when you look up scores. Your ear may catch an error that your eye misses.

STEP BY STEP: HOW TO SCORE THE DAS

In order to properly administer and score the DAS-II, there are several important terms and points that you must understand and master.

* Coauthored with Joe Salerno.

≡ Rapid Reference 4.1

Metrics for Standard Scores

Type of standard score	Mean	Standard Deviation	Range of Values
T score	50	10	10–90
GCA	100	15	30–170
Clusters	100	15	30–170

Calculating the Child's Age

Since the DAS-II is scored based upon the specific age of the child, it is extremely important that you calculate the age correctly.

On the record form, enter the date of testing followed by the child's date of birth. When a child is tested over multiple testing sessions, always use only the first testing date. Subtract the date of birth from the date of testing. Note that, on the record form, under the DAY column, you will find the reminder "(*Disregard the Days*)." You disregard the days only *after* first completely computing the correct age in years, months and days, and then use just the years and month when finding the correct norms tables. If you do not calculate the Test age by first using the days and only then disregarding them after the end of the calculation, you run the risk of scoring the DAS-II using the wrong normative table. See Figure 4.1, Incorrect and Correct Age Calculations, for an example of incorrect and correct age calculations. Note that in the first example the examiner disregarded the days *before* calculating the age, and incorrectly found the child to be 6 years 3 months old. In the second example, the examiner disregarded the days *after* the calculation and correctly found the child to be 6 years 2 months old.

RAW SCORE

A subtest's raw score is the number of points a child earns on a prescribed item set administered to that child. For most of the subtests on the DAS-II (those that use the 3 by 3 rule—see Chapter 3), a child does not obtain points for items not administered. Because different children take different item sets that span different ages and ability levels, raw scores for different children taking the same subtest are not comparable to each other. The raw scores are therefore converted to an *ability score*.

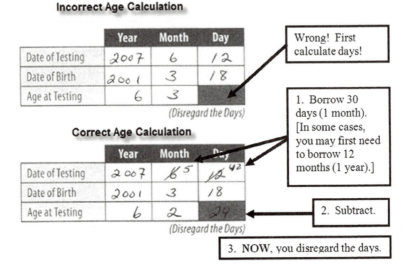

Figure 4.1 Incorrect and Correct Age Calculations

ABILITY SCORES

For each subtest, raw scores are transformed into ability scores using the Raw Score to Ability Score Tables found on the Record Form (see Figure 4.2). Ability scores are a reflection not only of the raw score a child obtains but also of the difficulty of the items administered to the child. For example, on the Word Definitions subtest, a raw score of 9 is equal to an Ability score of 92 for item set 1–13 (the first and easiest item set), but the same raw score of 9 is equal to an ability score of 156 for item set 19–35 (the last and hardest item set). Please see the black ovals on Figure 4.2. This scoring is slightly analogous to the scoring of competitive diving. The point value of a dive is a function both of quality of performance (raw score) and the degree of difficulty of the particular dive (item set). Note that the Raw Score to Ability Score tables on the Record Form also contain two additional and useful bits of information, outlined below.

Standard Error of Measurement (SEm). After each ability score, in parentheses, is the Standard Error of Measurement (SEm) of the ability score. This SEm should be used when a child has been administered two or more scorable item sets in the same subtest. When choosing the most appropriate of those item sets, choose the one for which the ability score has the lowest SEm.

Shaded Sections in the Raw Score to Ability Score Tables. The Raw Score to Ability Score table also includes several scores (at either the beginning or end of

Word Definitions
Raw Score to Ability Score

Raw Score	Item Set										
	1–13	1–18	1–24	5–18	5–24	5–30	11–24	11–30	11–35	19–30	19–35
0	10(15)	10(15)	10(15)								
1	27(13)	27(13)	27(13)	65(11)	64(11)	64(11)	82(11)	82(11)	82(11)	110(11)	110(11)
2	42(12)	42(12)	42(12)	73(8)	73(8)	73(8)	92(9)	92(9)	92(9)	119(9)	119(9)
3	55(10)	55(10)	55(10)	79(7)	79(7)	79(7)	99(8)	99(8)	99(8)	126(8)	126(8)
4	64(9)	64(9)	64(9)	85(7)	84(7)	84(7)	104(7)	104(7)	104(7)	132(7)	132(7)
5	71(8)	71(8)	70(8)	89(7)	89(7)	88(7)	109(7)	109(7)	109(7)	137(7)	137(7)
6	77(7)	76(7)	76(7)	94(7)	93(6)	93(6)	114(7)	113(6)	113(6)	142(7)	142(7)
7	82(7)	81(7)	81(7)	98(7)	97(6)	97(6)	118(6)	117(6)	117(6)	147(7)	146(7)
8	87(7)	85(7)	85(6)	103(7)	101(6)	100(6)	122(6)	121(6)	121(6)	152(7)	151(7)
9	92(7)	90(7)	89(6)	107(7)	104(6)	104(6)	126(7)	125(6)	125(6)	157(8)	156(7)
10	98(6)	94(7)	93(6)	112(7)	108(6)	108(6)	131(7)	128(6)	128(6)	164(9)	162(8)
11	105(9)	98(7)	97(6)	118(8)	112(6)	111(6)	136(7)	132(6)	132(6)	175(12)	169(8)
12	115(12)	103(7)	101(6)	124(9)	116(6)	115(6)	142(8)	136(6)	136(6)		176(9)
13		107(7)	105(6)	134(11)	119(6)	118(6)	151(11)	140(6)	140(6)		184(9)
14		112(7)	108(6)		123(6)	122(6)		144(6)	143(6)		193(9)
15		118(8)	112(6)		127(6)	125(6)		148(7)	148(7)		202(10)
16		124(9)	116(6)		131(7)	129(6)		153(7)	152(7)		214(12)
17		134(11)	119(6)		136(7)	132(6)		158(8)	157(7)		228(15)
18			123(6)	142(8)		136(6)		165(9)	163(8)		
19			127(6)	151(11)		140(6)		175(12)	169(8)		
20			131(7)			144(6)			176(9)		
21			136(7)			148(7)			184(9)		
22			142(8)			153(7)			193(9)		
23			151(11)			158(8)			202(10)		
24						165(9)			214(12)		
25						175(12)			228(15)		
26											

Figure 4.2 An Ability Score Table

item sets) that are shaded (see Figure 4.2). These shaded sections are reminders to you that the item set was not correctly administered. For example, in Figure 4.2, if a child had a raw score of 12 for item set 1–13, the ability score would be 115(12) and would be found in the shaded area (black rectangle in Figure 4.2). Remember that the item-set rule requires that the child pass three items and also fail three items (3 by 3 rule). Since the child took item set 1–13 and received a raw score of 12, the child would have failed only one item. If when calculating the ability

DON'T FORGET

If the ability score is in a shaded area, the item-set was not correctly administered.

- If the Raw Score is 1 or 2, you should administer an easier set of items
- For higher Raw Scores in shaded areas, you should administer a more difficult set of items

score, you discover that the ability score is in a shaded area, you know that you need to administer higher or lower item sets. Never promise a child that the evaluation is absolutely complete.

T SCORES, COMPOSITES AND CLUSTER SCORES

If you are unfamiliar with the types of normative scores in the DAS-II, refer to Rapid Reference 4.1 at the beginning of this chapter.

Convert subtest ability scores to T scores: After obtaining the ability score for each subtest, transfer these scores to the summary page of the Record Form. Each subtest's ability score is then converted to a *T* score with a range from 10 to 90 (please see Chapter 1 for a discussion of *T* score ranges).

To convert subtest ability scores to *T* scores within the examinee's own age group, use Table A.1 in the DAS-II *Normative Data Tables Manual* (Elliott, 2007c, pp. 2–101). Age groups are three-month intervals for children 2 years 6 months to 8 years 11 months, and six-month intervals for children 9 years and older. You may find it helpful to read the title of the table and the column and row headings aloud to make sure you are on the right part of the right page. If you wear bifocals or have the slightest difficulty with visual tasks, use one or even two straightedges to look up scores. If necessary, photocopy the age-appropriate table and draw lines and circles on the photocopy for that child. There is no excuse for looking up the wrong score, and the consequences of such an error can be devastating.

Determine the Sum of the Subtest T scores: Next, to obtain the standard scores for the GCA, SNC, and clusters, add together the *T* scores for the subtests that create each cluster (e.g., Word Definitions and Verbal Similarities for the School-Age Verbal Ability Cluster). Add carefully. Add twice. Mistakes in arithmetic are appallingly common even for experienced examiners. Use Table A.2 on pages 102–112 in the *Normative Data Tables Manual* to obtain the Cluster Standard Scores and Table A.3 on pages 113–122 for the GCA and SNC. The process is illustrated in Figure 4.3 for the clusters derived from the core subtests as well as the GCA, and in Figure 4.4 for the diagnostic clusters.

Age-equivalent scores: If you need to gauge growth or change over time and cannot do this by making age-referenced comparisons of *T* scores, age-equivalent scores are available. Age-equivalent scores are useful in certain situations and, indeed, may be the only way that we can express normative scores for some individuals who are at the extreme lower end of the ability range (for example, with profound mental retardation). However, in most cases, caution should be used

Core Subtest T Scores (Table A.1)		Ability Score	T Score	Verbal	Nonverbal Reasoning	Spatial	GCA	SNC
Recall of Designs	RDes	104	58			58	58	58
Word Definitions	WDef	66	27	▶ 27			27	
Pattern Construction ☑Std. ☐Alt.	PCon	234	55			55	55	55
Matrices	Mat	79	37		37		37	37
Verbal Similarities	VSim	86	35	▶ 35			35	
Sequential & Quantitative Reasoning	SQR	96	35		35		35	35

Cluster/Composite Scores (Tables A.2–A.4)				Verbal	Nonverbal Reasoning	Spatial	GCA	SNC
	Sum of Core Subtest T Scores			62	72	113	247	185
	Standard Score			69	77	111	82	93
	Percentile			2	6	77	12	32
	Confidence Interval (95 % level)			63–82	71–87	104–117	77–88	88–99
	Mean T Score						41	46
				Verbal	Nonverbal Reasoning	Spatial	GCA	SNC

Figure 4.3 Completion of Record Form, Showing T Scores and Standard Scores for the Core Subtests.

Diagnostic Subtest T Scores (Table A.1)		Ability Score	T Score	Working Memory	Processing Speed
Recall of Objects—Immediate	RObI	192	54		
Recall of Objects—Delayed	RObD	14	59		
Recall of Digits Forward	DigF	169	52		
Recognition of Pictures	RPic	114	40		
Recall of Sequential Order	SeqO	97	41	▶ 41	
Speed of Information Processing	SIP	112	40		40
Recall of Digits Backward	DigB	89	39	▶ 39	
Phonological Processing	PhP	78	35		
Rapid Naming	RNam	142	45		45

Diagnostic Cluster Scores (Tables A.2–A.4)		Working Memory	Processing Speed
Sum of Diagnostic Subtest T Scores		80	85
Standard Score		83	86
Percentile		13	18
Confidence Interval (95 % level)		78–90	79–96
		Working Memory	Processing Speed

Figure 4.4 Completion of Record Form, Showing T Scores and Standard Scores for the Diagnostic Subtests.

when using or reporting age-equivalents due to their common misinterpretation and psychometric limitations.

Table A.6 (pages 126–127) in the *Normative Data Tables Manual* provides age-equivalent scores for the cognitive subtests. No age-equivalent scores are available for the cluster scores or for the GCA or SNC.

SPECIAL CONSIDERATIONS IN SCORING

Prorating GCA scores: If for some reason one subtest score cannot be used in the calculation of the GCA, a prorating procedure is available. Prorating a Lower Early Years GCA would be done using the remaining three core subtests, while the Upper Early Years and the School-Age GCAs would be prorated based upon the remaining five core subtests. Prorating should be done only for the GCA, never for cluster scores (see Rapid Reference 4.2). Prorating should also be done only under the following circumstances: (a) A serious error in administration makes the subtest invalid; (b) a serious disruption in the testing process or a mechanical error with test materials (e.g., stopwatch malfunctions); (c) a child refuses to take or respond to a subtest; (d) evidence that coaching of the child has occurred or the child has "cheated" (e.g., having read the answers from the open manual).

Table A.5 (pages 123–125) in the Normative Data Tables Manual provides tables for converting the sums of three subtests (Lower Early Years) or five subtests (Upper Early Years and School-Age) to the prorated GCA. When more than one subtest is invalid, do not calculate a GCA or a SNC. Use prorated scores very cautiously. Wherever you refer to the score that was prorated (both in your tables and in the text of your report), remind the reader that their score was prorated. You must also explain the process, as most readers will not be familiar with it. Everyone needs to know that the total score is an estimate based on only 3/4 or 5/6 of the usual data.

Rapid Reference 4.2

Prorating on the DAS-II

If a subtest is spoiled, or a child's disability prevents you from administering a specific subtest, you may prorate the GCA or SNC

• You may NOT prorate a cluster

Scoring Using Substituted Subtests. Occasionally, when assessing a child between the ages of five and eight years, it may be necessary to substitute a core subtest. Discussion of this situation has already been made in Chapter 2 in the section titled 'Subtest Substitution' on p. 55. If one of the substitutions shown here has been made, it is permissible to obtain standard scores for the cluster, GCA or SNC in the normal way. As a reminder, Rapid Reference 4.3 shows the permissible substitutions:

Subtests with raw scores of zero: Because awarding *T* score points for no successes might be problematic, examiners should attempt to administer subtests from a lower level of the DAS-II battery whenever possible. This allows examiners to administer tasks that are closer to the child's ability level. Two of the problems are that you have no opportunity to observe the child actually doing anything and you don't know whether it was a "high zero" with the child barely missing earning one or more points or a "low zero" with the child utterly unable to even approximate a correct response. In cases where using a lower level is not possible, examiners can convert the 0 raw scores to ability and then *T* scores and interpret the results with extreme caution.

Ability scores and *T* scores from subtests with raw scores of zero are based on the assumption of a "high zero." Therefore, the child's *T* scores *may be an overestimate* of the ability of a very low-functioning child. You should consider this when interpreting any subtest in which the *T* score that results from the zero raw score is 25 or above, or when using the *T* score for the computation of a cluster or GCA score. If the subtest *T* score is somewhat inflated, this will also inflate the cluster, GCA or SNC scores.

In a case where a child refuses to do a task or to answer questions, the raw score would reflect the child's unwillingness to participate in the testing of that ability and not reflect the child's inability to do the task. *In such a case, the subtest score is invalid, and should NOT be reported, interpreted, or included in the calculation of cluster or*

≡ *Rapid Reference 4.3*

Acceptable DAS-II Core Subtest Substitutions at ages 5:0–8:11

Early Years Subtest		School-Age Subtest
Verbal Comprehension	↔	Verbal Similarities
Naming Vocabulary	↔	Word Definitions
Picture Similarities	↔	Sequential and Quantitative Reasoning
Copying	↔	Recall of Designs

Core Subtest Substitutions and Prorations For Ages other than 5:0–8:11

Remember, the DAS-II does not otherwise allow substituting one subtest for another like some other tests. If a subtest is spoiled, or a disability prevents you from administering a specific subtest, you may prorate the GCA or SNC, but you may not prorate a cluster or substitute some other subtest.

composite scores. When this happens, if only one subtest were considered invalid, the examiner might prorate the GCA or SNC based on the remaining, valid scores. When more than one subtest is considered invalid, the examiner should omit the calculation of the composite scores and restrict interpretation to the subtest level. The validity of the entire evaluation would obviously be open to question and the examiner's observations may be more important than any scores. If the child does not give a clear and believable reason for the lack of cooperation, refusal may suggest having another evaluator attempt working with the child.

CONFIDENCE INTERVALS

The DAS-II Normative Score Profile Page offers a good opportunity to record scores as confidence bands rather than as single points. The small cross bars on the vertical lines under the subtests and clusters make it easy to mark off precise score ranges. For the cluster scores and GCA or Special Nonverbal Composite, the confidence band is already provided when you look up the score, so all that is needed is an X or heavy cross bar at the score, smaller cross bars at the ends of the confidence interval, and a heavy, vertical line between the smaller cross bars as shown in Figure 4.5.

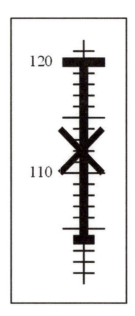

Figure 4.5 Marking Confidence Intervals on the Record Form

CONFIDENCE BAND

For individual subtests, the optional process for computing the confidence interval requires an extra step. When you look up the Ability Score for the student's raw score, you find the Standard Error of Measurement (SEm) or 68 percent confidence interval in parentheses to the right of the Ability Score. Multiply the SEm by 1.65 ($1\frac{2}{3}$) for a 90 percent confidence interval or by 1.96 (2) for a 95 percent confidence band. In the example in Figure 4.6, a Raw Score of 4 on Item Set 4–16 yields an Ability Score of 63 with an SEm of 6. The 90 percent confidence band for an SEm of 6 is 10 [1.65 × 6 = 9.90 ≈ 10 or $1\frac{2}{3}$ × 6 = $6\frac{2}{3}$ = 10]. The 95 percent confidence band for the SEm of 6 is 12 [1.96 × 6 = 11.76 ≈ 12 or 2 × 6 = 12].

When you look up the *T* score for the Ability Score, also look up the *T* score for the Ability Score minus the confidence interval and the *T* score for the Ability Score plus the confidence interval. In our example, for the 90 percent confidence band you would look up the *T* scores for 63 and for 63 ± 10 or for 53, 63, and 73.

Recall of Designs
Raw Score to Ability Score

Raw Score	Item Set 1–12	1–16	4–16	4–22	9–22
0	10(15)	10(15)			
1	26(13)	25(13)	44(11)	44(11)	60(11)
2	38(9)	38(9)	53(8)	53(8)	68(8)
3	45(8)	45(8)	58(7)	58(7)	74(7)
4	50(7)	50(7)	63(6)	62(6)	78(6)
5	55(6)	54(6)	66(6)	66(6)	82(6)
6	58(6)	58(6)	70(5)	69(5)	85(5)
7	61(6)	61(5)	72(5)	72(5)	88(5)
8	64(5)	64(5)	75(5)	74(5)	90(5)
9	67(5)	66(5)	78(5)	77(5)	93(5)
10	70(5)	69(5)	80(5)	79(5)	95(5)

Figure 4.6 Using Ability tables to form confidence bands

≡ Rapid Reference 4.4

Confidence Intervals (90% & 95%) For SEm of Ability Scores

	Confidence Intervals			Confidence Intervals	
SE$_m$	90%	95%	SE$_m$	90%	95%
3	5	6	12	20	24
4	7	8	13	22	26
5	8	10	14	23	28
6	10	12	15	25	30
7	12	14	16	27	32
8	13	16	17	28	34
9	15	18	18	30	36
10	17	20	19	32	38
11	18	22	20	33	40

You would make an X at the *T* score for 63, draw cross bars at the *T* scores for 53 and 73, and draw a heavy, vertical line between the cross bars. For the examiner's convenience, Rapid Reference 4.4 below shows 90 percent and 95 percent confidence intervals for SEm values from 3 through 20.

A "psychograph" (Wechsler's term) with 90 percent or 95 percent confidence bands encourages both examiner and reader to think of scores as intervals, not as single points. The confidence bands reinforce the requirements not to interpret non-significant differences between test scores and, conversely, to be sure to pay attention to statistically significant differences between scores.

EXTENDED GCA SCORES

Children ages 9:0 to 17:11 who are very low in ability may earn *T* scores of 10 on several of the School-Age core subtests by doing few if any of the tasks presented. For low-functioning children, ages 9:0 to 17:11, it is often desirable to administer the Upper Early Years level of the Cognitive Battery since the tasks may be more appropriate for the child. Going down to a lower age-level means that there will be the likelihood of a larger number of easy items on which older, low-functioning children may have greater chances of success, and which may give a more accurate measure of cognitive functioning. However, for these children the subtests do not have appropriate age norms. In cases where the examiner wishes to administer the Upper Early Years Cognitive Battery out-of-level, an Extended GCA or SNC score, together with extended Verbal, Nonverbal Reasoning, and Spatial cluster scores may be obtained through the "*Extended*

GCA and Cluster Score Norms" provided on the CD that accompanies this volume. These extended norms are based on an equating of the scales across ages. These norms enable users to obtain GCA scores as low as 25 and to administer the Upper Early Years Cognitive Battery out of level to children, ages 9:0 to 17:11, suspected of being very low in ability.

Extended GCA and Cluster scores are *not* available for children ages 2:6 to 8:11. For low-functioning children in this age range who earn *T* scores of 20 or less, appropriate age-based normative information is provided by the Early Years battery.

When May the Extended Norms be Used?

Extended norms based on administering the Upper Early Years battery may be used for low-ability children aged between 9:0 and 17:11, under the following conditions.

Extended GCA Scores. These may be used (a) if the child earns *T* scores of 20 or less on three or more of the School-Age Core subtests, using age-appropriate norms; AND (b) the sum of the child's core *T* scores on the School-Age Core subtests is 157 or less, using regular, age-based norms.

≡ *Rapid Reference 4.5*

When to Use Extended Norms

YOU MAY USE the Extended GCA, SNC, and Cluster norms if the child's age is between 9:0 and 17:11 and if the following conditions are met:

GCA Score
- Child earns *T* scores of 20 or less on three or more of the six School-Age Core subtests, using appropriate age-norms; AND
- The sum of the child's *T* scores on the six School-Age Core subtests is 157 or less, using regular age-based norms.

SNC Score
- Child earns *T* scores of 20 or less on two or more of the four School-Age Core subtests used for the SNC, using appropriate age-norms; AND
- The sum of the child's *T* scores on the four School-Age Core subtests used for the SNC is 107 or less, using regular age-based norms.

Cluster Scores
- Child earns *T* scores of 20 or less on one of the School-Age Core subtests used for the cluster, using appropriate age-norms; AND
- The sum of the child's *T* scores on the two School-Age Core subtests used for the cluster is 49 or less, using regular age-based norms.

Extended Special Nonverbal Composite Scores. These may be used (a) if the child earns *T* scores of 20 or less on two or more of the four School-Age Core subtests contributing to the SNC, using age-appropriate norms; AND (b) the sum of the child's core *T* scores on those four School-Age Core subtests is 107 or less, using regular, age-based norms.

Extended Cluster Scores. Extended scores for the Verbal Ability, Nonverbal Reasoning Ability, or Spatial Ability clusters may be used (a) if the child earns *T* scores of 20 or less on one of the two School-Age Core subtests contributing to a cluster, using age-appropriate norms; AND (b) the sum of the child's core *T* scores on those two School-Age Core subtests is 49 or less, using regular, age-based norms.

Rapid Reference 4.5 shows a summary of when to use extended norms.

Determining the Extended GCA and Extended Cluster Scores

If the School-Age battery has been administered and the conditions in Rapid Reference 4.5 have been met, administer the additional Core subtests from the Early Years battery (Verbal Comprehension, Naming Vocabulary, Picture Similarities or Copying) that are required for calculating the upper Early Years GCA, SNC, or Cluster scores. The procedure is then as follows:

Table 4.1 Example of Calculating Extended GCA and Cluster Scores for a Child Aged 9:3

	Ability Score	*T* Score (Age 3:6–3:8)	Verbal	Nonverbal Reasoning	Spatial	GCA	SNV
Verbal Comprehension	92	43	43			43	
Picture Similarities	87	54		54		54	54
Naming Vocabulary	102	50	50			50	
Pattern Construction	120	52			52	52	52
Matrices	53	54		54		54	54
Copying	39	41			41	41	41
Sum of Core *T* scores			93	108	93	294	201
Standard Score			34	55	25	38	39

1. Obtain the ability scores for each subtest in the normal way;
2. Generate *T* scores by *using the norms for ages 3:6–3:8* (known as the Reference age group); do *NOT* report these *T* scores anywhere;
3. Sum the *T* scores for the two subtests in each cluster;
4. Sum the six *T* scores required for the GCA, or the four *T* scores required for the SNC; and finally
5. Find the corresponding GCA, SNC, or Cluster scores for the child's chronological age from the Extended GCA, SNC, and Cluster tables in the CD accompanying this book.

For example, a child aged 9:3 obtains standard scores of 20 or below on the Word Definition, Verbal Similarities, and Recall of Designs subtests in the School-Age battery. He is given the Upper Early Years Level of the Cognitive Battery and obtains the ability scores shown in Table 4.1 on the core subtests. Using the norms for the Reference Age Group of 3:6–3:8, the examiner converts these ability scores (as shown) to *T* scores. For example, the Ability Score of 92 for Verbal Comprehension at the Reference Age of 3:6–3:8 (not at age 9:3) yields a *T* score of 43, which is entered in the *T* score, Verbal, and GCA columns. Do NOT report these *T* scores anywhere. Next, the examiner adds the *T* scores in each column. For example, the *T* scores of 43 and 50 in the Verbal Cluster column have a sum of 93. Then, to convert the sums of the *T* scores to GCA and Cluster scores, the examiner uses the Extended GCA and Cluster Scores norms. For example, the column for the child's chronological age of 9:3 shows that the sum of Verbal Cluster scores (93) yields a standard score of 34.

 TEST YOURSELF

. . . .

I. **When calculating the age of the child being tested, which of these statements is correct?**

   (a) You disregard the days only AFTER first completely computing the correct age and then use just the years and month when finding the correct norms tables.

   (b) You disregard the days BEFORE first completely computing the correct age and then use just the years and month when finding the correct norms tables.

(continued)

2. It is acceptable to prorate:

(a) the GCA

(b) any one of the three clusters (Verbal, Nonverbal Reasoning, Spatial)

(c) any one of the Diagnostic clusters (Working Memory, Processing Speed, School Readiness)

(d) all of the above

3. Prorating may be done for any of the following reasons EXCEPT:

(a) a serious error in administration

(b) a serious disruption in the testing process

(c) a child refuses to take or respond to a subtest

(d) prorating will increase the score significantly

4. It is possible to substitute a core subtest:

(a) at any age

(b) on the Early Years battery only

(c) between ages 5:0 and 8:11 on specified subtests

(d) on the School-Age battery only on specified subtests

5. Which of these statements is (or are) correct? You may choose more than one answer.

(a) Extended GCA and cluster scores can be calculated for children of any age.

(b) If a child earns *T* scores of 20 or less on two or more School-Age subtests, you should calculate extended GCA and cluster scores.

(c) Extended GCA and cluster scores are available for children over 9 years of age.

(d) You should be cautious about scoring and interpreting subtests with raw scores of zero.

(e) Subtests with raw scores of zero are invalid and should not contribute to the assessment.

Answers: 1. a; 2. a; 3. d; 4. c; 5. c, d.

Five

HOW TO INTERPRET THE DAS-II

INTRODUCTION

In this chapter, we advocate a method of interpretation of a child's or adolescent's performance on the DAS-II that is flexible but still based on firm psychometric evidence. We believe that test performance should be integrated with all other information that is available about the individual being evaluated to allow a comprehensive psychological report to be produced. The integrated, comprehensive evaluation also allows a plan of intervention, if needed, to be developed, implemented, and then evaluated. Meaningful interpretation of test results from the DAS-II not only depends on precise administration and flawless scoring, but also requires thorough knowledge of the test's background, psychometric properties, and materials as well as knowledge about the examinee gained from other sources of information (scores on other tests; medical, social, and educational history; behaviors observed during testing; observations in other settings; and interviews with the examinee and other persons knowledgeable about the examinee, such as teachers or parents).

For examinees referred for assessment of possible specific learning disabilities, the Response to Intervention (RTI) process may have generated detailed curriculum-based measurement or assessment (CBM or CBA) data and other records of attempted interventions and their outcomes. The No Child Left Behind Act of 2001 (P.L. 107-110; U.S. Congress, 2001) is another source of test data for students. Many schools routinely administer nationally normed, multiple-choice, group achievement tests. All of these sources of information must be considered skeptically. The quality and utility of tests created by individual states and schools vary. Tests that are scored by hand may be scored incorrectly. Other errors can occur when tests are administered to large groups and answer sheets are sent away for machine scoring. Nonetheless, such tests may help identify patterns or track trends in the examinee's performance and may allow you to generate additional questions and hypotheses for your assessment.

Report cards—both marks and comments—are notoriously subjective and unreliable. Again, though, they may alert you to patterns (e.g., math marks always higher than reading and language arts marks) and trends (e.g., marks beginning high and then dropping throughout each year; math grades steadily declining over the years).

Previous individual assessments should be studied carefully, but you should still consider the possibility that they contain errors. If possible, it is helpful to obtain the actual test protocols so you can check the accuracy of recording the birth date, calculating the age, administering and scoring the test, looking up scores, adding scores, and transferring scores to the report.

Before beginning the step-by-step process of interpreting the DAS-II, create a summary of all relevant scores. Report the standard scores associated with the Composites (GCA and or SNC) and core (Verbal, Nonverbal Reasoning, and Spatial) and any relevant diagnostic (Working Memory, Processing Speed, and School Readiness) clusters along with the T scores for each subtest administered. Report the name of each composite or cluster. Most of the information for this summary sheet can be easily found on the DAS-II Record Form. Figure 5.1 shows a portion of a completed DAS-II summary sheet that includes the scores of Marybeth, an 8-year-old second grader who was suspected of having a Nonverbal Learning Disability (NVLD) and was administered 14 subtests from the School-Age battery.

Note that for Composites and Clusters, standard scores may be reported at the 90 percent or 95 percent confidence intervals (CI), along with their corresponding Percentile Rank (PR) and the confidence interval's descriptive categories. Confidence intervals for the DAS-II Composite and Clusters scores, found in the Tables A.2, A.3, and A.4 (pp. 102–122) in the DAS-II *Normative Data Tables Manual,* are created using the Standard Error of Estimate (SEe) of the estimated "true" score, as opposed to the Standard Error of Measurement (SEm) of the actual obtained score. When we use this method, we find that the confidence intervals are asymmetrical around the obtained score when the obtained score is well above or below 100. Such confidence intervals based on estimated true scores are a correction for true-score regression toward the mean. For example, a GCA of 148 is associated with a 95 percent confidence interval of −8 to +4 points (140–152); a GCA of 100 is associated with a 95 percent confidence interval of −6 to +6 points (94–106); and a GCA of 64 is associated with a 95 percent confidence interval of −4 to +7 points (60–71). We find that these asymmetrical bands usually describe the examinee's performance most accurately, but Sattler (2008) generally recommends the use of symmetrical confidence bands around the obtained score, using the SEm, for reporting test scores. He suggests using the

Composite/Cluster/Subtest	Score	95% CI	PR	Description
General Conceptual Ability	110	(104 – 115)	75	**Average to Above Average**
Special Nonverbal Composite		(–)		
Verbal Ability	133	(120 – 139)	99	**High to Very High**
Word Definitions	74		99	
Verbal Similarities	65		93	
Nonverbal Reasoning Ability	104	(96 – 112)	61	**Average to Above Average**
Matrices	54		66	
Sequential & Quantitative Reasoning	52		58	
Spatial Ability	89	(83 – 96)	23	**Below Average to Average**
Pattern Construction	38		12	
Recall of Designs	50		50	
Working Memory	113	(106 – 119)	81	**Average to Above Average**
Recall of Digits Backward	54		66	
Recall of Sequential Order	60		84	
Processing Speed	53	(49 – 66)	<1	**Very Low**
Speed of Information Processing	28			
Rapid Naming	21		<1	
School Readiness		(–)		
Phonological Processing	49		46	
Early Number Concepts				
Matching Letter-Like Forms				
Diagnostic and out of level subtests				
Recall of Digits Forward	58		79	
Recall of Objects - Immediate	49		46	
Recall of Objects - Delayed	54		66	
Recognition of Pictures	47		38	

Figure 5.1 Summary of DAS-II Scores for Marybeth, Age 8:4

asymmetrical, SEe-based intervals only if you are predicting a future score on a re-evaluation. However, we find his clearly explained argument unconvincing.

For the Standard Scores, we encourage you to consider not only a single score value, but also its corresponding PR, confidence band, and classification label (i.e., Very High, High, Above Average, Average, Below Average, Low, and Very Low). Rapid Reference 5.1 DAS-II Classification Schema provides Standard Score, *T* score, and PR ranges that correspond to Descriptive, Proficiency, and Normative classification labels.

Note too that descriptive categories are given for the full range of scores conveyed by a Standard Score's confidence interval as opposed to simply reporting the description for the obtained score. If, however, the range of the confidence interval covers only one category, that single category is all that should be reported. For example, Marybeth's GCA score of 110 (PR 75) would have a confidence interval of 104 to 115 and she would be described as functioning at the Average to Above Average range of general conceptual ability. However, her Processing Speed score of 53 (PR <1) would have a confidence interval of 49 to

Rapid Reference 5.1

DAS-II Classification Schema

Standard Score (M=100, SD=15)	T Score (M=50, SD=10)	Percentile Rank	Descriptive	Proficiency	Normative
≥130	70+	98 to 99+	Very High	Very Advanced	Normative Strength / Highest / 16% of population (>+1 SD)
120 to 129	63–89	91 to 97	High	Advanced	
116 to 119	60–62	86 to 90	Above Average		
110 to 115	57–59	75 to 84	Above Average		
90 to 109	43–56	25 to 74	Average	Adequate	Normal Range / Middle / 68% of population (within ±1 SD)
85 to 89	40–42	16 to 24	Below Average		
80 to 84	37–39	9 to 15	Below Average	Limited	Normative Weakness / Lowest / 16% of population (<–1 SD)
70 to 79	30–36	3 to 8	Low		
≤69	≤29	1 to 2	Very Low	Very Limited	

66 and she would be described as functioning at the Very Low range of ability in processing speed. Using ranges and classification labels aids in the communication of results to parents, teachers, and other lay people who may not have any particular knowledge regarding tests and test results. It also prevents conveying the idea that a single number is accurate and error free. For subtests, only T scores and Percentile Ranks are reported.

STEP BY STEP: STEPS FOR INTERPRETING DAS-II RESULTS

This section addresses an example of how to interpret the DAS-II following a step-by-step interpretive method. Interpretation of DAS-II test results requires several steps, including evaluation of the GCA or SNC, Core and Diagnostic Clusters, and subtest scores for significant differences, and comparison with tests of achievement and adaptive behavior measurements. The name of this battery includes the terms *Differential* and *Scales,* which is an acknowledgement that most individuals have different levels of ability in various areas of functioning. Howard Gardner (1983) has said that the focus of psychological assessment should be to detect not how smart a person is, but rather, how the person is smart. This is the philosophy underlying assessment with the DAS-II.

Authorities disagree about the appropriate level of interpretation for tests of cognitive abilities. Many experts insist that the only appropriate use of such tests is to measure psychometric g or an overall, global, general intelligence. There are at least four popular ideas supporting this admonition.

One is that many theorists are persuaded that g is the most important, or even the only important aspect of intelligence. Total scores on various cognitive ability tests measure this psychometric g more or less accurately. From this viewpoint, any significant variations in subtest scores are believed to represent fluctuations around a basic level of intellectual ability or the consequences of disabilities, differences, or disadvantages. However, even when there is significant subtest variability, total test scores, as proxies for psychometric g, generally do predict school performance reasonably well.

Another reason that some authors recommend primary or exclusive attention to total scores on tests of cognitive ability is that the total score is usually more statistically reliable than subtests or scales with fewer items than are included in the total.

A related issue is the relatively low specificity of subtests on many cognitive ability batteries. There is often scant justification for interpreting subtests as anything except as parts of the larger scale or entire battery of which they are components. They have little separate variance of their own.

A fourth reason sometimes cited for focusing on the total score of a test of cognitive abilities is the idea that specific abilities are better measured by very narrow tests that are not contaminated with g than by cognitive-battery subtests that have moderate or high g loadings.

These are serious and thoughtful arguments, but we believe that there is good reason to use multifaceted scales in general and the DAS-II in particular and to interpret the DAS-II clusters and even, if necessary, subtests with confidence.

First, while psychometric g does predict academic achievement and other important outcomes more accurately than do most other variables, there is growing evidence that various combinations of specific abilities, such as Cattell-Horn-Carroll (CHC) broad and narrow abilities, can be even stronger predictors of specific areas of academic achievement. It is possible that some of the evidence for the predictive validity of total scores as proxies for psychometric g may be illusory. For example, a student with very strong verbal abilities and weak spatial, working memory, and fluid reasoning abilities would have a total score considerably lower than the student's verbal ability. The specific cognitive weaknesses would depress the student's reading achievement below the level predicted from the student's verbal ability. The superficial impression would be that the student had only a moderate level of g, which accurately predicted weak reading achievement. However, it might instead be a case of strong intellectual potential, as shown by the higher verbal score, with the total score and the achievement both depressed by specific weaknesses, producing a misleading impression of g mediated by the total score predicting achievement. Willis and Dumont (2002, pp. 131–132) and Dumont and Willis (http://alpha .fdu.edu/psychology/mnemonics_ for_ five_ issues.htm) call this situation the "Mark Penalty." It is true that total scores are generally more statistically reliable than the shorter subtests that make up the totals, although this is not always the case within Item Response Theory (IRT; e.g., Daniel, 1999; Elliott, 2007b; Embretson & Reise, 2000). However, reliability is a necessary, but insufficient virtue for cognitive tests. For example, head circumference has been used to estimate intelligence. Head circumference, except under very unfortunate circumstances, is a highly reliable measure for adults: one hopes not to experience changes in head circumference over time. However, it turned out not be to be an especially valid nor useful measure of intelligence. It is very important for evaluators to select batteries whose clusters have adequate reliability (which the DAS-II clusters do possess), but reliability alone is not enough.

It is also true that low specificity does render a subtest or cluster uninterpretable as a separate measure apart from the larger entity of which it is a component. However, one of the important design characteristics of the DAS-II is strong specificity of subtests and clusters, thereby enabling their scores to be individually interpreted.

The fourth argument—that specific abilities are better measured by highly specific tests with low *g* loadings—appears plausible at first sight. However, it has been well-known since the 1930s that specific abilities are intercorrelated. It is these intercorrelations that yield broad factors and the general factor. Therefore, there is also a strong argument for building an assessment around a single, multifaceted instrument that measures as many of the most germane abilities as possible. See, for example, Flanagan, Ortiz, and Alfonso (2007). Even though all of the subtests share *g* loadings (or at least correlate with the total score), they are also normed on the same sample of examinees and differ primarily in the different abilities they measure. If the battery is constructed well, the subtests will have their reliable specificity maximized, and the subtests will assess a range of abilities that are important for predicting and understanding achievement (e.g., Evans, Floyd, McGrew, & Leforgee, 2002; Fiorello, Hale, McGrath, Ryan, & Quinn, 2002; Floyd, Evans, & McGrew, 2003). The DAS-II is an example of such a case, and we would argue that the battery is ideally suited for differential assessment of cognitive abilities.

There are two contrasting extreme approaches to the interpretation of cognitive tests, although most test users will hopefully adopt a balanced, intermediate position. On the one hand, rigid adherence to a *g* theory of intelligence would focus attention exclusively on the GCA score of the DAS-II. On the other hand, the most extreme application of subtest analysis might lead interpreters of the DAS-II to examine the subtests, or even the items within those subtests, for evidence of specific abilities, while ignoring the broader abilities shared by the subtests. As discussed above, the difficulty with such a fine analysis at the subtest or item level is that with fewer items come diminishing levels of reliability. The GCA is therefore inherently more reliable than the Verbal, Nonverbal Reasoning, or Spatial cluster scores, or any one subtest, because the GCA includes all the items in those clusters. At the same time, we confidently assert that the DAS-II subtests and clusters *are* reliable, and focusing exclusively on the GCA can ignore significant (reliable) differences between scores on clusters or subtests. Such differences can provide us with valuable understanding about a child's or adolescent's relative abilities in various areas, which can be important in the design of interventions.

An intermediate approach is therefore the wisest. It makes sense to attack a DAS-II profile hierarchically, beginning with the most reliable groupings of subtests and working through successively less reliable, smaller groupings before finishing with the least reliable data: individual subtests. Again, if the evaluator adheres exclusively to a *g* theory, that analysis would be considered an investigation of deviations from the student's overall intellectual ability. An orientation emphasizing separate, specific abilities would consider the process one of separating the student's levels of intellectual abilities in various factors or "intelligences" (e.g., Gardner, 1983) Both orientations lead to investigation of the various components of the total GCA score.

If there are no significant differences between subtests within the various clusters and if there are no significant differences between clusters, then the GCA (or SNC) may be a reasonably complete summary of the child's core cognitive abilities. The Diagnostic subtests, responses to specific items, and test behaviors may provide additional information, but the GCA (or SNC) is clearly the primary information, summarizing results from the Core subtests.

Even if we adopt the extreme position that tests of cognitive abilities measure psychometric *g* and that other abilities are unimportant for understanding intelligence, there is still the critical problem that different tests produce their total scores (or measure *g*) differently. For one example, short-term and working memory (*Gsm*) subtests constitute 20 percent of the total score on the WISC-IV (Wechsler, 2003), approximately 10 percent to 14 percent of the total score on the Woodcock-Johnson III (WJ III; Woodcock, McGrew, & Mather, 2001), 20 percent of total score on the Stanford-Binet, 5th ed. (Roid, 2003), and 20 percent of the total FCI or 25 percent of the total MPI on the Kaufman Assessment Battery for Children, 2nd ed. (KABC-II; Kaufman & Kaufman, 2004a). No explicit short-term and working memory subtests contribute to the total scores on the DAS-II and the Reynolds Intellectual Assessment Scales Composite Index (RIAS; Reynolds & Kamphaus, 2003), but the RIAS does offer an optional total score (not recommended by the authors) that includes the two memory subtests, making short-term memory 33 percent of that total. The point of this example is that a person with unevenly developed cognitive abilities (which is the rule, not the exception, as demonstrated on the WISC-R by Kaufman, 1976) is likely to earn very different total scores (proxies for *g*) on different tests, depending on how the composition of the test matches the individual's profile of abilities. Well-constructed tests correlate highly with each other when administered to groups of people whose various strengths and weaknesses balance out. For one individual, however, the surprise should be that two tests give similar scores, not that they give different ones.

If the subtest scores within the Verbal, Nonverbal Reasoning, and Spatial Clusters are each tightly grouped within their clusters, but the three clusters scores are significantly different from one another, then it makes sense to consider the verbal (*Gc*), nonverbal reasoning (*Gf*), and spatial (*Gv*) domains separately: the student demonstrates significantly different levels of ability when dealing with verbal, with fluid reasoning, and with spatial tasks. Clearly, in such a case, the GCA by itself is not a complete description of the child's cognitive abilities

Sometimes scores of subtests within a cluster may be significantly different from one another, so we need to look even further. One or more of the three clusters may not be cohesive (the component scores differ significantly from each other) and may require additional subdivision. If there is notable scatter within one or more of the clusters, the next level of interpretation we would recommend would be the narrow ability interpretation which separates cognitive processes into more specific abilities. This is not an excuse to leap ahead to analysis of individual subtests. It is, instead, a signal to cautiously consider alternative groupings of subtest scores.

This approach takes into account the idea that, especially for children and adolescents referred for testing because of suspected learning problems, it is not reasonable to accept the GCA as the only measure of a student's intellectual ability. Instead, interpretation must take into account differential abilities, and must recognize the fact that a learning problem can affect scores on tests of cognitive ability as well as other measures of ability, achievement, and behavior. The following method is intended to demonstrate this argument. It is not our intention to suggest that this is the only way to carry out such an analysis. Sattler (2008), Flanagan, Ortiz, and Alfonso (2007), and Flanagan, Ortiz, Alfonso, and Mascolo (2006), for example, explain similar, but different approaches. Flanagan and Kaufman (2004) apply similar logic to the WISC-IV and Shrank, Flanagan, Woodcock, and Mascolo (2001) to the WJ III.

The interpretive steps outlined in Figure 5.2 and elaborated upon below involve a complete and thorough analysis of all the DAS-II data and results. You must evaluate the DAS-II results using a practical as well as statistical approach. After you have completed all the steps necessary for making logical decisions, hypotheses can be generated from the results.

The steps are presented in logical, sequential order, but, in reality, you will sometimes jump around among the steps and go backward to review a previous step in light of information revealed later. Finally, with all the data considered, you will attempt to proceed beyond the sequential or successive steps and consider the entire picture simultaneously or holistically.

Most interpretive schemes begin with the most general aspects (global scores) and progress to more detailed aspects of the individual's performance (factors or clusters, subtest variability, qualitative responses). These procedures allow for both a quantitative and qualitative interpretation of the test, which may lead

Step 1: Provisionally evaluate the GCA, SNC, and Core Clusters
  If the GCA or SNC is below 70, administer, score and evaluate an adaptive behavior checklist
Step 2: For the Core Clusters, Evaluate Between-Cluster Differences
  A. Identify any significant differences between DAS-II Clusters (Verbal vs. Nonverbal Reasoning vs. Spatial)
  B. Identify the base-rate frequency of any observed significant differences
  If differences are significant and unusual, tentatively focus interpretation on Clusters rather than on the GCA.
  If differences are significant but not unusual, consider whether to focus interpretation on Clusters or on the GCA.
Step 3: For the Core Clusters, Evaluate Within-Cluster Differences
  A. Identify any significant Within-Cluster differences between subtest T scores
  B. Identify the base-rate frequency of any observed significant differences
  If differences are significant and unusual, focus interpretation on narrow abilities rather than on the Cluster.
  If differences are significant but not unusual, consider whether to focus interpretation on narrow abilities or on the Cluster.
Step 4: Evaluate GCA—Diagnostic Cluster Differences
  A. Identify any significant differences between the GCA and each Diagnostic Cluster
  B. Identify the frequency of any observed significant differences
  Interpret Diagnostic Clusters in light of this information.
Step 5: For the Diagnostic Clusters, Evaluate Within-Cluster Differences
  A. Identify any significant Within-Cluster differences between subtest T scores
  B. Identify the base-rate frequency of any observed significant differences
  If differences are significant and unusual, focus interpretation on narrow abilities rather than the Cluster.
  If differences are significant, but not unusual, consider whether to focus interpretation on narrow abilities or on the Cluster.
Step 6: Narrow Ability Hypotheses
  A. Identify the narrow abilities assessed and any relevant differences between them
Step 7: Evaluate Subtest Variability (Core and Diagnostic subtests)
  A. Identify any significant subtest differences from the Mean Core T Score
  B. Identify the base-rate frequency of any observed significant differences
Step 8: Evaluate Shared Ability Hypothesis
  A. Identify any relevant shared ability groupings
Step 9: Evaluate Cultural and Linguistic Influences
  A. Generate hypotheses based upon how the person does in relationship to both cultural and linguistic demands of each subtest
Step 10: Evaluate relevant subtest comparisons
  A. Generate and test hypotheses based upon relevant subtest comparisons
Step 11: Evaluate Qualitative Responses and Observed Behaviors
  A. Generate and test hypotheses based upon the scores and also on relevant behaviors and observations
Step 12: (Optional) Compare DAS-II with Achievement Scores
Step 13: Evaluate all of this information and integrate it into a cohesive description of the examinee's cognitive functioning as revealed by the DAS-II
Step 14: Integrate this understanding with background information, previous testing, and concurrent testing

Figure 5.2 Steps to Interpreting the DAS-II

to an understanding of how the person obtained the results and performed the tasks presented by the test. As one moves through the successive steps presented here, readers are encouraged to consult the cluster and subtest information included later in the chapter. That section provides relevant information about the DAS-II subtests as well as possible interpretive hypotheses and various strategies for expanding understanding of the person's underlying processes.

The approach to DAS-II interpretation that is offered here is based upon a statistical and actuarial approach that leads into hypothesis generation. Without this statistical approach, any interpretation would be less valid and reliable, and would be more likely to be inaccurate. By developing interpretive hypotheses that are based upon a statistical and actuarial analysis of the data and then coupling these findings with clinical observation, evaluators are able to make statements about a child's abilities relative to others of the same age as well as make statements based on the child's own performance. As hypotheses are generated, they are checked by testing them against the child's test performance and behaviors found on this and other tests as well as other sources of information, such as interviews, historical data, concurrent testing by other evaluators, and classroom observations.

When interpreting any test, it is important, as noted above, to remember that interpretations should focus on the most general areas before moving to the less general areas. In the case of the DAS-II, the most general (and most reliable) areas are the General Conceptual Ability (GCA) or Special Nonverbal (SNC) composites, and then the cluster scores (Verbal, Nonverbal Reasoning, Spatial, Working Memory, Processing Speed and School Readiness). Below these measures are the Shared Ability factors and finally the individual subtests.

Since each successive step of a DAS-II interpretation requires examiners to judge the adequacy of certain scores, an analysis (without any hypotheses generated) should first be completed. The DAS-II Summary Page contains information to aid examiners with this task (critical significance values, Mean Core T score, etc.). Examiners may also find the DAS-II Analysis Sheets provided on the CD that accompanies this book and Appendix A: School-Age Interpretation Worksheet and Appendix B: Upper Early Years Interpretation Worksheet useful when beginning any interpretation of a DAS-II protocol. A completed DAS-II Analysis Sheet summarizes the statistical results that can then be used in each of the successive steps.

A Note on "Statistically Significant" Differences. In going through various steps for the analysis of a child's scores on the DAS-II, which are given below, we will often refer to statistically significant differences between scores. A "statistically significant" difference between any two measures is one that would be unlikely to occur by chance if there were truly no difference between the student's levels of ability on the different measures. Since there is always some chance fluctuation of scores, it is likely that a child with perfectly balanced abilities might show some difference between obtained scores for those abilities on any given administration of the test. Tests of statistical significance demonstrate the odds of a particular difference occurring by chance if there were really no difference between ability levels. A probability of less than 5 percent ($p < .05$) means that the odds of a difference that large or larger occurring by chance are less than 1 chance in 20, or 5 percent—not a good bet. A probability of less than 5 percent ($p < .05$) or less than one percent ($p < .01$) suggests that the difference probably did not occur by chance, but might have represented a genuine difference between levels of ability on the various measures. These probabilities are based on valid test administrations during the DAS-II norming. They do not include invalidating circumstances that would have caused the norming case to be discarded. Fire drills, administration errors, illness, and other extraneous threats to validity are not included in these probabilities. Table B.1 (p. 130) in the DAS-II *Normative Data Tables Manual* provides the examiner with information about the difference required for statistical significance for these Between-Cluster comparisons at the .15, .05, and .01 levels of significance. Rounded mean values at the .05 significance level are also found on the protocol Normative Score Profiles Page.

A simple, but essential rule that is ignored all too often is that a difference that is not statistically significant is not a difference at all. The definition of a significant difference (which is worth sharing with readers of your report) is a difference that is too large to be likely to occur simply by chance. Therefore, by definition, a nonsignificant difference is one that is small enough to be likely to occur simply by chance. We should not try to wiggle around that fact with weasel words such as, "The nonsignificant difference between these clusters suggests . . ." or "There was a nonsignificant trend toward. . . ." A nonsignificant difference is not a difference—full stop.

Having made these points concerning what we mean by statistically significant differences, we now turn to the steps that we go through to analyze a child's various scores on the DAS-II.

Step 1a: Evaluate the GCA or SNC

Because it contains the largest number and widest variety of items, the General Conceptual Ability (GCA) score is the most statistically reliable[1] score usually obtained on the DAS-II. It is an excellent measure of general cognitive ability (*g*) and, therefore, is the best predictor of overall academic achievement for most children with and without disabilities. Consequently, the GCA is the first score to consider.

The same descriptive classification system (e.g., Confidence intervals, PR, etc.) can be used to describe the SNC and the Core clusters as well as the GCA. But the point of writing a good psychological report is not necessarily to report

---

[1] It is worth recalling that statistically "reliable" means "internally consistent" or "likely to produce a closely similar score on retesting." It does not necessarily mean "trustworthy," "believable," or "meaningful." A test cannot be valid for a particular purpose unless it is reliable, and if a test is valid for a particular purpose, increased reliability should yield increased validity. However, reliability is not the same thing as validity. It is a necessary, but not sufficient foundation for validity. The Special Nonverbal Composite, for example, would be very reliable for a blind child, but it certainly would not be a valid measure of conceptual ability!

every score, but rather to find the best way to describe an individual's cognitive ability. Figure 5.3 shows a completed example of Step 1 for Marybeth.

Besides being a measure of overall general conceptual ability, the GCA measures several important cognitive factors, including crystallized knowledge (*Gc*), fluid ability (*Gf*), and visual-spatial ability (*Gv*). Because the GCA can be influenced by many different variables (e.g., cultural opportunities, access to early education and general education, the ability to process visual and verbal information), you must determine, over the next several steps, whether you believe the GCA score represents the best summary of the child's overall intellectual ability.

Note that Marybeth's overall functioning, as defined by her GCA of 110 would classify her as functioning in the Average to Above Average level of cognitive ability. However, note that the Core ability clusters (Verbal, Nonverbal Reasoning, and Spatial) range from a high of 133 to a low of 89 and provide levels that span the range from Below Average to Very High.

When you evaluate the GCA remember that the same variety of component subtests that makes the GCA a reliable and usually valid measure of *g* also means that the GCA for any particular individual may include subtests that may tap areas of disability or disadvantage. The most obvious situation is one in which disability (e.g., hearing loss or aphasia) or disadvantage (e.g., limited exposure to spoken English) turns the Verbal subtests into measures of disability or of achievement, rather than measures of intellectual capacity or potential. The Special Nonverbal Composite (SNC) is, of course, designed precisely for some circumstances of this nature. The SNC measures several cognitive factors, including fluid ability (*Gf*) and visual-spatial ability (*Gv*), without being strongly influenced by verbal abilities.

There are other circumstances that may render some components of the

	Score	(circle one) 90% or 95% confidence	PR	Classification
GENERAL CONCEPTUAL ABILITY (GCA):	110	104 - 115	75	Average to Above Average
SPECIAL NONVERBAL COMPOSITE (SNC):		-		
VERBAL (V):	133	120 - 139	99	High to Very High
NONVERBAL REASONING (NVR):	104	96 - 112	61	Average to Above Average
SPATIAL (Sp):	89	83 - 96	21	Below Average to Average

Figure 5.3 Step 1. Provisionally Evaluate the GCA, SNC, and Core Clusters

GCA suspect. For example, a child with severe visual-motor coordination challenges might be severely hindered on Recall of Designs and moderately hindered on Pattern Construction, even with the Alternative Procedure without bonus points for speed. In this instance, the Spatial and the GCA scores would not be good measures of the child's intellectual capacity or potential, but would instead reflect the child's disability.

The fact that the GCA is a good predictor of scores on intelligence tests and of scores on tests of academic achievement, even for children with disabilities, is often mistaken for proof that the GCA (and similar total scores on intelligence tests) is always a valid measure of overall conceptual ability or cognitive ability. It is not proof of any such thing. It is, instead, evidence that the same disability can impair scores on tests of both cognitive ability and achievement.

Therefore, at this first step, you should decide whether the GCA or the SNC represents a clinically meaningful measure of the individual's overall cognitive abilities or whether reporting and interpreting the various component constructs of the DAS-II would provide a more useful explanation of abilities. If the amount of "scatter"[2] within and between the clusters that make up the GCA is insignificant and not unusual compared to the scatter seen in the DAS-II norming sample, then the GCA score probably summarizes most of the useful information about the student available from that administration of the DAS-II core subtests. If, however, the three cluster scores that combine to create the overall GCA score deviate significantly from each other, more interpretation of those abilities seems warranted.

Rapid Reference 5.2 shows an example of how to describe the GCA in the opening of a psychological report. Note that we used an ordinal modifier after the percentile rank (-rd) to communicate to those unfamiliar with this statistic that the percentile rank is a description of the individual's performance in comparison to the standardization sample—and not a percent of correct answers.[3] We also used the descriptive classification system to describe a score's entire confidence interval—rather than a single score. Using classification labels, percentile ranks, and confidence interval ranges in this way aids in the communication of results to parents, teachers, and other lay people who may not have any particular knowledge regarding tests and test

---

[2] When writing reports, remember that the term "scatter" (simple difference between highest and lowest scores) is not familiar to readers who are not trained evaluators. Use familiar English words either to replace "scatter" or to define it.

[3] For the same reason, we also spell out "percentile rank" or use the abbreviation "PR" and never use the abbreviation "%ile" in our reports.

≡ Rapid Reference 5.2

Example of How to Describe the GCA in a Psychological Report

The General Conceptual Ability Score (GCA) is provided as a measure of the general ability of an individual to perform complex mental processing that involves the conceptualization and transformation of information. Erika earned a GCA of 109 (103–115, 73PR). While no one score is perfectly accurate, the chances are good (95 percent) that Erika's GCA is within the range of 103 to 115. This would classify her overall cognitive ability, as measured by the DAS-II, as Average to Above Average. Her GCA is ranked at the 73rd percentile, indicating that she scored as well or higher than 73 percent of other individuals of the same age in the standardization sample.

results. It also prevents conveying the idea that a single number is accurate and error free.

Step 1b: If the GCA or SNC is Below 70, Administer, Score, and Evaluate an Adaptive Behavior Checklist

The DAS-II is a test of cognitive ability; alone it cannot diagnose or provide recommendations to particular interventions. However, evaluators can and should use information provided by the DAS-II test results in combination with other sources of information about a particular individual to make diagnoses and provide recommendations. Mental retardation, cognitive impairment, or intellectual disability is one possible diagnosis that is based on information that can be provided by the DAS-II as well as other sources of information. We quote from the FAQ on the American Association on Intellectual and Developmental Disabilities (2008) website http://www.aamr.org/Policies/faq_intellectual _disability.shtml:

"Intelligence refers to a general mental capability. It involves the ability to reason, plan, solve problems, think abstractly, comprehend complex ideas, learn quickly, and learn from experience. Although not perfect, intelligence is represented by Intelligent (sic) Quotient (IQ) scores obtained from standardized tests given by a trained professional. With regards to the intellectual criterion for the diagnosis of intellectual disability, limitations in intellectual functioning are generally thought to be present if an individual has an IQ test score of approximately 70 or below. IQ scores must always be considered in light of the standard error of measurement, appropriateness, and consistency with administration guidelines. Since the standard error of measurement for most IQ tests is approximately 5, the ceiling may go up to 75. This represents a score approximately 2 standard deviations below the mean, considering the standard error of measurement. It is important to remember, however, that an IQ score is only one criterion: Significant limitations in adaptive behavior skills and evidence that the disability was present before age 18 are two additional criteria in determining if a person has intellectual disability."

We recommend that, whenever you suspect intellectual impairment based upon an individual's performance on the DAS-II, you obtain results from an adaptive behavior checklist completed by an individual who is knowledgeable about the examinee's adaptive behavior levels. Such checklists include the Vineland-II (VABS-II; Sparrow, Cicchetti, & Balla, 2005), the AAMR Adaptive Behavior Scales–School, 2nd ed. (ABS-S:2; Lambert, Nihira, & Lel, 1993), and the Adaptive Behavior Assessment System, 2nd ed. (ABAS: II; Harrison & Oakland, 2003). Various versions are available and rely on parent, childcare worker, or teacher report and can be administered as either paper-and-pencil checklists or through interview methodology. We recommend gathering data from both home and school and, when possible, using an interview format with parents.

Step 2a: Are There Any Significant Differences *Between* the Three Core Clusters?

Figure 5.4 shows a completed example of Step 2a using the scores obtained by Marybeth. Note that for Marybeth, the magnitude of the differences between the three core ability clusters are so large as to reach a statistical difference at the .01 level. You can assume that such large differences are real: there is less than one chance in 100 that they are the effect of some measurement error.

If there is a significant difference between any pair of Core cluster scores, the GCA must be interpreted with caution. In the example of Marybeth, she displays the following "profile" generated by her three core abilities: Her Verbal ability is significantly greater than her Nonverbal Reasoning (V>NV) and her Spa-

> **DON'T FORGET**
> ....
> A statistically significant and uncommon difference between ability scores does not necessarily imply the existence of a specific learning disability or any other problem for the individual. The absence of a statistically significant difference does not imply the absence of a specific learning disability or any other problem. Some children without learning disabilities show huge differences among ability scores. Some students with dramatic learning disabilities do not show significant differences among ability scores.

	Difference	Significant (.01)	Significant (.05)	Not Significant		Is Difference Significant?
V (133) vs. NVR (104):	29	17+	13-16	0-12	Yes	No
V (133) vs. Sp (89):	44	16+	12-15	0-11	Yes	No
NVR (104) vs. Sp (89):	15	14+	10-13	0-9	Yes	No

◆ Step 2a Interpretive Decision

Is at least one of the three comparisons marked "Yes"?	YES	NO

If the answer is NO, there are no significant differences between the cluster scores	⇨	You may interpret the GCA. **Skip to Step 3a**

If the answer YES, there are significant differences between the cluster scores	⇨	**Go to Step 2b**

Figure 5.4 Step 2a. Are There Any Significant Differences *Between* the Three Core Clusters?

tial abilities (V>Sp), and additionally her Nonverbal Reasoning is significantly greater than her Spatial ability (NV>Sp).

As with almost any cognitive test that assesses multiple cognitive abilities, differences among the abilities can often lead to important interpretive hypotheses. Focusing on a single score that represents an average between discrepant scores in different areas obscures important areas of strength and weakness. When interpreting differences between Core cluster scores, it is important to note that Between-Cluster differences can occur for a number of different reasons, including learning disabilities, different interests, different environmental opportunities, strengths/difficulties when working under time pressures, strengths/deficits in how one processes information, sensory impairments, cognitive styles, fluctuating attention or motivation, or brain injury. Neither the presence nor absence of Between-Cluster differences is by itself sufficient to diagnose or rule out any disability or recommend or dismiss any particular intervention. In fact, in the DAS-II standardization sample, many children displayed statistically significant (real) differences between at least one pair of the three Core clusters.

Table 5.1 shows the percent of children from the standardization sample who displayed various significant differences at the .05 level between the Core clusters. As you can see, when disregarding the specific comparison (e.g., Verbal versus Spatial), and the specific direction of any cluster difference (e.g., V>Sp or V<Sp), approximately 63 percent of all the children in the sample had at least one significant Core cluster difference. Interestingly, similar percentages of children had either no (37 percent), one (23 percent), or two (36 percent) significant

Table 5.1 Percentage of Standardization Sample Obtaining Various Core Cluster Differences

One cluster difference (Total = 23%)		Two cluster difference (Total = 36%)		Three cluster difference (Total = 4%)	
V=NV V<Sp NV=Sp	5%	V>NV V>Sp NV=Sp	7%	V<NV V<Sp NV<Sp	1%
V=NV V>Sp NV=Sp	5%	V=NV V<Sp NV<Sp	7%	V>NV V>Sp NV<Sp	1%
V=NV V=Sp NV<Sp	4%	V=NV V>Sp NV>Sp	6%	V>NV V>Sp NV>Sp	1%
V=NV V=Sp NV>Sp	3%	V<NV V<Sp NV=Sp	6%	V<NV V<Sp NV>Sp	1%
V<NV V=Sp NV=Sp	3%	V<NV V=Sp NV>Sp	5%	V<NV V>Sp NV>Sp	0%
V>NV V=Sp NV=Sp	3%	V>NV V=Sp NV<Sp	5%	V>NV V<Sp NV<Sp	0%

Note: V = Verbal; NV = Nonverbal Reasoning; Sp = Spatial

Approximately 37% of the sample had no significant differences between any one of the three core clusters (i.e., V=NV V=Sp NV=Sp)

cluster differences, while only about 4 percent of the children in the sample had all three Core clusters differing significantly from each other.

In the example of Marybeth, all three Core clusters differed significantly from each other, a fairly unusual occurrence, being found in only about 4 percent of the norm sample. Additionally, her specific profile (V>NV, V>Sp, NV>Sp) was found in only about 1 percent of the norming sample.

An examination of the intercorrelations between the subtests that make up the Verbal, Nonverbal Reasoning, and Spatial Ability clusters shows that they all do, as expected, correlate moderately (mean r = .43 to .66; Table 5.2). Note, however, that the Verbal and Spatial cluster subtests correlate almost equally to those of the Nonverbal Reasoning Cluster (Mean r Verbal/Nonverbal Reasoning = .53 and Spatial/Nonverbal Reasoning = .54, respectively) while they correlate lower with each other (Mean r Verbal/Spatial = .45). Nonverbal Reasoning, as measured by the DAS-II, requires the integration of both verbal and visual-spatial abilities, and because of this, it is not unusual to find that the Verbal and Spatial Ability cluster scores will differ significantly from each other, but at the same time the Nonverbal Reasoning Ability score a child receives will often be "in-between" the Verbal and Spatial Ability. In the norming sample, very few children had profiles in which the Nonverbal Reasoning ability score was significantly different from *both* the Verbal and Spatial clusters.

When each of the V/NV/Sp comparison differences is less than the critical value for significance, the GCA is most likely a useful total and the interpretative statement in Rapid Reference 5.2 can be sufficient to describe ability level.

Table 5.2 Average Intercorrelations of School-Age Subtests and Clusters

Clusters	Subtests	Verbal		Nonverbal Reasoning		Spatial	
		WD	VS	Mat	SQR	RDes	PC
Verbal	WD						
	VS	.66					
Nonverbal Reasoning	Mat	.50	.51				
			.53				
	SQR	.55	.55	.64			
Spatial	RDes	.43	.44	.50	.51		
			.45		**.54**		
	PC	.46	.47	.55	.59	.55	

If there is no compelling reason to bypass the statistical approach to interpretation (e.g., significant scatter between the scores that make up the clusters; the effects of retesting), one may infer that the person displays fairly equal abilities whether through verbal expression of concepts, knowledge, and reasoning; through complex nonverbal inductive reasoning; or through complex visual-spatial processing.

If significant differences between cluster scores are found in the profile then the examiner can still use the description of overall ability level recommended in Rapid Reference 5.2 but then add the statement in Rapid Reference 5.3 to make note of any significant differences that were found.

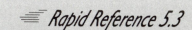

Rapid Reference 5.3

Statement to Add When the Clusters are Significantly Different But That Difference is Not Unusual

Rachel demonstrated significant variability in her performance across the three Indexes that make up the GCA score, specifically, her Verbal Ability Cluster score was significantly higher than both her Nonverbal Reasoning and Spatial Ability Cluster scores.

Step 2b: Are Significant Differences *Between* Core Clusters Unusually Large?

As seen before in Table 5.1, many people demonstrate statistically significant differences between their levels of ability in different areas. These differences, although important to the understanding of the child's overall functioning, simply reflect differences that did not occur by chance. As noted above, a statistically significant difference between certain cognitive abilities is often found frequently in the general population of children. If a DAS-II Core cluster differs significantly from any other Core cluster on the test, examiners should determine the base-rate frequency of the observed difference. If a given difference occurred in less than 10 percent of the norming sample ($f < 10\%$), we might consider that a notably uncommon difference.

The Between-Cluster differences shown by various percentages of the standardization sample are found in Tables B.2 (p. 130) in the DAS-II *Normative Data Tables Manual*. In general, the Lower Early Years Verbal and Nonverbal Clusters would need to differ by approximately 16 points in order to approach a level seen in only 10 percent of the population. For the Upper Early Years and the School-Age clusters, a difference between clusters must be between 15 and 19 points to be considered unusual. Note that these tables are derived from the absolute value of the difference but do take into account the direction of the discrepancy (e.g., V > NVR, NVR > V). Figure 5.5 shows a completed example of Step 2b for Marybeth.

For Marybeth, the magnitude of the difference between each of her core abilities not only is statistically significant, each difference also occurs fairly infrequently (V vs. NV ≈ 2 percent, V vs. Sp ≈ 1 percent, and NV vs. Sp ≈ 10 percent).

It is important to note that, when you are considering the magnitude of the differences between the three Core ability clusters, the size of the differences needed for unusualness (≤10 percent) may change substantially based upon the overall GCA ability level of the child. Tables C.1 and C.2 (pp. 140–142) in the DAS-II *Normative Data Tables Manual* provide the examiner with information, by ability level, about the difference obtained by various percentages (i.e., 15, 10, 5, 2, 1, and .5) of the norms sample.

Table 5.3 shows, for Upper Early Years and School-Age children, the Between-Cluster score differences displayed by approximately 10 percent of the norm sample for the total sample and by ability level. Note that there are often large differences between the magnitude of the difference needed for unusualness depending upon whether you compare the obtained difference to the entire sample or to children with similar ability levels. For example, the typical 5-year-old

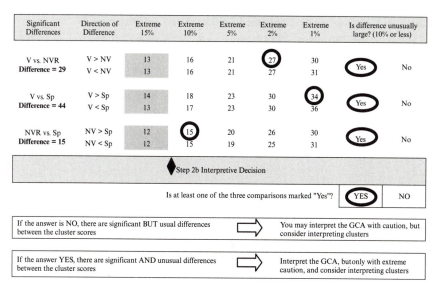

Significant Differences	Direction of Difference	Extreme 15%	Extreme 10%	Extreme 5%	Extreme 2%	Extreme 1%	Is difference unusually large? (10% or less)	
V vs. NVR Difference = 29	V > NV	13	16	21	27	30	Yes	No
	V < NV	13	16	21	27	31		
V vs. Sp Difference = 44	V > Sp	14	18	23	30	34	Yes	No
	V < Sp	13	17	23	30	36		
NVR vs. Sp Difference = 15	NV > Sp	12	15	20	26	30	Yes	No
	NV < Sp	12	15	19	25	31		

◆ Step 2b Interpretive Decision

Is at least one of the three comparisons marked "Yes"?	YES	NO

| If the answer is NO, there are significant BUT usual differences between the cluster scores | ⇨ | You may interpret the GCA with caution, but consider interpreting clusters |

| If the answer YES, there are significant AND unusual differences between the cluster scores | ⇨ | Interpret the GCA, but only with extreme caution, and consider interpreting clusters |

Figure 5.5 Step 2b. Are Significant Differences *Between* Core Clusters Unusually Large?

child administered the Upper Early Years battery would require a 19-point difference between Verbal and Spatial ability clusters to achieve a difference obtained by 10 percent or less. However, if that child's GCA were 120 or above, the 19-point difference between the Verbal and Spatial ability cluster scores would actually be quite common. For children with GCAs of 120 or higher, a Verbal-Spatial difference of 29 points is needed to reach the extreme 10 percent level.

Scatter

Another aspect to be taken into consideration when evaluating the GCA score's interpretability is the concept of test "scatter," or the range from the lowest to the highest subtest T score, conventionally determined by simple subtraction. The volumes of "WISC folklore" (Dumont's term; Dumont & Willis, 1995; Dumont, Farr, Willis, & Whelley, 1998) include a great deal of nonsense about test scatter. More than 30 years ago, Kaufman (1976) startled many examiners by demonstrating that the usual scatter on the WISC-R was about seven points, a span that many diagnosticians had considered indicative of a specific learning disability. Clearly, intersubtest scatter is not in itself diagnostic.

Tables C.4 (p. 144) in the DAS-II *Normative Data Tables Manual* provides the examiner with information about the magnitude of intersubtest scatter within

Table 5.3 Upper Early Years and School-Age Children, the Between-Cluster Score Difference Displayed by Approximately 10% of the Norm Sample for the Total Sample and by Ability Level.

		Extreme 10%				
			GCA			
	Total sample	<70	80–89	90–109	110–119	>120
Early Years						
V > NVR	19	23	16	18	22	24
V < NVR	18	17	16	17	20	22
V > Sp	19	21	19	17	21	29
V < Sp	19	15	16	18	20	22
NVR > Sp	19	21	20	16	23	25
NVR < Sp	19	18	16	19	19	25
School-Age						
V > NVR	16	13	18	17	15	11
V < NVR	16	18	15	15	16	25
V > Sp	18	14	20	17	18	20
V < Sp	17	22	15	16	17	25
NVR > Sp	15	10	14	13	17	21
NVR < Sp	15	14	13	14	16	17

Core subtests composites shown by various percentages of the norming sample. From this table, you will note that approximately 26 to 29 T score points (School-Age and Upper Early Years, respectively), between the highest and lowest Core subtest, is needed to reach a level of unusualness (equal to or less than 10 percent). For Marybeth, the 36-point T score difference between Word Definitions ($T = 74$) and Pattern Construction ($T = 38$) is found in only about 2 percent of the norming sample, adding strength to the notion that the GCA is not the best way to describe her abilities.

If the difference between the Core clusters is both significant and unusual, or if the intersubtest scatter itself is found to be unusual, it may be advisable to use a statement such as that given in Rapid Reference 5.4 and omit the discussion of the GCA used in Rapid Reference 5.2.

If you are submitting your report to people who are notorious for grabbing

≡ Rapid Reference 5.4

Example of How to Describe in a Psychological Report the Finding of a Significant and Unusual Difference Between the Core Cluster Scores

Victoria earned a GCA of 77, but this estimate of her ability in complex information processing may not be interpreted meaningfully because of the large differences between the three Core cluster scores that compose this overall score. Therefore, Victoria's cognitive ability is best understood by her performance on the separate core DAS-II clusters, namely, Verbal Ability, Nonverbal Reasoning Ability, and Spatial Ability, together with the Diagnostic clusters and subtests.

reports and circling poorly understood numbers so future readers can skip the words and just use the number, you might even want to omit the "of 77" from the statement in Rapid Reference 5.4 and relegate the number to an obscure appendix to your report.

Step 2c (Optional): Are There Any Significant Differences *Between* the GCA and the Core Clusters?

The DAS-II *Normative Data Tables Manual* does not provide tables enabling this question to be evaluated, although such tables were included in the first edition of the DAS (Elliott, 1990a). At least one research study (Joseph, Tager-Flusberg, & Lord, 2002) has used this method of identifying children with significant cognitive strengths and weaknesses. Researchers and practitioners alike may appreciate having these tables so that a continuity of approach to the identification of high and low cluster scores may be maintained.

Tables showing the significance of a difference between the GCA score and each of the Core clusters are provided on the CD accompanying this book. If a cluster score is significantly different from the GCA, this provides further support for caution in reporting the GCA score. Following a procedure similar to that described in Step 2a, you may compare the child's level of performance on the Core clusters to his or her overall level of performance as represented in the GCA. The table on the CD indicates that differences of between 7 and 8 points between the GCA and the Core clusters are statistically significant at the .05 level for both the Upper Early Years and the School-Age batteries.

Step 3a: Identify Any Significant Differences *Within* DAS-II Core Clusters

Because the clusters of the DAS-II assess not only broad cognitive ability factors, but also separate cognitive skills (narrow abilities) with higher levels of specificity than are found on some other scales, it is important to judge whether the clusters themselves are cohesive or unitary. Are the clusters, each composed of two subtests, valid measures of the abilities being assessed? Are the cluster scores complete summaries of the ability or is further explanation needed? Since broad cognitive skills, such as verbal ability, can be measured in numerous ways, it should not surprise examiners that subtests within factors or clusters do often deviate from each other. Because all the DAS-II Core clusters are composed of two subtests, the clusters use subtests that measure the same broad construct (e.g., Verbal ability), but do so with tasks that are different in their specific task demands. Each subtest can be delineated by one or more "narrow" abilities.

To determine the validity of a cluster score, examiners must first determine whether the subtests in that cluster differ statistically from one another. In Step 3a (Figure 5.6 with scores from Marybeth included), we identify any significant differences *within* the DAS-II core ability clusters. As noted above, both the DAS-II *Normative Data Tables Manual* (Tables B.5, p. 131) and the DAS-II Normative Score Profile Page of the Record Form include information regarding statistical discrepancy. The values from these sources indicate that, for the Early Years and the School-Age subtests included in the clusters, a difference of 8 to 12 points between the subtests may be considered significant at the .05 level.

If you determine that there are no significant differences between the subtest

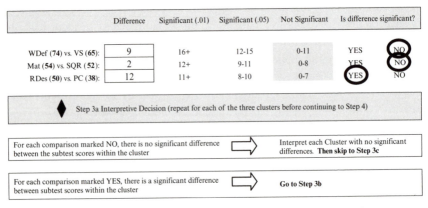

	Difference	Significant (.01)	Significant (.05)	Not Significant	Is difference significant?
WDef (**74**) vs. VS (**65**):	9	16+	12-15	0-11	YES **NO**
Mat (**54**) vs. SQR (**52**):	2	12+	9-11	0-8	YES **NO**
RDes (**50**) vs. PC (**38**):	12	11+	8-10	0-7	**YES** NO

◆ Step 3a Interpretive Decision (repeat for each of the three clusters before continuing to Step 4)

For each comparison marked NO, there is no significant difference between the subtest scores within the cluster	⇨	Interpret each Cluster with no significant differences. **Then skip to Step 3c**

For each comparison marked YES, there is a significant difference between subtest scores within the cluster	⇨	**Go to Step 3b**

Figure 5.6 Step 3a. Identify Any Significant Differences *Within* DAS-II Core Clusters

≡ Rapid Reference 5.5

Example of How to Describe a Cluster With No Significant Differences Between Subtest Scores

Verbal Ability, a measure of crystallized intelligence (*Gc*), represents Allison's verbal knowledge and ability to reason with previously learned information. *Gc* ability develops largely as a function of both formal and informal educational opportunities and language experiences and is highly dependent on exposure to mainstream U.S. culture. Allison's Verbal Ability was assessed by a task that required her to define words presented orally by the examiner (Word Definitions) and a task in which she had to identify the common concept linking three words (Verbal Similarities). Allison's performances on these two tasks (Word Definitions *T* = 52; Verbal Similarities *T* = 48) were not significantly different from each other, indicating that her Verbal Ability score is a good estimate of her verbal or *Gc* ability. Allison obtained a Verbal Ability score of 100 (94–106) which is ranked at the 50th percentile and is classified as Average.

scores within the clusters (i.e., the clusters appear to be cohesive or unitary), you can describe those clusters as representing broad measures of the separate abilities (e.g., Verbal, Nonverbal Reasoning, Spatial). (See Rapid Reference 5.5 for an example of such a description.)

Step 3b: Are Significant Differences *Within* Core Clusters Unusually Large?

As with all other comparisons, the base-rate frequency of any obtained within-cluster difference is evaluated for unusualness. Are significant differences between subtests *within* Core clusters unusually large? The DAS-II *Normative Data Tables Manual* (Tables B.6, p. 132) provides information regarding the frequency of occurrence of various within-cluster score differences. In the case of the DAS-II Early Years subtest comparisons, to reach a level of unusualness, defined as a difference shown by 10 percent of the sample or fewer, a difference of approximately 10 to 15 points is needed for all comparisons. For the School-Age clusters, differences of between 10 and 12 points are necessary. Figure 5.7 shows the steps used to determine the frequency of obtaining certain within-cluster differences.

In the case of Marybeth's scores, the differences between the subtests that make up her Verbal and Nonverbal Reasoning abilities were small (9 and 2 points, respectively) while the 12-point difference between the subtests of the Spatial cluster, with Recall of Designs (*T* = 50) being significantly higher than the Pat-

Significant Differences	Direction of Difference	Extreme 15%	Extreme 10%	Extreme 5%	Extreme 2%	Extreme 1%	Is difference unusually large? (10% or less)	
Verbal								
WDef vs. VS	WDef > VS	(8)	10	14	19	21	Yes	(No)
Difference = 9	WDef < VS	8	10	13	16	18		
Nonverbal Reasoning								
Mat vs. SQR	Mat > SQR	9	11	14	17	20	Yes	(No)
Difference = 2	Mat < SQR	9	11	14	20	24		
Spatial								
RDes vs. PC	RDes > PC	9	(12)	15	19	23	(Yes)	No
Difference = 12	RDes < PC	9	11	15	20	25		

◆ Step 3b Interpretive Decision for each cluster

Is at least one of the three comparisons marked "Yes"?	(YES)	NO

If the answer is NO, there are significant BUT not unusual differences between subtest scores <u>within</u> one or more clusters	⟹	You may interpret the cluster with caution, but consider interpreting subtests

If the answer is YES, there are significant AND unusual differences between subtest scores <u>within</u> the cluster	⟹	Interpret the cluster, but only with extreme caution, and consider interpreting subtests

Figure 5.7 Step 3b. Are Significant Differences *Within* Core Clusters Unusually Large?

tern Construction score ($T = 38$), is considered unusual, occurring in only about 10 percent of the norming sample.

If there are within-cluster differences that are significant and unusual, you may interpret the cluster, but only with extreme caution, and you should consider examining subtests (Step 6) rather than the cluster. When describing the child's functioning on these clusters, it is useful to take into account the overall level of functioning.

According to the classifications shown in Rapid Reference 5.1 (DAS-II Classification Schema), a T score below 40 can be described as being a Normative Weakness and a T score above 59 a Normative Strength. Therefore, if the variability among subtest scores comprising a cluster is unusually large and all scaled scores are ≤39, describe the individual's range of observed functioning in the ability presumed to underlie the Index as a notable limitation. Conversely, if the variability among subtest scores composing a cluster is unusually large and all scaled scores are ≥ 60, then describe the individual's range of observed functioning in the ability presumed to underlie the Index as a notable strength. See Rapid References 5.6 and 5.7 for examples of how to describe these occurrences.

≡ *Rapid Reference 5.6*

Example of How to Describe a Cluster With Significant and Unusual Differences Between the Subtest Scores Within It

The Nonverbal Reasoning Ability cluster, a measure of fluid intelligence (*Gf*), represents nonverbal inductive reasoning and requires complex mental processing. Fluid Intelligence refers to mental operations that an individual uses when faced with a relatively novel task that cannot be performed automatically. Kristin's *Gf* was assessed by a task that required her to select from among four or six choices the figure that correctly completes an incomplete matrix (Matrices, *T* Score = 30), and another task in which she was required to use reasoning to discover the underlying characteristic that governs a problem or set of materials (Sequential and Quantitative Reasoning, *T* Score = 60). The variability between her performances on these tasks was unusually large, indicating that her overall *Gf* ability cannot be fully summarized in a single score (i.e., the Nonverbal Reasoning Ability score).

≡ *Rapid Reference 5.7*

How to Describe the Overall Level of Observed Functioning

The Spatial Ability cluster, a measure of visual-spatial ability (*Gv*), requires the ability to perceive and remember spatial relations and shapes. Visual-spatial ability is the ability to generate, perceive, analyze, synthesize, store, retrieve, manipulate, transform, and think with visual patterns and stimuli. Joan's *Gv* was assessed by a task that required her to recall and reproduce an abstract line drawing that is presented to her for a brief period of time (Recall of Designs, *T* Score = 26) and a task in which she had to rapidly perceive and manipulate a relatively simple visual pattern of objects in space (Pattern Construction-Std., *T* Score = 38). The difference between Joan's performances on these tasks was unusually large, indicating that her overall *Gv* ability cannot be fully summarized in a single score (i.e., the Spatial Ability cluster). However, Joan's *Gv* ability is a notable limitation for her because her performance on both of the tasks that compose the Spatial Ability cluster ranged from Very Low to Below Average.

Note: If the variability among subtest scores that compose a cluster is unusually large and all scaled scores are ≥60, then describe the individual's range of observed functioning in the ability presumed to underlie the Index as a notable strength by changing the last sentence in the above paragraph, as follows:

However, Joan's *Gv* ability is a notable strength for her because her performance on the tasks that compose the Spatial Ability cluster ranged from Above Average to Very High.

Cluster Ability	Interpretable? (Y/N)	Standard Score	Normative Weakness <85	Within Normal Limits 85-115	Normative Strength >115
Verbal	Y	133			✓
Nonverbal Reasoning	Y	104		✓	
Spatial	N				

Figure 5.8 Step 3c. Determine Normative Strengths and Weaknesses in the Ability Score Profile

Step 3c: Determine Normative Strengths and Weaknesses in the Cluster Score Profile

For the cluster identified in Step 3b (Figure 5.7) as having small within-cluster subtest differences and therefore found to be interpretable as a cohesive whole, you should next determine Normative Strengths and Normative Weaknesses in the child's individual's profile (Figure 5.8). If the ability cluster's Standard Score is greater than 115, consider the Cluster Ability score a Normative Strength. If the ability cluster's standard score is less than 85, consider the Cluster Ability score is a Normative Weakness. If the ability cluster's standard score is between 85 and 115 (inclusive), then the ability measured by the cluster is Within Normal Limits. Remember that classification labels are arbitrary. For example, a score of 85 is only one point higher than a Normative Weakness and one of 115 is only one point lower than a Normative Strength.

In Step 3c, for each ability cluster found to be interpretable, record the standard score and place a checkmark in the box corresponding to the appropriate normative category for each Ability Cluster. In the case of Marybeth, her Verbal and Nonverbal Reasoning Clusters were found to be interpretable, and thus her Verbal functioning can be described as being a Normative Strength (standard score > 115) while her ability in the area of Nonverbal Reasoning can be described as Within Normal Limits (standard score = 85 through 115).

DON'T FORGET

All classification schemes for test scores are arbitrary. They are not what attorneys call "arbitrary and capricious." Publishers do not call low scores "high" or mid-range scores "low," but the decision to call the "average range" 85–115 or 90–109 or 90–110, though possibly thoughtful, is still arbitrary, as is the decision to call the next-lowest category "low average," "below average," or something else. We must be careful not to be misled by our own assignments of score classifications. No matter what they are called, standard scores of 84 and 85 are essentially identical. We must not forget that fact and we must not let our readers forget it.

Rapid Reference 5.8 shows how you might describe these normative strengths or weaknesses.

Before jumping to the narrow abilities of the Core subtests, it is important to examine the Diagnostic clusters and how to best interpret them. Repeat the process you have already done in Steps 2 and 3, but this time focus on the Diagnostic clusters.

≡ *Rapid Reference 5.8*

How to Describe a Normative Strength or Normative Weakness in a Psychological Report

Natalie's verbal ability is considered a significant Normative Strength compared to other individuals her age.

Melanie's verbal ability is considered a significant Normative Weakness compared to other individuals her age.

Step 4a: Are There Any Significant Differences *Between* the GCA and the Diagnostic Clusters?

The first step in interpreting the Diagnostic cluster scores is to compare each of them to the child's overall ability as represented by the GCA (or in some cases the SNC). Unlike instruments that include such abilities as processing speed and short-term and working memory in their total cognitive ability scores, the DAS-II excludes them from the total GCA or SNC, but still allows the examiner to compare scores on those diagnostic subtests to the examinee's GCA or SNC. Both the DAS-II *Normative Data Tables Manual* (Tables B.3, p. 131) and the DAS-II Normative Score Profile Page of the Record Form include information regarding statistical discrepancy. The values from these sources indicate that a difference of 9 and 11 points, respectively, between the Working Memory and Processing Speed clusters and the GCA may be considered significant at the .05 level.

Our question is this: Are there any significant differences *between* the GCA and the Diagnostic clusters? Following a procedure similar to that used previously in Steps 2 and 3, compare the child's level of performance on the Diagnostic clusters to his or her overall level of performance as represented by the GCA (Figure 5.9).

The difference between Marybeth's GCA and Working Memory was small (3 points) and nonsignificant, but the difference between her GCA and Processing Speed was large (57 points) and significant at the .01 level.

As was noted before, many children display considerable variability among their separate abilities. Table 5.4 shows the percentage of children from the standardization sample obtaining various differences between their GCA and

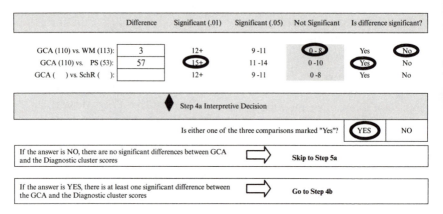

Figure 5.9 Step 4a. Are There Any Significant Differences *Between* the GCA and the Diagnostic Clusters?

Table 5.4 Percent of the standardization Sample Obtaining Various Differences (*p*<.05) Between the GCA and the Diagnostic Cluster Scores

	Diagnostic Cluster		
	Working Memory	Processing Speed	School Readiness
GCA is not significantly different from the Diagnostic Cluster	53	49	61
GCA is significantly less than the Diagnostic Cluster	21	26	20
GCA is significantly greater than the Diagnostic Cluster	26	26	19

Note: Percentages have been rounded.

the three diagnostic clusters. Between 49 and 61 percent of the standardization sample had no significant difference at the .05 level between the GCA and the individual Diagnostic cluster scores. Approximately equal percentages of children displayed Diagnostic cluster scores that were either significantly higher or lower than the GCA score.

Step 4b: Are Significant Differences *Between* GCA and the Diagnostic Clusters Unusually Large?

If you do find that any of the Diagnostic clusters differs significantly from the GCA, you should next determine the frequency of that occurrence (Figure 5.10).

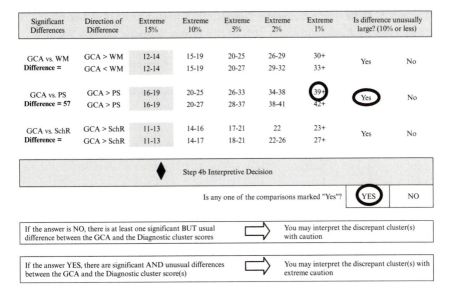

Significant Differences	Direction of Difference	Extreme 15%	Extreme 10%	Extreme 5%	Extreme 2%	Extreme 1%	Is difference unusually large? (10% or less)	
GCA vs. WM Difference =	GCA > WM	12-14	15-19	20-25	26-29	30+	Yes	No
	GCA < WM	12-14	15-19	20-27	29-32	33+		
GCA vs. PS Difference = 57	GCA > PS	16-19	20-25	26-33	34-38	39+	Yes	No
	GCA > PS	16-19	20-27	28-37	38-41	42+		
GCA vs. SchR Difference =	GCA > SchR	11-13	14-16	17-21	22	23+	Yes	No
	GCA > SchR	11-13	14-17	18-21	22-26	27+		

◆ Step 4b Interpretive Decision

Is any one of the comparisons marked "Yes"?	YES	NO

| If the answer is NO, there is at least one significant BUT usual difference between the GCA and the Diagnostic cluster scores | ⇨ | You may interpret the discrepant cluster(s) with caution |

| If the answer YES, there are significant AND unusual differences between the GCA and the Diagnostic cluster score(s) | ⇨ | You may interpret the discrepant cluster(s) with extreme caution |

Figure 5.10 Step 4b. Are Significant Differences Between GCA and the Diagnostic Clusters Unusually Large?

The DAS-II *Normative Data Tables Manual* (Tables B.4, p. 131) provides information showing that differences of 14 to 20 points between the GCA and the Working Memory, Processing Speed, or the School Readiness cluster scores would be expected to occur in only about 10 percent of children.

In our example, Marybeth's significant 57-point difference between her GCA (110) and her Processing Speed (53) is not only large and significant, but it also is highly unusual, being found in fewer than 1 percent of all children. Given such a large, unusual difference, we should next determine if such differences are related to the child's overall level of cognitive ability.

Table 5.5 shows the difference between the Diagnostic clusters and GCA scores displayed by approximately 10 percent of the norm sample for the total sample and by ability level, as measured by the GCA. Note that there are often large differences between the magnitude of the difference needed for unusualness depending upon whether you compare the difference found to the entire sample or to children with similar GCA ability levels. The largest differences typically occur at the extreme levels of functioning (e.g., GCA < 80 or GCA > 119). For example, consider Kate, a 7-year-old child with a GCA of 65 and a Processing Speed of 85. The 20-point difference, with the GCA being lower than the Processing Speed score (GCA < PS), would be considered unusual if we compared Kate to the entire norming sample—such a difference is found

Table 5.5 Difference Between Diagnostic Cluster and GCA Scores Displayed by Approximately 10% of the Norm Sample for the Total Sample and by Ability Level

	Total sample	Extreme 10% GCA				
		≤79	80–89	90–109	110–119	≥120
SchR > GCA	14	18	17	12	8	4
SchR < GCA	14	9	7	12	14	22
WM > GCA	15	26	19	15	7	3
WM < GCA	15	9	9	12	19	27
PS > GCA	20	37	27	18	8	2
PS < GCA	20	0	7	16	26	37

in 10 percent of the population. However, given Kate's overall ability (GCA = 65), the 20-point difference would actually be quite normal. For a child with a GCA of 79 or below, a difference of 37 points between the Processing Speed and GCA scores is needed to reach the extreme 10 percent level (these percentages are obtained from Tables B.4 and C.3 in the DAS-II *Normative Data Tables Manual*).

If a child has a significantly low score on the Working Memory cluster in comparison with the GCA, a comparison of the mean core T score with the child's T score on Recall of Digits Forward (RDf) may be helpful in determining whether poor auditory short-term memory can explain poor working memory performance. If Recall of Digits Forward is also significantly low, this finding may support a hypothesis that the child has a significant problem in holding information in auditory short-term memory long enough to work on it. If Recall of Digits Forward is not significantly low, this may support a hypothesis that the problem in working memory resides in inefficient strategies and factors such as those listed above, rather than in a specific difficulty in short-term storage.

We recommend that when you compare the Diagnostic clusters to the GCA, you always take into consideration the actual level of GCA functioning and refer to the tables in Section C of the DAS-II *Normative Data Tables Manual*. For convenience, Table 5.5 shows the differences shown by 10 percent of the sample for the total sample, and also for children in different ranges of GCA scores. In the case of Marybeth, with an overall ability level of 110, the 57-point difference between her GCA and her Processing Speed scores remains highly unusual.

Step 5a: For the Diagnostic Clusters, Are There Any Significant Differences *Within* Clusters?

Next, to determine the interpretability of the Diagnostic clusters, determine whether the subtests that make up a cluster differ significantly from each other. The DAS-II *Normative Data Tables Manual* (Tables B.5, p. 131) includes information regarding statistical discrepancy. The values from these sources (see Figure 5.11) indicate that a difference of 8 and 11 points between the subtests may be considered significant at the .05 level.

As you evaluate the separate clusters, if you find that the subtests that compose a Diagnostic cluster do not vary significantly, you can interpret the cluster score as a meaningful representation of the child's overall ability in that specific area. In our example, both of Marybeth's Working Memory and Processing Speed clusters can be interpreted since the subtests within them differ only slightly from each other and the differences do not reach a level of statistical significance.

If, however, you find that the subtests within a cluster do differ significantly, you next should determine the frequency of the difference(s).

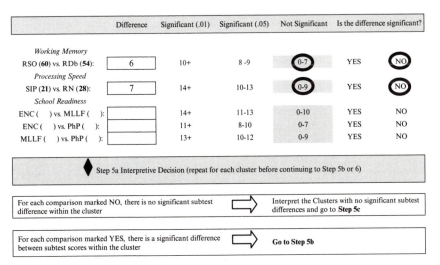

Figure 5.11 Step 5a. For the Diagnostic Clusters, Are There Any Significant Differences *Within* Clusters?

Step 5b: For the Diagnostic Clusters, Are Significant Differences *Within* the Clusters Unusually Large?

The DAS-II *Normative Data Tables Manual* (Tables B.6, p. 132) provides information regarding the frequency of occurrence of various within-cluster score differences. In general, differences of 11 and 14 points are considered unusual (occurring in 10 percent or less) and, when found, should lead you to interpret the Diagnostic cluster with extreme caution since the variability within the cluster is large.

In our example (Figure 5.12), none of the subtests that composed Marybeth's Diagnostic clusters differed significantly from each other and so Step 5b could have been skipped. If we had found any significant differences between the subtests within the clusters, we should have been cautious about interpreting the clusters as being meaningful representations of the skills and instead investigated, in Step 6, the separate abilities (narrow abilities) assessed by the subtests themselves.

Significant Differences	Direction of Difference	Extreme 15%	Extreme 10%	Extreme 5%	Extreme 2%	Extreme 1%	Is difference unusually large? (10% or less)	
Working Memory								
RSO vs. RDb	RSO > RDb:	9-10	11-14	15-20	21-24	25+	Yes	No
Difference = 6	RSO < RDb:	9-10	11-13	14-18	19-20	21+		
Processing Speed								
SIP vs. RN	SIP > RN:	11-13	14-17	18-23	24-29	30+	Yes	No
Difference =7	SIP < RN:	11-13	14-17	18-21	22-26	27+		
School Readiness								
ENC vs. MLLF	ENC > MLLF	11-13	14-18	19-24	25-26	27+	Yes	No
Difference =	ENC < MLLF	11-12	13-17	18-22	23-26	27+		
ENC vs. PhP	ENC > PhP	11-13	14-18	19-23	24-27	28+	Yes	No
Difference =	ENC < PhP	9-10	11-13	14-17	18	19+		
MLLF vs. PhP	MLLF > PhP	14-16	17-22	23-26	27-29	30+	Yes	No
Difference =	MLLF < PhP	9-11	12-15	16-19	20-22	23+		

Step 5b Interpretive Decision

Is at least one of the comparisons marked "Yes"?	YES	NO

If the answer is NO, there are significant BUT usual differences between subtest scores within one or both clusters	⇨	You may interpret the cluster(s) with caution but consider Narrow Abilities **(Step 6)**

If the answer is YES, there are significant AND unusual differences between the cluster subtest scores	⇨	Interpret individual clusters, but only with extreme caution. Examine Narrow Abilities **(Step 6)**

Figure 5.12 Step 5b. For the Diagnostic Clusters, Are Significant Differences *Within* the Clusters Unusually Large?

Cluster Ability	Interpretable? (Y/N)	Standard Score	Normative Weakness <85	Within Normal Limits 85-115	Normative Strength >115
Working Memory	Y	113		✓	
Processing Speed	Y	53	✓		
School Readiness					

Figure 5.13 Step 5c. Determine Normative Strengths and Weaknesses in the Ability Score Profile

Step 5c: Determine Normative Strengths and Weaknesses in the Diagnostic Ability Score Profile

For the cluster identified in Step 5b as having small within-cluster subtest differences and therefore found to be interpretable, you should next determine Normative Strengths and Normative Weaknesses in the child's individual's profile. If the ability cluster's standard score is greater than 115, consider the Diagnostic Cluster Ability score a Normative Strength. If the ability cluster's standard score is less than 85, consider the Cluster Ability Score as a Normative Weakness. If the ability cluster's standard score is between 85 and 115 (inclusive), then the ability is Within Normal Limits.

In Step 5c, for each Diagnostic ability cluster found to be interpretable, record the standard score and place a checkmark in the box corresponding to the appropriate normative category for each Ability Cluster. Marybeth's Working Memory (SS = 113) would be described as being within normal limits while her Processing Speed (SS = 53) would be described as being a Normative Weakness (see Figure 5.13).

Rapid Reference 5.9 shows how you might describe specific normative strengths or weaknesses for the Diagnostic clusters.

Step 6: Narrow Ability Hypotheses

As seen from the previous discussion, despite the fact that the subtests within each of the DAS-II clusters measure the same broad ability, one should not be surprised to find

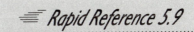

Rapid Reference 5.9

How to Describe a Normative Strength or Normative Weakness in a Psychological Report

Natalie's working memory ability is considered a significant Normative Strength compared to other individuals her age.

Melanie's working memory is considered a significant Normative Weakness compared to other individuals her age.

within-cluster differences. When interpreting clusters found to have divergent subtests, examiners may generate hypotheses relevant to the subtests themselves. In Step 6, you identify the narrow abilities assessed by the Core and Diagnostic subtests and any relevant differences between them. For example, knowing that Word Definitions and Verbal Similarities are both measures of Verbal Ability on the School-Age DAS-II and also knowing that Word Definitions measures that ability through Language Development and Lexical Knowledge while Verbal Similarities measures the ability through Language Development provides plausible explanations when the two subtest scores differ significantly. Note also that Verbal Similarities has a verbal reasoning component not possessed by Word Definitions. This is an example of a difference between two subtests that is not evident if we place a too-heavy reliance on descriptions of narrow abilities drawn from current CHC theory.

For those subtests within clusters found to be significantly different from each other, you should, as a preliminary hypothesis, consider the individual narrow abilities drawn from CHC theory as possible reasons for these differences. In the case of Marybeth, because the difference between her Recall of Designs and Pattern Construction scores was both significant and unusual, you should examine the subtest's narrow abilities as one possible explanation for the discrepancy. As seen in Rapid Reference 5.10a and defined in Rapid Reference 5.10b, Recall of Designs is considered to be a measure of Visual Memory while Pattern Construction is a measure of Spatial Relations. These CHC definitions are adapted from Kevin McGrew's (2004) Institute for Applied Psychometrics Cattell-Horn-Carroll (CHC) Definition Project at http://www.iapsych .com/chcdef.htm. See also Carroll (1983); Flanagan, Ortiz, and Alfonso (2007); Flanagan, Ortiz, Alfonso, and Mascolo (2006); McGrew (1997); and McGrew and Flanagan (1998) for definitions and explanations of these abilities. Be sure to consult these essential, original sources.

Again, the complete sources listed above are vital for a full understanding of CHC abilities. Additional data may be necessary to reach a meaningful and trustworthy interpretation. Specifically, we recommend that you read carefully the final section of this chapter, "Interpreting Clusters and Subtests." The section covers hypotheses concerning high and low cluster and subtest scores that are broader than the CHC definitions such as those listed in Rapid Reference 5.10b.

When a significant and unusual difference between subtests leads you to interpret narrow abilities rather than the broad ability represented by the cluster as a whole, be cautious! Although the DAS-II subtests are relatively reliable, and were designed to be individually interpretable, they only provide one source of information on the narrow ability that each one measures. Therefore, you

≡ *Rapid Reference 5.10a*

DAS-II Subtests Broad and Narrow Abilities

Narrow Abilities

Verbal Ability (Gc)
Verbal Comprehension	Listening Ability
Naming Vocabulary	Lexical Knowledge
Word Definitions	Language Development / Lexical Knowledge
Verbal Similarities	Language Development

Nonverbal Reasoning Ability (Gf)
Picture Similarities	Induction
Matrices	Induction
Sequential and Quantitative Reasoning	Induction / Quantitative Reasoning

Spatial Ability (Gv)
Pattern Construction	Spatial Relations
Pattern Construction–Alternative	Spatial Relations
Recall of Designs	Visual Memory
Copying	Visualization
Matching Letter-Like Forms	Visualization

Retrieval (Glr)
Recall of Objects–Immediate	Free-recall Memory
Recall of Objects–Delayed	Free-recall Memory

Memory (Gsm)
Recall of Digits Forward	Memory Span
Recall of Digits Backward	Working Memory
Recall of Sequential Order	Working Memory

Processing Speed (Gs)
Speed of Information Processing	Scanning
Rapid Naming	Complex

Auditory Processing (Ga)
Phonological Processing	Phonemic Coding

Additional
Early Number Concepts	Lexical Knowledge / General verbal knowledge / Piagetian reasoning

Adapted from Table 2.1, p. 19, *Introductory and Technical Handbook* (Elliott, 2007). Subtests in italic are Early Years Core subtests.

≡ Rapid Reference 5.10b

. . . .

CHC Narrow Ability (subtests): Definition*

Free Recall Memory (Recall of Objects–Immediate and Recall of Objects –Delayed): Ability to recall, without associations, as many unrelated items as possible, in any order, after a large collection of items is presented. (Note that Recall of Objects employs both visual *and* verbal input, not just visual.)

Induction (Picture Similarities, Matrices, Sequential and Quantitative Reasoning): Ability to discover the underlying characteristic (e.g., rule, concept, principle, process, trend, class membership) that underlies a specific problem or a set of observations, or to apply a previously learned rule to the problem. Reasoning from specific cases or observations to general rules or broad generalizations. Often requires the ability to combine separate pieces of information in the formation of inferences, rules, hypotheses, or conclusions.

Language Development (Word Definitions, Verbal Similarities): General development or understanding and application of words, sentences, and paragraphs (not requiring reading) in spoken native language skills to express or communicate a thought or feeling.

Lexical Knowledge (Naming Vocabulary): Extent of vocabulary (nouns, verbs, or adjectives) that can be understood in terms of correct word (semantic) meanings. Although evidence indicates that vocabulary knowledge is a separable component from LD, it is often difficult to disentangle these two highly corrected abilities in research studies.

Listening Ability (Verbal Comprehension): Ability to listen and understand the meaning of oral communications (spoken words, phrases, sentences, and paragraphs). The ability to receive and understand spoken information.

Memory Span (Recall of Digits Forward): Ability to attend to, register, and immediately recall (after only one presentation) temporally ordered elements and then reproduce the series of elements in correct order.

Perceptual Speed (Speed of Information Processing, Rapid Naming): Ability to rapidly and accurately search, compare (for visual similarities or differences) and identify visual elements presented side-by-side or separated in a visual field.

  Scanning (Ps) ability to scan, compare, and look up visual stimuli

  Complex (Pc) ability to perform visual pattern recognition tasks that impose additional cognitive demands such as spatial visualization, estimating and interpolating, and heightened memory span loads.

Phonetic Coding (Phonological Processing): Ability to code, process, and be sensitive to nuances in phonemic information (speech sounds) in short-term memory. Includes the ability to identify, isolate, blend, or transform sounds of speech.

Piagetian Reasoning (Early Number Concepts): Ability to demonstrate the acquisition and application (in the form of logical thinking) of cognitive concepts as defined by Piaget's developmental cognitive theory. These concepts include seriation (organizing material into an orderly series that facilitates understanding of relationships between events), conservation (awareness that physical quantities do not change in amount when altered in appearance), classification (ability to organize materials that possess similar characteristics into categories), and so on.

Quantitative Reasoning (Sequential and Quantitative Reasoning): Ability to inductively and/or deductively reason with concepts involving mathematical relations and properties.

Spatial Relations (Pattern Construction, Pattern Construction–Alternative): Ability to rapidly perceive and manipulate (mental rotation, transformations, reflection, etc.) visual patterns or to maintain orientation with respect to objects in space. Spatial Relations may require the identification of an object when viewed from different angles or positions. Differs from Visualization primarily by an emphasis on fluency.

Visual Memory (Recall of Designs, Recognition of Pictures): Ability to form and store a mental representation or image of a visual shape or configuration (typically during a brief study period), over at least a few seconds, and then recognize or recall it later (during the test phase).

Visualization (Copying, Matching Letter-Like Forms): The ability to apprehend a spatial form, object, or scene and match it with another spatial object, form, or scene with the requirement to rotate it (one or more times) in two or three dimensions. Requires the ability to mentally imagine, manipulate or transform objects or visual patterns and to predict how they would appear under altered conditions (e.g., parts are moved or rearranged). Differs from Spatial Relations primarily by a de-emphasis on fluency.

Working Memory (Recall of Digits Backward, Recall of Sequential Order): Ability to temporarily store and perform a set of cognitive operations on information that requires divided attention and the management of the limited capacity resources of short-term memory.

*CHC definitions adapted from http://www.iapsych.com/chcdef.htm. See also Flanagan, Ortiz, & Alfonso (2007); Flanagan, Ortiz, Alfonso, & Mascolo (2006); and McGrew & Flanagan (1998).

may also need to use other tests of the same abilities to more fully understand the student's strengths and weaknesses within the broad ability. Supplementing the DAS-II with other measures, when necessary, allows the examiner to select additional tests to complete the measurement of unusually scattered narrow abilities within a broad ability classification. The best source of information on constructing, implementing, and interpreting an assessment using two or more instruments in a CHC framework is *Essentials of Cross-Battery Assessment,* 2nd ed. (Flanagan, Ortiz, & Alfonso, 2007), which includes a CD with three very helpful programs as well as a clear explanation of current CHC theory and practice.

Step 7: Evaluate Subtest Variability (Core and Diagnostic Subtests)

Identify Any Significant Subtest Variation from the Mean Core T Score

A test battery such as the DAS-II provides a picture of an individual's cognitive strength and weaknesses. This type of evaluation is considered ipsative—within the individual. As such, when evaluating the test profile, the relative level of a subtest score, rather than the absolute level, is of great importance.

Although subtest scores are related, they differ in item content and test administration and thus these differences can cause the subtest scores to vary. In statistical terms, each subtest carries with it some components of shared common variance, some proportion of reliable, specific variance, and finally, components of error variance. Subtests can, and do, differ from each other. Before one can evaluate the differences between what appear to be high or low subtest scores, one must evaluate whether these apparent differences are large enough to warrant interpretation. To do so we must know if the difference is large, reliable, and significant.

Determining an individual subtest's strength or weakness requires that one examine how discrepant is each subtest, both Core and Diagnostic, from the mean of all the core subtests (Mean Core *T*). The DAS-II has provided the examiner easy access to both the child's mean of the core subtests (found in the DAS-II *Manual,* in Tables A.3 and A.4) and the discrepancy requirement for each subtest (on the Protocol Summary Page, as well as in the DAS-II *Normative Data Tables Manual,* Table B.7).

For statistical significance at the .05 level, the Early Years and School-Age Core subtests require between 5 and 8 points of difference between the subtest *T* score and the Mean Core *T* score, with slightly higher differences required when utilizing the Special Nonverbal Composite. Necessary differences for Diagnostic subtests vary between 7 and 13 points at the .05 level.

The first step in determining how

DON'T FORGET

Many of the most important readers of our reports are not familiar with our jargon. The phrase "Mean Core *T*" would strike most native speakers of English as absolute nonsense. It is prudent to ask a friend or relative who is not professionally involved in psychology, statistics, or education to proofread reports (with identifying information removed) from time to time and point out instances of gobbledygook. For example, most readers would better understand such an explanation as, "Myron's *T* score for the Verbal Similarities subtest, in which he was asked to explain how three different words (e.g., hope, fear, and love) could be related, was significantly higher than his own average *T* score on all the subtests that contribute to the GCA score." Even this explanation assumes that you have already explained the meaning of "*T* score."

each subtest compares to the student's overall mean for the test is to simply examine whether the subtest falls at, above (+), or below (−) the mean of the Core subtests. Next, determine if the subtest scores are statistically higher or lower than what would be expected. (We have chosen to use the terms High [H] or Low [L] rather than the more traditional Strength [S] or Weakness [W]. We do this to make clear that all analysis is done relative to the child and to emphasize that, for example, a subtest that does in fact deviate from the mean of the test may be "below the child's mean" but still within or even above the average range of scores. As Sattler [2008] repeatedly stresses, it is not appropriate to use the term "weakness" for a score that is average or higher by the test norms, nor the term "strength" for a score that is below the average range. Using the less value-laden terms of High and Low may prevent misinterpretation of the DAS-II results.)

Subtract the subtest score from the Mean Core *T* score. This difference is then compared to the number of points that represents a statistical difference between the scores. In Figure 5.14, this difference is referred to as "difference required." Any subtest that deviates from the mean at a level equal to or greater than the required difference is then identified as being either High (H) or Low (L).

Mean Core T: **56**	Circle one (GCA or SNC)	T Score	Difference from Mean	Difference required	High/ Low (H / L) (+ / −)	Frequency (Table B.8)
Word Definition (Gc)		74	+18	7	H	<1%
Verbal Similarities (Gc)		65	+9	8	H	<10%
Matrices (Gf)		54	−2	7	−	
Sequential & Quantitative Reasoning (Gf)		52	−4	6	−	
Recall of Designs (Gv)		50	−6	7	−	
Pattern Construction (Gv)		38	−18	5	L	<1%
Recall of Objects-Immediate (Glr)		49	−7	9	−	
Recall of Digits Forward (Gsm)		58	+2	7	+	
Recognition of Pictures (Gv)		47	−9	13	−	
Recall of Sequential Order (Gsm)		60	+4	7	+	
Speed of Information Processing (Gs)		28	−28	7	L	<1%
Recall of Digits Backward (Gsm)		54	−2	7	−	
Phonological Processing (Ga)		49	−7	9	−	
Rapid Naming (Gs)		21	−35	10	L	<1%

Figure 5.14 Are Single Subtest *T* Scores Significantly Different from Mean Core *T*?

Identify the Frequency of Any Observed Significant Differences

Tables B.8 in the DAS-II *Normative Data Tables Manual* provide approximate percentages of the norm sample that obtained specified differences between the Mean Core *T* score and the individual subtest scores. Using these tables allows the examiner to determine whether the differences observed reach a level of unusualness. Overall, for the Core subtests, differences of between 7 and 10 points on the Early Years battery and on the School-Age battery would be expected to occur in only about 10 percent of the children tested. For the Diagnostic subtest, differences of between 7 and 14 points would be needed. Identify the frequency of occurrence only for those subtests that you have already identified as being either a High (H) or Low (L) subtest. This procedure is similar to one developed for the original Kaufman Assessment Battery for Children (KABC; Kaufman & Kaufman, 1983) by Kamphaus and Reynolds (1987).

Figure 5.14 shows that when Marybeth's subtest scores were compared to her overall Mean Core *T* score (Mean Core *T* = 56), she demonstrated several High and Low scores. Of the Core subtests, Word Definitions and Verbal Similarities, the two subtests of the Verbal Ability cluster, were both significantly and unusually higher than her average while her performance on the Pattern Construction subtest was significantly and unusually lower than her average. The two Diagnostic subtests of the Processing Speed cluster, Speed of Information Processing and Rapid Naming, were both found to be significantly and unusually lower than her average.

Step 8: Evaluate Shared Ability Hypotheses

The DAS-II provides what are called "shared underlying processes" related to the DAS-II subtests. Subtests are grouped together, and labeled as "shared abili-

---

DON'T FORGET

Some authorities believe that a difference between scores must be statistically significant *and* unusual (such as a base-rate frequency of 10% or less) before we pay attention to it. We disagree. Although base rate is important, as Elliott (1990b, p. 92) states, "The fact that a particular, statistically significant discrepancy occurs relatively frequently, however, does not make the discrepancy unimportant in the assessment of an individual." Specific learning disabilities, lack of experience with spoken English, and poverty are all common, but obviously important. Part of the examiner's task is to consider significant differences among scores, even if they are not uncommon, and try to determine whether those differences are important to the individual's functioning.

ties," for sets of two or more subtests that appear to be assessing common capacities. The labels used for these sets of subtests are "suggestive" of the underlying processes. They are not meant to be definitive. They provide another avenue to pursue when generating hypotheses about a child's performance. Shared ability groupings are based on the assumption that a child who performs poorly on a particular subtest will be weak in some, but probably not all, of the aspects of abilities measured by that subtest. Conversely, the child who performs very well on a subtest is not necessarily expected to perform well on all aspects of the abilities that might contribute to performance on the subtest.

To examine shared abilities, you use the information regarding subtest High (H) and Low (L) and plus (+) and minus (–) that you generated at Step 7. (Figure 5.15 shows the DAS-II Analysis Sheet that represents the shared ability groupings with results from Marybeth's analysis entered.) Examiners begin the evaluation of each shared ability grouping by entering either + (higher), – (lower), H (significantly higher), or L (significantly lower) into the box below each subtest. The box would be blank if the subtest score were identical to the child's own Mean Core *T* score. These notations represent the relative standing for each of the DAS-II subtests when compared to the child's own overall mean on the test (Mean Core *T* score). Examiners then assess each grouping, noting especially those that contain subtests that are considered High (H) or Low (L). By noting whether the subtests within the groupings are consistent—all above the mean (+ and H) or all below the mean (– and L)—examiners can hypothesize possible strengths or weaknesses within the specific abilities. A shared ability with all subtests above the mean and additionally at least one subtest rated as H would be considered a "probable strength," while one with subtests all rated as "above the mean" but without any subtest being rated as H would be considered a "possible strength."

If one or more subtests that compose a shared ability at the examinee's age were not administered, we recommend not attempting to interpret that specific ability.

In Figure 5.15, the *Formulation and Testing of Hypotheses* shared ability would not be considered a potential strength or weakness because of the inconsistent pattern of subtest ratings. One subtest, Verbal Similarities, was rated as H while the remaining subtests were rated as either L (Pattern Construction) or below the mean (–) (Sequential and Quantitative Reasoning and Matrices). The *Use of Verbal Mediation to Solve Nonverbal Problems* shared ability would be hypothesized as a "probable weakness" since one of the subtests (Pattern Construction) was rated as L while the remaining subtests that make up the shared ability were rated as below the mean (–). Overall, Marybeth displayed a probable strength in

School-age Shared Ability	Shared Ability Subtests (includes out-of-level subtests) Enter H, L, +, or − in each box. (See below for definitions)							
Formulation and Testing of Hypotheses	VS	SQR	PC	Mat				
H / L or + / −	H	−	L	−				
Use of Verbal Mediation to Solve Nonverbal Problems	SQR	PC	Mat					
H / L or + / −	−	L	−					
Verbal Comprehension:	WD	RSO						
H / L or + / −	H	+						
Verbal Expression:	WD	VS	ROi	RDf	RSO	RDb	PhP	RN
H / L or + / −	H	H	−	+	+	−	−	L
Visual Analysis of Figures or Designs:	PC	Mat	RDes					
H / L or + / −	L	−	−					
Visual Verbal Integration:	SQR	Mat	ROi	RSO				
H / L or + / −	−	−	−	+				
Short-term Memory: (general):	RDes	ROi	RDf	RPic	RSO	RDb		
H / L or + / −	−	−	+	−	+	−		
Auditory Short-term Memory:	RDf	RSO	RDb					
H / L or + / −	+	+	−					
Visual Short-term Memory:	ROi	RPic						
H / L or + / −	−	−						
Verbal Long -term Information Retrieval:	WD	VS	RN					
H / L or + / −	H	H	L					
Knowledge of Quantitative Concepts:	SQR	SIP						
H / L or + / −	−	L						
Visual/holistic Information Processing:	PC	RDes	RPic					
H / L or + / −	L	−	−					
Sequential Information Processing:	ROi	RDf	RSO	SIP	RDb	RN		
H / L or + / −	−	+	+	L	−	L		

Figure 5.15 Step 8a. Determine Probable and Possible DAS-II School-Age Shared Abilities

the area of *Verbal Comprehension;* probable weaknesses in *Use of Verbal Mediation to Solve Nonverbal Problems, Visual Analysis of Figures and Designs, Knowledge of Quantitative Concepts,* and *Holistic Information Processing;* and a possible weakness in *Visual Short-term Memory.*

It is possible to compute standard scores (Mean = 100, SD = 15) for each of the shared abilities for which all subtests in the grouping has been administered. However, we recommend doing so only for those shared abilities that you have identified in Step 8 as being either possible or probable. To calculate a Shared Ability's Standard Score, first add together the *T* scores for each of the subtests

School-age Shared Ability	Subtests	Sum of T scores¹	Multiplier	Additive	Score	.05 SEm
Formulation and Testing of Hypotheses	VS, SQR, PC, Mat		.46	7.94		6
Use of Verbal Mediation to Solve Nonverbal Problems	SQR, PC, Mat	144	.59	12.15	96	6
Verbal Comprehension	WD, RSO	134	.87	13.11	130	8
Verbal Expression	VS, WD, ROi, RDf, RSO, RDb, PhP, RN		.27	-7.59		5
Visual Analysis of Figures and Designs	PC, Mat, RDes	142	.60	9.64	95	7
Visual Verbal Integration	SQR, Mat, ROi, RSO		.42	-4.33		7
Short-Term Memory (general)	RDes, ROi, RDf, RPic, RSO, RDb		.35	-5.89		6
Auditory Short-Term Memory	RDf, RSO, RDb		.59	10.92		6
Visual Short-Term Memory	ROi, RPic	96	.91	9.38	96	12
Verbal Long-Term Information Retrieval	VS, WD, RN		.64	3.35		9
Knowledge of Quantitative Concepts	SQR, SIP	80	.93	6.97	81	8
Holistic Information Processing	PC, RDes, RPic	135	.63	6.09	91	8
Sequential Information Processing	RORDf, RSO, SIP, RDb, RN		.36	-7.94		6

PC = Pattern Construction; Mat = Matrices; RDes = Recall of Designs; WD= Word Definitions; VS = Verbal Similarities; SQR =Sequential & Quantitative Reasoning; RDf = Recall of Digits – Forward; RPic = Recognition of Pictures; ROi = Recall of Objects – Immediate; ROd = Recall of Objects – Delayed; PhP = Phonological Processing; RSO = Recall of Sequential Order; RDb = Recall of Digits – Backward; SIP = Speed of Information Processing; RN = Rapid Naming

¹All subtests in a shared ability grouping must have been administered in order to use the individual formulae.

Figure 5.16 Step 8b (optional). School-Age Shared Ability Formulae for Converting Sums of T Scores to Deviation Scores (Mean = 100, SD = 15)

that make up the shared ability. Next multiply this Sum of T scores by the Multiplier, and finally to this add the Additive. The converted standard scores for each relevant shared ability should be reported as a range of scores by using the SEm provided in Appendix A Step 8b.

Figure 5.16 presents T score to Standard Score conversions for the seven probable and possible shared abilities identified for Marybeth in Step 8. *Use of Verbal Mediation to Solve Nonverbal Problems* (SS = 96 ±6), *Verbal Comprehension* (SS = 130 ±8), *Visual Analysis of Figures and Designs* (SS = 95 ±7), *Knowledge of Quantitative Concepts* (SS = 81 ±8), *Holistic Information Processing* (SS = 91 ±8), and *Visual Short-term Memory* (SS = 96 ±12).

Once you have calculated standard scores for each of the relevant shared abilities, you should look for other corroborating evidence from other sources (parent or teacher report, other testing results, etc.) to support any interpretation of these specific abilities. *Never* present a laundry list of hypotheses for the reader to sort through. We have, to our sorrow, seen reports with such lists, sometimes even including hypotheses that were obviously contrary to well-known facts about the examinee.

Step 9: Evaluate the Cultural and Linguistic Influences That May Impact Subtest Scores

The subtests of the DAS and the DAS-II have been categorized by McGrew, Flanagan, and Ortiz (1998, pp. 427–438), Flanagan, McGrew, and Ortiz (2000, pp. 305–310), and most recently further elaborated on by Flanagan, Ortiz, and Alfonso (2007) according to both their presumed cultural loading and degree of linguistic demand. Regarding cultural content, it was reasoned that subtests that are typically less influenced by U.S. culture, contain abstract or novel stimuli, and require simple, less culturally bound communicative responding (e.g., pointing) might yield scores that are less affected by an individual's level of exposure to mainstream U.S. culture. Cultural content was evaluated and classified as high, moderate, or low. Linguistic demands were classified according to the extent to which the examiner was required to use expressive and receptive language to administer the tasks, and the level of language proficiency needed by the examinee in order to understand and appropriately respond to the task directions. Linguistic demands were classified as high, moderate, and low. Table 5.6 shows the DAS-II subtests and their levels of linguistic demand and cultural loading, according to the analysis by Flanagan, Ortiz, and Alfonso (2007).

For the 20 DAS-II subtests, nine were assessed by Flanagan, Ortiz, and Alfonso (2007) as having low linguistic demands while nine had low cultural demands. Only six subtests were deemed to be high in either cultural or linguistic demand and only two (Word Definitions and Verbal Similarities) were high in both demands. Six subtests were found to be low in both areas, and of these four (Matrices, Sequential & Quantitative Reasoning, Pattern Construction, and Recall of Designs) make up the School-Age Special Nonverbal Composite. Of the four subtests that make up the Upper Early Years Special Nonverbal Composite, three (Matrices, Pattern Construction, and Copying) were identified as being low in both areas, with the fourth (Picture Similarities) being identified as medium/low.

The "low/low" properties of the DAS-II subtests have contributed to making it a very popular pre-school and bilingual assessment tool. The DAS-II is unusual among cognitive assessment batteries in that it provides one of the widest ranges of coverage of the broad *Gf-Gc* abilities, and does so with the lowest overall culture-language demands.

Step 10: Compare Relevant Subtest Groupings

Besides the within-cluster subtest comparisons that you make during Steps 3a and 5a, there are several other subtest comparisons that you may wish to consider

Table 5.6 Linguistic and Cultural Influences on DAS-II Subtests

DAS-II Subtest	Linguistic/Cultural Influence
Matrices	Low/Low
Sequential & Quantitative Reasoning	Low/Low
Pattern Construction	Low/Low
Recall of Designs	Low/Low
Matching Letter-like Forms	Low/Low
Copying	Low/Low
Recall of Digits Backward	Low/Medium
Speed of Information Processing	Low/Medium
Recall of Digits Forward	Low/High
Picture Similarities	Medium/Low
Recognition of Pictures	Medium/Low
Recall of Objects–Immediate	Medium/Low
Early Number Concepts	Medium/Medium
Rapid Naming	Medium/Medium
Recall of Sequential Order	Medium/Medium
Phonological Processing	Medium/High
Verbal Comprehension	High/Medium
Naming Vocabulary	High/Medium
Verbal Similarities	High/High
Word Definitions	High/High

Note: Core subtests are in bold print.

Adapted from Flanagan, Ortiz, & Alfonso 2007

in your interpretation of the DAS-II results. Rapid Reference 5.11 provides a summary of several meaningful Core and Diagnostic subtest comparisons and their possible implications. Sattler (2008) also presents possible implications of relationships between scores, which may be especially useful in comparison with similar lists Sattler creates for other tests of cognitive abilities. Tables B.11 (p. 137) and B.12 (p. 138) in the DAS-II *Normative Data Tables Manual* provide differences between subtest *T* scores required for statistical difference at the .15 and .05 levels when making paired comparisons. We recommend using the .05 level of significance. Depending upon the specific subtest comparison that you choose to make, a difference between 7 to 13 *T* score points will be required.

Comparison of Memory and Retrieval Subtests
The Recall of Designs (RDes), Recognition of Pictures (RPic), Recall of Digits Forward (RDf), Recall of Digits Backward (RDb), Recall of Sequential Order (RSO), Recall of Objects–Immediate (ROi), and Recall of Objects–

≡ Rapid Reference 5.11

Core and Diagnostic Subtest Comparisons and Implications

DAS-II Subtest Comparison	Possible Implication
RDf vs. RDb	Non-meaningful auditory memory span versus Non-meaningful auditory working memory
RDf vs. RSO	Non-meaningful auditory memory span versus Meaningful auditory/visual working memory
RDf vs. RPic	Non-meaningful auditory memory span versus Visual recognition memory
RDf vs. RDes	Non-meaningful auditory memory span versus Non-meaningful visual memory
RDb vs. RSO	Non-meaningful auditory working memory versus Meaningful auditory/visual working memory
ROi vs. ROd	Meaningful visual memory immediate versus Meaningful visual memory delayed
ROi vs. RDf	Meaningful visual memory immediate versus Non-meaningful auditory memory span
ROi vs. RDb	Meaningful visual memory versus Non-meaningful auditory working memory
RDes vs. RPic	Non-meaningful visual memory versus Meaningful visual memory, or, visual recall versus recognition
SIP vs RN and ROi vs. RN	These comparisons are made jointly since SIP and RNam are part of the Processing Speed cluster and should, typically be close. When the two differ significantly (14+ point) examine whether the RNam subtest is more similar to the ROI subtest. RNam has been presumed to include aspects of long term lexical retrieval, whereas such retrieval in ROi is intermediate-term (information only retained for approximately half an hour)

RDf = Recall of Digits Forward; RDb = Recall of Digits Backward; RN = Rapid Naming; ROi = Recall of Objects Immediate; RPic = Recognition of Pictures; RSO = Recall of Sequential Order; SIP = Speed of Information Processing.

Delayed (ROd) subtests all involve aspects of memory and retrieval. Differences exist among the subtests, however, in the stimuli used to elicit responses—that is, whether the stimuli are meaningful or non-meaningful, whether the items are presented orally or visually, whether the materials must be transformed in some way after presentation, and whether the memory requirement is short- or long-term. On Recall of Designs, the stimuli are non-meaningful and presented visually, and require a motor response with no transformation of the stimuli necessary. On Recognition of Pictures, the stimuli are meaningful and presented visually, a pointing response is required, and no transformation of the stimuli is necessary. On Recall of Digits Forward, the stimuli are non-meaningful and presented orally, and an oral response is required. No transformation of the stimuli is necessary. On Recall of Digits Backward, the stimuli are non-meaningful and presented orally, and an oral response is required. The stimuli must be transformed (reordered). On Recall of Sequential Order, the stimuli are meaningful and presented visually (early items) and orally, and an oral response is required. The stimuli must be transformed (reordered) on the basis of the visual-spatial location of parts of the body. On Recall of Objects–Immediate, the stimuli are meaningful and presented visually (and once verbally), and a verbal response is required. No transformation or sequencing of items is required. On Recall of Objects–Delayed, the stimuli are retrieved from memory, and a verbal response is required. No transformation or sequencing of items is required.

Comparison of Processing Speed and Long-Term Retrieval Subtests

The last comparisons listed in Rapid Reference 5.11 evaluate the two subtests that combine to create the Processing Speed cluster (SIP and RN) and, if they differ significantly, secondly evaluate the relationship between the ROi and RN subtests. Usually, SIP and RN will be similar (within 9 points of each other). As seen previously in Steps 5a and 5b, when the subtests do vary significantly, we might generally interpret that the reason for the difference is in the person's skill on the specific narrow abilities being assessed by the two subtests (Rapid References 5.10a and 5.10b). However, under certain circumstances, a second possible interpretation seems warranted. Although Rapid Naming is generally assumed to be a measure of Processing Speed, the speed component concerns speed of access to, and retrieval from, the individual's lexicon, or long-term store of words. Several tests that include subtests of Rapid Naming [e.g., Comprehensive Test of Phonological Processing (CTOPP; Wagner, Torgesen, & Rashotte, 1999), Gray Diagnostic Reading Test, 2nd ed. (GDRT-2; Bryant, Wiederholt, Bryant, 2004), and Rapid Automatized Naming and Rapid Alternating Stimulus Test (RAN/RAS; Wolf & Denckla, 2005)] classify the skill as both Processing Speed (Gs) and Long-term Retrieval (Glr).[4] Therefore, whenever there appears

---

[4]In the opinion of one of us (CDE), such a classification is incorrect. The so-called "long-term retrieval" factor (Glr) applies to tests requiring retention of information stored usually for no more than half an hour. It does not apply to tests such as Rapid Naming, Naming Vocabulary, or Word Definitions, that require the retrieval of words or

| SIP vs. RN
(58) vs. (31) | 27 | 10 | Processing Speed Cluster: If significant difference is evidenced, examine ROi vs. RN comparison |
| ROi vs. RN
(35) vs. (31) | 4 | 12 | * Make this comparison only if the SIP vs. RN is significant. RN could involve Glr |

Figure 5.17 Comparison of Kate's Processing Speed and Long-Term Retrieval Subtests

to be a difference between the SIP and RN subtests (*Gs*), compare the RN to ROi subtests (*Glr*). There are aspects of general speed of mental operations, fluency of retrieval, and motor speed (finger, oral, or both) that connect and divide these subtests in different ways. In some instances, you may need to use additional information (teacher reports, classroom observations, informal testing, or other formal tests) to help sort out these abilities for an examinee. The complete Woodcock-Johnson III (WJ III; Woodcock, McGrew, & Mather, 2001) offers more than 50 tests of cognitive abilities and academic achievement from which you could select follow-up measures. Mather and Jaffe (2002) provide valuable information and recommendations to help in the use of those tests. Flanagan, Ortiz, and Alfonso (2007) and Flanagan, Ortiz, Alfonso, and Mascolo (2006) explain and classify tests of cognitive ability and achievement by CHC broad and narrow abilities. Sattler (2008) and Sattler and Hoge (2006), among others, provide critical reviews of many tests.

For example, Kate (Figure 5.17) obtained a significant, 27-point difference between her SIP (*T* = 58) and RN (*T* = 31) subtest scores. This would lead to a cautious interpretation of her Processing Speed abilities. However, when we compare Kate's RN to her ROi scores (31 to 35, respectively), we note that there is very little difference between the scores. Thus, it may be that Kate is slow in long-term word-retrieval, but apparently not in processing speed for a paper-and-pencil test of making simple comparisons and decisions.

Figure 5.18 shows the DAS-II worksheet completed using Marybeth's subtest *T* scores. None of the planned paired comparisons found any relevant differences between her scores.

Comparison of Out-Of-Level Subtests
Because the DAS-II provides overlapping subtest norms at ages 5 through 8, examiners are able to test certain hypotheses about the child without the need

---

information from long-term memory, which may have been laid down years beforehand. In normal parlance (not that of experimental psychology), *Glr* tests measure retention of recently-acquired information.

Comparison	Difference	Difference needed for significance	Possible implication
RDf vs. RDb (58) vs. (54)	4	8	Non-meaningful auditory memory span versus Non-meaningful auditory working memory
RDf vs. RSO (58) vs. (60)	2	8	Non-meaningful auditory memory span versus Meaningful auditory/visual working memory
RDf vs. RPic (58) vs. (47)	9	12	Non-meaningful auditory memory span versus Visual memory
RDf vs. RDes (58) vs. (50)	8	9	Non-meaningful auditory memory span versus Non-meaningful visual memory
RDb vs. RSO (54) vs. (60)	6	8	Non-meaningful auditory working memory versus Meaningful auditory/visual working memory
ROi vs. ROd (49) vs. (54)	5	11	Meaningful visual memory immediate versus Meaningful visual memory delayed
ROi vs. RDf (49) vs. (58)	9	10	Meaningful visual memory immediate versus Non-meaningful auditory memory span
ROi vs. RDb (49) vs. (54)	5	14	Meaningful visual memory versus Non-meaningful auditory working memory
RDes vs. RPic (50) vs. (47)	3	12	Non-meaningful visual memory versus Meaningful visual memory
SIP vs. RN (28) vs. (21)	7	10	Processing Speed Cluster: If significant difference is evidenced, examine ROi vs. RN comparison
ROi vs. RN (49) vs. (21)	28	12	* Make this comparison only if the SIP vs. RN is significant. RN could involve Glr

Figure 5.18 Step 10. Additional Subtest Pair Comparisons

to switch to another test. For example, a 7-year-old child who does poorly on the Word Definitions subtest may be demonstrating poor verbal expression yet may, in fact, understand the meaning of certain words. The child may have an expressive, rather than a receptive vocabulary problem. At this age, the examiner could administer the Naming Vocabulary subtest of the Early Years battery, since that subtest taps into more receptive vocabulary skills than does the Word Definitions subtest. Below are several of the most relevant out-of-level subtest comparisons that you may find useful during testing.

Word Definitions versus Verbal Comprehension: Poor performance on the Word

Definitions subtest may be the result of an expressive language problem. Administering Verbal Comprehension allows you to compare the child's ability to demonstrate understanding of language using verbal expression (expressive language) on Word Definitions to the child's demonstration of the understanding of oral directions without the demand of expression (receptive language) on Verbal Comprehension. Pay close attention to the quality of the child's verbal expression on all tests and be alert to instances of difficulty with word-finding or word retrieval, including hesitations and fillers (e.g., "um," "ah," "er," "you know"), overt expressions of attempts to retrieve words (e.g., "What do you call it?"), circumlocutions or paraphrastic language (e.g., "One of those round things that makes it move"), and non-specific words and phrases (e.g., "thing," "thingy," "gizmo," "whachamacallit").

Word Definitions versus Naming Vocabulary: Poor performance on the Word Definitions subtest may be the result of an inability to accurately express one's word knowledge. Word Definitions measures the child's ability to demonstrate understanding of language and word knowledge typically requiring verbal expression using sentences (much expression). On the other hand, Naming Vocabulary measures word knowledge without the demand of extended verbal expression (little expression). In some cases, however, you may need to add a receptive vocabulary test, such as the Peabody Picture Vocabulary Test, 4th ed. (PPVT-4; Dunn & Dunn, 2006), which requires no verbal expression at all.

Verbal Similarities versus Picture Similarities: Poor performance on the Verbal Similarities subtest may be the result of an expressive language problem. Administering Picture Similarities allows you to compare the child's ability to demonstrate verbal reasoning requiring verbal expression with the ability to reason without the demand of verbal expression.

Recall of Designs versus Copying: Recall of Designs requires the child to copy a design that has been presented for only five seconds. A child may do

DON'T FORGET

When you notice and begin to keep track of instances of a specific behavior, such as word-finding difficulty or lapses of attention, be sure also to keep track of opposite instances, such as fluently employing highly specific words or sustaining attention. Otherwise, you may create a confirmatory bias for yourself, just as referral information may create a confirmatory bias for you. For example, a referral question about attention-deficit/hyperactivity disorder is likely to make us more prone to noticing and recording instances of inattention, but our own recognition of one instance of inattention may have the same affect. It is easy to let a few random instances of a behavior persuade us that there is a pattern when there actually is not. "Many" is a potentially misleading word.

poorly on this subtest because of a memory problem or problems with attention. Administering the Copying subtest allows you to compare the child's ability to recreate designs from memory using pencil and paper versus copying designs on a task that has no memory demand at all.

Sequential and Quantitative Reasoning versus Early Number Concepts: Sequential and Quantitative Reasoning requires the child to solve reasoning problems that, at least on later items, utilize numerical concepts and reasoning. A child may do poorly on this subtest because of a lack of number concepts (poor math facts or concepts). Administering Early Number Concepts to a child below 9 years of age allows one to examine whether or not the child actually has an adequate grasp of math concepts to perform. For children 9 years of age and older, if you are not including a formal test of math computation in your battery, informal assessment can tell you whether the child lacks solid skills in addition, subtraction, multiplication, division, and computation of common fractions.

Step 11: Evaluate Qualitative Responses, Subtest Demands, *and* Observed Behaviors

Another important step in DAS-II interpretation is the qualitative evaluation of both the responses given and the task requirements of the subtests. As noted earlier we find it helpful, whenever we begin to study a new test, first to have someone administer the test to us so that we can personally experience the process of trying to perform the tasks. This introspection (Titchener, 1924; Wundt, 1858–1862), although influenced by your own pattern of abilities and the appropriateness of the test to your age, does help illuminate the thinking processes required for taking the various subtests. Taking a test before you study it is also a good way to become intimately familiar with the subtests and items.

Rapid Reference 5.12 shows input/output requirements for each of the DAS-II subtests. Examiners may wish to examine the demands of a subtest with which a child has had particular problems and contrast that with the child's performance on another subtest having different demands. For example, a child may have done well on the Verbal Comprehension subtest and poorly on the Naming Vocabulary subtest. Contrasting the input/output demands of the subtests, input for Verbal Comprehension involved both auditory and visual meaningful stimuli while Naming Vocabulary included primarily visual input. Additionally, the mode of output for Verbal Comprehension is motoric while the mode for Naming Vocabulary is verbal. Examiners using this comparative approach could investigate further the hypotheses generated by qualitative analysis. Again, to really understand the demands of each subtest, have someone

≡ *Rapid Reference 5.12*

Step 11. Method of Input and Output for DAS-II Subtests

	Input			Output	
	Auditory	Visual		Verbal	Motor
		Meaningful	Symbolic		
Verbal Subtests					
Verbal Comprehension	✓	✓			✓
Naming Vocabulary		✓		✓	
Word Definition	✓			✓	
Verbal Similarities	✓			✓	
Nonverbal/Spatial Subtests					
Picture Similarities		✓	✓		✓
Copying		✓	✓		✓
Recall of Designs		✓	✓		✓
Pattern Construction			✓		✓
Nonverbal (Fluid Reasoning) Subtests					
Matrices		✓	✓	✓	✓
Sequential and Quantitative Reasoning		✓		✓	✓
Diagnostic Subtests					
Early Number Concepts	✓		✓	✓	✓
Matching Letter-Like Forms			✓		✓
Recall of Digits Forward	✓		✓	✓	
Recall of Digits Backward	✓			✓	
Recall of Sequential Order	✓			✓	
Recognition of Pictures		✓			
Recall of Objects–Immediate		✓		✓	
Recall of Objects–Delayed		✓		✓	
Rapid Naming		✓		✓	✓
Phonological Processing	✓	✓		✓	
Speed of Information Processing		✓			✓

administer the subtest to you. Even with preschool tests, there is no substitute for this experience in helping you understand all the demands of a subtest.

An Example of Qualitative Examination of a Child's Responses and Response Patterns

Specific responses and response patterns may also provide valuable information when attempting to interpret results. Figure 5.19 shows a sample of Kenny's DAS-II Word Definitions subtest. Kenny was referred for testing because of his extreme difficulty in acquiring early academic skills in reading and writing. Teachers voiced concerns about his memory abilities as well as the possibility of speech and language difficulties.

On the Word Definitions subtest, Kenny received credit for only 3 of the 12 items administered to him, resulting in a *T* score of 31. By evaluating his responses qualitatively, we can generate some interesting and important hypotheses.

Throughout the subtest, Kenny demonstrated retrieval and/or initiation difficulties, evidenced by the long pauses (shown on the record form as: ..... LP. . . . .) he exhibited before beginning, and while giving his responses.

On the very first item (Scissors), his response of "You can 'cup' with it" dem-

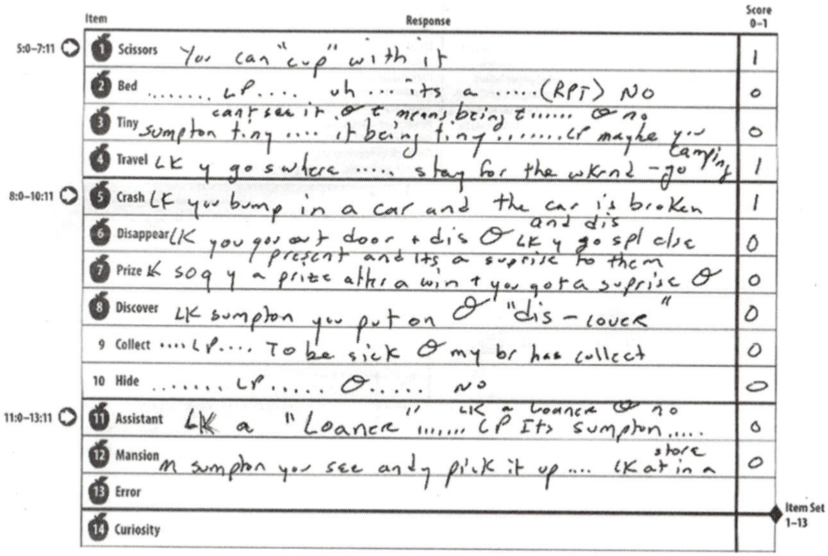

	Item	Response	Score 0–1
5:0–7:11	1 Scissors	You can "cup" with it	1
	2 Bed	.... LP.... uh ... its a .....(RPT) NO	0
	3 Tiny	sumpton tiny .... it being tiny .... LP maybe you can't see it. Q it means being t...... Q no	0
	4 Travel	LK you go swhere ..... stay for the wkend - go camping	1
8:0–10:11	5 Crash	LK you bump in a car and the car is broken	1
	6 Disappear	LK you go out door + dis Q LK you go spl else and dis	0
	7 Prize	LK so you a prize a thing win + you got a suprise Q present and its a suprise to them	0
	8 Discover	LK sumpton you put on Q "dis - cover"	0
	9 Collect	....LP.... To be sick Q my br has collect	0
	10 Hide	.... LP..... Q..... NO	0
11:0–13:11	11 Assistant	LK a "Loaner" ...... LP Its sumpton..... LK a "Loaner" Q no	0
	12 Mansion	m sumpton you see and pick it up .... LK at in a store	0
	13 Error		
	14 Curiosity		

Item Set 1–13

Figure 5.19 Kenny

Note: All responses are written verbatim. The following notations were used: LP = Long Pause, RPT = Repeat the item, Q = "Tell me more," LK = "Like." Dots (e.g., ...) were used to denote pauses (one dot per second) in responses.

onstrates an apparent knowledge of the word but a problem of either misarticulation of certain words or incorrect word retrieval, or both—problems demonstrated several more times on this subtest and throughout the rest of the DAS-II. An additional example of misarticulation is the way that, on several items, Kenny pronounced the word "something" as "sumpton."

On two items (8 and 9), he gave peculiar responses that actually become clear with questioning. For Item 8 (Discover), Kenny responded with the explanation: "Like sumpton you put on." Asked to elaborate, he demonstrated pulling something over his body while saying, "Dis cover." He was evidently referring to something that covers the body ("This cover").

For Item 9 (Collect), Kenny, after approximately a 10-second pause, responded, "to be sick." When questioned, he explained, "My brother has collect." He had evidently been attempting to explain the word "colic."

These qualitative examples, from a single subtest, in and of themselves may not be indicative of any particular problem or interpretation. However, when qualitative examples of this sort are found consistently throughout the test, and when they are validated through independent confirmation (e.g., additional testing, other observation, or parent or teacher report), they may lead to better-informed decisions. Kenny was referred to a speech and language expert and was later identified as having a central auditory processing disorder (CAPD).

Step 12 (Optional): Compare DAS-II with Achievement Scores

The DAS-II can aid examiners in determining if there is a cognitive explanation for certain academic achievement problems. The DAS-II GCA score (or if there is a compelling reason to do so, the SNC or one of the Core Cluster scores) can be used to determine if a child's achievement is below expectations and whether a severe discrepancy between cognitive ability and achievement exists. This can help determine eligibility for special education services in the public schools.

One of the problems inherent in the ability/achievement discrepancy method for determining severe discrepancy is the over-reliance on the ability score (e.g., FSIQ, GCA, GIA) as the cornerstone for decision-making. Over 10 years ago, Kelman and Lester (1997) coined the phrase "IQ Fetishism" to describe the often mindless fixation on IQ-Achievement discrepancy despite the lack of empirical support for such distinctions. We know that the relationship between IQ and achievement is not necessarily a strong relationship and that it varies based upon the measures used. Knowing that a child has a high or a low GCA score may tell us something about what he or she might or should be doing on achievement tests, but that information is typically not very meaningful. Just because we know a GCA score does not mean that we can predict all things from it. IDEA 2004 or IDEIA (U.S. Congress, 2004) forbids states from requiring local educational agencies to use discrepancy measures for identification of specific learning disabilities, although states may still elect to permit the practice.

Table 5.7 shows the relationship between the DAS-II GCA and the three core composites, on the one hand, and the mean of three measures of academic achievement on the other, for non-clinical samples. The GCA correlated slightly lower with Reading (Mean $r = .61$) than with Written language tests (Mean $r = .69$) and had its highest correlation with measures of mathematics abilities (Mean $r = .78$). The Verbal ability cluster related almost equally to Reading, Math, and Written Language achievement measures (Mean $r = .60, .62,$ and $.61$, respectively), while Nonverbal Reasoning and Spatial abilities correlated best with Math achievement (Mean $r = .72$ and $.62$, respectively). Given these imperfect relationships between ability and achievement, it is often difficult to make accurate predictions of one score from another.

Unless correlations are perfect ($r = 1.00$), high ability scores do not predict equally high achievement scores, and low ability scores do not predict equally low achievement scores. It is only when the ability score is close to the mean (Mean $= 100$) that the ability and achievement are predicted to be equal. Predicted achievement normally falls between the predictor score and the population mean (e.g., Standard Score 100). The lower the correlation between the tests, the more closely the predicted score is likely to approach the population mean. Galton (1886) published data and an explanation of this "regression toward mediocrity" or "regression toward the mean" more than 120 years ago. Consequently, high ability scores do predict high achievement scores, but the achievement is predicted to be below the ability score. For example, examination

Table 5.7 Average Correlation Between DAS-II Composites and Achievement Measures

	Reading	Math	Written Language
Verbal (V)	.60	.62	.61
Nonverbal Reasoning (NVR)	.52	.72	.57
Spatial (Sp)	.45	.62	.55
General Conceptual Ability (GCA)	.61	.78	.69

Note: Based upon non-clinical samples only.

Source: Adapted from Elliott (2007b, pp. 164–170). *Differential Ability Scales–Second Edition.* Adapted by permission. Reproduced by permission of the Publisher, The Psychological Corporation. All rights reserved. "Differential Ability Scales–Second Edition" and "DAS-II" are trademarks of The Psychological Corporation.

of Table D.1 in the DAS-II *Normative Data Tables Manual* (pp. 146–147) shows that, with a GCA of 140, a child's WIAT-II achievement composite scores would be predicted to range from 133 (Total achievement) to 126 (Written Language), differences of 7 to 14 points from the GCA of 140. Conversely, a child with a GCA score of 70 would be expected to obtain an achievement composite score from 75 (Total achievement) to 80 (Written Language), differences of 5 to 10 points.

Besides the problem with the imperfect prediction of achievement scores, it is also important to remember that if achievement can be depressed by the impact of a "disorder in 1 or more of the basic psychological processes" (U.S. Congress, 2004, Sec. 602 (30) (A)), we should also expect that the ability score itself would be depressed by the very same disorder. This is what we refer to above as the "Mark Penalty." Because of this "double-whammy," school multidisciplinary teams often find a student ineligible for special education services because, despite the low achievement scores, the student's ability is not high enough above the achievement to create a "severe discrepancy." The team has accepted that the disorder may depress the achievement while ignoring the possibility that the IQ has also been similarly depressed by the very same disorder.

Under IDEA 2004 (U.S. Congress, 2004), states no longer may require local education agencies to use discrepancy measures to identify specific learning disabilities, but states may still permit the use of discrepancy measures for this purpose if they choose to do so. In any event, "the Team must apply reasoned, professional judgment, not simply indulge in an exercise in arithmetic. By our interpretation of federal law and by most state laws, it is not lawful to deny services to a student who truly has a learning disability simply because of the results of a statistical exercise" (Willis & Dumont, 2002, pp. 182–183).

While there are several methods that can be used for comparing cognitive ability scores to achievement, the method explained in this section utilizes the predicted difference method. This method accounts for regression effects and avoids overestimation of the frequency of a severe discrepancy for children with above average ability scores and underestimation of the frequency of such a discrepancy for children with below average ability scores.

Tables to compare DAS-II ability scores and WIAT-II achievement scores are provided in the *Normative Data Tables Manual* (Tables D.1–D.17, pp. 146–161) and are discussed on page 99 of the DAS-II *Technical Manual*. Additionally, page 33 of the School-Age Battery Record Form provides a table for use when comparing WIAT-II to DAS-II results. However, there are times when it may be advisable to administer a different test of academic achievement and use the scores from that battery in the consideration of whether there is a severe discrepancy between ability and achievement. The CD accompanying this book provides similar tables to compare DAS-II ability scores with achievement scores for the WJ III and KTEA-II.

Tables 5.8, 5.9, and 5.10 provide the differences between predicted achievement and actual WIAT-II, WJ III, and KTEA-II scores shown by 5 percent of the normal school population. Note that the values for the WIAT-II discrepancies are identical to those in the DAS-II *Normative Data Tables Manual* (Tables D.7–D.11), using the 5 percent columns for the WIAT-II composites. The values of discrepancy between predicted and actual achievement are *always* higher than those required for statistical significance. In other words, all the values in Tables 5.8 to 5.10 are statistically significant. Some professionals define a "severe discrepancy" as one shown by 5 percent or fewer in the population. That is what these tables show.

Those wishing an extensive discussion of the differences between various ways of determining discrepancy should see the discussion by Cecil Reynolds (1990) in Conceptual and Technical Problems in Learning Disability Diagnosis. in C. R. Reynolds and R. W. Kamphaus (Eds), *Handbook of psychological and educational assessment of children: Intelligence and achievement* (ch. 24).

Using the predicted difference method of calculating whether a severe discrepancy between ability and achievement exists requires three steps. First, se-

Table 5.8 Differences (Critical Values) Between Predicted and Actual WIAT-II Achievement Score Needed for "Severe Discrepancy" *

| Composite | KTEA-II Achievement Composite | | | | |
	Total Achievement	Reading	Mathematics	Written Language	Oral Language
Verbal	17	19	20	21	18
Nonverbal Reasoning	18	20	19	21	21
Spatial	19	21	19	21	21
General Conceptual Ability	15	18	16	19	17
Special Nonverbal Composite	17	19	17	20	20

*Five percent of the school population show these differences or greater. The table applies to those individuals whose Actual achievement is *lower* than their Predicted achievement score.

Table 5.9 Differences (Critical Values) Between Predicted and Actual KTEA-II Achievement Score Needed for "Severe Discrepancy" *

	KTEA-II Achievement Composite								
Composite	CAC	RCC	MCC	WLC	OLC	SSC	DCC	RFC	OFC
Verbal	17	19	20	19	17	22	22	21	23
Nonverbal Reasoning	16	20	17	21	17	23	23	22	23
Spatial	19	21	20	22	19	24	23	22	23
General Conceptual Ability	15	18	17	19	15	22	22	21	22
Special Nonverbal Composite	15	19	16	20	16	23	22	21	22

KTEA-II abbreviations are: CAC = Comprehensive Achievement Composite, RCC = Reading Composite, MCC = Math Composite, WLC = Written Language Composite, OLC = Oral Language Composite, SSC = Sound Symbol Composite, DCC = Decoding Composite, RFC = Reading Fluency Composite, OFC = Oral Fluency Composite

* Five percent of the school population show these differences or greater. The table applies to those individuals whose Actual achievement is *lower* than their Predicted achievement score.

lect the DAS-II ability score that you deem most relevant (GCA, SNC, Verbal, Nonverbal Reasoning, or Spatial). Second, use Tables D.1 to D.5 in the DAS-II *Normative Data Tables Manual* (if you are using the WIAT-II) or the tables in the CD accompanying this book (if you are using the WJ III or the KTEA-II), to determine the predicted achievement test score. Third, calculate the difference between the actual achievement test score and the predicted achievement test score using simple subtraction (Actual Achievement – Predicted Achievement). Finally, the difference between these two scores is compared to the Critical values in Tables 5.8, 5.9, and 5.10 for the WIAT-II, WJ III, and KTEA-II. If you are working with a different criterion of severe discrepancy than the "5 percent or less" definition, you will need to use the appropriate tables on the CD (for the WJ II or KTEA-II) or in the *Normative Data Tables Manual* (if you are using the WIAT-II).

Whichever definition we use, differences equal to or greater than the critical value indicate that a severe discrepancy exists between the actual level of achievement and that predicted by cognitive ability. Note that when considering the presence of a severe discrepancy between ability and achievement, what we are generally concerned about are those times when the actual achievement is much lower than the predicted achievement and not the opposite (actual achievement much higher than predicted achievement). Therefore, our statistics are "one-tailed" rather than "two-tailed."

Table 5.10 Differences (Critical Values) Difference Between Predicted and Actual WJ III Achievement Score Needed for "Severe Discrepancy" *

Composite	WJ III Achievement Composite											
	TOT	OE	LC	Bread	BRS	RC	BMath	MCalc	MR	BWL	BWS	WE
Verbal	17	19	19	18	20	16	18	21	18	20	18	21
Nonverbal Reasoning	18	23	20	21	21	20	16	18	16	20	19	21
Spatial	19	22	21	21	22	22	19	21	18	20	20	21
General Conceptual Ability	15	20	18	18	19	17	14	17	13	17	16	19
Special Nonverbal Composite	17	22	19	20	20	20	15	18	14	19	18	20

WJ III abbreviations are: TOT = Total Achievement, OE = Oral Expression, LC = listening Comprehension, BRead = Broad Reading, BRS = Basic Reading Skills, RC = Reading Comprehension, BMath = Broad Math, MCalc = Math Calculation, MR = Math Reasoning, BWL = Broad Written language, BWS = Basic Writing Skills, WE = Written Expression

* Five percent of the school population show these differences or greater. The table applies to those individuals whose Actual achievement is *lower* than their Predicted achievement score.

DAS-II Composite Score Used for this Comparison: **GCA**

DAS- II Composite Standard Score: **84**

WJ III ACH Composite	Actual WJ III Score	Predicted WJ III Score	Difference (Actual – Predicted)	Critical Value (.05)	Significant Difference
Total	84	87	-3	15	
Oral Expression	99	90	9	20	
Listening Comprehension	94	89	5	18	
Broad Reading	85	89	-4	18	
Basic Reading Skills	89	90	-1	19	
Reading Comprehension	88	88	0	17	
Broad Math	70	87	-17	14	YES
Math Calculation	72	89	-17	17	YES
Math Reasoning	67	86	-19	13	YES
Broad Written Language	86	89	-3	17	
Basic Writing Skills	88	88	0	16	
Written Expression	92	90	2	19	

Figure 5.20 Predicted Difference Method—DAS-II versus WJ III ACH

The predicted difference method is illustrated in Figure 5.20 (DAS-II versus WJ III ACH) for Joe, a 9-year-old with a GCA of 84. The GCA was used to predict the WJ III score. The differences between the actual WJ III scores and the predicted WJ III scores are recorded in the Difference column. These differences are compared to the values needed for a severe discrepancy (Critical Values). Any negative value for a difference that is equal to or greater than the critical value is recorded as being a Significant Difference by placing a "yes" in that column. In the example, Joe's actual achievement was fairly close to the predicted achievement scores in all areas except Math. For Broad Math, Math Calculations, and Math Reasoning, his actual scores were severely discrepant from the predicted achievement based upon his overall ability (GCA).

Step 13 (Optional): Summarize DAS-II Scores and Findings

Before beginning to write your interpretive report, it is often useful to summarize your findings in a way that allows you to focus your interpretations on the relevant findings from Steps 1 through 12. Figure 5.21 shows a completed summary page for Marybeth.

Composite/Cluster/Subtest	Score	95% CI	PR	Description	Cluster Difference		Subtest	
					Between	Within	High	Low
General Conceptual Ability	110	(104 – 115)	75	Average to Above Average				
Special Nonverbal Composite		(–)						
Verbal Ability	133	(120 – 139)	99	High to Very High	V>NV			
Word Definitions	74		99			NS	H	
Verbal Similarities	65		93				H	
Nonverbal Reasoning Ability	104	(96 – 112)	61	Average to Above Average	NV>Sp			
Matrices	54		66			NS		
Sequential & Quantitative Reasoning	52		58					
Spatial Ability	89	(83 – 96)	23	Below Average to Average	SP<V			
Pattern Construction	38		12			Sign.		L
Recall of Designs	50		50					
Working Memory	113	(106 – 119)	81	Average to Above Average	NS			
Recall of Digits Backward	54		66			NS		
Recall of Sequential Order	60		84					
Processing Speed	53	(49 – 66)	<1	Very Low	GCA>PS			
Speed of Information Processing	28					NS		L
Rapid Naming	21		<1					L
Diagnostic and out of level subtests								
Recall of Digits Forward	58		79					
Recall of Objects - Immediate	49		46					
Recall of Objects – Delayed	54		66					
Recognition of Pictures	47		38					
Phonological Processing	49		46					

Figure 5.21 DAS-II School-Age Summary Sheet

INTERPRETING CLUSTERS AND SUBTESTS

What follows are brief descriptions of the DAS-II clusters and subtests. The specific information may be useful as you work your way through the steps of interpretation. The key to interpreting a child's performance on the DAS-II is to integrate all the relevant information you have (from both a statistical standpoint and a clinical standpoint) and to generate hypotheses that you can use to help explain how and why the child obtained the scores that he or she did. We recommend that interpretation focus on the abilities being measured by groups of subtests (for example clusters and/or shared abilities) rather than on any individual subtest score. The information provided here is to help you understand how each subtest contributes to the DAS-II. The shared or overlapping abilities that two or more subtests provide are crucial to the understanding of the child's DAS-II performance. Although we want examiners to be aware of the unique aspects of each subtest, the hypotheses generated by groups of subtests are generally more reliable and relevant to understanding the child.

Verbal Ability

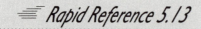

Rapid Reference 5.13

Verbal Ability Cluster

- Measures acquired verbal concepts and knowledge
- Early Years: Verbal Comprehension and Naming Vocabulary
- School-Age level: Word Definitions and Verbal Similarities

The Verbal Ability cluster is based on accumulated experience and may be influenced by experience with language at home, educational experiences and opportunities, cultural differences in language use and richness of verbal expression, or language impairments due to neurological or cognitive processing problems. The items in this cluster usually assess the examinee's repertoire of verbal knowledge and concepts. Questions are presented either verbally or visually, and the child gives the responses orally or, on the Early Years Verbal Comprehension subtest, through actions.

Children with extremely low scores on the Verbal Ability cluster may show the characteristics of children with verbal learning disabilities, expressive and/or receptive language disorders, hearing impairments, or English as a second language (ESL).

Nonverbal Ability and Nonverbal Reasoning Ability

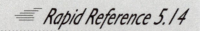

Rapid Reference 5.14

Nonverbal Ability and Nonverbal Reasoning Ability Cluster

- Ages 3–6 to 17–11, a measure of fluid ability (Gf)
- Ages 2–6 to 3–5, a measure of fluid ability (Gf) and visual-spatial ability (Gv)
- Early Years Lower level: Picture Similarities and Pattern Construction
- Early Years Upper level: Picture Similarities and Matrices
- School-Age level: Matrices and Sequential and Quantitative Reasoning

The Nonverbal Ability and Nonverbal Reasoning Ability clusters measure several cognitive factors, including, for ages 3:6 to 17:11, fluid ability (Gf), and for ages 2:6 to 3:5, both fluid ability (Gf) and visual-spatial ability (Gv). At the Early Years Lower Level, the Nonverbal cluster score represents complex, nonverbal mental processing and is assessed with subtests that require no verbal responses and use only simple verbal instructions.

At the Upper Early Years and the School-Age level, the Nonverbal Reasoning cluster score is a measure of nonverbal, inductive reasoning and requires complex mental processing. Each of the subtests requires the child to identify important elements of stimuli, to formulate and test hypotheses about relationships among those stimuli, and to apply the relationship to new stimuli. The subtests are visually presented and are nonverbal in the sense that they require minimal verbal instructions to the child and either minimal or no verbal response. Despite the apparent nonverbal nature of these problems, they do allow for (and are considerably aided by) verbal mediation in the solution of each item. Although visual-spatial ability (*Gv*) is separated from the fluid reasoning (*Gf*) ability of the Nonverbal Reasoning Ability cluster at the Upper Level Early Years and School-Age levels, severe weaknesses in visual perception might impair performance on Matrices. The Copying subtest could be used to check that hypothesis.

Children with extremely low scores on the Nonverbal Reasoning Ability cluster, especially when in relationship to higher Verbal and Spatial Ability cluster scores, may show difficulty with tasks that require the integration and analysis of both verbal and visual stimuli at the same time. Elliott (2001, 2005) found that a large number of children with reading and learning disabilities displayed difficulty in the areas of nonverbal reasoning when compared with non-disabled children. Despite everything that is written about "visual" and "verbal" learning, most schoolwork requires integration of visual and verbal input, thinking, and output.

Spatial Ability

The Spatial Ability cluster measures complex visual-spatial processing (*Gv*) through subtests that are nonverbal and require only simple verbal or nonverbal instructions to the child about the nature of the tasks. The subtests require the abilities to perceive and to remember spatial relationships and shapes. Responses require some degree of eye-hand coordination for drawing or for constructing block

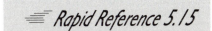

Rapid Reference 5.15

Spatial Ability Cluster

- A measure of visual-spatial processing ability (Gv)
- Early Years Upper Level: Pattern Construction and Copying
- School-Age level: Pattern Construction and Recall of Designs

patterns but do not require verbalization. Pattern Construction may also require inductive reasoning for forming hypotheses about how to synthesize a pattern. These visual-spatial problems do not permit as much verbal mediation in their solutions as do the subtests in the Nonverbal Reasoning Ability cluster.

DON'T FORGET

There is a difference between using verbal mediation to help solve a problem and merely talking to oneself. "This goes here and this goes here and this goes here" usually is not useful verbal mediation. It may just be an effort to avoid what broadcasters call "dead air." However, "Oh! I need to put the two half-and-half sides together to make a big triangle" probably does represent an effort to use verbal skills to help solve a nonverbal problem. It is important to make this distinction in considering and reporting test behaviors.

One of the Spatial Ability subtests, Recall of Designs, requires the examinee to draw designs from memory after the model has been removed. Although this task requires aspects of visual memory, the correlations of Recall of Designs with other subtests involving memory (e.g., Recall of Objects, Recognition of Pictures, and Recall of Digits Forward) are much lower than the correlation with Pattern Construction (*Introductory and Technical Handbook*, Elliott, 2007b, p. 152). Apparently, if the perception of the figure is precise and clear, it is easy to remember, but if the figure is not clearly perceived, then memory does not help very much.

Children with extremely low scores on the Spatial Ability cluster may show the characteristics of nonverbal learning disabilities (NVLD; Rourke, 1995). As well as showing poor spatial imagery and inattention to visual details, children with NVLD are often disorganized and distractible. There are several different definitions of NVLD in current use. However, some children simply have visual, spatial weaknesses without some or any of the other characteristics cited in various descriptions of NVLD. Unless you have considered all aspects of the child's situation and are contemplating a diagnosis of NVLD by one of the several current definitions (which you should make explicit in your report), be sure to describe a "visual/spatial" weakness or learning disability so your formulation is not confused with one of the other definitions of NVLD.

Working Memory

The Working Memory cluster score is primarily a measure of the broad ability of short-term memory and specifically of the narrow ability of working memory. The subtests that contribute to this cluster are Recall of Digits Backward and Recall of Sequential Order. The Recall of Digits Backward is an entirely verbal test using non-meaningful strings of numbers while Recall of Sequential Order is verbally presented and lists parts of the body that must be reordered in correct sequence from highest to lowest (e.g., shoulder, foot, head → head, shoulder, foot). The characteristic of all items in both subtests is that they require the child to listen to a list of items and to hold that list in short-term memory while the list is worked on and put into a different order than the order of presentation.

Rapid Reference 5.16

Working Memory Cluster

- A measure of short-term memory ability (Gv)
- All levels: Recall of Digits Backward and Recall of Sequential Order

Working memory is a process underlying many cognitive abilities. Most of the DAS-II core subtests require that the information and hypotheses about problems to be held in verbal or visual short-term memory while the child is working on a solution. The working memory subtests have high g loadings similar to the core subtests but in contrast to the Recall of Digits Forward subtest's relatively low g loading. However, it cannot be assumed that, because a child scores well on the core subtests, his or her working memory is also normal. We need to test working memory directly.

Much classroom information is presented orally and sequentially, and a low working memory score may suggest that the child has specific problems in organizing, transforming, and storing sequences of verbal information. This finding has implications for instruction and suggests that the child may need additional visual cues to support his or her verbal working memory. Multi-sensory teaching methods may help in such cases (Birsh, 1999). Also, a relative weakness in working memory suggests that the amount and the pace of verbal information being presented to the child at any one time should be moderated. The child may need to have multiple-step operations broken down into a series of single steps.

If a child has a low score on the Working Memory cluster, and is also noted to be distractible and inattentive, the examiner should consider whether this is a possible causal factor, or whether this is an effect of difficulties experienced on these tasks. If the distractibility and inattention are limited to these subtests, and there is no evidence that this behavior is generalized to all of the child's activities, the possibility should be considered that this behavior is reactive to the problems posed by the tasks. If there is clear evidence of generalized attentional problems, this would suggest that working memory problems may be one of the causal factors underlying the low score.

Processing Speed

Rapid Reference 5.17

Processing Speed Cluster

- A measure of general cognitive processing speed (Gs)
- All levels: Speed of Information Processing and Rapid Naming

The Processing Speed cluster measures several cognitive factors, including processing speed, ability to work fast under time pressure, ability to integrate visual and verbal processing efficiently, scanning ability, attention, and concentration. The Processing Speed cluster is also related to rate of motor activity, motivation and persistence, visual acuity, and ability to delay responding until appropriate.

Processing speed may be important for children's learning because of the concept of "attentional resource allocation" (Hunt, 1980; Roberts, Beh, & Stankov, 1988; Stankov, 1983). A child's ability to rapidly encode, store, and retrieve information would enable attentional resources to be switched rapidly and to be devoted to incoming information from various sources. Since information is processed faster, the individual should be able to handle more information and thus to develop a larger store of information over time.

Children whose processing speed is significantly slow may need special accommodations, particularly when taking timed educational achievement tests. In the classroom, these children may need instructional materials to be presented at a rate that enables them to be processed, and preferably in small amounts at a given time. Such children would require further investigation of the specific areas in which they have difficulty in processing information fast enough.

Processing speed is likely to interact with memory span. If one has a tremendous memory span, one can afford to process information more slowly. If one processes very swiftly, the demand on memory is reduced. However, combined weaknesses in both memory span and processing speed can be devastating.

While scores on the Processing Speed cluster are intended to provide a helpful summary of a child's overall cognitive speed, it is recommended that the results for each of the two subtests in the cluster should be considered and compared carefully. Use the interpretive guidelines provided above (Steps 6 and 10) for Speed of Information Processing and Rapid Naming. If the Rapid Naming score is lower than Speed of Information Processing, consider whether fluency in speech, general language development (particularly if words in Rapid Naming are unfamiliar), and speed of access and efficiency of retrieval of available words from the lexicon are possible explanations. On the other hand, if the Speed of Information Processing score is lower than Rapid Naming, consider the specific aspect of making quantitative comparisons rapidly and possible motivational problems with numbers (where there is evidence of math difficulties).

Examiners should note that Processing Speed has positive, but generally low (on average between .2 and .3 across the age groups), correlations with other cognitive subtests. The proportion of variance attributed to g for the Speed of Information Processing (24 percent) and Rapid Naming (18 percent) subtests was the lowest of all the DAS-II subtests. These finding are important especially with regard to children you test who are of high or low cognitive abilities. Children with high cognitive abilities often do less well on processing speed tasks when compared to their other scores (and conversely those of low ability may do better on these tasks). For example, for a sample of intellectually gifted children whose mean GCA was 125.4, the Processing Speed scores was 112.0.

School Readiness

The School Readiness cluster measures several cognitive factors, including development of skills underlying literacy and numeracy, language and conceptual ability, ability to match objects, auditory and visual discrimination ability, and phonological processing. It is also related to richness of early environment and quality of early education and general education.

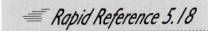

Rapid Reference 5.18

School Readiness Cluster

- Available at ages 5:0 to 8:11
- A measure that represents the growth of skills fundamental to early school learning
- All levels: Early Number Concepts, Matching Letter-Like Forms, and Phonological Processing

Seven- and eight-year-old children who are normal in their development of early quantitative concepts and reading and writing skills may obtain maximum or near-maximum scores on the Early Number Concepts and Matching Letter-Like Forms subtests. For such children, the School Readiness cluster score is inappropriate. The cluster has served its purpose—establishing school readiness—without your needing to report a score. However, for lower-functioning children—those for whom school learning presents some difficulty—the cluster yields useful information on some of the important processes underlying early school achievement.

Subtest-by-Subtest Analysis (Subtests are listed in alphabetical order)

Copying

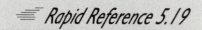

=== *Rapid Reference 5.19*

Copying Subtest

- Contributes to estimates of Spatial Ability, the Special Nonverbal Composite, and the GCA
- Requires the examinee to copy geometric figures
- Typically administered at ages 3:6 to 5:11
- Extended range at ages 6:0 to 8:11
- Input is visual
- Output is nonverbal (paper and pencil task)
- Measure of visual-spatial ability (Gv) and the narrow ability of Visualization (Vz)

The Copying subtest assesses fine-motor ability and the ability to perceive similarities between figures. Copying is a measure of visual-spatial ability (*Gv*) and the narrow ability of Visualization (Vz).

The subtest, containing 20 untimed items, requires the examinee to copy, using paper and pencil, abstract geometric figures. Items vary from a simple straight line to complex geometric figures. Early items are simple figures (e.g., straight line or a circle); later items include letter shapes that commonly cause reversal difficulties for young children (e.g., p, b); and the final items are more complex geometric figures. For all items, the drawing remains in view while the child attempts to reproduce it.

For each item, the child must utilize graphomotor abilities to copy the designs as well as visual spatial abilities to recognize the similarities between the original design and the figure being drawn. Since copying, writing, and perceptual matching are particularly important in the emergence of early academics, a child's performance on the Copying subtest may be useful in determining readiness for, or facility with, these pre-academic skills.

Children who do well on the Copying subtest may be demonstrating developed skills in matching visual shapes using paper and pencil, good fine-motor coordination, and good visual spatial perception and orientation.

Poor performance on the Copying task may reflect poor experience or lack of opportunity with drawing and writing tasks, poor motor control, and or poor matching skills.

When administering the subtest, be mindful to observe not only the child's posture and hand position relative to the paper (does the child move his or her body around in order to recreate the drawing), but also the pencil grip. Does the child have a relaxed, tripod grip, a thumb-wrap grip, or a tight, clenched fist grasp? Does the child apply so much pressure to the page that the pencil tip breaks? Does the copying appear fluent and comfortable or slow and difficult? Are there many erasures when trying to recreate the designs? This could be a sign of a compulsive style—the design must be perfect—or recognition that the copies are not accurate. Is the child left handed, right handed, or mixed dominant?

It is sometimes helpful to examine with the child any designs that are particularly poorly drawn. Show the child the original design as well as his or her own drawing and ask, "Does your design look like this one" (pointing to the original design). If the child responds that the designs are similar, this may indicate a visual perceptual difficulty (the child does not see the design correctly). In contrast, if the child recognizes that the design does not match the target design, the poor copy may be the result of a graphomotor difficulty.

Early Number Concepts

The Early Number Concepts subtest measures such number abilities as reciting, counting, matching, comparing, recognizing, and solving number problems. Early Number Concepts is a mixed measure of crystallized and fluid intelligence (*Gc/Gf*) and measures the narrow abilities of Language Development (LD), General Verbal Information (K0), and Piagetian Reasoning (RP).

The subtest contains 33 items that requires the examinee to demonstrate knowledge of number abilities. None of the items requires an extended verbal response. Despite the fact that this subtest assesses the child's acquired knowledge of concepts of number and quantity, the subtest should not be considered a

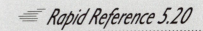

Rapid Reference 5.20

Early Number Concepts Subtest

- Contributes to the School Readiness Composite
- Requires the examinee to demonstrate knowledge of number abilities
- Administered at ages 2:6 to 8:11
- Input is visual and auditory
- Output is verbal (typically a single word) or nonverbal (pointing)
- Measure of crystallized and fluid intelligence (*Gc/Gf*) and measures the narrow abilities of Language Development (LD), General Verbal Information (K0), and Piagetian Reasoning (RP).

complete assessment of general mathematical concepts as it does not include concepts of measurement. The subtest assesses the following number concepts and skills: reciting by rote numbers up to ten; counting up to ten objects in one-to-one correspondence; matching and classifying according to qualitative attributes (numbers); making comparisons of sets by concepts such as more, less, same/equal; recognizing number names and numerals, and ordinal relationships such as first, second, or last; understanding numerical order shown by identifying larger or smaller numbers; solving basic addition and subtraction word problems; and counting by tens and recognizing place value of tens and ones. Analysis of failures on specific subtest items may reveal concepts that the child has not yet mastered. Information about gaps in the child's conceptual knowledge may be useful for planning early learning activities. For example, the child may have missed an item that asks the child to "point to the cake with one more candle than this one." The concept of "more" or "one more" is basic to many primary instructional activities.

Because there is a fundamental relationship between conceptual knowledge and verbal knowledge, scores on this subtest may also reflect more general aspects of language development. Low scores may reflect relatively poor general cognitive or verbal development. Poor performance may also result from disadvantage or a lack of experience in using language to express number or quantity. If necessary, the Bracken Basic Concept Scale, 3rd ed. (Bracken, 2006) could provide additional information.

Observe the way in which the child attempts to solve problems, for example counting on his or her fingers, drawing with a finger on the table, closing eyes and imagining the numbers in his or her head, or talking out loud. Is the child able to count correctly with correct pointing, or is the counting correct but the pointing incorrect? You will find that children will show varying types of response styles, such as thinking through the questions; responding quickly and correctly, slowly and correctly, quickly and incorrectly, or slowly and incorrectly; or simply guessing. If the child does appear to be guessing at the answers, are the guesses reasonable or inappropriate?

Item analysis may be helpful when trying to interpret a child's successes and errors. Were errors found that demonstrate a misunderstanding of the mathematical operation of addition and or subtraction, of ordinal numerical relationships (e.g., first, third), of numerical order, or of quantitative relations (e.g., larger, smaller)? You can check many such hypotheses by making up a few additional questions after the DAS-II is completed.

Matching Letter-Like Forms

The subtest measures visual discrimination and spatial orientation. This type of task is difficult for most children below the age of 4 years, but develops very rapidly thereafter, usually reaching a ceiling after the age of 7 years. This subtest is therefore most suitable for most children in the age range of 4:0–6:11, but it can also be administered to children ages 7:0–7:11 of average or low ability and to children ages 8:0–8:11 of very low ability. The task appears to be highly relevant to young children's development of visual discrimination skills, which in turn are relevant to the acquisition of reading and writing skills. It is a measure of visual-spatial ability (*Gv*) and measures the narrow ability of Visualization (Vz).

The subtest contains 27 items that require the child to look at a figure on one page and identify, by pointing, that same figure on another page that contains six identical figures, five of which have been rotated to varying degrees. The examinee must

Rapid Reference 5.21

Matching Letter-Like Forms Subtests

- Contributes to the School Readiness Composite
- Requires the examinee to look at a figure on one page and identify that same figure on another page that contains six identical figures, five of which have been rotated to varying degrees
- Typically administered at ages 4:0 to 6:11
- Extended ages 7:0 to 8:11
- Input is visual
- Output is nonverbal (pointing)
- Measure of visual-spatial ability (*Gv*) and measures the narrow ability of Visualization (Vz).

select the one figure whose orientation is identical to the target figure's orientation. The task requires relatively fine discriminations to be made between the orientations of similar figures.

Performance on this task may be indicative of the child's general abilities in distinguishing between letter-like shapes and the development of visual discrimination skills. Performance may be influenced by the child's perception and discrimination of the spatial orientation of the figures; the strategies used for scanning and making visual comparisons; and the ability to follow verbal instructions and visual cues.

Low scores on this subtest may be caused by the child's impulsiveness (responding without checking the response); lack of experience in visual matching activities; or normal developmental pattern (the child is simply not ready to understand the task).

When interpreting scores on this task, be sure to take into consideration whether the child understood the directions. Examine the responses to see if there was any indication of impulsive responding (e.g., the child responds without carefully scanning all the choices) or of perseveration (e.g., child consistently points to the same position on the page or makes the same type of error on many items). Since vision problems could affect the task, be attuned to any visual problems that may hamper the child on this task. Did the child have to adjust his or her position to view the pages, leaning very close to the page or pushing the booklet farther away? Does the child squint or rotate the booklet? We strongly urge examiners to obtain an assessment of at least near vision acuity before beginning the assessment. It is easy to purchase near vision test cards and instructions in case you must check near vision yourself. If you do, do not report anything that might lead parents to think their child has now had a comprehensive vision exam, unless you are qualified and equipped to check astigmatism, binocular function, and other essential characteristics. If the child passes the near vision assessment, simply continue with the DAS-II. If the child does very badly on the near vision assessment, consider referring the child for an optometric or ophthalmological evaluation before continuing your evaluation.

Matrices

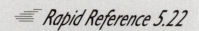

Rapid Reference 5.22

Matrices Subtest

- Contributes to estimates of Nonverbal Reasoning Ability, the Special Nonverbal Composite, and the GCA
- Requires the examinee to select the response that best completes a matrix
- Administered at ages 3:6 to 17:11
- Correct responses are highlighted in bold ink
- Input is visual
- Output is nonverbal (pointing) or minimally verbal (name a letter)
- Measure of the broad ability of fluid intelligence (*Gf*) and the narrow ability of Induction (I).

The subtest assesses nonverbal inductive reasoning ability, ability to formulate and test hypotheses, verbal mediation, and visual perception. Matrices is a measure of the broad ability of fluid intelligence (*Gf*) and the narrow ability of Induction (I).

The Matrices subtest contains 56 items presented nonverbally, and requiring no oral response. Set A (Items 1 through 19 in Stimulus Book 3) are colored items intended for younger children. Set B (items 20 through 56 in Stimulus Book 2) are black and white and intended for older children. Each matrix problem is a square of four or nine cells, with a blank cell in the lower right-hand corner.

For each item, the child must determine the relationship between the pictures or diagrams in the matrix and then, on the basis of that relationship, must select, from among the answer choices, the one that is most closely associated with the perceived relationship. Because

Matrices is a measure of reasoning ability, children with good nonverbal, inductive reasoning, which would include the ability to formulate and test hypotheses about relationships, and the ability to identify rules governing features or variables in abstract figures, will often do well on this subtest. Although the items are nonverbal, verbal mediation of the problems (e.g., labeling the pictures in Set A or the diagrams in Set B) is possible and can help the child formulate a correct solution.

Poor performance on the Matrices subtest may indicate poor reasoning ability. For example, the child may not be able to independently rationalize the pattern of the first two rows and to apply this pattern to the third row to supply the missing element. Problems with language, specifically in understanding the instructions or in the inability to use verbal mediation, may impact the child's performance on Matrices. Specific visual-spatial difficulties and/or the inability to gain meaning from the visual cues may also possibly cause poor performance on this subtest. Finally, an impulsive response style (choosing quickly from the multiple-choice answers without adequately evaluating the subtle differences between them) or an inflexible response style (choosing one solution and being unable to formulate any other solution) may hinder performance on this test.

Although the subtest is not timed, it may be useful to monitor how long it takes the child to respond to the items. Are the child's responses deliberate and carefully thought out, very fast or very slow, or are they impulsive in nature? Children who respond quickly but poorly may be demonstrating an impulsive response style. In contrast, children who spend a lot of time and arrive at a correct answer may be demonstrating a contemplative, trial-and-error approach to the task.

Comparing passed and failed items will sometimes reveal better performance on items that are perceptually simple, even if conceptually difficult, and weak performance on items that seem to be visually confusing. Such a pattern might suggest visual perceptual difficulties. Review the child's performance on Copying, Pattern Construction, and Recall of Designs.

It may be useful to examine the differences between the child's responses on the early picture items and to the later items that are geometric shapes and designs. Problems on later items may be the result of problems with complex visual stimuli.

Naming Vocabulary

The Naming Vocabulary subtest assesses recognition language, expressive language ability, general language development, and word retrieval from long-term

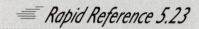

Rapid Reference 5.23

Naming Vocabulary Subtest

- Contributes to the Verbal Ability and the GCA
- Requires the examinee to name real objects or pictured objects, or to provide a verb, noun, or synonym
- Typically administered to ages 2:6 to 6:11
- Extended ages 7:0 to 8:11
- Input is visual
- Output is verbal (typically a single word)
- Measures the broad ability of crystallized intelligence (Gc) and the narrow ability of Lexical Knowledge (VL)

memory. In contrast to the receptive language demands of the Verbal Comprehension subtest, Naming Vocabulary measures expressive language ability. It measures the broad ability of crystallized intelligence (*Gc*) and the narrow ability of Lexical Knowledge (VL).

The subtest contains 34 items that require the child to name real objects (Items 1–2) or pictured objects (Items 3–30), or to provide a verb, noun, or synonym for specific queries related to the pictured items (Items 31–34).

Performance on the subtest may be influenced by the child's vocabulary knowledge and, on the most difficult items, knowledge of verbs and adjectives. The items require the child to recall words from long-term memory rather than to recognize or to understand the meaning of words. Is the child hesitant to respond? Are there apparently excessive "I don't know" responses? Does the child typically respond with an item's function as opposed to its name? Does the child typically respond by providing a related object rather than the name for the pictured item? Since the task demands much less expression than the more open-ended responses involved in the Word Definitions subtest, observe whether the child gives multiple-word definitions as opposed to single-word responses. The child who "talks his or her way around an answer" (circumlocutions) may have word-retrieval difficulties that should be explored further. Word-retrieval or word-finding difficulties may also be indicated by the child who responds slowly, as if searching for the correct word.

Pattern Construction

Pattern Construction Set A measures visual-perceptual ability, problem-solving ability, hand-eye coordination, and spatial orientation; it may also involve verbal encoding strategies. Set A tasks measure the same abilities measured by the Copying subtest, but were designed for young children not yet able to manipulate

≡ Rapid Reference 5.24

Pattern Construction Subtest

- Contributes to estimates of Nonverbal Ability (Lower Early Years), Spatial Ability (Upper Early Years and School-Age), Special Nonverbal Composite, and the GCA
- **SET A** requires the examinee to copy two- and three-dimensional models or diagrams using wooden blocks
- **SETS B and C** require the examinee to reproduce pictured designs using three-dimensional bi-colored foam or plastic blocks
- Administered at ages 2:6 to 17:11
- Scored in two ways: standard and alternative
- Input is visual
- Output is nonverbal (motoric)
- Measure the broad ability of visual-spatial ability (Gv) and the narrow ability of Spatial Relations (SR)

a pencil. Sets B and C assess visual-spatial ability, perception of spatial orientation, analysis of visual data, and nonverbal reasoning.

The subtest contains 38 items that require the child to analyze and synthesize sample designs demonstrated by the examiner or presented in a picture. Items 1 through 12 measure the child's ability to copy a design with wooden blocks. On Items 1 and 2, the child builds a tower, using either two or eight blocks. For the remaining Set A items (3 to 12), the examiner constructs, and leaves in view, a two- or three-dimensional design that the child then attempts to copy with the remaining blocks. Items 10 and 12 are more challenging two-dimensional designs that emphasize orientation and sequence. Items 14 to 19 require the child to construct patterns with foam squares that have each side either solid yellow or solid black. The final items (20 to 38), typically administered to older children, require the child to construct patterns with plastic blocks. The block items begin with easy two-block patterns and increase in complexity to nine-block patterns. Daniel (1986) demonstrated that items with flat squares and items with cubes assess the same abilities, but that the flat squares allow assessment of younger children.

Pattern Construction Sets B and C allow an alternative scoring procedure. If you believe that time limits will invalidate the subtest (e.g., a motor impairment hampers the examinee or the examinee is overly slow or overly thoughtful), use the alternative scoring procedure. Usually, you will need to administer more items if you use the alternative scoring procedure.

Items 36–38 are only administered as part of the alternative scoring procedure. You do not need to choose between the two types of procedures in advance. However, you must decide which one to use before you complete the subtest. If you are not sure which procedure you will use, be sure to administer the extra items to keep your options open.

Interpretation of Performance

For very young children, successful performance requires not only motor skills and visual-perceptual ability, but also requires the child to have developed the notion of copying models. A child's performance on this subtest may be enhanced if he or she has begun to develop efficient verbal-encoding strategies.

For harder items, the task requires the child to make two-dimensional constructions and to ignore the third dimension of the block. Poor scores may indicate poor visual-spatial ability resulting from the child being distracted by the sides of the blocks, or an inability to perceive the correspondence between the pattern on the blocks and the pattern in the Stimulus Book.

Be observant of the problem-solving approach used by the child. Does the child use a trial-and-error approach to the blocks or a more systematic block-by-block approach? Does the child change the approach from item to item, and which approach, if any, is more successful than others? Is the child quick and impulsive or slow and reflective when deciding how to recreate the designs? Does the child methodically check each block placement against the design or rarely check? Is the child careless with block placement or overly compulsive, attempting to line up the blocks perfectly? Are the designs built using a left-to-right approach or the less common right-to-left or bottom-to-top approach? Note whether the child seems to benefit from feedback given when teaching items are incorrect. How does the child react when you say that a construction is wrong, demonstrate the correct construction, and ask the child to try again?

Note whether the child does better on items that have a model to copy

DON'T FORGET

Rotation of Designs

On the DAS-II, if the child constructs a pattern correctly it is scored correct regardless of the degree of rotation. Do make note if a child rotates the designs on a number of items, since this information may be useful when interpreting overall performance even though it does not affect the obtained score.

from rather than just the picture. Be careful to observe if there are any indications of fine-motor difficulties such as tremor or clumsiness.

Phonological Processing

The Phonological Processing subtest assesses knowledge of sound structure of the English language and the ability to manipulate sound, and it measures auditory processing (*Ga*) and the narrow ability of Phonetic Coding (PC).

The subtest contains four tasks (a total of 53 items) that require the child to rhyme, blend, segment, identify, and delete syllables, sounds, and phonemes in words. These tasks are considered to be fundamental abilities necessary for the early acquisition reading and writing skills. Rhyming and deletion are considered to be analytic skills that reflect whether the child has an "ear" for the sounds within words. Blending is a fundamental skill that a child needs when he or she is reading unfamiliar words that have to be decoded phonetically. Segmentation is a fundamental skill needed for spelling.

≡ *Rapid Reference 5.25*

Phonological Processing Subtest

- Contributes to the estimate of the School Readiness Composite
- Require the examinee to rhyme, blend, segment, identify, and delete syllables, sounds, and phonemes in words
- Administered at ages 5:0 to 12:11
- Provides only a global phonological processing subtest *T* score
- Input is auditory
- Output is verbal
- Measures auditory processing (*Ga*) and the narrow ability of Phonetic Coding (PC)

Each sub-task has four to seven teaching items, and a total of 11 to 15 test items. Blending is presented orally with no pictorial stimuli, while the other three tasks have both an oral and pictorial presentation.

Children who do well on these tasks often have well-developed auditory processing abilities as well as good oral language development and the ability to manipulate sounds within words. These are necessary but not sufficient foundations for development of reading skills. Children who have been exposed to word and sound games at home and at school and who have been read to during the preschool years may also do well on these tasks.

Observe the child's responses on this subtest. Are the tasks familiar to the child or do you need to teach them? If taught, does the child pick up the tasks quickly and easily, slowly and painfully, or not at all? Are the child's responses given in a fairly quick and automatic way or are they given in a slow and laborious fashion? Do the responses seem to suggest any particular problems with hearing? Since difficulties with attention, concentration, short-term memory, or working memory can impact the child's abilities on this subtest, pay close attention for signs of these issues. If there is any possibility of a hearing loss, refer the child for an evaluation by an audiologist. The audiometers and methods typically used in schools and physicians' offices are not adequate for the task.

Picture Similarities

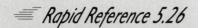

Rapid Reference 5.26

Picture Similarities Subtest

- Contributes to the estimate of Nonverbal Ability, Nonverbal Reasoning Ability, Special Nonverbal Composite, and GCA
- Requires the examinee to place a picture card below the picture that it best goes with
- Typically administered at ages 2:6 to 6:11
- Extended ages 7:0 to 8:11
- Input is visual
- Output is nonverbal (placing a picture card)
- Measures the broad ability of fluid intelligence (Gf) and the narrow ability of Induction (I)

Picture Similarities assesses nonverbal reasoning abilities, including the ability to solve nonverbal problems, identify pictures, formulate and test hypotheses about the relationship among different pictures in a set, use verbal mediation, and attach meaning to pictures. Although many similarities tests (including the Verbal Similarities subtest of the DAS-II) require a verbal response, this subtest was designed to be entirely nonverbal, requiring no oral response from the child. It is a test of the broad ability of fluid intelligence (Gf) and the narrow ability of Induction (I).

The subtest contains 32 items, most of which are representational rather than abstract, that require the child to place a picture card below the picture (one of four) with which it goes best. To do well, the child must recognize various, possibly relevant, features of the drawings and then engage in developing and testing hypotheses regarding a relevant feature that the target picture shares with one and only one of the four drawings.

Performance on the Picture Similarities subtest may be influenced by the child's ability to formulate and test hypotheses and to identify the rules governing the common features or variables in pictures. Some children use good verbal skills to label the pictures, thus aiding themselves in solving the problems.

Observation of testing behaviors may help in interpreting the results of Picture Similarities. Does the child demonstrate impulsive behaviors, such as responding too rapidly without carefully checking their response or not carefully examining the pictures to determine the subtle differences between them? Does the child have difficulty placing the pictures accurately on the target page, possibly indicating a fine-motor problem? Does language help or hinder the child's responses? Is there any indication that the child does not know what many of the pictures represent? Does the child appear to have problems understanding the directions, or does the child appear to use verbalization to help solve the items? Does the child require many items to be explained on the specific items that require teaching after failure?

Rapid Naming

Rapid Naming assesses automaticity of integration of visual symbols with phonologically referenced naming. It is a diagnostic subtest that contributes to the estimate of the Processing Speed Composite. It is a measure of Processing Speed (*Gs*) and measures the narrow ability of Perceptual Speed–Complex (Pc). The Rapid Naming subtest measures speed of lexical access and retrieval. That is the speed with which words can be identified and retrieved from the child's personal dictionary of words. These words are held in the child's long-term verbal memory. Despite the fact that the strongest relationship of Rapid Naming is

> ### ≡ Rapid Reference 5.27
>
> #### Rapid Naming Subtest
>
> - Contributes to the estimate of the Processing Speed Composite
> - Requires the examinee to name colors, pictures, and colored pictures as quickly as possible
> - Administered at ages 5:0 to 17:11
> - Includes Simple and Complex Naming
> - Input is visual
> - Output is verbal
> - Measure of Processing Speed (*Gs*) and measures the narrow ability of Perceptual Speed–Complex (Pc)

with Speed of Information Processing, and that these two subtests combine to form the Processing Speed cluster, it is clear from an examination of the content of this subtest that name retrieval is required and this specific retrieval process is linked to a visual analysis of the pictures. Thus, the CHC long-term retrieval ability (*Glr*) may also contribute to a child's success or failure on this subtest.

The subtest contains three items, each with 35 stimuli that requires the child to first name colors, then name pictures, and finally to name both the color and the picture as quickly as possible (120-second time limit).

Because of its greater complexity, all children are slower on Item 3 (Color-Picture Naming). However, some children who are able to name colors and pictures with ease will have relatively greater difficulty (as shown by norms) when two words per stimulus have to be retrieved from their lexicon. Children who obtain low scores on the Rapid Naming subtest, or who have significant differences between their abilities on the Simple Naming (Items 1 and 2) and the Complex Naming (Item 3) tasks, may be demonstrating that one of their processing difficulties is concerned with lexical access and retrieval. The relative slowness in speed of lexical access when faced with greater verbal complexity may have an impact on the child's development of reading skills.

Comparing a child's score on Rapid Naming with his or her score on Word Definitions may provide insight as to whether there is a discrepancy between the available store of words (as measured by Word Definitions) and speed of retrieval of words from the lexical store. If Rapid Naming is significantly lower, this may suggest the need for instruction to be at a measured pace, with a reduced emphasis on speed of presentation or response. If reports, observations, or additional testing reveal poor reading fluency, special attention may need to be given to helping the child develop reading fluency. Poor reading fluency can impair comprehension because it increases the memory load of the slowed and lengthened reading task. (Poor reading fluency may also be a subtle indication of weak and not fully automatic reading decoding skills. In that case, another consequence is likely to be that attention is diverted from comprehension to the struggle with decoding. See, for example, Brody, 2001, Wolf, 1997, and Wolf and Bowers, 1999.)

To do well on the Rapid Naming subtest, a child must be able to efficiently and fluently retrieve available words from the lexicon by integrating both visual and verbal processing. Since low scores on this subtest may reflect an inefficient balance between speed and accuracy, examine the performance of the child, observing whether he or she was either overly cautious, sacrificing speed for the sake of accuracy, or overly impulsive, sacrificing accuracy for the sake of speed. Was the approach taken on Rapid Naming similar to that taken on the Speed of Information Processing subtest? If a child makes any uncorrected errors on this subtest, the child may be demonstrating difficulties in dealing with interference from competing stimuli; perseveration of responses; or impulsivity and disinhibition of responses.

Recall of Designs

Recall of Designs assesses the ability to encode and retain visual-spatial information and use motor skills, short-term visual recall, spatial orientation, and drawing skills. It is a measure of Visual-Spatial Ability (*Gv*) and Visual Memory (MV).

The subtest contains 22 items that require the child to reproduce pictured designs that are exposed to view for five seconds and then removed. The nonpictorial line drawings are sufficiently complex and the exposure time is sufficiently brief to make verbal encoding of the designs difficult. Thus, the contribution of verbal mediation is minimized. Performance on the subtest requires not only visual-spatial perception, encoding, and retention, but also an adequate level of motor skills.

Rapid Reference 5.28

Recall of Designs Subtest

- Contributes to the estimate of the Spatial Ability Composite, the Special Nonverbal Composites and the GCA
- Requires the examinee to reproduce pictured designs that are exposed to view for five seconds and then removed
- Typically administered at ages 7:0 to 17:11
- Out of level at ages 5:0 to 6:11
- Input is visual
- Output is nonverbal (paper and pencil task)
- Measure of Visual-Spatial Ability (*Gv*) and Visual Memory (MV)

Performance on this subtest may be influenced by the child's short-term visual recall (the ability to retain and recall the stored designs), perception of spatial orientation, and drawing skills. Designs that are copied easily but incorrectly may reflect memory or visual-spatial difficulties while designs drawn slowly and with difficulty may reflect a graphomotor difficulty. Many erasures may indicate compulsivity (drawing has to be exactly right) or recognition that the erased attempts were genuinely inadequate.

As with the copying subtest, it is sometimes helpful to examine with the child designs that are particularly poorly drawn. Show the child the original design as well as his or her own drawing and ask, "Does your design look like this one" (pointing to the original design). If the child responds that the designs are similar, this may indicate a visual perceptual difficulty (the child does not see the design correctly). In contrast, if the child recognizes that the design does not match the target design, the poor copy may be the result of a graphomotor difficulty.

Both physical and behavioral aspects of the child's approach to this task may be important when interpreting the results. Carefully observe whether or not the child uses a comfortable pencil grip and whether the child changes the grip during the subtest. Does the manner of gripping the pencil seem to affect performance? Does the child appear to be comfortable with the use of the preferred hand (left or right or alternating handedness)? Does the child apply too much, or too little, pressure while drawing the items?

Note whether the behaviors of the child impact on the quality of the drawings. If the child is quick and impulsive when drawing the items, does the quality of the drawings suffer? Some impulsive children may attempt to begin to draw before the exposure time has elapsed while others look away from the picture before the exposure time has elapsed. When evaluating the drawings, examine whether the child misses major aspects of the items or adds unnecessary elaborations.

Recall of Digits Forward

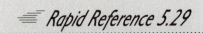

Rapid Reference 5.29

Recall of Digits Forward Subtest

- Contributes to no Composite
- Requires that the examinee to recall a sequence of digits that you read aloud
- Administered at ages 2:6 to 17:11
- Digit sequences are arranged in eight blocks, each block containing four to five sequences of digits
- Input is auditory
- Output is verbal
- Measure of Short-term Memory (*Gsm*) and Memory Span (MS)

The Recall of Digits Forward subtest measures short-term auditory sequential memory. It is a measure of Short-term Memory (*Gsm*) and Memory Span (MS).

The subtest contains 38 items that require the child to recall a sequence of digits that you read aloud. Sequences range from two to ten digits in length. The digit sequences are arranged in eight blocks, with each block containing four to five sequences of digits. The items are presented to the child at the rate of *two digits per second*. Faster than the usual presentation rate in other digit-recall subtests, this speed was chosen because it prevents the child's use of verbal rehearsal strategies during the presentation, thus making the subtest a purer measure of short-term auditory memory.

Record the child's responses verbatim for interpretive analysis. Examine errors to determine if they represent a problem in memory (forgetting numbers but otherwise correct repetition) versus poor sequencing (recalling all the original numbers but repeating them in the wrong order). Also be attuned to responses in which the numbers repeated have very little relationship to those intended. Does the child seem to make the same kind of error throughout the subtest? These types of responses may be indicative of inattention, impulsivity, anxiety, or distractibility. Impulsivity may also be evident when the child begins to repeat the numbers back before you have completed the series.

Be sensitive to environmental distractions (visual or auditory distractions) that may cause lower scores. Hearing difficulties may also impact on the final score. Does the child watch your face intently as you read the numbers?

It may be useful to compare the child's performance on the short-term memory task of Recall of Digits Forward to that of the working memory task of Recall of Digits Backward (Hale, Hoeppner, & Fiorello, 2002). If the child's *T* score on Recall of Digits Forward is *significantly greater than* that on Recall of Digits Backward (7 points for the Early Years battery and 6 points for the School-Age Battery), this difference may reflect a specific strength with auditory short-term memory, specifically memory span, in comparison with auditory working memory. Before coming to this conclusion, variables listed above, such as impulsiveness, lack of understanding of instructions, and distractibility, should be excluded as possible causes.

If the child's *T* score on Recall of Digits Forward is significantly *less than* that on Recall of Digits Backward (7 points for the Early Years battery and 6 points for the School-Age battery), this may reflect inattention or other interfering conditions that may have lowered the child's Recall of Digits Forward score. If both scores, Forward and Backward, appear valid and not impacted by behavioral (e.g., impulsivity, anxiety, etc.) concerns, this may suggest that the child has a relative strength in conceptualizing and transforming information in comparison with simple retention. Some children are bored by Recall of Digits Forward but challenged by Recall of Digits Backward. One aspect of executive function weaknesses can be difficulty assessing the difficulty of tasks and marshalling appropriate mental resources. That difficulty can lead to overestimating the difficulty of Recall of Digits Backward and underestimating the difficulty of Recall of Digits Forward, resulting in a much better performance on Recall of Digits Backward than on Recall of Digits Forward.

Recall of Digits Backward

The Recall of Digits Backward subtest measures short-term auditory sequential memory that contributes to the estimate of Working Memory. It is a measure of Short-term Memory (G*sm*) and Working Memory (MW).

≡ *Rapid Reference 5.30*

Recall of Digits Backward Subtest

- Contributes to the estimate of Working Memory
- Requires the examinee to recall a sequence of digits that you read aloud and repeat them backward
- Typically administered at ages 5:6 to 17:11
- Out-of-level norms for ages 5:0 to 5:6
- Input is auditory
- Output is verbal
- Measure of Short-term Memory (*Gsm*) and Working Memory (MW)

The subtest contains 30 items that require the child to immediately recall a sequence of digits that you read aloud to them and then have them repeat back to you in reverse order. Sequences range from two to seven digits in length. The digit sequences are arranged in six blocks, with each block containing five to seven sequences of digits presented at a pace of two digits per second. The rapid presentation of the items has several advantages to you as a tester. It allows more items to be given in the same amount of time (thus adding to the overall reliability of the score); it provides a parallel condition for comparing scores on Recall of Digits Forward (a test of memory span) with those on Recall of Digits Backward (a test of working memory); and it prevents a child from using verbal rehearsal strategies to recall the items (thus turning the test into one of verbal mediation rather than working memory).

Although the score a child obtains on this subtest may be affected by anxiety or by inattention, under normal circumstances the scores may be taken as an estimate of the child's ability to remember (memory span) and manipulate (working memory) sequential information (specifically, numbers). Performance on this subtest is limited by the child's immediate auditory recall ability (short-term auditory memory), oral recall of sequences of numbers (non-meaningful memory), and concentration and attention. As such, it is always useful to compare the score a child obtains on the Recall of Digits Backward subtest with that obtained on the Recall of Digits Forward subtest.

Scores on this subtest may be influenced by the child's ability to process information that is being held in verbal short-term memory, by the use of effective strategies for transforming the digit sequence, and by the ability to hold the original digit sequence in short-term auditory memory during processing.

Several factors may be reflected by a child's poor performance on this task. The child may be attempting to use inappropriate or ineffective strategies for storing and then retrieving the correct digit sequences. For example, the child may attempt to start rehearsing the sequence or recalling the items before you have finished presenting all the items. Impulsive children may respond rapidly by repeating back the digits but not in correct or reversed order. Other children may simply not understand the nature of the task and respond by simply recalling the numbers in the same order as you present them. Be observant of any behaviors that may indicate that distractibility, inattention, or anxiety has impacted the score.

Record the child's responses verbatim for interpretive analysis. Examine errors to determine if they represent a problem in memory (forgetting numbers but otherwise correct repetition) versus poor sequencing (recalling all the original numbers but repeating them in the wrong order). Also be attuned to responses in which the numbers repeated have very little relationship to those intended. Does the child seem to make the same kind of error throughout the subtest? These types of responses may be indicative of inattention, impulsivity, anxiety, or distractibility. Impulsivity may also be evident when the child begins to repeat the numbers back before you have completed the series.

Be sensitive to environmental distractions (visual or auditory distractions) that may cause lower scores. Hearing difficulties may also impact on the final score. Watch for evidence of speech reading ("lip reading").

Because of the specific memory demands and the similarity in the tasks, it is often useful to compare a child's performance on the Recall of Digits Forward to that of the Recall of Digits Backward subtests. If the child's *T* score on Recall of Digits Forward is *significantly greater than* that on Recall of Digits Backward (7 points for the Early Years battery and 6 points for the School-Age battery), this may reflect a specific problem with working memory in comparison with auditory short-term memory. Before coming to this conclusion, variables listed above, such as impulsiveness, lack of understanding of instructions, and distractibility, should be excluded as possible causes.

If the child's *T* score on Recall of Digits Forward is significantly *less than* that on Recall of Digits Backward (7 points for the Early Years battery and 6 points for the School-Age battery), this may reflect inattention or other interfering conditions that may have lowered the child's Recall of Digits Forward score. If both scores, Forward and Backward, appear valid and not impacted by behavioral (e.g., impulsivity, anxiety, etc.) concerns, this may suggest that the child has a relative strength in conceptualizing and transforming information in comparison with simple retention.

Recall of Objects—Immediate & Delayed

Rapid Reference 5.31

Recall of Objects Subtest

- Contributes to no Composite
- Requires the examinee to recall objects from memory
- Administered at ages 4:0 to 17:11
- Input is visual
- Output is verbal
- Measures the broad ability of Long-term Storage and Retrieval (*Glr*) and the narrow ability of Free Recall Memory (M6)

The Recall of Objects–Immediate and Recall of Objects–Delayed subtests are diagnostic subtests that require the examinee to recall objects from memory. The subtest assesses (a) short-term verbal memory, including verbal encoding, rehearsal, and retrieval strategies (e.g., use of a semantic clustering strategy— retrieving all the animals and then all the vehicles—versus use of a serial clustering strategy—retrieving the items in the exact order in which they are presented on the page); (b) short-term visual memory; or (c) a combination of the two. It measures the broad ability of Long-term Storage and Retrieval (*Glr*) and the narrow ability of Free Recall Memory (M6).

The examinee is shown a card with pictures of 20 common objects. Three trials are given, with exposure times of 45 seconds, 20 seconds, and 20 seconds, respectively. On the first trial, during the 45 seconds, you say the names of the objects aloud for the examinee. After the card is removed, the examinee is asked to recall as many objects as possible in any order (with time limits of 45 seconds on trial 1 and 40 seconds each on trials 2 and 3). After you complete the three trials, you administer two nonverbal subtests (which together take about 10 to 30 minutes) and then, with no warning and no review, administer the delayed-recall trial (time limit of 45 seconds). Usually, the delayed-recall trial will be about 10 to 15 minutes after the initial subtest. Examinees are not informed that they will be asked to recall the objects again.

Although the manual suggests recording the child's responses by simply placing a checkmark in the Response Column next to the item the child recalls, for interpretive purposes we would suggest one of two alternative recording procedures. Record the order in which the child recalls each item by using a number (i.e., 1, 2, and 3) rather then a simple checkmark, or simply record the responses verbatim as the child recalls them, ignoring the alphabetized list. You can use abbreviations, such as omitting vowels. Just be sure that no two words have the same abbreviation in your system.

Regardless of how you record the responses, it is important to observe how the examinee recalls the objects. Note whether the child recalls the items in the order in which they appear on the card or by categories (e.g., all animals, all toys). Examine the overall performance of the child looking to see if her or his performance improves or worsens on each trial. Are only some types of items remembered? Are items recalled primarily by their position on the card? Some children have difficulty remembering new items after having already "remembered" a group of items. Examine whether or not items from the first trial are also recalled in the second or third trials. Some children use a "replacement" strategy in which, in order to remember new items, they must "forget" the learned items. Each trial will contain new items that were not recalled in previous trials, but each trial will also not contain the previously learned item.

When interpreting this subtest, keep in mind that the scores a child obtains may be very different from those obtained on the Recall of Digits Forward subtest. Although both tests are tapping a child's memory abilities, Recall of Objects, with its strong visual component and the method of presentation of the objects, does not correlate highly with the auditory memory demands of Recall of Digits. Examining the difference between the scores on these two subtests may provide information regarding strengths or weaknesses in general memory or, more specifically, strengths or weaknesses in integrating verbal and visual components in short-term memory. When discussing Recall of Objects in your report, be careful not to describe it as a purely visual task. There are both visual and verbal demands. Performance on Recall of Objects may also be influenced by problems with attention and concentration.

Always compare the T score obtained for the Recall of Objects–Immediate trial to that of the delayed trial, but do not interpret the delayed score unless there is a difference of 11 or more points between the two scores. A difference of less than 11 points indicates that the child's performance on the Delayed recall trial did not differ from that expected from his or her performance on the Immediate recall trials. Do not discuss the normal, expected difference. It is not a real difference. If the child's normative scores on the Immediate and Delayed recalls are reliably different (11 or more points), both scores should be recorded, compared, and interpreted; otherwise only the Immediate recall score is reported and interpreted.

Performance on this subtest may be influenced by the child's ability to use effective strategies for storage and retrieval of the information (e.g., serial order versus semantic clustering), the ability to easily use both visual and verbal information, and the ability to maintain appropriate attention and concentration (e.g., attending to the stimulus picture for the entire exposure time).

In the standardization sampling for the DAS-II, approximately 82 percent of the school-age children obtained a Recall of Objects–Immediate score that was within 10 points of the Delayed score. When a significant difference between the Immediate and Delayed scores was found, it was only slightly more common (10 percent versus 7 percent) to find an Immediate score greater than the Delayed score (ROi > ROd) than it was to find the Immediate score below the Delayed score (ROi < ROd). If you find that the Recall of Objects–Delayed score is significantly lower than the Immediate recall score, this difference may suggest problems with the utilization of encoding strategy on the Immediate trials as well as a rapid loss of stored information possibly caused by the interference of intervening tasks. In contrast, a Delayed recall score significantly higher than the Immediate recall score may reflect the child's efficient consolidation of memory trace, or use of "deep" encoding and rehearsal strategies on Immediate trials.

Recall of Sequential Order

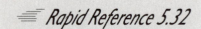
Rapid Reference 5.32

Recall of Sequential Order Subtest

- Contributes to the Working Memory Composite
- Requires the examinee to listen to a list of parts of the body and then reorder that list from highest to lowest
- Administered at ages 5:0 to 17:11
- Unlike the other verbally presented recall subtests, Recall of Sequential Order is presented at a rate of one word per second
- Input is auditory
- Output is verbal
- Measure of Short-term memory (Gsm) and measures the narrow ability of Working Memory (MW)

Recall of Sequential Order is a measure of Short-term memory (*Gsm*) and measures the narrow ability of Working Memory (MW). It is different from many other purely verbal tests of working memory in that it is designed to require some degree of visualization in conjunction with the manipulation of lists of words.

The subtest contains 32 items that require the examinee to listen to a list of parts of the body and then reorder that list from highest to lowest (head to toe). Early items use a drawing of a human figure, while later items are done from memory alone. The most difficult items also include non-body parts that must be grouped and recalled separately. Unlike the other verbally presented recall subtests, Recall of Sequential Order is presented at a rate of one word per second.

Scores on the Recall of Sequential Order subtest may be influenced by the child's ability to process information that is being held in verbal short-term memory, the ability to use effective strategies for encoding and recalling the word sequences, and the ability to integrate the visualization of body parts with verbal short-term memory.

Several influences may be reflected by a child's poor performance on this task. The child may be attempting to use inappropriate or ineffective strategies for storing and then retrieving the correct word sequences. For example, the child may attempt to start rehearsing the sequence or recall the items before you have finished presenting all the items. Impulsive children may respond rapidly with the body parts but not in correct sequence. Other children may simply not understand the nature of the task and respond by merely repeating the words in the same order as you presented them. Be observant of any behaviors that may indicate that distractibility, inattention, or anxiety have impacted the score.

Try to discern what specific strategies the child has used in his or her attempt to recall the items (e.g., closing eyes to visualize the picture or touching his or her own body to aid in recall, etc.). Examine the types of errors that the child makes to see if there is a specific pattern that will help in interpretation (e.g., remembers all items but mis-sequences them, forgets certain items, etc.). Also examine whether the child appears to do much better on the early items that utilize the picture and less well on items without it.

Recognition of Pictures

Recognition of Pictures measures short-term visual memory. It is a measure of Visual-Spatial Ability (*Gv*) and the narrow ability of Visual Memory (MV).

The Recognition of Pictures subtest contains 20 items that require the examinee to find, among a group of pictures, one or more pictures that were previously shown to him or her. All of the pictured objects in each item represent a single category (e.g., toys or vehicles). A picture of one to four target objects is shown for five seconds. Then another picture is shown that contains the target object

≡ Rapid Reference 5.33

Recognition of Pictures Subtest

- Contributes to no Composite
- Requires the examinee to find, among a group of pictures, one or more pictures that were previously shown to him or her
- Administered at ages 2:6 to 17:11
- Input is visual
- Output is nonverbal (pointing)
- Measure of Visual-Spatial Ability (*Gv*) and the narrow ability of Visual Memory (MV)

plus distracter objects. The task is to point to the target objects. Success depends on recall of visual images. Performance on some of these items in the subtest may be aided by verbal mediation and rehearsal strategies.

Scores on the Recognition of Pictures subtest may be influenced by the child's short-term visual memory abilities, specifically recognition memory, visual imagery, and memory for picture details and orientation. Children who do poorly on this test often have difficulty because they tend to be distracted by competing visual information; the use of inappropriate memory strategies (e.g., attempting to name all of the pictures aloud); or problems with anxiety, attention, or concentration.

Careful observation of the child during the test and an analysis of the responses given may aid in interpreting the results. Were there any signs of problems with anxiety, attention, or concentration? Did the child attend to the stimulus picture for the entire exposure time and, if not, did it appear that the child had a short attention span or did he or she appear to believe that all pictures have been memorized? If the child does not attend to the stimulus picture for the entire exposure time and then acknowledges failing the item, does he or she learn from the mistakes and begin attending to the subsequent pictures for the entire exposure time?

Review the answers given to determine if there are there any signs of perseveration [e.g., child points to the same position(s) on the page for each item]. This may be an indication of the child's motivation on the task or a recognition on the part of the child of a memory problem leading to giving up and not investing the energy to attempt the discouraging tasks.

Sequential and Quantitative Reasoning

Sequential and Quantitative Reasoning assesses the child's ability to perceive relationships, draw conclusions (inductive reasoning), formulate and test hypotheses, use analytic reasoning, and retrieve long-term information. Overall, the subtest measures nonverbal reasoning ability. It is a measure of Fluid Reasoning (*Gf*) and the narrow ability of Induction (I) and, in Set B, Quantitative Reasoning (RQ).

The subtest contains 50 items presented visually and with minimal verbal instruction. The early items measure visual perceptual-motor skills, and the later items require arithmetic computation skills. Items 1 through 23 are presented in a stimulus book as a linear array of between three and seven colored pictures with a blank space placed somewhere in the array (beginning, end, somewhere in middle). For Items 24–50, the examinee responds orally, typically with a single oral response, to problems presented in the stimulus book. The stimuli are two pairs of numbers related by the same arithmetic rule (e.g., the second number is 3 greater than the first number, or the second number is twice as great as the first number less 1). The examinee must derive the rule from the two pairs and apply the rule to another number to create a third pair that follows the same rule. Answers are typically given orally (telling the correct number), however, written answers also are acceptable (but examinees may not use paper to work out answers).

Poor performance on the early items of Set A may reflect low nonverbal reasoning ability and or weak sequential information processing, while poor performance on the later items may also be due to poor basic

> ### ≋ *Rapid Reference 5.34*
>
> ### Sequential and Quantitative Reasoning Subtest
>
> - Contributes to the estimates of Nonverbal Reasoning Ability, the Special Nonverbal Composite, and the GCA
> - Requires the examinee to solve problems dealing with sequential and quantitative material
> - Typically administered to ages 7:0 to 17:11
> - Extended ages 5:0 to 6:11
> - Input is visual
> - Output is nonverbal (pointing) or minimally verbal (a number)
> - Measures the broad ability of Fluid Reasoning (*Gf*) and the narrow ability of Induction (*I*) and Set B Quantitative Reasoning (RQ)

arithmetic skills and or inflexibility in selecting solution strategies. Poor performance may also be indicative of a general lack of knowledge of numerals, basic number facts, and basic arithmetic operations (for Set B), or inflexibility in choosing solution strategies.

To aid in interpretation, we have found it useful to actually write on the Record Form the numerical operations (e.g., $+, -, \times, \div$) that a child must use in order to arrive at the correct answer. If for example the problem was:

6   8
9   11
15   __

the solution would be 17, arrived at by adding 2 to each number. On the Record Form we would have written +2. When analyzing the test result, examine whether any incorrect answers have a logical explanation. If, for our example, the child responded with the number 13, we could surmise that the child discovered the underlying concept of utilizing the number 2, but confused the operation, in this case subtracting the number instead of adding it or solved the item as if the blank were on the left and the 15 were on the right. It is essential to distinguish between a weakness in logical reasoning and a failure of concentration, attention to detail, or left-right orientation. All of these aspects of solving problems are important and all can affect schoolwork, but weaknesses in them have very different instructional implications.

Although the arithmetic required is designed to be fairly easy for children of the appropriate ages, a child with a severe weakness or learning disability in math may be at a disadvantage on Set B. Be sure to check the child's acquired math skills by formal or informal testing, by review of background information, or by asking a parent or teacher. Because *Gf* is an important predictor of math achievement, a low score on Sequential and Quantitative Reasoning might actually reflect a reciprocal relationship between *Gf* and math achievement.

Several aspects of the subtest may provide information when interpreting the child's results. For example, you should compare the child's abilities on the later items involving numbers versus the abilities on the early items using pictures, as well as noting whether the child appears to have had difficulty on later items that do not involve multiple choices. Examine the child's incorrect responses to determine if they show a pattern of difficulties (e.g., failing all items that involve multiplication). By carefully examining the incorrect responses, you may be able to discern if the child attempted to perform the correct arithmetic operation but arrived at the wrong answer, or whether incorrect responses occur more often on the items that require multi-step math solutions as opposed to those involving single-step math solutions.

Speed of Information Processing

The Speed of Information Processing subtest measures mental speed. Although the subtest requires the child to make simple quantitative comparisons, it measures a general speed of processing information regardless of domain or task content. It is a measure of Processing Speed (*Gs*) and measures Perceptual Speed-Scanning (Ps). The Speed of Information Processing subtest correlates more highly with Rapid Naming than with any other subtest.

Three booklets are used, each requiring the examinee to mark the circle with the most boxes in each row or to mark the highest number in each row. The basic task of Speed of Information Processing is relatively easy, and almost all children can solve the items correctly. The variation in performance lies in the time the child takes to complete the task. Booklet B uses single-digit numbers while Booklet C uses two- or three-digit numbers. Each booklet contains eight pages—two practice pages and six test pages. Each page contains five to eight rows of figures (e.g., circles containing one to four small squares) or numbers.

Remember that the subtest is designed to measure a child's speed of *accurate* information processing, and because of this any item responses that have more than two errors are scored 0. Very few children older than 6 years make more than a very small number of errors. If a child you test does make numerous errors, the subtest is probably not measuring the ability it was designed to measure, and the subtest and cluster scores should be interpreted with appropriate caution. If you do believe that the child did not understand the task or that the score is not an indication of the child's ability to accurately process the information, it is probably

Rapid Reference 5.35

Speed of Information Processing Subtest

- Contributes to the Processing Speed Composite
- Requires the examinee to mark the circle with the most boxes in each row or to mark the highest number in each row
- Administered at ages 5:0 to 17:11
- Input is visual
- Output is nonverbal (motoric)
- Measure of Processing Speed (*Gs*) and measures Perceptual Speed-Scanning (Ps)

prudent to disregard interpretation of the subtest and cluster scores entirely. Conversely, do *not* even mention that the child made few or no errors. Making very few errors is the norm; making more than a very few errors is the exception. Mentioning the small number of errors will mislead the reader.

Scores on the Speed of Information Processing subtest may reflect the child's willingness and ability to work fast under time pressure and the speed in performing simple mental operations. If it seems likely that the child was unable or unwilling to work at top speed, do not interpret low scores as necessarily indicating a weakness in the capacity as opposed to the output. Some cultures do not reinforce speed or hastiness. Some children who are deaf or hard of hearing do not seem to work at top speed on such tasks. Motivation for tasks involving numbers (particularly for Items 7–18) or problems with attention and concentration may also influence the scores.

Poor performance on this subtest may not always be due to poor speed of information processing but may in fact be due to differences in cognitive style. For example, some children may approach the task as if they are trying to "beat the clock," and while doing this they make a large number of careless errors. Some children make exaggerated hand movements and pant loudly to convey to themselves or to the examiner the impression of making a great effort to work at high speed. In contrast might be the child who, at the expense of speed, places an obsessive overemphasis on accuracy. A few children work quickly until the last row on the page and then nearly double their time finishing that last row. Observe the child's performance to determine if the score is the result of one of these, or some other, response style. Was the child's performance influenced by motivation to perform quickly or possibly a misunderstanding of the need to do so?

As with all subtests, it is important to be an astute observer of the child's behaviors and performance on this subtest. Does the child appear to understand the directions and proceed correctly after you give an explanation to teaching items? Do you need to encourage the child to work quickly or does he or she do so naturally? Are there any indications of impulsiveness, frustration, anxiety, physical problems (e.g., pencil grip, tremors) that interfere with the child's ability to perform the tasks? When an error is pointed out to the child, how does he or she react?

Verbal Comprehension

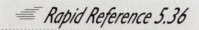

Rapid Reference 5.36

Verbal Comprehension Subtest

- Contributes to the estimate of Verbal Ability and the GCA
- Requires examinee to show understanding of oral instructions by pointing or by performing action you request
- Typically administered at ages 2:6 to 6:11
- Extended ages 7:0 to 8:11
- Input is auditory and visual
- Output is nonverbal (demonstrating)
- Measures the broad ability of Crystallized Intelligence (Gc) and the narrow ability of Listening Ability (LS)

The Verbal Comprehension subtest measures the child's understanding of language (including understanding of syntax and prepositional and relational concepts), the ability to follow verbal directions, and short-term auditory memory. It is a measure of receptive, rather than an expressive, language that assesses understanding of oral instructions involving basic language concepts. Verbal Comprehension measures the broad ability of Crystallized Intelligence (Gc) and the narrow ability of Listening Ability (LS).

The subtest contains 42 items, none of which requires the child to respond orally. For Items 1 through 5 the child is shown a picture of a teddy bear and asked to point to several features (e.g., eyes) named by the examiner. For Items 6 through 12, which samples the child's understanding of object names and commands, the child is shown a set of toys and asked to do certain manipulations with the objects identified by name (e.g., "Give me the box") or function (e.g., "Give me the one that goes on your wrist"). For Items 13 through 23, the child uses wooden objects to follow instructions that demonstrate the child's understanding of prepositions (e.g., "Put the child *under* the bridge"). For Items 24 through 36, the child views a set of four pictures, each of which depicts a distinct situation or outcome; the child is asked to indicate the picture that goes best with the story (e.g., Kate and her mother played cards with John). To perform this task, the child must perceive various, possibly relevant, features of the drawings. Then, the child must engage in hypothesis testing to select the single drawing that accurately reflects an event or outcome consistent with the story. For the final items, 37 through 42, the child uses colored chips of different shapes to demonstrate understanding of more complex instructions (e.g., "Give me all of the black chips except the triangle").

Performance on the Verbal Comprehension subtest can be influenced by the child's understanding of the spoken language, by the ability or inability to formulate and test hypotheses, and to follow instructions. Does the child easily pass the vocabulary items (1–8) and then suddenly begin failing the items calling for more complex understanding or responses? Is the child's performance influenced by the length or complexity of the instructions?

The ability to utilize short-term memory for meaningful sentences is also important for success on this test. Does the child need the reminder to "listen carefully" before each item? Does the child ask for repetitions? Does the child follow the easy one-step directions but have more than expected difficulty on the multi-step ones?

Observe whether the child is distracted by the toys and manipulatives. Does the child miss the instructions because of being distracted by the toys? Is the child impulsive, responding quickly to instructions without hearing the entire question? For the multiple-choice items, does the child frequently pick the same answer?

Be careful to note whether there are any indications of limited hearing, poor auditory perception, or difficulty understanding even very simple language? Does the child watch your face intently while you speak? Does he or she ask that questions to be repeated or appear confused by the complexity of the questions?

Verbal Similarities

The Verbal Similarities subtest measures the ability of the child to identify the common concept linking three words. The subtest assesses acquired verbal knowledge, language comprehension, language fluency, verbal inductive reasoning, vocabulary and verbal development, logical and abstract thinking, and abil-

Rapid Reference 5.37

Verbal Similarities Subtest

- Contributes to estimates of Verbal Ability and the GCA
- Requires the examinee to tell how three words go together, what they all are, or how they are similar
- Typically administered at ages 7:0 to 17:11
- Extended ages 5:0 to 6:11
- Input is auditory
- Output is verbal
- Measure of Crystallized Intelligence (Gc) and measures the narrow ability of Language Development (LD)

ity to distinguish between essential and superficial features. It is a measure of Crystallized Intelligence (*Gc*) and measures the narrow ability of Language Development (LD)

The subtest contains 33 three-word items presented orally to the child. The task is for the child to express the underlying common concept that could define what the three words all are, how they go together, or how they are alike. Children who perform well often have well-developed verbal inductive reasoning skills, along with good logical and abstract thinking abilities. Occasionally a child will not know the meaning of one of the three words, but using well-developed thinking skills, will create an answer based upon the two remaining words. [Do *not* suggest this strategy to the child!] Poor performance may reflect poor lexical knowledge (they don't know what the words mean), possibly poor word-retrieval abilities, an inability to distinguish essential from superficial features, or an inability to formulate and test hypotheses about the words.

Observe how the child approaches the solution to the items. Does the child have any problems keeping the three items in memory or does the child drift into making other associations between the words? Is the child thinking through the questions; responding quickly and correctly, slowly and correctly, quickly and incorrectly, or slowly and incorrectly; or simply guessing?

Distinguish between the child who frequently says, "I know this answer, but I can't think of it" and one who answers with "I don't know." Observe the quality of the child's responses. Some children give responses that are very specific while others give vague responses. Note the differences between the child who seems to have a need to supply long, wordy answers and the one who responds with one or two words.

Word Definitions

Word Definitions assesses acquired verbal knowledge, language comprehension, expressive language ability, and fluency. It is a measure of Crystallized Intelligence (*Gc*) and the narrow abilities of Language Development (LD) and Lexical Knowledge (VL).

The Word Definitions subtest contains 35 words and requires the examinee to define the words that you present orally. All items (except Items 1 and 3, which allow demonstration) require the child to orally give the meaning of the word rather than merely to use it correctly in context. This task contrasts with the task of the Naming Vocabulary subtest, which is far less open-ended and which assesses a child's acquired knowledge of object names.

A child's performance on this test may be influenced by his or her experience as well as education. Low scores may be generally attributable to poor verbal development. Because of the influence of experience on language acquisition, low scores may be associated with disadvantaged environmental circumstances. Children who are very inhibited, who lack fluency, or who lack confidence may also score poorly on this subtest.

It may be useful to distinguish between the children whose responses are expansive, using much expression, versus those whose responses are terse, one-word replies. Children with good word knowledge but poor verbal fluency may reply correctly using very few words, while other children may find it difficult to retrieve the one word that could be used as a definition. Some children need to "talk themselves into a definition."

Be attuned to children who provide definitions for words that are close approximations of the target word. If a child does give a "strange" definition for a word, it is often useful to ask, "What word did you hear me say?" (see Figure 5.20 for an example).

As noted previously, you can use Naming Vocabulary to follow up on low scores on Word Definitions. If necessary, you can delve deeper with instruments such as the Peabody Picture Vocabulary Test–4 (Dunn & Dunn, 2006) and Expressive Vocabulary Test–2 (Williams, 2006).

🖋 TEST YOURSELF 🖋

1. **When beginning to interpret a child's DAS-II results, which of the following scores is typically not important in the process and need not be reported?**
   (a) Raw score
   (b) *T* score
   (c) Standard Score
   (d) Percentile Rank

2. **If the Verbal, Nonverbal Reasoning, and/or Spatial scores differ significantly from each other, the examiner should usually**
   (a) completely ignore the GCA score and not record it anywhere.
   (b) report and discuss only the GCA and the highest cluster.
   (c) report and discuss only the GCA and the two lowest clusters.
   (d) emphasize the cluster scores over the GCA.
   (e) emphasize the GCA over the cluster scores.

3. **Significant differences between subtest or cluster scores usually**
   (a) should be emphasized if they are also uncommon (low base rate).
   (b) should be ignored unless they are also uncommon (low base rate).
   (c) totally invalidate the cluster, GCA, or SNC of which they are components.
   (d) are never statistically reliable.
   (e) are valid only for the School-Age level of the DAS-II.

4. **Which of the following statements is NOT true:**
   (a) A statistically significant and uncommon difference between ability scores is a sign of the existence of a specific learning disability.
   (b) Many children without learning disabilities show huge differences among ability scores.
   (c) Many students with dramatic learning disabilities do not show significant differences among ability scores.

5. **The Cattell-Horn-Carroll theory of cognitive abilities provides a framework by which one can interpret the DAS-II.** True or False?

6. **Since interpretation should focus on the most general areas before moving to the less general areas, rearrange these areas so they go from most to least general and reliable:**
   (a) Cluster scores
   (b) Individual subtests
   (c) General Conceptual Ability
   (d) Shared Ability factors

7. An evaluation report based on the DAS II should:

(a) take the reader step-by-step through the examiner's entire interpretive process in sequence.

(b) report in the narrative both the probability and base rate of each score and each difference between scores.

(c) focus on the interpretation of the findings and other information.

(d) focus on the DAS-II results without introducing other information that might be distracting.

(e) All of the above.

Answers: 1. a; 2. d; 3. a; 4. a; 5. True; 6. c, a, d, b; 7. c

Six

STRENGTHS AND WEAKNESSES OF THE DAS-II*

O bviously, the authors of this book believe that, on balance, the DAS-II is a very good instrument. One of the book authors is also the creator of the test (and did not contribute to this chapter) and the other two authors thought enough of it and of the original DAS to use them in our own practices, to teach them to our captive audiences of graduate students, and to write this book. All of us had had extensive experience with many other cognitive assessment instruments long before the original DAS was published.

ASSETS OF THE DAS-II

The DAS-II provides an efficient, thorough, reasonable, and statistically reliable and valid assessment of cognitive abilities. It is designed with features that enhance useful interpretation. With variations in structure and content, the DAS-II covers the age range from 2:6 through 17:11. (See Rapid Reference 6.1.)

Composition of the General Conceptual Ability Score

Tests of cognitive abilities vary considerably in the cognitive abilities they assess and in which abilities are included in total scores or are relegated to supplementary status.

We believe that the composition of the General Conceptual Ability (GCA) score is an important asset of the DAS-II. At the School-Age and Upper Early Years levels, the DAS-II GCA is based on two subtests each of verbal comprehension/knowledge or crystallized ability (Gc), fluid reasoning ability (Gf), and visual-spatial thinking ability (Gv). At the Lower Early Years Level, the GCA includes four subtests: two verbal (Gc) and two nonverbal (Gf and Gv).

Obviously, there are many opinions on this issue, but we believe that fluid reasoning, verbal comprehension/knowledge, and visual-spatial thinking are key

* This chapter was written by John Willis and Ron Dumont.

≡ *Rapid Reference 6.1*

ASSETS OF THE DAS-II

- Composition of the General Conceptual Ability Score
- Special Nonverbal Composite
- Special administration guides
- Record forms
- Efficiency
- Cattell-Horn-Carroll (CHC) structure
- Respect for examiner's judgment:
  GCA vs. SNC
  Pattern Construction Alternative Procedure
  Extended Age Ranges
- Assessment of differential abilities
- Fairly easy administration
- Item Sets
- Generally easy scoring
- Developmental appropriateness
- Diagnostic subtests and clusters
- Normative sample
- Reliability
- Specificity
- Evidence of validity
- Evidence of validity with special groups
- Fairness
- Introductory & Technical Handbook

components of thinking and conceptualizing ability. We believe that other cognitive abilities, such as memory or auditory processing, are essential for higher-level cognitive functioning and must be measured, as is done with the DAS-II *Diagnostic Subtests,* but that these important additional abilities should not be included in the total score of a test of cognitive ability, such as the DAS-II.

To the extent that evaluators, diagnosticians, teams, admissions committees, parents, and government agencies depend on total scores (e.g., FSIQ, GCA, GIA, MPI, FCI, CIX, etc.), the composition of those total scores is very important. We absolutely do *not* support basing any important decision about a human being on one score from one test. We recognize that any two different tests of cognitive abilities may give very different scores to the same individual

DON'T FORGET

Composition of the DAS-II GCA

The GCA "*is not a global composite score such as is found in other batteries.* It is not derived from a heterogeneous mix of all subtests, but is derived only from either six or four subtests that are the best measures of conceptual and reasoning abilities" (Elliott, 2007b, p. xiii, emphasis in original). The GCA includes only subtests that primarily assess fluid reasoning (*Gf*), verbal comprehension (*Gc*), and visual-spatial thinking (*Gv*). Other CHC abilities are measured by the diagnostic subtests.

on the same day. However, we also understand that total scores on tests do weigh heavily on many important decisions.

If an examiner wishes to interpret and use the total score from a test of cognitive abilities, or knows that the total score will be used by others, the examiner needs to accept the composition of that total score as reasonable. For example, some examiners, parents, teachers, and administrators were concerned when some children who had been tested with the Wechsler Intelligence Scale for Children, 3rd ed. (WISC-III) (Wechsler, 1991) obtained much lower scores on re-evaluations with the WISC-IV (Wechsler, 2003). In addition to the expected Flynn Effect (Flynn, 1994, 1997, 1998), the WISC had been reorganized so that oral question-and-answer and picture and puzzle subtests were reduced from 80 percent to only 60 percent of the Full Scale IQ, and subtests of auditory short-term and working memory and clerical processing speed were doubled from 20 percent to 40 percent of that total score. Children with relatively strong verbal comprehension/knowledge, spatial, and fluid reasoning abilities and relatively weak abilities in short-term and working memory and clerical processing speed tended to score notably lower on the new version of the Wechsler Intelligence Scale for Children (Farrall, 2004). Children with the opposite pattern scored higher. People who believed that abilities such as short-term memory and processing speed should be only small parts of a total cognitive ability score preferred the composition of the old WISC-III to that of the new WISC-IV. The WISC-IV General Ability Index (Saklofske, Prifitera, Weiss, Rolfhus, & Zhu, 2005) helps address this concern.

People who believe that short-term and working memory, processing speed, and phonological abilities are important to measure but should not be included in a total cognitive ability score might prefer the composition of the DAS-II than either the WISC-III or the WISC-IV (see, for an earlier example, Dumont, Cruse, Price, & Whelley, 1996).

One of the great virtues of the Woodcock-Johnson III (WJ III) (Woodcock, McGrew, & Mather, 2001) and the two earlier editions is the wide variety of cognitive abilities included in the cognitive battery. However, some practitioners (e.g., Willis & Dumont, 1994) prefer to assess memory, processing speed, and other basic abilities separately from reasoning or conceptual ability, although the issue should be interpretation of performance, not a single number (e.g., McGrew, 1994b). For an example with the original DAS, see Dumont, Willis, Farr, McCarthy, & Price (2000).

Unfortunately, state education departments, school special education teams, private school admissions officers, teachers, parents, courts considering the death penalty, and others often do focus inappropriately on a single number, such as the WISC-IV

CAUTION

Different Tests Measure Different Cognitive Abilities

Although the major tests of cognitive abilities have high correlations with each other for groups of examinees, each instrument measures different mixes of cognitive abilities in different proportions with subtests that demand different skills (e.g., visual-spatial (Gv) tests with or without fine-motor performance or verbal comprehension (Gc) tests with and without demands for complex expressive language). Therefore, different tests are more likely than not to give different scores to any individual.

FSIQ, the WJ III GIA, or the DAS-II GCA. Although such unwise decisions are obviously not the fault of the various tests and should be opposed by evaluators (McGrew, 1994b), they do raise concerns about the apparent "double jeopardy" of assessing, for example, both fluid reasoning ability (Gf) and the working memory (Gsm MW) and processing speed (Gs) abilities that contribute to fluid reasoning. If the examinee had a weakness in one of the essential components of fluid reasoning, then the examinee's total score might be depressed by the low score on the component and then again by the low score on the fluid reasoning.

To the extent that the examiner (or the audience to whom the examiner will present the findings) is concerned about the total score on the test (FSIQ, GCI, MPI, GIA, GCA, CIX, etc.), the composition of that total score becomes important. In those cases, the examiner should, we believe, select a test that, in addition to satisfying other important criteria for reliability, validity, norms, fairness, relevance, and efficiency, bases its total score on the components preferred by the examiner and suited to the needs of the particular examinee.

Although any examinee may present individual needs that may dictate a different choice of ideal core subtests to include in a total score, we find that the DAS-II selection of fluid reasoning, verbal comprehension/knowledge, and visual-spatial thinking is, for most examinees, the best choice of components for the total, General Conceptual Ability. For most purposes, we find that plac-

	Abilities Measured by Total Score						
	Gf	Gv	Gc	Ga	Glr	Gsm	Gs
DAS-II GCA [1]	✓	✓	✓				
DAS-II SNC [1]	✓	✓					
KABC-II MPI [2]	✓	✓			✓	✓	
KABC-II FCI [2]	✓	✓	✓		✓	✓	
RIAS CIX [3]		✓	✓				
RIAS CIX + CMX [3]		✓	✓			✓	
SB5 FSIQ [4]	✓	✓	✓	✓			✓
WISC-IV FSIQ [5]		✓	✓			✓	✓
WJ III GIA [6]	✓	✓	✓	✓	✓	✓	✓

[1]DAS-II GCA or SNC = Differential Ability Scales – Second Edition General Conceptual Ability or Special Nonverbal Composite (Elliott, 2007a), [2]KABC-II MPI or FCI = Kaufman Assessment Battery for Children – Second Edition Mental Processing Index or Fluid Crystallized Index (Kaufman & Kaufman, 2004), [3]RIAS CIX or CIX+CMX = Reynolds Intellectual Assessment Scales Composite Intelligence Index or Composite Intelligence Index + Composite memory Index (Reynolds & Kamphaus,2003), [4]SB5 FSIQ = Stanford Binet Fifth Edition Full Scale IQ (Roid, 2003), [5]WISC-IV FSIQ = Wechsler Intelligence Scale for Children-Fourth Edition Full Scale IQ (Wechsler, 2003), [6]WJ III GIA = Woodcock Johnson Third Edition Tests of Cognitive Ability General Intellectual Ability (Woodcock, McGrew, & Mather, 2001).

Figure 6.1 Summary of Primary CHC Broad Abilities Measured by Total Scores on Several Representative Tests

ing other ability measures in the Diagnostic subtest category to be a good choice. Figure 6.1 shows the major broad ability components of the total scores of several representative tests. For more information, please see Flanagan (2001).

Special Nonverbal Composite

The DAS-II provides normative data and complete support in the *Normative Data Tables Manual* for the Special Nonverbal Composite (SNC) at the Upper Early Years and School-Age levels. At the School-Age level, only one of the subtests in the Nonverbal Reasoning cluster and in the Special Nonverbal Composite requires much explanation to the examinee for administration: the numerical items in Set B of Sequential and Quantitative Reasoning, which are at the normal start-point for 11-year-olds. The other Special Nonverbal Composite subtests are very easy to administer by demonstration. Practice and Teaching items further facilitate the process of administration. None of the Special Nonverbal Composite subtests requires an oral response—the numerical responses for Sequential and Quantitative Reasoning Set B can be written by the examinee.

The examiner is permitted to use the Special Nonverbal Composite and its Mean Core T score instead of the General Conceptual Ability score and its Mean Core T for almost all purposes. The choice of SNC or GCA is left up to the examiner's professional judgment and the examiner's knowledge of the examinee.

Special Administration Guides in American Sign Language and Spanish

The DAS-II includes instructions for administration and a demonstration Signed Standard Sentences CD in American Sign Language (ASL) developed with the help of Dr. Steven Hardy-Braz and Poorna Kushalnagar. Administration instructions in Spanish were developed with the aid of Dr. Jonathan Sandoval, Malú Antúnez-Bellatin and Mercedes Ibañez-Clark. These valuable materials allow examiners who are fluent in ASL and Spanish to administer appropriate subtests of the DAS-II correctly and in a standardized manner,

DON'T FORGET

Special Nonverbal Composite

At the Upper Early Years Level and School-Age Level, the Special Nonverbal Composite (SNC) is an alternative to the General Conceptual Ability (GCA) score, and is based only on *Gf* and *Gv* subtests requiring no spoken responses. At the Lower Level Early Years Level, the Nonverbal Cluster serves the same purpose. The examiner is encouraged to substitute these composite non-oral scores for the GCA whenever, in the examiner's judgment, the SNC or Nonverbal Cluster provides a more accurate representation of the child's conceptual abilities.

CAUTION

Administration in American Sign Language and Spanish

The instructions for administration in Spanish by Dr. Jonathan Sandoval, Malú Antúnez-Bellatin and Mercedes Ibañez-Clark and the instructions and Signed Standard Sentences CD by Dr. Steven Hardy-Braz and Poorna Kushalnagar standardize and greatly facilitate administration of appropriate DAS-II subtests in Spanish or American Sign Language. The materials do not permit an examiner with limited fluency in American Sign Language or Spanish to attempt administration of the test in those languages!

greatly reducing inter-examiner variability. These supporting materials enhance the use of the Nonverbal Cluster and Special Nonverbal Composite. The materials *do not* permit an examiner with some knowledge of, for example, classroom Signed English or vague memories of high school Spanish to attempt administration of the test!

Record Forms

For the most part, the DAS-II Record Forms, which were improved over those of the DAS, are easy to use. There is space to record all but the most verbose responses. Only one consumable booklet (rather than the two on the original DAS) is needed for each examinee except under extremely rare circumstances. Each subtest begins with tables clearly listing the needed materials, start points, any alternative stop points, any time limits administration details, special scoring rules, decision points, discontinue rules, and, where appropriate, rules for establishing basals and ceilings. Starting points and decision points are clearly marked. The tables of Raw Score to Ability Score conversions are easy to use and as close as possible to the test items. The Standard Error of Measurement (SEm) is printed in parentheses next to each ability score. The back pages of the Record Forms provide additional useful information. The procedures for comparing separate tasks on Rapid Naming and Phonological Processing look complicated, but are not difficult to use if you follow the directions carefully step by step. The Ability-Achievement Analysis, Core Analysis, and Diagnostic Analysis pages are clear and feature large print and big boxes. The Normative Score Profiles page clearly displays the differences between scores needed for significance at the .05 level, which is a very valuable feature unique, as far as we know, to the DAS and DAS-II.

Efficiency

Although the DAS-II is not designed or designated as a "brief test," it is not unduly long. The core battery includes only six subtests (four for the Lower Early Years), none of which requires a great deal of time for most examinees. The use of item sets rather than traditional basal and ceiling rules for most subtests (all core subtests) helps limit the time required. Administration of the core subtests of the DAS-II takes just under 40 minutes, on average (Elliott, 2007b, p.18). Therefore, it does not take much longer than administration of some of the more popular brief tests, but it provides scores for verbal ability, fluid reasoning, and visual-spatial thinking ability at the School-Age and Upper Early Years level and verbal ability and nonverbal ability at the Lower Early Years level, as well as the GCA and SNC. The GCA is not a shortened version of a longer test nor is it a "brief" test with a diminished sampling of cognitive abilities. It is an efficient measure of the core cognitive abilities needed to assess general conceptual ability.

Cattell-Horn-Carroll (CHC) Structure

Cattell-Horn-Carroll (CHC) theory has become a common language—a periodic table of cognitive ability elements—for evaluators (e.g., Carroll, 1997/2005; Horn & Blankson, 2005). CHC theory allows evaluators to compare and contrast different measures of cognitive ability and achievement for research and for

DON'T FORGET
....

The DAS-II is Efficient

If the examiner desires only a reliable and valid measure of general conceptual ability, the DAS-II GCA requires only six subtests at the Early Years Upper Level and School-Age Level and only four at the Early Years Lower Level. The starting and stopping rules for item sets reduce testing time by eliminating items not necessary for assessment of abilities. Although not much longer than many "brief" or "short-form" tests, the GCA is neither; it is a complete and unaltered assessment of general conceptual abilities.

the McGrew, Flanagan, and Ortiz Integrated Cross-Battery Assessment (e.g., Flanagan & McGrew, 1997; Flanagan, Ortiz, & Alfonso, 2007; Flanagan, Ortiz, Alfonso, & Mascolo, 2006).

Like most recently published tests of cognitive abilities, the DAS-II is explicitly organized by CHC broad and narrow abilities. However, unlike some tests, the DAS-II is intended to focus subtests on specific narrow as well as broad abilities as precisely as possible. There are practical limits to this effort because, inevitably, more than one narrow ability is involved in almost any non-trivial mental task. For example, defining words, an important component of most intelligence tests back to the Binet-Simon scale (Binet & Simon, 1916/1980), requires both lexical knowledge (VL) to know the words and language development (LD) to define them. We believe, though, that the DAS-II does well in focusing subtests as sharply as possible.

As noted above, the Core subtests have high g loadings and high loadings on their specific broad abilities: Gf, Gc, and Gv. The subtests with lower g loadings and the subtests measuring broad abilities other than Gf, Gc, and Gv are included in the DAS-II, and are designated as Diagnostic subtests. We believe that this arrangement makes the DAS-II an excellent choice as the anchor for a McGrew, Flanagan, and Ortiz Integrated Cross-Battery Assessment (e.g., Flanagan & McGrew, 1997; Flanagan, Ortiz, & Alfonso, 2007; Flanagan, Ortiz, Alfonso, & Mascolo, 2006).

Respect for Examiner's Judgment in Administrative Choices

The DAS-II leaves several important decisions up the professional judgment of the evaluator. "Rather than impose rigid guidelines, the DAS-II still respectfully defers to the judgment of the expert examiner in deciding which battery, subtests and items are most appropriate for an individual child" (Elliott, 2007b, p. 1). Some evaluators are uncomfortable with this philosophy and would prefer to have all administrative and interpretive decisions governed by inflexible rules to be followed blindly under all circumstances. We, however, believe strongly that inflexible rules risk diminishing the validity of assessments. Willis and Dumont (2002, p. 182) recommend that you "maintain a bias in favor of reality" over blind application of arbitrary rules and arithmetic procedures.

GCA versus SNC   It would be impossible to make a rule or even a complex set of rules that would always tell an examiner when to use the GCA and when to use the SNC as the more accurate measurement of a child's cognitive abilities without creating occasional situations in which the wrong measure would be used. The examiner must consider the child's language background; medical, personal, family, social, and educational history; previous and concurrent testing; modifications and accommodations included in the child's Individualized Education Program (IEP); and other variables in reaching the best decision for most validly characterizing the child's cognitive abilities with either the GCA or SNC. This decision cannot be made blindly by application of some simple rule.

Alternative Procedure for Pattern Construction   The DAS-II provides an Alternative Procedure for scoring the Pattern Construction subtest as a pass-fail test within the normal time limit for each pattern without any bonus points for faster completion of the designs. This procedure avoids a penalty for moderately slow, deliberate, thoughtful, or poorly coordinated completion of the patterns, although, by maintaining the time limits for completion of patterns, the Alternative Procedure still penalizes extremely slow completion. The WISC-IV (Wechsler, 2003) also offers a No Time Bonus score for Block Design, but that No Time Bonus score may not be used to compute the Perceptual Reasoning Index nor Full Scale IQ. The DAS-II Alternative Procedure may be used entirely at the examiner's discretion, and the choice may be made at any time (as long as the examiner includes the additional items required in most item sets to permit calculation of the Alternative Procedure score).

Extended Age Range   The examiner is free to take advantage of the overlapping Age Ranges for eight core subtests at ages 5 through 8, to give School-Age subtests and clusters to 5- and 6-year-old children, and to give Upper Level Early Years subtests and clusters to children of ages 7 and 8. Once again, this option is left to the informed clinical judgment of the examiner rather than being imposed by some rule or numerical cut-off. If the examiner does in fact use good, thoughtful judgment, the result should be more accurate and useful assessments better meeting the special needs of individual children.

DON'T FORGET

Examiner Judgment is Encouraged on the DAS-II

The examiner decides whether to use the GCA or the SNC or Nonverbal Cluster as the best representation of the child's conceptual abilities. The examiner selects either the standard or the Alternative Procedure for administering and scoring Pattern Construction. The examiner, within the limits of the overlapping Early Years Upper Level and School-Age norms, chooses which subtests to use to obtain the best measurement of a child's abilities. These decisions are left to the examiner's expert judgment

Assessment of Differential Abilities

Elliott (2007b) explicitly directs the examiner to be cautious in lumping together scores that differ significantly from each other. Even statistically significant differences that are not "uncommon" (differences with relatively high base rates) are considered a signal to consider the total cluster, GCA, or SNC score skeptically. The DAS-II truly is intended and designed to assess differential abilities and the examiner does so with the blessing of the test author rather than, as with many other tests, independently and without support from the test manual.

Fairly Easy Administration

The DAS-II is not effortless to administer, but it is not unduly or unnecessarily difficult. As with most individual tests covering a wide range of ages, there is more hardware to cope with when testing younger children, but it is not too challenging to learn to keep track of and manipulate the cards and objects needed for Picture Similarities and Verbal Comprehension. You do need to use both the Administration Manual and the Record Form along with the several Stimulus Books for some subtests, especially Word Definitions, Copying, and Recall of

Designs, but this divided-attention task is not difficult to master. Elsewhere in this book, we discuss simplification of administering Copying and Recall of Designs. Just as most people will always love their first car and their first computer, most of us come to think of our first cognitive ability test as clear, simple, and easy to administer and score. People trained on one of the Wechsler scales will naturally find anything different to be a little off-putting at first, but our (RP's and JOW's) experiences learning and teaching the DAS and then the DAS-II suggest that the DAS-II really is efficient to administer even for people initially trained on and experienced with other tests. See Sattler (2008) for a discussion of the difficulty of administering each DAS-II subtest.

Item Sets

One of the greatest differences between the DAS-II and many other tests is the use of item sets based on Item Response Theory (IRT) (Daniel, 1999; Elliott, 2007b, Appendix D, pp. 265–272; Embretson & Hershberger, 1999; Embretson, & Reise, 2000; Rasch, 1960; Woodcock, 1999) to tailor the testing to the ability levels of the examinee. Anyone who is long used to testing down to a level of utter boredom to gain a basal and up through levels of frustration to finally escape through a ceiling knows the feeling of secretly and guiltily hoping the examinee will fail one last item and end the suffering. That should make the adaptive testing model a welcome relief, but many examiners used to the traditional model approach it with caution or even suspicion. The rules seem difficult to understand and apply (which they are not), but just a little study and practice makes most examiners wonder why more tests do not use adaptive testing based on Item Response Theory.

The *Introductory and Technical Handbook* (Elliot, 2007b, Appendix A, pp. 225–240) also uses IRT to provide item difficulties for all items on the DAS-II. This information, which should be provided for all tests, can be used to enhance interpretation of an examinee's performance.

When the original DAS first be-

DON'T FORGET

Item Sets

Most subtests of the DAS-II do not use traditional basal and ceiling rules. Item sets developed through application of Item Response Theory (IRT) allow administration of only a set or adjacent sets of items that contain enough items that are difficult for the child (usually three failures anywhere in the set or sets) and easy for the child (usually three passes anywhere in the set or sets) to accurately assess the child's abilities. Testing need not continue through excessive numbers of too-easy and too-difficult items.

came available, one of us (JOW) was so suspicious of the use of Item Sets and basing scores on sets of items on which the lowest item might be failed and the highest item might be passed, that he routinely administered additional Item Sets below and above the set or sets that were actually needed, treating the DAS like the WISC (Wechsler, 1949) and 1960 Stanford-Binet L-M (Terman & Merrill, 1960) he had first used. After wasting a lot of examinees' time and going to the trouble of computing scores based on two or three different combinations of Item Sets for each subtest for each examinee, he eventually realized that he almost always obtained approximately the same score by all possible computations.

Generally Easy Scoring

Difficult judgments and subjectivity in scoring rules cause inter-examiner variation and errors in scores. Some mistakes are frequent and some result in serious errors in subtest and total test scores (e.g., Alfonso & Pratt, 1997; Belk, LoBello, Ray, & Zachar, 2002; Willis, 2001). With the exception of four Verbal Similarities items, all verbal subtests on the DAS-II are scored pass-fail (1 or 0) rather than 2, 1, or 0, and the scoring rules strike us as generally clear and unequivocal. The scoring of Copying and especially of Recall of Designs does take careful attention and some practice, but becomes reasonably quick and easy with experience. See Sattler (2008) for a discussion of the difficulty of scoring each DAS-II subtest.

Developmental Appropriateness

"The DAS-II is child-centered—it was created from a developmental and educational perspective. It is not a downward extension of an adult battery" (Elliott, 2007b, p. xiv). Children and adolescents throughout the DAS-II age range generally find the test engaging. Of course, some examinees are resistant to the entire testing process and some have short spans of attention or energy (one young, nonvocal boy explained to JOW that the test session was over by carefully placing a Pattern Construction foam tile in his mouth and biting deep teeth marks into it). In most cases, though, we have found administration of the DAS-II to be enjoyable and easy at all ages without overwhelming young children with poorly developed skills nor offending older examinees with high levels of abilities.

The blending of visual-spatial thinking (Gv) and fluid reasoning (Gf) abilities at the Lower Level of the Early Years and their separation at the Upper Level Early Years and School-Age Level agrees with the differential development of

DON'T FORGET

....

Overlapping Batteries and Extended Age Ranges

The DAS-II Early Years and School-Age batteries are co-normed between ages 5:0 and 8:11. These extended age ranges and the out-of-level norms for some subtests allow the examiner considerable flexibility in selecting the most appropriate subtests and level for each examinee. You may, in your expert judgment, consider referral information, concurrent testing, and the examinee's performance to select the subtests and level that will provide the most accurate assessment of the child's abilities.

children's abilities. The lack of demand for complex expressive language at the Lower Level of the Early Years avoids penalizing children who are shy or withdrawn or who have communication disabilities or disadvantages. (Naturally, you would want to assess speech and language skills separately, but this aspect of the DAS Early Years Lower Level makes it less likely that we would confound speech and language skills with cognitive abilities.)

The availability of Extended Range norms for ages 5 through 8 also makes it very easy to accommodate the developmental needs of children with unusually high, low, or scattered levels of abilities.

Diagnostic Subtests and Clusters

As noted above, we strongly support the limitation of the Core clusters and GCA to fluid reasoning (*Gf*), verbal comprehension (*Gc*), and visual-spatial thinking (*Gv*) abilities. However, it is also essential to assess other abilities, especially those that strongly influence school achievement. The DAS-II Working Memory, Processing Speed, and School Readiness clusters and the subtests Recall of Objects, Recall of Digits Forward, Recognition of Pictures, Matching Letter-Like Forms, and Phonological Processing greatly enhance the utility of the DAS-II for assessment of children. United States schools are beginning to implement the mandate (U.S. Congress, 2004) for use of Response to Intervention (RTI) for identification of specific learning disabilities, and comprehensive, individual assessments may come to be reserved mostly for other disabilities and for children with suspected specific learning disabilities who have not responded to intervention (e.g., McBride, Dumont, & Willis, 2004; Willis & Dumont, 2006). If this trend does continue, we can anticipate that our evaluations will increasingly focus on children with severe and complex learning problems that cannot be resolved by routine interventions. The DAS-II, with its combination of core tests of *Gf, Gc,*

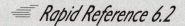

Rapid Reference 6.2

Diagnostic Clusters and Subtests

The DAS-II Diagnostic clusters and subtests greatly enhance the interpretive utility of the test and should be used whenever appropriate to the referral concerns and whenever performance on core subtests suggests further investigation. The Diagnostic clusters and subtests are listed below.

School Readiness Cluster	Early Number Concepts
	Matching Letter-Like Forms
	Phonological Processing
Working Memory	Recall of Sequential Order
	Recall of Digits Backward
Processing Speed	Speed of Information Processing
	Rapid Naming
Other diagnostic subtests	Recall of Objects–Immediate
	Recall of Objects–Delayed
	Recognition of Pictures

and *Gv* abilities and a wide variety of other important abilities not included in the GCA score, may prove to be a very good choice.

The Diagnostic subtest clusters can be compared to each other and to the examinee's GCA (or SNC). Each Diagnostic subtest score can also be compared to the examinee's own Mean Core T score from the GCA or SNC subtests. This comparison of Diagnostic subtests to the student's own average score on only the core subtests is particularly useful. (See Rapid Reference 6.2.)

Normative Sample

Normative samples are important for tests, just as for opinion polls. If the normative sample does not resemble the population to whom examinees will be compared, scores will be misleading. An opinion poll on milk subsidies given only to Vermont dairy farmers might not accurately reflect the overall pattern of opinions of the entire United States population. There have been instances in which a test has been normed on a non-representative sample and has consequently yielded inaccurate scores. The normative sample of the DAS-II is described in Chapter 6 of the *Introductory and Technical Handbook* (Elliott, 2007b) and in Sattler (2008), and we consider it to meet or exceed good current practice and to provide a trustworthy basis for an individual's scores.

Children with mild disabilities that presumably would not impair the validity of test performance were included in the statistical sampling procedure, but not children with severe disabilities, for whom the DAS-II GCA would be inappropriate. This exclusion does not mean that the DAS-II cannot be used, at least in part (for example, the Special Nonverbal Composite, SNC) for some children with severe disabilities. The exclusion does mean that the normative comparison for children with severe disabilities will be the same-age population of the United States in 2002, which provides a useful yardstick. The child's disability or disabilities absolutely must be taken in consideration when interpreting the DAS-II scores. However, the attempt to assemble a representative sample of, for example, children with cerebral palsy, would be futile. We simply do not know how many children with cerebral palsy have gifted levels of cognitive ability or mental retardation or live in poverty or wealth. It would be impossible to interpret scores based on a comparison with some essentially random sample of the incredible diverse population of children with various types and a wide range of severity of cerebral palsy, some with additional disabilities and some without.

Reliability

The DAS-II subtests generally have strong reliability. This topic is discussed at length in Chapter 7 of the *Introductory and Technical Handbook* (Elliott, 2007b) and in Sattler (2008). Test scores cannot be trusted unless the tests are internally consistent and likely to yield very similar scores for the same person under similar circumstances, so reliability is an essential foundation for any responsible use of test scores. It is a necessary, but not sufficient, foundation for application of test scores. A test can be reliable but still not valid for a particular purpose, but without reliability, it cannot be valid for any purpose.

It is still too early to be able to measure long-term stability of DAS-II scores, and long-term stability statistics are depressed by genuine changes in the abilities of the persons being retested. Short-term stability coefficients for all subtests at all tested ages (Elliott, 2007b, p. 138), as noted previously, ranged from .63 (marginally reliable) to .91 (reliable). For the core subtests, short-term stability coefficients were .67 to .91, with a median of .79.

Specificity

In large part, most subtests in tests measure the larger factor or factors of which they are components. This characteristic is necessary if the larger factors are to be coherent and make sense. If the component subtests in a factor or in the total test are not correlated reasonably strongly with each other, then the factor scores and the total score would not be measuring a single ability and simply would not make sense. If the subtests within a factor did not correlate higher with each other than with subtests in other factors, the factor structure would be meaningless. All tests also contain error variance—random fluctuation of scores. However, there are often situations in which we want to consider individual subtests and contrast them with other similar, but not identical, subtests in the same or other factors. That is often an imprudent procedure because the individual subtests may not have sufficient specificity, or unique variance, separate from their shared variance with the other subtests in the factor or total score. They are simply measuring whatever the larger factor or total score measures. If you "just say no to subtest analysis" (McDermott, Fantuzzo, & Glutting, 1990), lack of specificity is not a problem, but the information derived from the test may be of limited utility ("Thanks for the referral. Yes, he does have a low score on the test. Please contact me with any questions.") Subtest scores are simply used to compute total scores and are then forgotten. Adequate specificity allows us to consider the unique information about an examinee's functioning that may be provided by a particular subtest and allows us to consider patterns of strengths and weaknesses—differential abilities.

Unlike the subtests of some other instruments, all of the DAS-II subtests have sufficient (ample or adequate) specificity to allow us to interpret specific subtest functions (Chapter 1 of this book, Chapter 7 of Elliott, 2007b, and Sattler, 2008).

Evidence of Validity

Validity does not exist in a vacuum. The DAS-II is, for example, a highly valid measure of cognitive abilities and has good validity for predicting academic achievement. It is not, however, a valid predictor of athletic performance. (Actually, in our unfair world, the correlation probably would be greater than zero with measures of athletic performance and height for age, but the correlations would be too low to be considered adequately valid, a comfort to those of us who are clumsy or short.)

Validity data for the DAS-II are discussed in Chapter 1 of this book, in the DAS-II *Introductory and Technical Handbook* (Elliott, 2007b, pp. 163–207), and in Sattler (2008). Validity evidence from comparisons with tests of cognitive abilities and tests of academic achievement supports the use of the DAS-II for cognitive assessment and prediction of achievement.

Evidence of Validity with Special Groups

As discussed above, the DAS-II is not normed on children with severe disabilities or disabilities likely to invalidate test scores. However, studies were done with 12 special groups, as discussed in Chapters 1 and 7 of this book, Elliott (2007b, Ch. 8, pp. 184–224), and Sattler (2008). When you are assessing children with special characteristics, the information in Elliott (2007b) is extremely helpful.

Fairness

Chapter 9 of the *Introductory and Technical Handbook* (Elliott, 2007b, pp. 219–224) discusses the careful procedures used to make the DAS-II as fair as possible to various groups of people. Statistical item bias analyses were conducted for the following contrasts: male vs. female, African American vs. White, Hispanic vs. White non-Hispanic (Elliott, 2007b, p. 220). Fairness of prediction of academic achievement was also analyzed statistically.

Introductory and Technical Handbook

The *Handbook* (Elliott, 2007b) provides, in our opinion, coverage of technical information about the test that is as good as any and better than many test manuals on the market, and it is included in the DAS-II kit, so examiners cannot be deprived of it by excessively frugal purchasing agents. However, the *Handbook* also offers a wealth of information about the construction, selection, application, administration, and interpretation of cognitive tests in general, including a clear and helpful explanation of the Rasch (Item Response Theory) model that underlies the development of most recent psychometric tests. We (RP and JOW) consider the *Handbook* to be, in part, a brief but good general text on cognitive assessment.

LIMITATIONS OF DAS-II

Age Range

The DAS-II norms extend only to age 17:11, which is a nuisance for evaluators wishing to do evaluations for students in the last years of high school.

Although there is continuity of structure and conceptual basis across the entire age range, only one subtest is used at all ages. This limitation is a necessary accommodation for developmental appropriateness and for subtest cohesiveness and specificity. We believe, for example, that it is better to have separate Naming Vocabulary and Word Definitions subtests (with the option at ages seven and eight of using the Early Years Naming Vocabulary when appropriate) rather than creating a single vocabulary test that would mix the two item types in different proportions for different individuals. (See Rapid Reference 6.3.)

≡ Rapid Reference 6.3

LIMITATIONS OF DAS-II

- Age range
- "Intelligence"
- Administration and scoring considerations
- Record forms
- One item
- Range of scores
- Expressive language
- Number of subtests in each cluster

"Intelligence"

Elliott (2007b, pp. 17–18) explains the rationale for not using the terms "intelligence" and "IQ" with the DAS-II. The reasons are, we believe, very sound, and many examiners avoid those terms in their reports. "Although some researchers may (for their own purposes) refer to the DAS-II as an 'IQ test,' the fact that they have used this label does not make it so. The DAS-II certainly produces a second-order composite score called the General Conceptual Ability Score (GCA). However *this is not a global composite score such as is found in other batteries*. It is not derived from a heterogeneous mix of all subtests, but is derived only from either six or four subtests that are the best measures of conceptual and reasoning abilities" (Elliott, 2007b, p. xiii; emphasis in the original). Sattler (2008), however, disagrees about the use of the term "intelligence" and many school teams, administrators, school admissions committees, and government agencies demand a measure of "intelligence." A word search in IDEA 2004 (U.S. Congress, 2004) did not find a single instance of "intelligence," "I.Q.," nor "IQ," (although many of "unique" and "technique." A search of the IDEA Regulations (34 CFR Parts 300 and 301) did not locate "I.Q." The word "intelligence" appeared three times, once in the commentary and twice in the actual regulations. Section 300.304(c) (2) states, "Assessments and other evaluation materials include those tailored to assess specific areas of educational need and not merely those that are designed to provide a single general intelligence quotient." Section 300.304 (c) (4) requires that "The child is assessed in all areas related to the suspected disability, including, if appropriate, health, vision, hearing, social and emotional status, general intelligence, academic performance, communicative status, and motor abilities." The term "IQ" appeared 12 times in the commentary, but we could not find it in the actual regulations.

The composition of the GCA core subtests, the correlations of the GCA with the total scores of intelligence tests, and the correlations of the GCA with measures of academic achievement all make it clear that the DAS-II does fulfill all the statutory and practical demands for a measure of intelligence, but examiners may sometimes need to go to some effort to make this point.

Administration and Scoring Considerations

Although we noted above that the DAS-II is not unduly difficult to administer and score, and easier than many comparable tests, it is a complex instrument that does require training, practice, and careful attention, especially with Verbal Comprehension, Recall of Designs and Recall of Objects. It is possible to make tests that are very simple, even machine-scored, multiple-choice tests, but that simplicity sacrifices depth and breadth of measurement. We (RP and JOW) did not find the original DAS difficult to learn, administer, and score, but new examiners also will need to be thoughtful and thorough in their preparation.

The procedures for analyzing task strengths and weaknesses on the subtests of Rapid Naming and Phonological processing seem daunting, but they provide

CAUTION

Keep Record Forms out of Sight

On all tests, it is good practice to make absolutely certain that you are keeping record forms completely out of the examinee's line of vision. Not only do many record forms contain correct answers, some of which can easily be read upside down, but your writing will give the examinee information about the correctness of answers, which violates the standardization and may invalidate norms, even if the examinee's hypotheses are incorrect. It is helpful to learn to make a *1* with a down-and-up stroke so that the sound and movement of your pen (pencils are even noisier) does not distinguish between a *1* and a *0*. Failing to record correct responses verbatim not only deprives you of potentially useful interpretive information (not all correct responses are the same) and the essential opportunity of rechecking your scoring, but it also becomes a signal that writing means an incorrect response. Examinees are resourceful and most hate not knowing if they are right or wrong. One student correctly observed to one of the authors (JOW) that, "When you say, 'UM hm,' it means I am right, but when you say, 'um HM,' it means I am wrong."

explicit directions that are easier than they appear to be. We think the results justify the effort.

Record Forms

As noted above, the DAS-II Record Forms have been improved from the original DAS Record Forms. Examiners must, however, be very careful not to allow the child to see the Record Form, especially during administration of Recall of Objects—Immediate and Delayed—and Recall of Designs. Pictures of the items are clearly printed on the Record Forms. The risk is smaller on Picture Similarities, Matrices, Recognition of Pictures, Early Number Concepts, and Sequential and Quantitative Reasoning, where correct answers are in slightly bolder print than the other choices. Correct answers are written on the Record Form for Recall of Digits Forward and Phonological Processing and the stimuli are written on the Record Form for Recall of Digits Backward. One of us (JOW) has encountered over several decades three children who appeared to be able to read better upside down (like some experienced teachers) than right side up.

Although the SEm value printed next to each Ability Score in each Raw Score to Ability Score table makes it easy to calculate a 95 percent confidence band for each subtest score, and the cross-marks on the Normative Score Profile page make it easy to draw lines showing the confidence bands, the procedure does take several steps and is not encouraged because of the poor trade-off between time taken and information gained.

One Item

A single item on the Phonological Processing subtest lists an incorrect answer. The word "crutch" does not contain a /t/ sound. In English, final /ch/ sounds are pronounced differently from initial /ch/ sounds, but there is no separate /t/ sound as there is, for example, in "meat chops." Both responses, the listed one and the one that is actually correct, are to be scored as correct. This error will be corrected in future printings of the Record Form.

Range of Scores

Sattler (2008) observes that many subtests do not provide the full potential range of T scores and not all potential GCA standard scores at all ages. However, these truncations of possible scores are small. Where they occur is usually at the youngest or oldest extremes of the operating range of a subtest, and they tend to occur more in diagnostic than in core subtests. With all tests, examiners must always make sure that extremely low or nearly perfect raw scores do not yield average-range derived scores (Bracken, 1988; Goldman, 1989). The truncations of DAS-II subtest, cluster, and GCA scores never rise to that level, but should, of course, be checked in the case of extremely low scores for young children and extremely high scores for older adolescents. (See Rapid Reference 6.4.)

Expressive Language

To avoid confounding hearing, speech, and language issues with cognitive abilities and to permit effective use of the DAS-II with children who are shy, withdrawn, or otherwise uncommunicative, the DAS-II Early Years subtests minimize demands for expressive language. Naming vocabulary requires the most spoken language. On the whole, this limitation is a substantial virtue of the DAS-II, but it sometimes requires the use of expressive language tests for a comprehensive assessment of younger children.

The DAS-II also excludes any subtests comparable to the WISC-IV (Wechsler, 2003) Comprehension subtest with its long, complex questions and requirement for long, complex, sometimes two-part verbal responses. This deliberate omission is likely to diminish scoring errors and depressed scores for laconic exam-

---

☰ Rapid Reference 6.4

95 percent Confidence Bands

To obtain a 95 percent confidence band for a subtest *T* score, first look up in the Raw Score to Ability Score table the Ability Score core corresponding to the raw score. Double the SEm listed in parentheses next to the Ability Score. Add that doubled value to the Ability Score and subtract it from the Ability Score. When you look up the *T* score for the Ability Score, also look up the *T* scores for the Ability Score plus the doubled SEm and the Ability Score minus the doubled SEm. Those two additional *T* scores mark off the 95-percent-confidence band for the child's score on the subtest.

Test manuals and textbooks tend to emphasize confidence bands most for the most reliable scores (e.g., GCA, FSIQ, GIA, MPC, GCF, or CIX), no more (or even less) for the slightly less reliable groups of scores (e.g., clusters, indexes, or scales), and least (if at all) for the least reliable scores—individual subtests. Examiners might consider reporting confidence bands for subtest scores, even if significant-difference values are readily available in the test manual or, on the DAS-II, on the Record Form.

inees, but it may leave the examiner wishing to have had more of a conversation with the examinee. There is an obvious solution: have that conversation.

Number of Subtests in Each Cluster

Each DAS-II cluster is based on two subtests. If two subtests measuring separate narrow CHC abilities (which is usually the case with the DAS-II) are not significantly different from each other, they should be sufficient to measure the broad ability of which they are components (see, for example, Flanagan, Ortiz, & Alfonso, 2007). However, if the two subtests do differ significantly from each other, interpretation must be cautious, as directed by Elliott (2007b), and complementary assessment tools may be needed.

ALTERNATIVE AND COMPLEMENTARY ASSESSMENT TOOLS

As noted above, there are instances in which divergent subtest scores in a cluster or divergent cluster scores in the GCA or SNC require further investigation. Flanagan, Ortiz, and Alfonso (2007) provide detailed, specific, practical instructions and a CD with eminently useful programs for conducting a McGrew, Flanagan, and Ortiz Integrated Cross-Battery Assessment. We strongly recommend their procedures when additional testing is needed.

The Woodcock-Johnson III (WJ III; Woodcock, McGrew, & Mather, 2001) is usually the first place to look for complementary cognitive measures. The WJ III offers 53 tests explicitly organized within the CHC framework and explicitly permits the examiner to select specific tests for various purposes. Each easel includes a useful chart showing how each test fits into the CHC factors or other categories. If an examiner is using the DAS-II as the core battery for a cognitive assessment, the WJ III is an outstanding source for any needed follow-up.

In some extreme instances, with children who have language, hearing, or other challenges to verbal skills or who are constrained in verbal interaction, for example by autism, the SNC may suggest stronger Nonverbal Reasoning (*Gf*) and Spatial (*Gv*) abilities. Nevertheless, even though the reliabilities of these measures and that of the SNC are high, you may wish to give the child an additional nonverbal test in order to come to a more definitive conclusion about the child's nonverbal cognitive abilities. In those cases, we would recommend a factorially complex, multiple-subtest, entirely nonverbal test such as the Leiter International Performance Scale-Revised (Roid & Miller, 1997) or the Universal Nonverbal Intelligence Test (UNIT; Bracken & Walker, 1997). The Leiter assesses several CHC abilities and also includes an Attention and Memory Battery. See Braden (2000), McCallum, Bracken, and Wasserman (2001), and Braden and Athanasiou (2005) as well as Elliott (2007b) for more information on nonverbal assessment, including the distinction between assessment of nonverbal abilities (e.g., visual-spatial thinking [Gv]) and nonverbal assessment of abilities.

Unlike most tests of cognitive ability, except for the WJ III, the DAS-II includes some essential abilities underlying academic achievement, such as short-term and working memory, orthographic discrimination, rapid naming, and phonological processing. In some cases, these measures may suggest additional assessment with highly specialized measures such as the WJ III, Comprehensive Test of Phonological Processing (CTOPP) (Wagner, Torgesen, & Rashotte, 1999), or Rapid Automatized Naming and Rapid Alternating Stimulus Test (RAN/RAS; Wolf & Denckla, 2005).

The DAS-II provides tables linking DAS-II scores with scores from the Wechsler Individual Achievement Test, 2nd ed. (WIAT-II; The Psychological Corporation, 2001). This book provides a CD containing such tables linking DAS-II scores with the WJ III, and the Kaufman Test of Educational Achievement, 2nd ed. (KTEA-II; Kaufman & Kaufman, 2004b). All three of these achievement batteries represent the best examples of academic achievement tests that offer a variety of useful subtests. They are not interchangeable. They measure some different skills, and they measure skills in different ways. Although the tests correlated highly with each other for groups of students, differences in format and content can make large differences in scores for an individual. We find that the coverage and format of the KTEA-II make it especially useful for academic assessment of most students and a very good match with the DAS-II. See Flanagan, Ortiz, Alfonso, & Mascolo (2006) for a very thorough, detailed review of achievement tests within a CHC Framework and for valuable guidelines for the use of achievement tests in the assessment of specific learning disabilities. Willis and Dumont (2002) offer other suggestions for achievement testing for students who may have specific learning disabilities.

TEST YOURSELF

1. The GCA includes only subtests that primarily assess fluid reasoning (*Gf*), verbal comprehension (*Gc*), and visual-spatial thinking (*Gv*). The other CHC abilities are not measured by the DAS-II. True or False?

2. DAS-II examiners are permitted to use the Special Nonverbal Composite and its Mean Core T score instead of the General Conceptual Ability score and its Mean Core T only if there is serious medical or language-based reasons to do so. True or False?

3. The instructions for administration and the demonstration of Signed Standard Sentences in American Sign Language (ASL) provided on the CD allow an examiner with some knowledge of classroom Signed English to administer appropriate subtests of the DAS-II correctly and in a standardized manner. True or False?

4. The Cattell-Horn-Carroll theory of cognitive abilities provides a framework by which one can interpret the DAS-II. True or False?

5. Extended Range norms, used to accommodate the developmental needs of children with unusually high, low, or scattered levels of abilities, are available for ages:

   (a) 3 through 6
   (b) 5 through 8
   (c) 6 through 12
   (d) 5 through 17

6. The normative sample of the DAS-II is problematic because it does not meet acceptable standards for providing trustworthy individual scores. True or False?

Answers: 1. False, the other CHC abilities are measured by the diagnostic subtests; 2. False, the choice of SNC or GCA is left up to the examiner's professional judgment and the examiner's knowledge of the examinee; 3. False, these materials allow examiners who are *fluent* in ASL to administer appropriate subtests of the DAS-II correctly and in a standardized manner; 4. True; 5. b; 6. False

Seven

CLINICAL APPLICATIONS OF THE DAS-II

Clinical assessment is all about reaching an understanding of an individual. Typically, such assessment takes place in the context of stated referral problems or specific presenting behaviors or psychological characteristics of the person being assessed. Our understanding of the processes underlying the referred problem can lead to interventions that take the characteristics of that individual into account.

When we are asked to evaluate an individual's cognitive development or aspects of the individual's ability in information processing, we need to do this in a way that will clearly identify distinctive, interpretable cognitive factors, systems, or processes with as little overlap and ambiguity as possible. That is the reason we need subtests and composites that are not only reliable but which also have high specificity. As explained in earlier chapters, the DAS-II has been designed for this purpose. It has between 10 percent and 20 percent more reliable specificity in its subtests and clusters than other cognitive test batteries. This specificity maximizes the likelihood of a clinician identifying real intra-individual strengths and weaknesses in cognitive abilities.

Sometimes the nature of an information-processing difficulty that underlies a problem is so specific that it leads to a straightforward and successful intervention. For example, one of the authors (CDE) has come across school-aged children who (sometimes through traumatic brain injury, sometimes with unknown causes) have problems at school because they forget what teachers tell them to do. In some of these cases, where the problem is a highly specific deficit in auditory short-term memory, if we recommend the student to write down everything that has to be remembered in a notebook, this often works like a charm! In other cases, we find that problems in information processing are so generalized and intractable that attempts at intervention are unsuccessful. In such cases, it may be that the most we can do is to bring to parents, teachers and student an understanding of the nature of the problem so that they might adapt and learn to live with the problem.

This leads us to a key point of understanding: *A profile of test scores can never lead us directly to a specific intervention.* There is no one-to-one link. Four broad steps are necessary that take us from testing to intervention. At Step 1, test profiles tell us the areas in which an individual has reliable, significant, real (these words are broadly equivalent) differences in scores between different subtests and composites. We then typically go to Step 2 and evaluate patterns of scores among all these measures in developing hypotheses that these high and low scores represent cognitive strengths and weaknesses. At Step 3, we try to understand the causes of these strengths and weaknesses by examining the child's medical and developmental history. Finally, at Step 4, we develop intervention strategies based on both our hypotheses of strengths and weaknesses together with our knowledge of the child's history. Tests alone can never tell us the cause of a problem. Our understanding of causation is dependent on social and medical factors in conjunction with our psychological test data. Any intervention or treatment has to be related to causes and therefore cannot be based solely on an individual's test profile.

In this chapter, we will discuss a number of clinical areas in which the DAS-II is commonly applied: (a) assessment of specific learning disabilities (SLDs); (b) assessment of Attention-Deficit/Hyperactivity Disorder (ADHD); (c) assessment of mental retardation; (d) assessment of gifted children; (e) assessment of preschool children; (e) assessment of language disabilities; and (f) assessment of children with autism spectrum disorder.

Before doing this, we need to make another key point. It is this: The six areas to be discussed are diagnostic *categories* of conditions. Such categories are conceptualized and incorporated into law and regulations based upon certain relatively crude criteria. For example, children categorized as having mental retardation show low levels of cognitive abilities together with a low level of social adaptation for their ages. It is well known that children who are in this category are there for a variety of reasons. A range of genetic disorders is shown among this group, while others have histories of trauma such as anoxia at birth. We would therefore expect to see a wide range of presenting behaviors and referral problems. Other than the individuals being uniformly low in terms of a crude single measure such as a full scale IQ or GCA, we would not be surprised to find a range of relative cognitive strengths and weaknesses in this population.

Similarly, children with SLDs are categorized this way if their school achievements lag behind their age peers, if their cognitive abilities appear to be in the average range, and if there are no obvious extraneous influences causing the low achievement. Here, their appearance and medical history often give us no clue as to the cause of their problems. However, there is ample evidence that children with SLDs in reading fall into distinct subgroups or subtypes (for recent

DON'T FORGET

1. A profile of test scores can never lead us directly to a specific intervention.

2. Within various clinical categories or categories of handicap, there is a range of causal influences.

3. There is no single cognitive ability profile within each clinical category.

4. Each child needs distinctive, individualized methods of intervention based on our hypotheses of strengths and weaknesses together with our knowledge of the child's history and likely causal influences.

examples, see Bakker, 2006; Bakker et al., 2007; Katzir et al., 2008; Maner, 2006; Piasta & Wagner, 2008). Moreover, there are distinct differences between children with specific difficulties in reading, and those with specific difficulties in math. And yet all come under the category of SLD. However, even within the content categories of, say, Reading and Math, there is ample evidence of subgroups of individuals that have distinctively different cognitive profiles of strengths and weaknesses. This leads us to conclude that across the whole spectrum of children identified as having SLD there is a range of causal influences, with strengths and weaknesses needing distinctive methods of intervention tailored to each child's needs (Townend & Turner, 2000).

PRESENTATION OF MEANS OF CLINICAL GROUPS

In presenting group data, the chief measure in this chapter will be a standard difference measure. This is a measure of *effect size*. Effect sizes are in standard deviation (SD) units. An effect size of 1.0 indicates that two means are one SD apart. Cohen (1988) defined effect sizes below .50 as small, .50 to .79 as medium, and .80 and above as large. In this chapter, for the sake of clarity, only relatively large effect sizes of .70 or greater will be reported. Readers should consult the DAS-II *Introductory and Technical Handbook,* pages 184–207, if more detail is desired.

APPLICATION OF THE DAS-II IN THE ASSESSMENT OF SPECIFIC LEARNING DISABILITIES (SLD)

Over approximately the past 30 years, a SLD has been diagnosed when a person's achievement on standardized tests is significantly below the level expected from the person's age and level of intelligence. Although IDEA (U.S. Congress, 2004) no longer permits states to require use of a "severe discrepancy" formula for determination of SLD [34 C.F.R. § 300.307 (a) (1)], state departments of education may still permit this approach, many evaluation teams still consider it in their determinations, and it can be part of a pattern of strengths and weaknesses [34 C.F.R. § 300.309 (a) (2) (ii)]. Two basic methods have been used to determine whether there is a significant difference between ability and achievement.

Simple Difference Method

This method makes a direct comparison between an obtained achievement score and an ability score. Table D.12 in the *DAS-II Normative Data Tables Manual* gives statistically significant differences (at the levels $p < .05$ and $p < .01$) between DAS-II composite and cluster scores, on the one hand, and WIAT-II subtests and composite scores, on the other hand. Thus any subtest or composite from the WIAT-II may be directly compared with the DAS-II GCA score, the Special Nonverbal Composite, or the Verbal Ability, Nonverbal Reasoning Ability or Spatial Ability cluster. Tables D.13 to D.17 also provide the frequency or unusualness of differences between a given achievement measure and a given ability measure.

Predicted Difference Method

There is a major technical problem with the simple difference method. This problem is due to the phenomenon of regression to the mean: Children who have *below*-average ability scores tend to have achievement scores that are higher than their ability level. Similarly, children who have *above*-average ability scores tend to have achievement scores that are lower than their ability level. Therefore, smaller numbers of children in the below-average range of ability will be identified as having SLD (that is, with achievement below the level of their ability), and larger numbers will be identified if their ability is in the above-average range.

For this reason, many professionals use (and we strongly prefer) the *predicted difference method,* which makes a comparison between an obtained achievement score and a *predicted* achievement score. The prediction of the achievement score is made on the basis of an ability score, but because we are using a predicted achievement score and are *not* using the ability score directly, this takes the problem of regression to the mean into account. In order to use this method with the WIAT-II and the DAS-II, it is first necessary to obtain predicted achievement scores on the WIAT-II subtests and composites, based upon DAS-II ability scores. These predicted achievement scores are provided in Tables D.1 to D.5 in the *DAS-II Normative Data Tables Manual.* Having obtained the predicted scores, we then make a comparison between the predicted and obtained scores on the WIAT-II. Table D.6 gives statistically significant differences (at the levels $p < .05$

DON'T FORGET
....

1. Use of predicted achievement rather than simple differences compensates for regression toward the mean.

2. Evaluators can consider both the significance of differences and the frequency of differences (base rate).

3. Tables on the CD accompanying this book allow evaluators to use the KTEA-II and WJ III achievement tests as well as the WIAT-II with the DAS-II and still determine whether differences are significant and uncommon.

and $p < .01$) between obtained and predicted WIAT-II subtest and composite scores. Predicted scores may be derived from the DAS-II GCA score, the Special Nonverbal Composite, or the Verbal Ability, Nonverbal Reasoning Ability or Spatial Ability clusters. Having determined whether the difference between obtained and predicted scores is statistically significant, we may then turn to Tables D.7 to D.11 to evaluate their frequency or unusualness.

In addition to these tables relating the DAS-II to the WIAT-II, the CD that accompanies this book provides full tables for comparisons of the DAS-II with the WJ III Achievement subtests and composites, and with the KTEA-II subtests and composites. Thus, using any one of the three major achievement batteries, the DAS-II user may evaluate the significance of differences between ability and achievement scores and apply these to the diagnosis of SLD, if local or state regulations require such differences to be evaluated in order to determine whether a child has SLD and to provide him or her with appropriate services.

Determination of Significant Cognitive Strengths and Weaknesses

Another method of determining if a child has SLD is to evaluate (a) whether the child's achievement is markedly below expectation for the child's age—typically achievement scores below 85; and (b) whether in addition the child shows evidence of specific difficulties in cognitive processing that might be related to the child's impaired achievement. Such a method is closely aligned with the Federal Definition of SLD: "Specific Learning Disability means a disorder in one or more of the basic psychological processes involved in understanding or in using language, spoken or written, that may manifest itself in the imperfect ability to listen, think, speak, read, write, spell, or to do mathematical calculations, including conditions such as perceptual disabilities, brain injury, minimal brain dysfunction, dyslexia, and developmental aphasia" [IDEA, U.S. Congress, 2004; 34 C.F.R. 300.8 (c) (10)]. The DAS-II is specifically designed to be sensitive to the detection of a child's strengths and weaknesses in basic psychological processes, and is therefore well suited for the purpose of diagnosis of SLD.

DAS-II Mean Scores of Children with SLD

At the time when data were collected for the DAS-II standardization sample, a number of independent examiners also provided data for special group studies. Children included in three Learning Disorder samples were aged between 7:0 and 13:11, and had previous scores of 80 or higher on a standardized measure of cognitive ability. They either (a) showed a discrepancy of 15 points or more between ability and achievement scores on standardized tests in one, and only one, of the following three areas: Reading only, Reading and Written Expression, Mathematics only; or (b) they met specific school or district criteria for learning disorder in only one of the three areas.

Children in each of the three groups of children with SLD were individually matched with children drawn from the standardization sample, thereby forming three separate control groups. The matching variables were age, sex, race/ethnicity, parent education level, and geographic region.

Table 7.1 shows the mean scores of the *children with Reading disorder* and their matched control group on those subtests and composites that show effect sizes of .70 or greater. Note that subtest scores are expressed in a *T* score metric (Mean 50; SD 10) and that clusters and composites are standard scores (Mean 100; SD 15).

We emphasize that these mean scores are for the *total* sample of children diagnosed with an SLD in Reading. The earlier comments in this chapter mentioned the strong likelihood that within groups of children with reading disabilities there will be subgroups displaying varied, often contrasting, profiles of strengths and weaknesses in abilities. If this is the case, some weaknesses in one subgroup may not show as weaknesses in the total sample because the same processes are strengths in another subgroup: If the number of individuals in each subgroup were similar, their mean scores on the relevant subtests or clusters might be close to the mean scores of the control group. The contrasting patterns would, in effect, cancel each other.

Having stated this, it is still interesting to examine the data shown in Table 7.1. Starting with the composites, the SLD group has significantly lower scores on both the GCA and the SNC. This is not altogether surprising, since the nature of SLD is that it reflects a disorder in one or more basic psychological processes. Thus if one or more subtests or clusters have low scores because of the presence

Table 7.1. Mean Performance of Children with SLD in Reading, Showing Subtests, Clusters and Composites with Relatively Large Effect Sizes (Standard Differences)

Subtest/Cluster Composite	Reading Disorder			Matched Controls		Group Comparison	
	Mean	SD	N	Mean	SD	Difference	Standard Difference
Subtest							
NVoc	45.4	8.2	22	53.0	9.9	7.6	.84
RObjI	43.1	11.9	46	50.9	9.6	7.8	.73
DigF	42.9	9.8	46	52.0	10.6	9.1	.90
MLLF	45.5	10.4	22	53.3	7.7	7.8	.85
PhP	44.9	7.2	46	52.3	7.9	7.4	.98
RNam	43.6	9.5	46	49.9	8.2	6.3	.71
Cluster							
NVR	91.2	11.8	46	99.3	10.8	8.1	.72
SchR	92.9	10.9	22	104.0	9.7	11.1	1.08
PSp	89.8	12.1	46	100.9	13.4	11.1	.87
Composite							
GCA	90.6	10.4	46	99.8	12.5	9.2	.80
SNC	91.2	10.5	46	99.4	11.9	8.2	.73

Key: NVoc = Naming Vocabulary; RObjI = Recall of Objects, Immediate; DigF = Recall of Digits Forward; MLLF = Matching Letter-Like Forms; PhP = Phonological Processing; RNam = Rapid Naming; NVR = Nonverbal Reasoning; SchR = School Readiness; PSp = Processing Speed; GCA = General Conceptual Ability; SNC = Special Nonverbal Composite .

of an SLD, this weakness will in its turn lower any composite score derived from the subtest or composite. The lower scores obtained by the SLD sample illustrate a major problem with using discrepancy models to identify and diagnose children with SLD: The disability pulls down the composite score, thereby reducing any discrepancy between ability and achievement! [This paradox is called the "Mark Penalty" (Willis & Dumont, 2002, p. 172).]

For younger children, the School Readiness cluster shows a large effect size, indicating that children with SLD in reading have difficulties in the areas of phonological processing, letter discrimination and the development of early concepts of number—these school-related skills are slow to develop. Other notable weaknesses for this group are shown in Nonverbal Reasoning and Processing Speed.

Table 7.2. Mean Performance of Children with SLD in Reading and Written Expression, Showing Subtests, Clusters, and Composites with Relatively Large Effect Sizes (Standard Differences)

Subtest/Cluster Composite	Reading and Written Expression Disorder			Matched Controls		Group Comparison	
	Mean	SD	N	Mean	SD	Difference	Standard Difference
Subtest							
RDes	42.7	10.2	44	50.5	7.8	7.8	.86
SQR	42.8	6.8	44	50.6	9.4	7.8	.95
ENC	41.9	8.5	22	51.3	10.4	9.4	.99
DigB	43.3	7.6	44	49.4	8.5	6.1	.77
PhP	43.9	7.9	40	50.4	8.0	6.5	.82
RNam	42.3	9.2	44	53.0	8.5	10.7	1.22
Cluster							
NVR	90.4	10.1	44	99.2	13.7	8.8	.73
Spat	89.6	14.0	44	99.6	11.4	10.0	.78
SchR	87.8	10.6	22	99.6	11.8	11.8	1.06
WMem	90.2	11.1	44	99.8	13.5	9.6	.77
PSp	87.7	14.3	44	102.6	16.3	14.9	.97
Composite							
GCA	89.5	12.2	44	99.3	11.9	9.8	.82
SNC	89.0	12.0	44	99.3	12.2	10.3	.86

Key: RDes = Recall of Designs; SQR = Sequential and Quantitative Reasoning; ENC = Early Number Concepts; DigB = Recall of Digits, Backward; PhP = Phonological Processing; RNam = Rapid Naming; NVR = Nonverbal Reasoning; Spat = Spatial; SchR = School Readiness; WMem = Working Memory; PSp = Processing Speed; GCA = General Conceptual Ability; SNC = Special Nonverbal Composite.

Low-scoring subtests reflect these clusters. In addition, a general tendency for low scores should be noted on two memory subtests—Recall of Digits Forward and Recall of Objects.

We now turn to a sample of children identified as having *a disorder in both Reading and in Written Expression*. Do they have similar weaknesses when compared with their matching Controls? To answer this question, we turn to Table 7.2.

Once again, the GCA and SNC composite scores for this SLD group are significantly below those of their matched controls. For this group with problems not only in reading but also in written expression, there are more significantly low cluster scores. Again, the largest effect size is shown by the School Readiness cluster, and Nonverbal Reasoning and Processing Speed are again low. However, for this group, there is evidence of general problems in the areas of Spatial ability and Working Memory. The subtests underlying these clusters also tend to have low scores.

Finally, in this comparison of clinical SLD samples with matched controls, we look at the results for the sample of *children with a disorder in Mathematics.* Their results, and those of the controls, are shown in Table 7.3.

As with the samples of children with SLD in literacy, the GCA and SNC

Table 7.3. Mean Performance of Children with SLD in Mathematics, Showing Subtests, Clusters, and Composites with Relatively Large Effect Sizes (Standard Differences)

Subtest/Cluster Composite	Mathematics Disorder			Matched Controls		Group Comparison	
	Mean	SD	N	Mean	SD	Difference	Standard Difference
Subtest							
RDes	45.7	8.0	39	52.4	7.8	6.7	.86
Mat	42.7	8.3	39	49.5	9.3	6.8	.77
SQR	42.5	7.7	39	50.2	10.4	7.7	.84
DigF	43.3	10.3	39	51.1	9.8	7.8	.77
ENC	34.4	10.3	20	50.4	9.6	16.0	1.61
SIP	39.0	8.6	39	49.5	12.4	10.5	.98
RNam	45.3	9.3	39	52.3	10.0	7.0	.73
Cluster							
NVR	87.8	11.2	39	99.2	14.3	11.4	.89
Spat	90.2	10.4	39	100.6	12.1	10.4	.92
PSp	85.5	14.2	39	101.7	18.1	16.2	1.00
Composite							
GCA	89.3	10.6	39	98.9	12.2	9.6	.84
SNC	87.8	10.4	39	100.0	12.5	12.2	1.06

Key: RDes = Recall of Designs; Mat = Matrices; SQR = Sequential and Quantitative Reasoning; DigF = Recall of Digits, Forward; ENC = Early Number Concepts; SIP = Speed of Information Processing; RNam = Rapid Naming; NVR = Nonverbal Reasoning; Spat = Spatial; PSp = Processing Speed; GCA = General Conceptual Ability; SNC = Special Nonverbal Composite.

scores of these children with SLD in Math are significantly lower than those of the matched control group. Also once again, we note significantly low mean scores in Nonverbal Reasoning Ability, Spatial Ability and in Processing Speed. When we turn to subtests, the subtest with the largest effect size is Early Number Concepts, which is entirely consistent with the nature of these children's disability.

For all three SLD samples, the clusters that consistently show significantly low scores, together with relatively large effect sizes, are Processing Speed and Nonverbal Reasoning. Again, however, we reiterate that while group data for conditions as diverse as learning disabilities may be interesting, they do not enable us to state general rules about cognitive processing difficulties in SLD.

We should always be aware, first, of the probability that there are distinctive subgroups within children identified as having SLD, and second, that we should make no assumptions about an individual child's difficulties until we have carried out a full evaluation. While our research efforts to identify characteristics of dyslexic or SLD children are fascinating (to us, and maybe to some others) and help generate hypotheses about an individual child, there is no substitute for investigation of each individual and discovering his or her specific processing problems, rather than being tempted to treat dyslexia or SLD as a unitary disorder.

ARE THERE SUBGROUPS OF DAS-II SCORE PROFILES WITHIN SLD CATEGORIES?

In order to answer this question, we examined score profiles of children who were poor readers, and who were drawn from the DAS-II standardization sample, and compared them with the samples of SLD children previously described.

Definition of Samples

The analysis of children drawn from the standardization sample provides baserate data. All 2,400 children in the *DAS-II standardization sample* aged between 6:0 and 17:11 were given the Word Reading subtest of the WIAT-II. Those who were poor readers were identified, "poor reading" being defined as having a Word Reading standard score of 85 or less. Children were excluded from this sample if their Verbal, Nonverbal Reasoning, and Spatial Ability cluster scores were all below 70, thereby excluding from the sample of poor readers those who may more properly be considered to be in the range of mental retardation. This sample of 219 poor readers was subdivided into those who showed a significant discrepancy ($p < .05$) between their obtained and predicted WIAT-II Word Reading scores ($N = 172$) and those with no significant discrepancy ($N = 47$). Prediction of the reading scores was done on the basis of the children's DAS-II GCA scores.

The *clinical samples* are as described above. For the purpose of this analysis, the samples of children with SLD in Reading and with SLD in Reading and Written Expression were combined to form a single sample of children with reading difficulties. In addition, a separate analysis was conducted of the sample of children with a Learning Disorder in Mathematics. Results for the sample showing combined Attention-Deficit/Hyperactivity Disorder and Learning Disorder (ADHD/LD) are reported later in this chapter.

Definition of Subgroups

Subgroups of children in all these samples were formed based upon whether they show distinctively different cognitive strengths and weaknesses. The following analyses examine the frequency found in each sample of different profiles of DAS-II cluster scores (Verbal, Nonverbal Reasoning, Spatial, Working Memory, and Processing Speed), together with scores on the Phonological processing subtest.

Children in the two clinical samples (SLD in Reading and SLD in Math) were placed into subgroups based upon the presence or absence of significant discrepancies between scores that were significant at the 5 percent confidence level. The differences between cluster scores were obtained from Tables B.1. and B.3. in the DAS-II *Normative Data Tables Manual* (Elliott, 2007c), and the difference between the Phonological Processing subtest and the mean of the core subtests used to estimate the GCA is taken from Table B.7. in the same Manual. Note that these differences are also shown on the Normative Score Profiles Page of the DAS-II School-age Record Form.

The subgroups were defined according to the possible combinations of high and low scores that may be found among the school-age clusters, and also included subgroups with flat cluster profiles. Even among poor readers with a significant discrepancy between GCA and Word Reading (or more properly between observed Word Reading and Word Reading predicted from the GCA), it would be expected that there would be a proportion of children with flat cognitive test profiles. Poor reading has many causes, and there is no reason to believe that children who have failed to read because of lack of exposure to teaching through absences from school, or because of poor teaching, or because of poor motivation, or because of adverse home circumstances, should have anything other than normal (i.e., flat) cognitive profiles. Other poor readers may show a range of different high and low cluster scores. The DAS-II core clusters (Verbal, Nonverbal Reasoning and Spatial Ability) may reveal some children who have verbal disabilities linked to literacy (e.g., British Psychological Society, 1999; Snow, Burns, & Griffin, 1998) or spatial processing difficulties linked to a nonverbal learning disability (Rourke, Del Dotto, Rourke, & Casey, 1990). Additionally, we may find some whose nonverbal reasoning ability is lower than both their verbal and spatial abilities. Elliott (2001, 2005) reported findings from a number of samples in which between 25 percent and 40 percent of students identified as dyslexic or SLD in Reading had this profile on the first edition of the DAS. Finally, there may be some individuals who show the reverse pattern, with nonverbal reasoning ability higher than both verbal and spatial, although no research studies have identified such a subgroup.

It also seems likely that some children will have problems with tasks involving Working Memory and/or Processing Speed, although others will not. We may well expect to find large numbers of poor readers with significantly low scores in Phonological Processing, although some poor readers will not have a problem in this area.

The various profiles are defined in Table 7.4. A child is placed in a particular profile subgroup if he or she shows statistically significant differences between scores at the $p<.05$ level of significance. Clearly, with five clusters and one subtest being analyzed, there are many possible combinations of high and low scores. To reduce this possible number, the following steps were taken:

a. Four possible combinations of high and low scores were defined for the Core clusters, seen in Groups 2 to 5;

b. The Processing Speed and Working Memory clusters defined two groups each, to enable us to determine how many children with SLD show high or low scores on them;

c. Six groups were defined that showed combinations of low scores among the Core and Diagnostic clusters;

d. The Phonological processing subtest defined two groups to enable us to determine how many SLD children showed significantly low or high scores; and

e. Three additional groups were defined in terms of having low scores on Phonological Processing together with low Verbal, Spatial, or Nonverbal Reasoning scores.

Table 7.4. Definition of Profile Subgroups

Group	Cluster Score Profiles	Definition
1.	Flat Cluster Profile	There are no statistically significant differences among the three DAS-II Core cluster scores, and neither the Processing Speed nor the Working Memory clusters have significantly high or low scores.
2.	Low Spatial (S), High Verbal (V)	The S cluster score is significantly lower than the V cluster, with NVR being intermediate.
3.	Low V, High S	The V cluster score is significantly lower than the S cluster, with NVR being intermediate.
4.	High Nonverbal Reasoning (NVR)	The NVR cluster score is higher than *both* the V and S cluster scores, and significantly higher than at least one of them.
5.	Low NVR	The NVR cluster score is lower than *both* the Verbal and Spatial scores, and significantly lower than at least one of them.
6.	High Processing Speed (PS)	The PS cluster score is significantly higher than the child's GCA score.
7.	Low PS	The PS cluster score is significantly lower than the child's GCA score.
8.	High Working Memory (WM)	The WM cluster score is significantly higher than the child's GCA score.
9.	Low WM	The WM cluster score is significantly lower than the child's GCA score.
10.	Low S, High V *and* Low PS	The child is a member of Groups 2 and 7.
11.	Low V, High S *and* Low PS	The child is a member of Groups 3 and 7.
12.	Low S, High V *and* Low WM	The child is a member of Groups 2 and 9.
13.	Low V, High S *and* Low WM	The child is a member of Groups 3 and 9.
14.	Low NVR *and* Low PS	The child is a member of Groups 5 and 7.
15.	Low NVR *and* Low WM	The child is a member of Groups 5 and 9.
	Phonological Processing and Clusters	
16.	High Phonological Processing (PhP)	The PhP subtest *T* score is significantly higher than the mean subtest score on the 6 Core subtests (the Mean Core *T* score).
17.	Low PhP	The PhP subtest *T* score is significantly lower than the mean subtest score on the 6 Core subtests (the Mean Core *T* score).
18.	Low S, High V *and* Low PhP	The child is a member of Groups 2 and 17.
19.	Low V, High S *and* Low PhP	The child is a member of Groups 3 and 17.
20.	Low NVR *and* Low PhP	The child is a member of Groups 5 and 17.

Results

Base Rates are shown in Table 7.5. The third column of this table gives the percentages of children with each profile in the total standardization sample for ages 6:0 through 17:11. Interestingly, only about 10 percent of the total standardization sample has a flat profile of cluster scores. Although individuals with "flat" profiles may show some scores that seem relatively high or low, none of them reaches a level where we have confidence that they are real, and not attributable to measurement error. When we look at all five cluster scores together with children's scores on Phonological Processing, about 90 percent of all children in the total standardization sample show one or more significantly high or low scores.

The most important base rate tables for our comparisons, however, are those for the Poor Readers, shown in the first two columns of Table 7.5. There are interesting base-rate contrasts between those poor readers with a significant discrepancy between their obtained and predicted WIAT-II Word Reading scores and those showing no significant discrepancy. The profile frequencies for the two groups have very little in common. For example, 17 percent of those with a significant discrepancy had significantly low scores on the Phonological Processing (PhP) subtest, whereas *no* individual in the group with no significant discrepancy had such a low score on PhP. A similar pattern was shown for Processing Speed, for which 22 percent and zero, respectively, had significantly low scores. The Poor Readers with significant discrepancy also have a much higher percentage of children with low Working Memory (27 percent versus 9 percent). In contrast to this, 40 percent of those with no significant discrepancy had significantly *high* Working memory scores and 51 percent of them had high Processing Speed scores. This information may be helpful to an evaluator attempting to ferret out the possible causes for an individual's low achievement in reading.

We now turn to the clinical samples. Table 7.6 shows the percentages of profile types shown in the combined clinical samples of children with SLD in Reading and SLD in Reading and Written Expression. The percentages of each profile are somewhat similar to the percentages found in the members of the standardization sample with significant discrepancies between obtained and predicted word reading scores.

The results for the group with SLD in Mathematics are shown in Table 7.7. No results concerning Phonological Processing are reported for this group because this variable does not appear to have much relevance for math achievement. Because relatively few children in the DAS-II standardization sample were given math subtests from the WIAT-II, there were insufficient data to provide base rates for children who are poor in math on the same lines as Table 7.5. Therefore, the

Table 7.5. Base Rates of DAS-II Profiles, Showing the Percentage of Poor Readers in DAS-II Standardization Sample with Each Profile, and the Percentage with Each Profile Found in the Total DAS-II Standardization Sample for Ages 6:0–17:11

Group	Cluster Score Profiles	Poor Readers with Significant Discrepancy (N = 172)	Poor Readers with no Significant Discrepancy (N = 47)	Total Standardization Sample Ages 6:0–17:11 (N = 2,400)
1.	Flat Cluster Profile	15.1	19.1	11.0
2.	Low Spatial (S), High Verbal (V)	10.5	4.3	13.3
3.	Low V, High S	18.6	17.0	13.3
4.	High Nonverbal Reasoning (NVR)	14.5	6.4	18.5
5.	Low NVR	18.0	6.4	18.8
6.	High Processing Speed (PS)	26.2	51.1	25.3
7.	Low PS	21.5	0.0	25.0
8.	High Working Memory (WM)	15.7	40.4	22.1
9.	Low WM	26.7	8.5	24.2
10.	Low S, High V *and* Low PS	2.9	0.0	4.0
11.	Low V, High S *and* Low PS	2.9	0.0	3.0
12.	Low S, High V *and* Low WM	3.5	0.0	3.0
13.	Low V, High S *and* Low WM	5.2	0.0	2.8
14.	Low NVR *and* Low PS	4.1	0.0	4.4
15.	Low NVR *and* Low WM	7.6	2.1	5.3
	Phonological Processing and Clusters	**Ages 6:0–12:11 (N = 123)**	**Ages 6:0–12:11 (N = 24)**	**Ages 6:0–12:11 (N = 1,400)**
16.	High Phonological Processing (PhP)	5.7	12.5	11.4
17.	Low PhP	17.1	0.0	9.4
18.	Low S, High V *and* Low PhP	0.8	0.0	1.4
19.	Low V, High S *and* Low PhP	4.1	0.0	1.5
20.	Low NVR *and* Low PhP	4.1	0.0	1.4

Table 7.6. Percentage of Children with SLD in Reading and SLD in Reading and Written Expression Who Show Each Profile

Group	Cluster Score Profiles	LD-R plus LD-RW (N = 99)	DAS and BAS-II Data: LD/Dyslexic w/ Word Reading < 85 (N = 277)[a]
1.	Flat Cluster Profile	9.1	
2.	Low Spatial (S), High Verbal (V)	13.1	6.1
3.	Low V, High S	17.2	16.6
4.	High Nonverbal Reasoning (NVR)	11.1	5.1
5.	Low NVR	18.2	34.7
6.	High Processing Speed (PS)	23.2	
7.	Low PS	29.3	
8.	High Working Memory (WM)	26.3	
9.	Low WM	22.2	
10.	Low S, High V *and* Low PS	5.1	
11.	Low V, High S *and* Low PS	3.0	
12.	Low S, High V *and* Low WM	1.0	
13.	Low V, High S *and* Low WM	2.0	
14.	Low NVR *and* Low PS	7.1	
15.	Low NVR *and* Low WM	9.1	

	Phonological Processing and Clusters	Ages 6:0–12:11 (N = 89)	
16.	High Phonological Processing (PhP)	6.7	
17.	Low PhP	15.7	
18.	Low S, High V *and* Low PhP	1.1	
19.	Low V, High S *and* Low PhP	2.2	
20.	Low NVR *and* Low PhP	4.5	

[a]See text for full explanation. Frequency for flat profile omitted due to lack of comparability. Frequencies for groups 6–20 omitted due to unavailability of data on the DAS.

DON'T FORGET

1. Never assume that children with SLDs in Reading have a single, defining profile of cognitive strengths and weaknesses. They don't.
2. Always investigate the specific cognitive processing strengths and weaknesses of an individual child, and validate them wherever possible against information from home and school.

most relevant comparison is with the total standardization sample, shown in Table 7.5. As might be expected, a relatively large number of children in this sample have low Spatial Ability scores (16 percent), and only 7 percent have high Spatial scores. A large percentage have significantly low NVR scores (28 percent), low Processing Speed (35 percent), and low Working Memory (28 percent). The evidence suggests that there are multiple possible causes for SLD in Mathematics, requiring the evaluator to investigate each possible cause carefully.

All these results for the various SLD samples demonstrate considerable diversity in cognitive processing in children with learning disabilities. Every SLD group has some children who have significantly high scores on a given cluster, and others who have significantly low scores. The majority of children (86 percent to 91 percent, depending on the sample) have at least one significantly low or high cluster score. Moreover, only about one sixth of those with SLD in Reading have significantly low scores in Phonological Processing, showing that this is a problem for some, but by no means all, poor readers. There is no single profile for children with SLD in Reading or with SLD in Mathematics. The evidence strongly shows that these are not unitary conditions. All children must be assessed individually in order to reveal their specific processing strengths and weaknesses.

Previous Results from the DAS

The frequency of profiles of core cluster scores that have been found for the DAS first edition are also summarized in Table 7.6. These data were obtained for substantial clinical samples of children with SLD in Reading or with dyslexia, gathered during the late 1990s. Note that no data are available for the DAS on anything other than the core clusters because the first edition did not have Processing Speed or Working Memory clusters, nor did it contain a Phonological Processing subtest. However, the findings on frequencies in the core cluster groups for five DAS and BAS-II samples, which were drawn from various states in the United States and also from the United Kingdom, were astonishingly consistent (see Elliott, 2001, 2005). Compared with the DAS-II sample, the DAS/BAS-II

Table 7.7. Percentage of Children with SLD in Mathematics Who Show Each Profile

Group	Cluster Score Profiles	LD-M (N = 43)
1.	Flat Cluster Profile	14.0
2.	Low Spatial (S), High Verbal (V)	16.3
3.	Low V, High S	7.0
4.	High Nonverbal Reasoning (NVR)	16.3
5.	Low NVR	27.9
6.	High Processing Speed (PS)	20.9
7.	Low PS	34.9
8.	High Working Memory (WM)	16.3
9.	Low WM	27.9
10.	Low S, High V *and* Low PS	7.0
11.	Low V, High S *and* Low PS	0.0
12.	Low S, High V *and* Low WM	9.3
13.	Low V, High S *and* Low WM	2.3
14.	Low NVR *and* Low PS	11.6
15.	Low NVR *and* Low WM	7.0

low-frequency groups had lower frequencies, and the high-frequency groups had higher frequencies. The order of frequency for these groups is the same, however, for both the DAS/BAS-II and the DAS-II. Children with high NVR form the lowest-incidence group, followed closely by the low-Spatial, high-Verbal group. The third largest group in both samples comprises children with the low-Verbal, high-Spatial cluster scores. Finally, on both the DAS/BAS-II and the DAS-II, children with significantly low-NVR profiles form the largest group. The difference in incidence, though, is striking, with nearly twice as many being in that group from the DAS/BAS-II sample.

We repeat: When tested with the DAS or BAS-II, more than one third of the children with reading difficulties fell into the low-NVR group. Considering the different times and settings when these data were gathered, the results were remarkably similar, providing mutual cross-validation of these findings. The mean profile for the children in this low-NVR group—dyslexic and SLD—is shown in Figure 7.1. The differences between the mean scores are dramatic—Nonverbal Reasoning is lower than both the Verbal and Spatial means by more than one standard deviation.

Why should we have such a difference between results from the DAS and the DAS-II? It is unlikely to be due to differences in test materials. The test items in the DAS-II core subtests are generally not very different between the two editions. It is possible that the different criteria for gathering the clinical samples

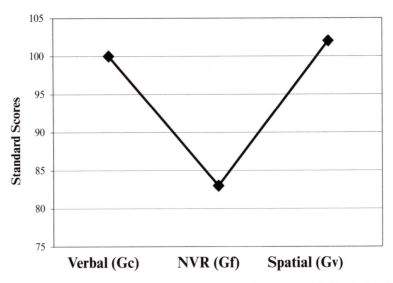

Figure 7.1. Mean Scores on DAS Clusters for 96 Students with Dyslexia/CD in the Low NVR Group

at the time of the DAS-II standardization resulted in the SLD samples not being fully representative of the population of children who are SLD in reading. Whatever the reason for the difference, we would advise readers and users of the DAS-II to be prepared for a substantial number of children with dyslexia or SLD in reading to have difficulties in solving the reasoning problems in the Matrices and Sequential and Quantitative Reasoning subtests, thereby showing the low-NVR profile.

Why should children with reading disabilities score poorly on the two DAS-II subtests measuring nonverbal reasoning? The answer seems most plausibly to lie in the nature of the tasks of reading and "nonverbal" reasoning. Reading requires a high level of visual/verbal integration in order to convert visual printed codes into sounds and words. For fluent reading, and for recognition of common words or letter strings, an individual needs information in the auditory/verbal and visual processing systems to be effectively integrated. Similarly, to perform well on the DAS-II Nonverbal Reasoning tasks (or indeed any good measures of fluid reasoning) one needs good integration of the visual and verbal processing systems. These tasks are presented visually—hence the term "nonverbal" that describes them—but to solve the problems effectively, the use of internal language to label and to mediate the solution of the problems is generally essential. In the case of an individual who has excellent verbal and spatial abilities, if the two brain processing systems specialized for those abilities do not "talk" to each other effectively, this may have an adverse effect on performance both in reasoning and in reading acquisition.

Readers may wonder why these striking findings, on two independent samples, have not been reported previously for other test batteries. The simple and short answer (because there is insufficient space to elaborate on it) is that all other psychometric batteries used with children, with one exception, do not have three separate measures of Verbal ability (*Gc*), Spatial ability (*Gv*), and Nonverbal Reasoning ability (*Gf*). The exception is the WJ III whose *Gf* measures are described by Mather and Woodcock (2001) as "controlled learning" tasks, and as such differ in a number of important respects from the DAS Nonverbal Reasoning subtests.

In the last resort, we can say that while discussions of differences between samples or between instruments in the frequencies of particular profile types are of some academic interest, they don't help us much when we are faced with an individual child to assess who has learning difficulties. Although there may be common features between some children in the cognitive processes and background circumstances that underlie their difficulties, we should treat each one as unique. The DAS-II illuminates many of these individual differences

APPLICATION OF THE DAS-II IN THE ASSESSMENT OF ATTENTION-DEFICIT/HYPERACTIVITY DISORDER (ADHD)

Attention-Deficit/Hyperactivity Disorder (ADHD) is one of the most common disorders of childhood. According to the American Psychological Association (APA, 2000) it is found in approximately 3 percent to 7 percent of the school population. At the time of the DAS-II standardization, a sample of 98 ADHD children was obtained, representing the various ADHD subtypes (i.e., they met the *DSM-IV-TR* criteria for the predominantly inattentive type, or the predominantly hyperactive-impulsive type, or they had been diagnosed as ADHD by a physician or psychiatrist). Children ranged in age from 5 years to 17:11. Additionally, they had existing scores of 80 or more on a standardized cognitive ability measure.

In addition, data were also collected for a sample of 56 children with Attention-Deficit/Hyperactivity Disorder (ADHD) who also had a Learning Disorder. Such co-morbidity is well documented (Mayes, Calhoun, & Crowell, 1998; Shanahan et al., 2006; Swanson, Mink, & Bocian, 1999; Wilcutt et al., 2001). To be selected for this group, children met the criteria for both the SLD and the ADHD groups.

The groups of children with ADHD were individually matched with children from the DAS-II standardization sample, the matching being done on the basis of age, sex, race/ethnicity, parent education level, and geographic region.

Sample with ADHD Only

As in the case of the children with SLD, the ADHD sample was compared with their matched controls on all the DAS-II subtests, clusters, and composites. Significant differences were found for all cluster and composite scores, with generally small to moderate effect sizes. Only one cluster showed a relatively large effect size between the ADHD and control group: the School Readiness cluster. Data were only obtained from 36 children on this cluster, because its operating age range is only between 6 years and 8:11. On this cluster, the mean standard scores for the ADHD sample and the control group were 97.9 and 106.5, respectively. The standard difference (effect size) was .73. This finding is neither surprising nor particularly large (only about three fourths a standard deviation difference in scores). The ADHD sample had scores on other clusters that were lower than the controls by between 4 and 7 standard score points. At the subtest level, only small to moderate effect sizes were observed, with T score differences generally in the range of about 2 to 5 points in favor of the control group. The findings are consistent with research indicating that children with ADHD typically achieve cognitive test scores near the average range of intellectual functioning.

Sample with Combined ADHD and SLD

The results for this sample, and those of the controls, are shown in Table 7.8. Clusters with the largest effect sizes are School Readiness, Working Memory, and Processing Speed. This group also has a lower mean score on the Sequential and Quantitative Reasoning and Phonological Processing subtests. These findings are consistent with current research indicating that children with ADHD/LD typically experience a wide variety of cognitive weaknesses on measures of working memory, attention, executive functioning, processing speed, and phonological processing (Bonafina et al., 2000; Pennington et al., 2003). It is also interesting to note that this ADHD/LD group performed significantly worse than the ADHD group on tasks measuring processing speed, working memory, and auditory short-term memory, suggesting that these processes play a larger role in ADHD/LD than in ADHD alone, and underscoring the need for careful assessment of cognitive abilities in children referred for evaluation of suspected ADHD.

The data for the sample with ADHD/LD were also analyzed to evaluate how many children in this sample have various cognitive profiles on the DAS-II. The

Table 7.8. Mean Performance of Children with ADHD-LD, Showing Subtests, Clusters, and Composites with Relatively Large Effect Sizes (Standard Differences)

Subtest/Cluster Composite	ADHD and Learning Disorder			Matched Controls		Group Comparison	
	Mean	SD	N	Mean	SD	Difference	Standard Difference
Subtest							
SQR	45.1	8.7	56	52.2	10.6	7.1	.72
DigF	42.7	9.1	56	50.5	10.8	7.8	.78
ENC	43.4	10.7	22	51.8	8.5	8.4	.88
SIP	44.2	9.3	56	51.6	11.9	7.4	.70
DigB	42.2	10.2	56	50.8	9.5	8.6	.87
PhP	46.2	8.5	47	52.3	8.5	6.1	.72
Cluster							
SchR	90.7	13.4	22	102.1	9.4	11.4	.99
WMem	88.5	13.5	56	101.4	15.1	12.9	.90
PSp	90.3	13.9	56	100.6	15.7	10.4	.70

Key: SQR = Sequential and Quantitative Reasoning; DigF = Recall of Digits, Forward; ENC = Early Number Concepts; SIP = Speed of Information Processing; DigB = Recall of Digits, Backward; PhP = Phonological Processing; SchR = School Readiness; WMem = Working Memory; PSp = Processing Speed.

percentages of children with each profile are shown in Table 7.9. When compared with the poor readers with significant discrepancy shown in Table 7.5, the ADHD/LD group has more children with flat cluster profiles. They have more children who have significantly low scores on Processing Speed (28 percent) and Working Memory (32 percent). There are more who are in the Low Spatial, High Verbal group, and also more who have significantly *high* scores on Phonological Processing (15 percent).

As with the samples of children with SLD, these frequencies underline the diversity of cognitive profiles found between ADHD and ADHD/LD children.

APPLICATION OF THE DAS-II IN THE ASSESSMENT OF MENTAL RETARDATION

A sample of 72 children identified as having mild to moderate mental retardation was compared with a matched control group drawn from the DAS-II standard-

Table 7.9. Percentages of Children with Combined ADHD and Learning Disorder Who Show Various Profiles

Group	Cluster Score Profiles	ADHD plus Learning Disorder ($N = 57$)
1.	Flat Cluster Profile	19.3
2.	Low Spatial (S), High Verbal (V)	19.3
3.	Low V, High S	10.5
4.	High Nonverbal Reasoning (NVR)	12.3
5.	Low NVR	19.3
6.	High Processing Speed (PS)	24.6
7.	Low PS	28.1
8.	High Working Memory (WM)	12.3
9.	Low WM	31.6
10.	Low S, High V *and* Low PS	12.3
11.	Low V, High S *and* Low PS	5.3
12.	Low S, High V *and* Low WM	7.0
13.	Low V, High S *and* Low WM	1.8
14.	Low NVR *and* Low PS	5.3
15.	Low NVR *and* Low WM	10.5
	Phonological Processing and Clusters	**Ages 6:0–12:11 ($N = 41$)**
16.	High Phonological Processing (PhP)	14.6
17.	Low PhP	8.3
18.	Low S, High V *and* Low PhP	2.1
19.	Low V, High S *and* Low PhP	2.1
20.	Low NVR *and* Low PhP	2.1

ization sample. Children in the clinical sample were drawn from an age range of 2:6 through 17:11, and all children met the DSM-IV-TR criteria for Mental Retardation, Mild or Moderate Severity. All had previously obtained IQ scores on standardized cognitive ability tests of between 40 and 70.

Not surprisingly, the mean scores of the Mentally Retarded sample were lower than the control group on every subtest, every cluster, and every composite in the DAS-II battery. Results showed:

1. Mean T scores on the subtests ranged from a low of 21 on Verbal Similarities to a high of 33.5 on Rapid Naming, with an overall mean T score of 26.2. In contrast, the control group subtest means were, as expected, centered around a mean T score of 50. Standard differences (the measure of effect size) for subtests ranged from a low of 1.58 for Rapid Naming to a high of 3.32 for Early Number Concepts, with a mean effect size of 2.54.

Table 7.10. Means and Standard Deviations of DAS-II Cluster and Composite Scores Obtained by a Sample of 74 Children with Mental Retardation

Cluster or Composite	Mean	SD
Verbal	54.1	14.1
Nonverbal Reasoning	60.7	12.5
Spatial	58.8	17.5
School Readiness	49.9	15.0
Working Memory	57.3	17.1
Processing Speed	67.8	17.7
GCA	51.0	13.7
Special Nonverbal Composite	55.1	14.6

2. On the clusters, the Mentally Retarded group had standard score means ranging from 49.9 (School Readiness) to 67.8 (Processing Speed), with an overall mean standard score of 58.1. Effect sizes for clusters ranged from 2.16 to 3.88 (mean effect size 3.05).
3. Finally, the composite scores reflected the low subtest and cluster scores, with the mean GCA score for this group being 51.0 and the mean Special Nonverbal composite being 55.1, with effect sizes of 3.77 and 3.38 respectively.

Clearly every effect size in this analysis can be considered extremely large. The results clearly demonstrate that the DAS-II subtests, clusters, and composites are able effectively to measure the cognitive abilities of children with mild to moderate mental retardation and to discriminate between them and non-retarded children. Means and SDs of cluster and composite scores for this sample are shown in Table 7.10.

As indicated earlier in this book, the low floors of the DAS-II on most subtests—with T scores going down as low as 10—makes the instrument suitable for use for cognitive assessment in cases where mental retardation is suspected. Rapid Reference 7.1 shows the lowest possible scores for children taking the Upper Early Years and the School Age batteries, using age-appropriate norm tables. Scores of 30 are 4.67 standard deviations below the mean of 100. For children in the age range of 9:0 to 17:11 who obtain very low scores on the School Age battery, and for whom the Early Years battery is developmentally most appropriate, Rapid Reference 7.1 shows the lowest

≡ *Rapid Reference 7.1*

Lowest Possible Standard Scores Obtainable

Core Cluster or Composite	Lowest Possible Standard Score	
	Early Years Battery	School Age Battery
Verbal Ability	30	31
Nonverbal Reasoning Ability	32	31
Spatial Ability	34	32
GCA	30	30
Special Nonverbal Composite	30	30
Extended Cluster or Composite (ages 9:0—17:11)		
Verbal Ability	25	N/A
Nonverbal Reasoning Ability	25	N/A
Spatial Ability	25	N/A
GCA	25	N/A
Special Nonverbal Composite	25	N/A

≡ *Rapid Reference 7.2*

Das-II Features Making It Suitable for Use With Low-Functioning Children

1. The DAS-II has very low floors on clusters and composites.
2. Extended cluster and composite scores are provided for very low-scoring children in the CD accompanying this book.
3. Varied test materials, including low number of entirely verbal subtests.
4. Age appropriate norms are available for the Early Years battery to age 8:11.

scores obtainable using extended cluster and composite scores. Tables enabling you to obtain these extended cluster and composite scores are provided on the CD accompanying this book. These and other features that make the DAS-II suitable for assessing children with mental retardation are shown in Rapid Reference 7.2.

APPLICATION OF THE DAS-II IN THE ASSESSMENT OF INTELLECTUALLY GIFTED CHILDREN

A sample of 68 children identified as intellectually gifted was compared with a matched control group drawn from the DAS-II standardization sample. Children in the clinical sample were drawn from an age range of 5:0 through 17:11, and all children had previously obtained IQ scores on standardized cognitive ability tests of 130 or greater. That is, they were previously assessed as being 2 SDs or more above the mean for their age.

Results are shown in Table 7.11. The mean scores of these children on the DAS-II core subtests and core clusters were all well above-average, and discriminated this intellectually gifted sample significantly from the control group. Their highest mean scores of 125.4 were obtained on the Verbal cluster and on the GCA composite. Their mean scores on the Copying and Recall of Designs subtests were a little lower ($T = 56.4$ and 57.9, respectively) with small effect sizes. It is important to remember that, because of regression toward the mean, children selected for extremely high scores are likely to, on average, score lower on a second test of intellectual abilities. This is the most important reason for relatively low scores for intellectually gifted groups reported in the manuals of most well-designed tests of intellectual abilities. This normal and expected pattern should not discourage evaluators considering tests for assessment of intellectually gifted children..

Among the diagnostic clusters and subtests there were somewhat lower mean scores and effect sizes. The Processing Speed cluster had the lowest mean score (112.0), and indeed all the diagnostic clusters had scores below the level of the GCA score. This finding is consistent with previous research on the WISC-III showing that children identified as intellectually gifted had more variability and lower mean performance on tests measuring processing speed (Sparrow & Gurland, 1998; Watkins, Greenawalt, & Marcell, 2002).

The results from this sample provide strong evidence that the DAS-II provides scores that are useful in the assessment of intellectual giftedness. The results are, of course, limited to children who have been identified as *intellectually* gifted and should not be generalized to children who are gifted in other domains.

APPLICATION OF THE DAS-II IN THE ASSESSMENT OF YOUNG CHILDREN DEVELOPMENTALLY AT RISK

Part C of the *Individuals with Disabilities Education Act* (U.S. Congress, 2004) recognizes children at risk as having developmental delay in one or more of the

Table 7.11. Mean Performance of Intellectually Gifted Children, Showing Subtests, Clusters, and Composites with Relatively Large Effect Sizes (Standard Differences)

Subtest/Cluster Composite	Intellectually Gifted			Matched Controls		Group Comparison	
	Mean	SD	N	Mean	SD	Difference	Standard Difference
Subtests (Core)							
VComp	66.7	12.1	33	54.0	10.0	−12.7	−1.15
PSim	59.7	12.0	33	51.1	7.6	−8.6	−.86
NVoc	64.8	9.7	33	53.3	8.2	−11.5	−1.29
WDef	63.8	7.6	68	54.1	8.2	−9.7	−1.23
PCon	61.7	9.4	68	53.6	7.1	−8.1	−.98
Mat	63.1	8.4	68	53.5	8.8	−9.6	−1.12
VSim	64.2	7.5	68	53.6	7.6	−10.6	−1.40
SQR	63.7	11.6	68	53.0	9.1	−10.7	−1.03
Subtests (Diagnostic)							
DigF	59.7	9.3	68	52.9	8.8	−6.8	−.75
RSO	61.5	9.2	68	53.6	7.3	−7.9	−.96
PhP	58.8	6.8	50	52.8	7.1	−6.0	−.85
Cluster							
Verbal	125.4	12.2	68	106.2	12.5	−19.2	−1.55
NVR	121.4	12.8	68	104.8	11.4	−16.6	−1.36
Spatial	117.8	12.3	68	106.0	10.8	−11.8	−1.01
SchR	114.6	9.0	33	104.6	11.7	−10.0	−.96
WMem	116.7	12.0	68	105.2	11.2	−11.5	−1.00
Composite							
GCA	125.4	10.3	68	106.8	11.0	−18.6	−1.74
SNC	121.8	10.9	68	106.3	10.7	−15.5	−1.44

Key: VComp = Verbal Comprehension; PSim = Picture Similarities; NVoc = Naming Vocabulary; WDef = Word Definitions; PCon = Pattern Construction; Mat = Matrices; VSim = Verbal Similarities; SQR = Sequential and Quantitative Reasoning; DigF = Recall of Digits Forward; RSO = Recall of Sequential Order; PhP = Phonological Processing; NVR = Nonverbal Reasoning; SchR = School Readiness; WMem = Working Memory; GCA = General Conceptual Ability; SNC = Special Nonverbal Composite.

following areas of development: physical, cognitive, communication, social or emotional, and adaptive. There are clearly a number of biological and environmental factors that can place a child at risk of delay in his or her development. The DAS-II Early Years battery was administered to a sample of 49 children in the age range of 3:0–4:11 if they met one of the following criteria placing them at risk for a developmental or cognitive delay: (a) one or more developmental risk factors including chromosomal abnormalities, genetic/congenital disorders, respiratory distress as a newborn, brain hemorrhage, infection, and nutritional deprivation; or (b) were diagnosed with a physical or mental condition that typically results in developmental delay; or (c) were born prematurely, weighing less than 5.51 lbs; or (d) were born at less than 36 weeks gestation. Risk factors were not included that are due to social conditions, socioeconomic status, or parent education level.

Scores obtained by the at-risk sample were compared with those of a matched control group drawn from the DAS-II standardization sample. Results are shown in Table 7.12, which presents mean scores on those subtests, clusters, and composites that have moderate (above .50) to large effect sizes.

For the developmental risk group, the lowest cluster or composite score was the GCA, which was about 12 points below the mean of the control group, but it should be said that all clusters and composites have very similar mean scores. The largest effect size was on the Verbal cluster. At the subtest level, there were large effect sizes for Matching Letter-Like Forms and Early Number Concepts, with moderate effects for Recall of Digits Forward, Naming Vocabulary, and Pattern Construction. Taken together, these results are consistent with recent evidence that there is a relationship between developmental risk and difficulties on measures of language processing, memory, and learning (Briscoe, Gathercole & Marlow, 2001; Korkman, Kettunen, & Autti-Ramo, 2003; O'Leary, 2004).

The DAS-II has been designed to be very appealing to young children. The subtests have good floors. Rapid Reference 7.3 shows the T scores obtainable on each subtest for low-scoring children at various ages from 2:6 to 3:11 who only obtain a raw score of 1 point on each subtest. For the core subtests, even for the youngest age of 2:6, all T scores are at least two standard deviations below the mean. If a child of age 2:6 obtained those core subtest scores, he or she would have a GCA score of 59. Age 3:6 is the lowest age level for the Matrices and Copying subtests, so at that age, T scores are at their highest level for a raw score of 1. However, if a child of that age had great difficulty with those subtests, the examiner would be able to use the Lower Early Years subtests in order to obtain estimates of scores for Verbal and Nonverbal ability and for the GCA. At age

Table 7.12. Mean Performance of Young Children Who are Developmentally At-Risk, Showing Subtests, Clusters and Composites with Moderate to Large Effect Sizes (Standard Differences)

Subtest/Cluster Composite	Developmentally At Risk			Matched Controls			Group Comparison	
	Mean	SD	N	Mean	SD		Difference	Standard Difference
Subtests (Core)								
VComp	46.2	12.5	49	52.9	9.9		6.7	.60
NVoc	46.4	12.0	49	53.4	8.5		7.0	.68
PCon	47.4	13.3	49	53.9	10.9		6.5	.54
Subtests (Diagnostic)								
DigF	43.6	14.6	49	52.3	8.3		8.7	.73
RPic	45.7	10.7	49	52.0	10.0		6.3	.61
ENC	45.8	8.3	49	53.6	8.2		7.8	.94
MLLF	40.2	11.3	26	50.2	10.9		10.0	.91
Cluster								
Verbal	94.0	18.1	49	105.7	14.3		11.7	.72
NVR	92.8	16.1	49	100.6	14.4		7.8	.51
Spatial	95.8	20.7	37	105.3	16.4		9.5	.51
Composite								
GCA	92.5	18.4	47	104.4	15.6		11.9	.70
SNC	93.0	19.9	37	103.5	16.6		10.5	.57

Key: VComp = Verbal Comprehension; NVoc = Naming Vocabulary; PCon = Pattern Construction; DigF = Recall of Digits Forward; RPic = Recognition of Pictures; ENC = Early Number Concepts; MLLF = Matching Letter-Like Forms; NVR = Nonverbal Reasoning; GCA = General Conceptual Ability; SNC = Special Nonverbal Composite.

3:6, if a child obtained raw scores of 1 on the Lower early Years core subtests, he or she would have a GCA of 43.

Clearly, if a very young child is suspected of being in the cognitive range of mental retardation, it would be advisable to supplement the DAS-II with a test such as the *Bayley Scales for Infant and Toddler Development—Third Edition* (Bayley, 2006), which starts at a younger age and therefore has low floors for children in the 2:6 to 3:6 age range. In general, however, the DAS-II materials and subtest floors make it a suitable and attractive battery for the evaluation of children referred as at risk of developmental or cognitive delay.

≡ Rapid Reference 7.3

T Scores Equivalent to a Raw Score of 1 for Each Early Years Subtest from Ages 2:6 to 4:2

Early Years Subtests	T Scores Obtained by a Raw Score of 1 at These Ages:			
	2:6	3:0	3:6	4:0
Core Subtests				
Verbal Comprehension	24	19	14	10
Picture Similarities	30	25	21	17
Naming Vocabulary	24	20	15	11
Pattern Construction	28	23	18	11
Matrices	N/A	N/A	31	28
Copying	N/A	N/A	34	26
Diagnostic Subtests				
Recall of Digits, Forward	39	34	28	23
Recognition of Pictures	40	38	34	28
Early Number Concepts	31	28	24	22

APPLICATION OF THE DAS-II IN THE ASSESSMENT OF LANGUAGE DISABILITIES

According to *DSM-IV-TR,* children diagnosed with mixed Receptive-Expressive Language Disorder (RELD) generally have lower scores on measures of both receptive and expressive language than on nonverbal ability measures (American Psychiatric Association, 2000). Results from studies on children with RELD suggest that they have great difficulties with rapid naming and picture naming tasks (Lahey & Edwards, 1999), as well as in reading and language comprehension (Bishop, 1992).

The DAS-II was administered to two samples of children with language disabilities. One sample consisted of 54 children with Expressive Language Disorder—not fully reported here—and another of 62 children with RELD in the age range of 3:0–13:11, which is the sample we shall focus on. Children were selected for this sample according to *DSM-IV-TR* criteria or they had existing scores on a comprehensive assessment of language that were in the clinically significant range for both receptive and expressive language. Moreover, they had existing scores of 80 or more on a standardized measure of cognitive ability, or had been assessed as having at least low-average intellectual functioning by a speech/language professional. Their language impairment was judged not to be due to a deficit in speech proficiency or fluency only. As before, this sample was individually matched with children from the DAS-II standardization sample who formed a control group for comparison purposes.

Table 7.13 shows the mean scores for the RELD and control samples on those subtests, clusters, and composites that have relatively large effect sizes of 0.7 and above. All mean scores on every DAS-II subtest, cluster, and composite were lower than those of the matched controls, and all differences except one were statistically significant at or beyond the $p < .01$ level.

The core cluster scores all show very large differences between the samples, with the Verbal cluster being marginally the lowest for the RELD group. Among the diagnostic clusters, the RELD sample has even lower means on the School Readiness and Working Memory clusters. The School Readiness result is not surprising, as children with this disorder may be expected to have major problems in acquiring reading and numeracy skills. Working Memory, too, requires much rehearsal of word strings in order to get the word lists into correct order, and language disability is likely to have a major impact on such tasks. Similarly, the low score of the RELD group on the Nonverbal Reasoning cluster and its component subtests suggests that children with RELD are unable to solve visually presented problems that require internal verbal mediation. We conclude that *a verbal disorder has a major impact on a wide range of cognitive domains, some of which do not appear at first sight to be verbal.*

The mean of the RELD sample on the Processing Speed cluster, although well below that of the controls, has a smaller effect size due to the large SD of scores in the RELD group. This suggests that some children with RELD obtain relatively high scores on Processing Speed, even though the majority does not.

Elliott (2007b, p. 201) has commented that the results for the sample with Expressive Language Disorder (receptive language being intact) are almost identical to those for the RELD sample, which is the reason we present only the results for the latter group here.

In developing the DAS-II, decisions were made to keep the number of specifically verbal subtests relatively small in comparison with some other batteries. Children with RELD have low scores on the verbal subtests in the DAS-II, and this provides evidence on the construct validity of those verbal measures. However, in order to make a full diagnosis of a language disorder of any kind, the DAS-II should be supplemented with a comprehensive assessment of language.

Table 7.13. Mean Performance of Children with Mixed Receptive-Expressive Language Disorder, Showing Subtests, Clusters, and Composites with Relatively Large Effect Sizes (Standard Differences)

Subtest/Cluster Composite	Expressive Language Disorder			Matched Controls		Group Comparison	
	Mean	SD	N	Mean	SD	Difference	Standard Difference
Subtests (Core)							
VComp	40.1	8.3	40	49.5	7.9	9.4	1.16
NVoc	39.6	7.2	41	48.5	8.0	8.9	1.17
WDef	35.9	9.1	44	49.7	8.8	13.8	1.54
PCon	37.0	10.3	62	47.5	9.4	10.5	1.06
Mat	39.7	9.9	59	48.9	10.5	9.2	.90
Copy	41.7	10.7	35	48.1	6.3	6.4	.74
VSim	39.6	8.7	44	50.9	9.5	11.3	1.25
SQR	37.7	9.3	44	49.1	8.8	11.4	1.26
Subtests (Diagnostic)							
DigF	41.1	10.1	62	50.0	10.3	8.9	.87
RPic	42.1	9.5	62	49.4	8.5	7.3	.82
ENC	40.0	8.6	41	48.6	9.0	8.6	.99
MLLF	40.2	11.7	31	51.7	9.9	11.5	1.06
RSO	35.1	11.1	42	51.0	12.6	15.9	1.34
DigB	35.3	12.4	44	49.6	9.3	14.3	1.31
PhP	40.5	11.4	40	49.1	9.9	8.6	.81
RNam	40.9	10.6	44	49.3	10.6	8.4	.79
Cluster							
Verbal	80.8	12.2	62	98.7	12.5	17.9	1.45
NVR	81.7	12.8	62	96.8	13.8	15.1	1.14
Spatial	81.4	14.0	57	96.2	13.0	14.8	1.10
SchR	79.2	15.2	23	100.1	14,7	20.9	1.40
WMem	76.2	15.7	42	101.1	15.6	24.9	1.59
PSp	86.2	14.6	44	97.9	17.9	11.7	.71
Composite							
GCA	78.5	11.0	60	96.6	13.2	18.1	1.49
SNC	79.8	12.9	57	96.3	13.3	16.5	1.26

Key: VComp = Verbal Comprehension; NVoc = Naming Vocabulary; WDef = Word Definitions; PCon = Pattern Construction; Mat = Matrices; Copy = Copying; VSim = Verbal Similarities; SQR = Sequential and Quantitative Reasoning; DigF = Recall of Digits Forward; RPic = Recognition of Pictures; ENC = Early Number Concepts; MLLF = Matching Letter-Like Forms; RSO = Recall of Sequential Order; DigB = Recall of Digits, Backward; PhP = Phonological Processing; RNam = Rapid Naming; NVR = Nonverbal Reasoning; SchR = School Readiness; WMem = Working Memory; PSp = Processing Speed; GCA = General Conceptual Ability; SNC = Special Nonverbal Composite.

Overall, the results of these studies are consistent with research showing that children with language disorders tend to have global deficits in cognitive functioning, and relatively better performance on nonverbal than verbal tasks (Beitchman et al., 1996; Bishop, 1992; Doll & Boren, 1993; Rose, Lincoln, & Allen, 1992). These results highlight how children diagnosed with RELD might be at increased risk for classroom difficulties, even on tasks that rely minimally on receptive or expressive language skills.

APPLICATION OF THE DAS-II IN THE ASSESSMENT OF CHILDREN WITH AUTISM SPECTRUM DISORDER (ASD)

A study using the first edition of the DAS was reported by Joseph, Tager-Flusberg and Lord (2002). One of the issues addressed by the study was whether children with autism exhibit characteristic patterns of unevenness in their cognitive abilities, and if so, whether such patterns or profiles differ as a function of age or overall ability.

Of the 120 children participating in the study, 73 were given the DAS Preschool battery (now called the Early Years battery in the DAS-II) and 47 were tested on the School-Age battery. Of the 73 who were administered the Preschool DAS, 35 (48 percent) had Verbal (V) cluster scores that were significantly lower than their Nonverbal (NV) cluster scores, which we denote as V < NV. Six individuals (8 percent) had V scores significantly higher than NV (V > NV), and 32 (44 percent) exhibited no discrepancy (V = NV). The frequency of children having any discrepancy between the V and NV scores (56 percent) was significantly higher than the 30 percent shown in the DAS standardization sample. Of those who were administered the School Age battery, 16 (34 percent) had V < NV, 18 (38 percent) exhibited a V = NV profile, and 13 (28 percent) exhibited a V > NV profile. Once again, the number of individuals showing significant discrepancies between their V and NV scores (62 percent) was significantly higher than in the standardization sample.

Discrepantly high and low subtest scores were also examined, and the authors found a higher frequency of these than would be expected in the general population. There was a high degree of individual variation in cognitive profiles, and no evidence for a modal profile in either the preschool or the school-age group. As in the case of children with learning disorder (reviewed earlier in this chapter), the results from the study by Joseph and his colleagues point to the wide range of individual differences exhibited by children within clinical diagnostic categories.

While a brief review does not do justice to a detailed and complex study on children with ASD, it is worth reporting some conclusions of the authors about the DAS: "One of the main advantages of the DAS, and particularly of the School-Age version, is that it groups subtests in conceptually homogeneous clusters that allow a clearer comparison of differential abilities than is possible with other measures such as the Wechsler scales. Further, the extended range of possible standard scores on the DAS, and the relatively brief amount of time required for its administration, contribute to its usefulness in identifying reliable and valid distinctions in the cognitive abilities of children with developmental disorders" (Joseph et al., p. 818). The DAS-II enhances those desirable features listed above, and should prove to be an illuminating, engaging and efficient instrument for the assessment of children with ASD.

CHAPTER SUMMARY

We have reviewed a number of clinical areas in which special group studies were made of children's response to, and performance on, the DAS-II. The battery was designed to be suitable for a wide range of clinical applications. It is widely used in the evaluation and diagnosis of specific learning disabilities. It is designed for use with children of a wide range of chronological ages and developmental levels, and to be suitable for the evaluation of children at both ends of the ability spectrum: those with mental retardation, those who are intellectually gifted, and all gradations in between. Further research is needed to provide further data on the characteristics of the DAS-II when applied to clinical samples, and on the nature of subgroups of children within clinical categories when given the DAS-II.

Examiners can use data on the DAS-II scores of groups of children with various disabilities to help themselves understand the unique needs of an individual, but they should never succumb to the temptation to compare a child's DAS-II profile (or profile of scores on any other scale) to a "template" to arrive at a diagnosis. Especially in view of the variability within diagnostic and eligibility categories, it is essential to evaluate each child individually and to incorporate data beyond test scores.

Eight

ILLUSTRATIVE CASE REPORTS

The goal of this chapter is to demonstrate how you might present, in written form, the results of the DAS-II. Each case uses the step-by-step analysis explained in Chapter 4 to arrive at the results, although the reports are not written directly following those steps. The steps should guide the examiner's initial thinking, but the report should not drag the reader through every step the examiner followed. It is an evaluation report, not the examiner's personal diary. The report should be organized to explain, to illustrate, and to guide, and it should take into account (but not necessarily retell) the complete set of information about the examinee and the examinee's situation, not just the statistical outcomes of the testing. Complete statistical tables, descriptions of tests used, details of tests of significance and base rates, and other data can be placed at the end of the report or in an appendix, which allows the examiner to cite in text only the information that is necessary and germane to most readers. Please see Lichtenberger, Mather, Kaufman, and Kaufman (2004), Sattler (2008), and Sattler and Hoge (2006) for additional suggestions about writing reports. As with most comprehensive reports, interpretation must go beyond simply an examination of scores. All information gathered must be sifted for its relevance and then what remains is integrated into the evaluation report. In all cases, the following information is provided: reason for referral, background information, behavioral observations, test results and summary, diagnostic impressions, and recommendations.

This chapter contains several real case reports of children referred to their school multidisciplinary teams for a comprehensive psychoeducational evaluation. Obviously there is no one way to write or interpret test data, and so we have chosen to provide several examples written by different evaluators using their own individualized styles. Examiners must always strive to integrate all relevant information gathered from multiple sources. Parents, teachers, and the students themselves make important contributions to the evaluation, and they must be included in the process. It is especially important that examiners elicit genuine referral *questions,* not just "issues" to be answered by the evaluation, either in a permanent, promulgated record of the evaluation team meeting or in the examiner's report. Interviews and questionnaires are often essential parts of a complete evaluation. Evaluation results must be as clear as possible with any jargon and statistics defined clearly. Again, the total evaluation must be integrated, which is not achieved with a staple (Willis & Dumont, 2002, pp. 4, 178, 286).

First case report: Marybeth. Marybeth's scores were presented in Chapter 4 to illustrate the step-by-step interpretation of the DAS-II. The entirety of that process is presented here in Marybeth's case report.

Second case report: Jenna. This report was intentionally written in a way that would not only explain the results from the DAS-II testing but would additionally describe and explain the rationale for using the DAS-II in that specific assessment. Jenna's evaluation was done as part of an ongoing Special Education Due Process and as such may not reflect the same style of writing as would be used for a more traditional psychoeducational report.

Third case report: Allison. This report illustrates the use of stanine scores in a school system in which all evaluators use the same statistical system to provide a lingua franca that allows parents, teachers, advocates, attorneys, and judges to more easily integrate reports from the various disciplines. Scores are also reported in *T* scores and standard scores with 90 percent confidence bands and in percentile ranks, but stanine scores are added in staggered columns. The stanine classification labels subdivide the broad average range into three educationally meaningful classifications: low average, average, and high average, which teachers usually find especially useful.

The report text attempts to describe subtests in sufficient detail to allow the reader to follow the discussion, but a complete description of the DAS-II and the statistics are relegated to the appendix, where interested readers can readily find them. Some information that would attract only a limited audience is put in footnotes.

Conclusions are offered with even more than the normally appropriate caution, and recommendations are omitted because the results of the academic achievement, speech and language, and occupational therapy reports have not yet been shared.

Fourth case report: John. This report concerns a child evaluated because of nonresponse to reading interventions.

CASE REPORT I

Name: Marybeth
Chronological Age: 8 years, 4 months

Reason for Referral

Marybeth is an 8-year-old second-grader referred for evaluation because of continued academic and behavioral problems at school. Marybeth's mother has requested this evaluation to "help explain difficulties in social, behavioral, and academic functioning."

Background Information

A comprehensive interview with Marybeth's mother, Mrs. XX, indicated that Marybeth lives with her birth mother, birth father, and 22-month-old brother. The duration of the pregnancy was 38 weeks, and labor lasted about 18 hours with many hours of pushing and subsequent caesarian section. Her birth weight was 8 pounds, 11 ounces. Marybeth was hospitalized for seven days after delivery. Her mother reported that Marybeth has a congenital birth defect in her spine. Marybeth's mother indicated that, during infancy, Marybeth had disturbed sleep due to breathing problems and that she developed allergies or asthma between five and six months. Developmental milestones were reported to be early to normal with the one exception of language. Mrs. XX reports that Marybeth's language development was slow to begin. Until about the age of four, she remained relatively language free, relying on grunts and gestures to convey her wants and needs. Mrs. XX reports that, between four and five years old, there was "an explosion of language" with Marybeth beginning to speak in almost complete sentences. Mrs. XX indicated that Marybeth's activity level increased as she reached toddlerhood and that her ability to pay attention depends on the topic. Mrs. XX reported that Marybeth still does not sleep through the night without disruption and is a restless sleeper. Marybeth's mother reported that Marybeth's adaptability (how well she deals with change) and her approach/withdrawal (how well she responds to new things) have developed "not well, but getting much better." She indicated that others are "very aware of Marybeth's feelings and that she is happy most of the time, but she went through a very tough time from the past summer until about February." During these months Marybeth was particularly depressed and vocal about her lack of lasting relationships with her friends.

Mrs. XX indicated that Marybeth did well academically in pre-school. However, she reports that, since Marybeth entered first grade, apparent problems have been noted. Marybeth repeated the first grade because the school felt she had not made sufficient progress during that year and attributed Marybeth's difficulties to her "lack of focus" and "her need to mature physically and mentally." Her problems have continued on into second grade. Marybeth's teachers have described the following as significant classroom problems: "She doesn't sit still in her seat, she frequently gets up and walks around the classroom, talks out and doesn't wait to be called on." At home, Marybeth's mother reports that she exhibits the following behaviors to an excessive or exaggerated degree when compared to other children her age: "She fidgets with hands, feet, or squirms in her seat, has difficulty remaining seated when required to do so, and is easily distracted by extraneous stimulation. She has difficulty awaiting her turn in games or group situations, blurts out answers to questions before they have been completed, and has problems following through with instructions (usually not due to opposition or failure to comprehend). She often talks excessively, interrupts or intrudes on others (often not purposeful or planned), has boundless energy, impulsivity and poor self-control, temper outbursts, acts like she is driven by a motor, and frustrates easily." Mrs. XX said that the type of discipline that she uses with Marybeth is time-outs. She indicated that Marybeth works well for a short-term reward. Although Marybeth has difficulty waiting her turn while playing with peers, she seeks friendships but has difficulty starting them and maintaining peers as friends. Her interaction with her peers is described as "bossy," and she seems to take little interest in the wants and desires of her playmates. Mrs. XX stated, "Marybeth is a very kind, smart, and loving little girl, but she just can't seem to get along with others."

In an effort to help Marybeth socialize, her parents have encouraged her to participate in organized group activities (youth soccer and Girl Scouts). Unfortunately, neither of these has been successful. Both her fine- and gross-motor skills are generally underdeveloped, and her experience at youth soccer was, as described by Mrs. XX, "a disaster." When attempting to play in a game, Marybeth walked around the playing field as opposed to running, generally avoided the ball and the game action as best as she could, and was injured when a ball was kicked to her and she did not respond quickly enough. The ball hit her directly in the face and she ended up with a bloody nose and a black eye. Her experience in Girl Scouts was not any more successful. Mrs. XX reports that Marybeth went to the meetings enthusiastically but returned angry, stating that the other girls refused to play with her. When Mrs. XX spoke with the scout leader, she learned that Marybeth had attempted to play with the other girls but had been vocally loud, talked incessantly, and made generally off-task or irrelevant comments.

Tests Administered

Differential Ability Scales–Second Edition (DAS-II)

Behavior Assessment System for Children–Second Edition (BASC-II); Parent & Teacher Scales

Developmental/Readiness informal screening

Childhood History Form (Revised)

Woodcock Johnson Third Edition Tests of Achievement (WJ III Ach)

Delis-Kaplan Executive Functioning System (D-KEFS) selected subtests

Observations

During the first evaluation session, Marybeth, when asked to write her name, wrote only "M b." With some verbal encouragement and prodding, Marybeth correctly spelled her name as she said the letters out loud while writing them down properly. She wrote slowly and in capital letters, and each letter was progressively larger. When asked for her address, she knew both the street address and what town she lives in and could say her telephone number. She correctly stated her birthday and her current age in years. She correctly sang the alphabet. When letters of the alphabet were printed randomly and she was asked to name the letters, she correctly named only five (O, X, T, A, and Y) of the 10 letters presented. Marybeth was able to correctly name the colors, orange, red, blue, green, brown, black, white, gray, and yellow, but confused purple for pink. She named a rectangle, circle, square, star, and triangle, but said that she did not know the names of the diamond and oval shapes. She counted from one to eight correctly, skipped nine, and then said ten. Later, during the same session, she correctly counted out loud from one to 29, but had difficulty recognizing several numbers written as digits on paper.

Behavior Rating Scales

Marybeth's mother and her second grade teacher each completed the BASC-II, which is an integrated system designed to facilitate the differential diagnosis and classification of a variety of emotional and behavioral problems of children. The BASC-II evaluates behavior according to Externalizing Problems, Internalizing Problems, and School Problems. Any score within the clinically significant range suggests a high level of maladjustment. Scores within the at-risk range may identify either a significant problem that may not be severe enough to require formal treatment or a potential of developing a problem that needs careful monitoring.

The Validity Indexes (measures of consistency of responding) were within the Acceptable range on both the mother's and teacher's BASC-II forms, which suggests that these results may be considered valid. On the BASC-II, both raters identified Marybeth as having problems with Externalizing behaviors (Externalizing Problems T score = 65 and 68, respectively) and within that area both rated Hyperactivity as being in the clinically significant range (Hyperactivity T = 72 and 75, respectively). Both Marybeth's mother and her teacher report that she tends to engage in many disruptive, impulsive, and uncontrolled behaviors. In the area of adaptive skills, the raters found that Marybeth demonstrated poor adaptability and social skills.

Test Results and Interpretation

The General Conceptual Ability Score (GCA) is provided as a measure of the general ability of an individual to perform complex mental processing that involves the conceptualization and transformation of information. Marybeth earned a GCA standard score of 110 (104–115, 75PR). While no one score can be perfectly accurate, the chances are good (95 percent) that Marybeth's GCA is within the range of 104 to 115. This would classify her overall cognitive ability, as measured by the DAS-II, as Average to Above Average. Her GCA is ranked at the 75th percentile (PR), indicating that she scored as high as or higher than 75 percent of other individuals of the same age in the standardization sample. However, additional information is needed.

Marybeth demonstrated significant variability in her performance across the three indexes that make up the GCA score. Specifically, the Verbal Ability Cluster score was significantly[1] higher than both the Nonverbal Reasoning and the Spatial Ability Cluster scores, and the Nonverbal Reasoning score was itself significantly higher than the Spatial Ability score. Because of these large differences among her abilities, the GCA may not be a sufficiently meaningful descriptor of her skills. Therefore, Marybeth's cognitive ability may be better understood by her performance on the separate DAS-II Clusters, namely, Verbal Ability, Nonverbal Reasoning Ability, and Spatial Ability.

The Verbal Ability, a measure of Crystallized Intelligence (Gc), represents Marybeth's ability to reason with previously learned information. Gc ability develops largely as a function of both formal and informal educational opportunities and experiences and is highly dependent on exposure to mainstream U.S. culture. Marybeth's Gc was assessed by a task that required her to define words

---

[1]A "significant" difference between scores is one too large to be likely to occur by chance unless the measured abilities really are different from each other.

Marybeth's Intellectual Assessment using the Differential Ability Scales–Second Edition (DAS-II)

Composite/Cluster/Subtest	Score[b]	95% C[c]	PR[d]	Description
General Conceptual Ability	**110**	**(104–115)**	**75**	**Average to Above Average**
Verbal Ability	**133**	**(120–139)**	**99**	**High to Very High**
Word Definitions	74		99	
Verbal Similarities	65		93	
Nonverbal Reasoning Ability	**104**	**(96–112)**	**61**	**Average to Above Average**
Matrices	54		66	
Sequential & Quantitative Reasoning	52		58	
Spatial Ability	**89**	**(83–96)**	**23**	**Below Average to Average**
Pattern Construction	38		12	
Recall of Designs	50		50	
Working Memory	**113**	**(106–119)**	**81**	**Average to Above Average**
Recall of Digits Backward	54		66	
Recall of Sequential Order	60		84	
Processing Speed	**53**	**(49–66)**	**<1**	**Very Low**
Speed of Information Processing	28		<1	
Rapid Naming	21		<1	
Diagnostic subtests				
Recall of Digits Forward	58		79	
Recall of Objects–Immediate	49		46	
Recall of Objects–Delayed	54		66	
Recognition of Pictures	47		38	
Phonological Processing	49		46	

[a]Please see the explanation of test scores attached to this report.

[b]A "significant" difference between scores is one too large to be likely to occur by chance. It indicates that the measured abilities really are different from each other.

[c]These are T scores for subtests and standard scores for clusters. Please see the explanation of test scores attached to this report.

[d]Test scores can never be perfectly accurate. Lucky and unlucky guesses, momentary inattention, variations in working speed and other influences cause scores to vary. This interval shows how much scores are likely to vary by chance 95% of the time.

[e]Percentile Rank

presented orally by the examiner (Word Definitions) and a task in which she had to identify the common concept linking three words (Verbal Similarities). Marybeth's performances on these two tasks (Word Definitions $T = 74$; Verbal Similarities $T = 65$) were not significantly different from each other, indicating that her total Verbal Ability score is a good estimate of her Crystallized Intelligence. Marybeth obtained a Verbal Ability standard score of 133 (120–139), which is ranked at the 99th percentile and is classified as High to Very High. Marybeth's verbal ability is considered a significant normative strength as compared to other individuals her age.

The Nonverbal Reasoning Ability Cluster, a measure of Fluid Intelligence (Gf), represents nonverbal inductive reasoning and requires complex mental processing. Fluid Intelligence refers to mental operations that an individual uses when faced with a relatively novel task that cannot be performed automatically. Marybeth's Gf was assessed by a task that required her to select from among four or six choices the figure that correctly completes an incomplete matrix (Matrices $T = 54$) and a task in which she was required to induce the underlying characteristic that governs a problem or set of materials (Sequential and Quantitative Reasoning $T = 52$). The difference between her scores on these tasks was not significantly large, indicating that her Nonverbal Reasoning Ability score is a good estimate of her Fluid Intelligence. Marybeth obtained a Nonverbal Reasoning Ability score of 104 (96–112), which is ranked at the 61st percentile and is classified as Average to Above Average.

The Spatial Ability Cluster, a measure of Visual-Spatial Ability (Gv), requires the ability to perceive, remember, and manipulate spatial relations and shapes. Visual-spatial ability is the ability to generate, perceive, analyze, synthesize, store, retrieve, manipulate, transform, and think with visual patterns and stimuli and mental images. Marybeth's Gv was assessed by a task that required her to recall and draw an abstract line drawing that had been shown to her briefly (Recall of Designs $T = 50$) and a task in which she had to rapidly perceive and manipulate a relatively simple visual pattern of objects in space (Pattern Construction-Std. $T = 38$). The significant 12-point difference between the subtests of the Spatial cluster, with Recall of Designs being significantly higher than the Pattern Construction score, is considered unusual, occurring in only about 10 percent of the norming sample. Marybeth appeared to struggle with the Pattern Construction task, working extremely slowly. Although the task allows a child to obtain "bonus points" for successful completion within strict time limits, Marybeth was unable to gain any extra points. On several of the later items, although it did not affect her score, she rotated the designs from their intended orientation. She appeared to apply little planning or organization to her responses and seemed to use a trial-and-error approach when placing each block.

Marybeth's short-term memory, both memory span and working memory, was assessed by the DAS-II and found to be in the Average to Above-Average range. On the Recall of Digits Forward subtest (memory span), she was read a series of increasingly long non-related numbers and asked to repeat them back to the examiner. Although she did not appear to have any difficulty remembering and repeating the numbers, she did need several prompts to gain her attention before having the items presented to her. Her score (Recall of Digits Forward T score = 58) was not significantly different from the average (mean) of her core T scores and suggests that her memory span is well developed and equal to or greater than approximately 79 percent of children her age.

Two subtests (Recall of Digits Backward and Recall of Sequential Order) were administered to Marybeth to assess her abilities in the area of working memory. These working memory tasks required her to listen to a list of words (body parts) or numbers, and to hold that list in her short-term memory while she manipulated the items and put them into a different order. On this Working Memory cluster (SS = 113, PR = 81, Range = 106–119), she obtained a score in the Above-Average range. She had no difficulty in listening to body parts named in random order or numbers read in random order and then repeating the body parts from highest to lowest position on the body (Recall of Sequential Order T score = 60) or repeating the numbers in reversed order (Recall of Digit Backward T score = 54).

Marybeth's long-term retrieval ability, as measured by the Recall of Objects subtest, was found to be in the average range (Recall of Objects–Immediate T = 49). She was shown a page with 20 objects, which were named for her once, and was asked to remember all that she could. Over 3 trials, she correctly recalled 27 items (6, 9, 12 items on successive trials) and after a 15-minute delay recalled 11 items (Recall of Objects–Delayed T = 54). Her score on both trials of this subtest (immediate and delayed) were not significantly different from each other, nor were they different from her overall average.

Marybeth demonstrated the most difficulty, and her lowest scores, on the Processing Speed cluster, on which she obtained a standard score of 53 (49–66), which is ranked low in the 1st percentile and is classified as Very Low. The score she obtained on the cluster is significantly different from her overall ability score and the size of the difference between her overall ability and her processing speed is highly unusual. The Processing Speed cluster measures several cognitive factors, including processing speed, the ability to work fast under time pressure, the ability to integrate visual and verbal processing efficiently, scanning ability,

Marybeth's Academic Assessment using the Woodcock-Johnson III Achievement Battery.

Test	Score	PR	95% CI	Description
Total Achievement	92	30	89 to 95	Low Average to Average
Letter Word Identification	115	84	111 to 119	High Average to High Average
Reading Fluency	101	53	97 to 105	High Average to High Average
Passage Comprehension	116	86	108 to 124	Average to Superior
Calculations	82	12	74 to 90	Low to Average
Math Fluency	81	10	75 to 87	Low to Low Average
Applied Problems	70	02	66 to 74	Very Low to Low
Spelling	84	14	78 to 90	Low to Average
Writing Fluency	87	19	75 to 99	Low to Average
Writing Samples	89	23	73 to 105	Low to Average

attention, and concentration. The Processing Speed cluster is also related to rate of motor activity, motivation and persistence, visual acuity, and ability to delay responding until appropriate. Marybeth showed great difficulty with both the motor aspects of the Speed of Information Processing subtest ($T = 28$) and the verbal fluency task of Rapid Naming ($T = 21$). Although, as expected, she made few if any errors on either of these very simple tasks, the speed with which she was able to complete them was typically extremely slow. She found the tasks especially difficult and this appeared to hinder her motivation to complete the tasks and her willingness to continue. She had to be prompted on both tests to work quickly and to keep going.

Marybeth was administered the Woodcock Johnson Third Edition Tests of Achievement (WJ III Ach) to obtain an estimate of the levels of her academic ability. On the WJ III, she obtained a Total Achievement standard score of 92, placing her at the 30th percentile and in the Low Average to Average range. She had varied performance across the achievement domains, with her scores on reading measures generally much higher than those on either math or writing measures. When compared to her overall cognitive ability as measured by her GCA (SS = 110) her scores on reading are close to what one might predict of a child with this ability. Her scores on the math and writing sections of the WJ III were, however, well below what was predicted.

Marybeth read words aloud from the WJ III Letter Word Identification list with good accuracy for her age. She relied more on instant recognition of familiar words than on strategies to attack unfamiliar words, but her automatic reading was strong, yielding a High Average score. She did attempt to sound out some unfamiliar words. Marybeth's passage comprehension score was equally strong as her accuracy in reading words aloud from a list. She read short sentences written with omitted words and supplied the missing words that confirmed that she understood what she had read.

Marybeth's math abilities were not as well developed as her reading abilities. She was able to demonstrate understanding of certain mathematical concepts, to count items, and to add one-digit whole numbers. When presented with simple word or story problems, she used her strong memory to work the problems in her head without using the available scratch paper. As the word problems became more complex, Marybeth seemed to have difficulty distinguishing relevant from irrelevant information. Her paper-and-pencil computations were disorganized and, as she set up the problems on the paper, she occasionally misaligned numbers, resulting in incorrect solutions. She did slightly better on those problems that were presented to her on written computation sheets, although her paper-and-pencil math computation was very slow and laborious.

Marybeth's written language abilities were also found to be lower then expected given her overall cognitive skills. She wrote answers using her right hand, but she used an awkward pencil grip that resulted in letter formation that was at times difficult to read. Her letters and the spacing between them were messy and

Comparison of Marybeth's Achievement and Predicted Achievement Scores

Predicted Difference Method—DAS-II versus WJ III ACH

DAS-II Composite Score Used for this Comparison: GCA

DAS- II Composite Standard Score: ___110___

WJ III ACH Composite	Actual WJ III Score	Predicted WJ III Score	Difference (Actual–Predicted)	Critical Value (.05)	Significant Difference
Broad Reading	114	107	7	18	
Basic Reading Skills	110	107	3	19	
Reading Comprehension	116	107	9	17	
Broad Math	72	108	−36	14	Yes
Math Calculation	82	107	−25	17	Yes
Math Reasoning	77	109	−32	13	Yes
Broad Written Language	82	107	−25	17	Yes
Basic Writing Skills	93	108	−15	16	
Written Expression	88	107	−19	19	Yes

disorganized. Although Marybeth was able to spell many words using a phonetic approach, she often missed silent letters and reordered some letters in words.

Achievement test scores can be predicted from scores on tests of cognitive abilities on the basis of the relationship, or *correlation,* between the two tests. Predicted scores on achievement tests fall between the cognitive ability test score and the average score for all students (standard score 100). We can determine statistically whether an examinee's actual achievement score is significantly different from the prediction, as shown in the table on page 292. The "critical value (.05)," for example, is the size of a difference that is so great it would occur simply by chance less than 5 times in 100.

Executive Functioning Assessment

Marybeth was administered the Trail Making subtest of the Delis-Kaplan Executive Functioning System (D-KEFS). The D-KEFS measures cognitive processes involved in self-monitoring, problem solving, planning and organization, and inhibition. It also includes higher-order aspects of attention, including divided attention, vigilance, and multitasking. On this specific measure of cognitive flexibility that involve shifting mental sets, Marybeth generally performed poorly (D-KEFS Trail Making – Composite = 2nd percentile). She performed slightly better when asked to simply connect, in order, a series of numbers scattered on a page (Visual Scanning = 16th percentile) than she did when asked to quickly switch between putting letters and numbers in sequence (e.g., A 1 2 B 3 . . .) (Number letter Switching = 5th percentile). She had difficulty locating on the page the desired number or letter, suggesting that she has difficulty scanning a visual field for a desired target. Marybeth's performance on the Motor Speed subtest was below the 1st percentile of students her age.

These scores are similar to Marybeth's DAS-II score for speed of scanning

Marybeth's Scores on the D-KEFS Trail Making Test

	Scaled Score*	Percentile Rank
Trail Making		
Composite Scaled Score	4	2
Visual Scanning	7	16
Number Sequencing	3	1
Letter Sequencing	6	9
Number-Letter Switching	5	5
Motor Speed	2	0.4

*Scaled Score Mean = 10, SD = 3

rows of numbers and marking the greatest number in each row, another visual scanning task.

Summary

Marybeth is an 8-year-old second grader referred for evaluation because of continued academic and behavioral problems at school. Mrs. XX provided relevant medical, developmental, and educational histories. Marybeth has fallen behind her peers in both academic achievement and social functioning. She has repeated the first grade and is now in second grade, where she continues to struggle both academically and socially.

Several aspects of Marybeth's abilities and her behaviors observed and evaluated throughout the current assessment seem notable for understanding her present difficulties. Despite her slow early development of oral language, Marybeth now has highly developed oral, verbal abilities and reading skills. These abilities stand in stark contrast to several of her other cognitive and academic skills. Marybeth appeared impulsive and disorganized in her approach to several of the tasks she was asked to perform during the evaluation. As the task demands shifted from those that allowed verbal mediation and rote-memory abilities to those that were less structured and much more novel and abstract in their nature, her performance, both qualitatively and quantitatively, declined. On a social level, Marybeth's highly verbal presentation can mask the facts that she has difficulty in certain social settings and that she does not easily pick up on the nonverbal social cues given to her by adults and her peers. These skills are sometimes called "language pragmatics."

Marybeth's overall cognitive ability, as represented by the DAS-II GCA was 110 (percentile rank 75; Average to Above Average). Her separate abilities were, however, very differently developed, with her verbal and memory abilities being generally much higher than her nonverbal, spatial, or processing speed abilities. Her performance on tasks that required her to respond in a rapid manner, even orally, was especially problematic for her (Processing Speed Score = 53, Low: in the first percentile). Marybeth's overall poorer performance on these abilities also appeared to impact her academic achievement, most notably in her math and writing abilities. Her strong verbal and memory skills appear to have helped her in acquiring early reading skills but are not sufficient in themselves to aid her in acquiring appropriate age and grade levels in math and writing.

Observations made during this assessment seem to suggest that Marybeth was better able to attend to and perform certain tasks when comfortable and given clear expectations, encouragement, and praise. It seems that the high level of disorganization, impulsivity, and distractibility that was observed and reported by her mother and teacher may be related to a possible attention deficit disorder with a comorbid nonverbal learning disability.

RECOMMENDATIONS

1. The information contained in the report should be shared with Marybeth's school multidisciplinary team, including her parents, for consideration of whether Marybeth meets the criteria for classification as a student with a disability that requires special education remediation or a formal plan of special accommodations under §504 of The Rehabilitation Act (Public Law 93-112).

2. Marybeth's emotional and behavioral difficulties should continue to be monitored. Mrs. XX reported that Marybeth has seen a therapist during difficult times, and she may continue to benefit from additional individual counseling during stressful situations. Given Marybeth's difficulty with peer relationships and socialization, it might be useful to enroll Marybeth in a social skills group where she can learn to successfully interact with children her own age. Marybeth needs to be taught social skills and language pragmatics directly, as she will not learn them easily through observation. The social skills training program should provide direct, practical training and include components that involve modeling, role playing, feedback, and transfer of training. Her current public school offers such groups.

3. Marybeth may benefit from a behavior modification plan that is consistently implemented at home and in school with short-term rewards and immediate consequences and that focuses on following directions, on her activity level, and on impulse control. Traditional behavior modification techniques may not be effective with Marybeth because many of her inappropriate behaviors may be a result of a neurological impairment (possibly both an attention deficit disorder and a nonverbal learning disability). Behavior techniques that focus on and employ verbal strategies that will help her to learn more appropriate behaviors should be stressed. Close communication between home and school is crucial to the success of any behavior intervention plan.

4. Marybeth's teachers should recognize that students with cognitive profiles like Marybeth's often demonstrate severe difficulties in subjects that involve complex problem solving and concept formation. Also, Marybeth can use her excellent verbal skills and her excellent

rote memory abilities to help her succeed with many tasks in the lower grades, but she may continue to experience increasing difficulties in school as the academic demands in each grade shift to more complex applications.

5. Given Marybeth's extreme difficulties on tasks that require her to respond quickly and without conscious deliberation, and particularly when under pressure to maintain focused attention, it might be beneficial to Marybeth for her teachers to allow her more time to complete assignments whenever possible. For some assignments, it might be useful to reduce the quantity of work expected of Marybeth. When evaluating her acquisition of skills, it might be more reasonable to focus on the quality of what is produced rather then on the overall quantity. She will have difficulty successfully completing tasks that she views as overwhelming or time consuming.

CASE REPORT 2

Name: Jenna D.
Grade: 1st
Age: 7 years 6 months

Reason for Referral

Jenna was referred for evaluation because of an apparent dispute between Jenna's parents and her school about the accuracy of prior testing used to identify Jenna as being disabled due, at least in part, to mental retardation. Jenna's parents have raised the concern that prior cognitive testing by the school and independent evaluators did not accurately reflect Jenna's abilities because of her "language difficulties" as well as her possible attention problems. They are seeking a re-evaluation of Jenna's cognitive abilities and specifically asked for testing that would be sensitive to any of Jenna's possible non-cognitive difficulties.

Background

Jenna is a 7-year, 6-month-old first-grader who was retained in kindergarten because of her "limited ability to learn the academic material." After two years in kindergarten, she is now in first grade and continues to struggle with the academic demands.

From a review of the school records and communications with parents, teachers, and prior evaluators, there appears to be no disagreement about Jenna's current adaptive skill limitations. Dr. A.M., whom Mrs. D. has described as "the professional who knows Jenna best," administered both the Vineland Adaptive Behavior Scales (VABS) and the Adaptive Behavior Scales–school (ABS-S). On both these measures (which are questionnaires on which adults describe the child's skills), she was found to have "significant limitations in a number of areas, among them the social, communications, and self-help areas."

Prior evaluations of Jenna's cognitive abilities have generally been consistent. Within the past two years Jenna has been administered the Wechsler Preschool and Primary Scale of Intelligence–Third Edition (WPPSI-III) and the Kaufman Assessment Battery for Children–Second Edition (KABC-II). The results from these tests were typically in agreement and found Jenna to be functioning in the range of mental retardation or intellectual disability.

Over the past three years, Jenna has been independently evaluated by a number of professionals who have described Jenna as presenting with "apraxia," "verbal dyspraxia," "Pervasive Developmental Disorder," "Developmental Verbal Dyspraxia," "severe speech and language disability," "a global pattern of developmental immaturities and delay," and "processing and sequential difficulties in addition to Attention Deficit Disorder." Because of these possible problems and diagnoses, Jenna's parents doubt that the results from the prior intellectual measures are accurate because they believe that the tests are "auditory verbal language loaded intelligence" tests and are impacted by Jenna's many other problems.

Choice of Test

The determination of intellectual functioning requires the use of global measures that include different types of items and different factors of intelligence. When formulating this assessment, great thought was given to if, and how, an accurate assessment might be undertaken. For this evaluation, the Differential Ability Scales–Second Edition (DAS-II, 2007) was chosen. It was chosen specifically to match the perceived (nonverbal-visual) strengths and the language-based weaknesses of Jenna. The DAS-II allows the examiner, within the context of a standardized administration, considerable flexibility to adjust to the needs of the child. It is considered a comprehensive measure of cognitive ability, assessing for a child of Jenna's age three major components of cognitive skills: Verbal, Nonverbal Reasoning, and Spatial. The test is designed to be user and child friendly and very adaptable for the individual child. Items are constructed so that a child need not fail in order to assess maximum ability. Children taking the DAS-II can often complete a task "while succeeding" and obtain a valid score, unlike other tests that require the child to fail a certain number of prescribed items before the examiner stops. Because of Jenna's language difficulties, the DAS-II was considered appropriate because it also provides the Special Nonverbal Composite (SNC), which removes the language-based tests from the computation of the overall ability score. Additionally, the DAS-II teaching items were an especially useful feature since these items allowed the examiner to evaluate whether or not Jenna understood the individual subtest tasks and, if she did not, to teach her those tasks through multiple teaching items and through explanations, modeling, and demonstrations. Because of Jenna's possible motor and sensory issues, the DAS-II was also deemed appropriate because only one subtest, Pattern Construction, requires a motoric response. The DAS-II procedures for Pattern Construction would also have allowed for "alternative scoring" of Jenna's performance if it had been determined that either her motor skills or her speed of performing the task had been greatly impacting on her scores. The DAS-II also allows for confirmation of strengths and weaknesses through the use of out-of-level subtests generally intended for older or younger children. These tasks typically would not be given to a child of Jenna's age, but when the examiner wishes to test some hypothesis about the performance of a child, they are available.

When Jenna was tested, all appropriate strategies were employed during the testing session. Because of the flexibility offered by the DAS-II, no departure from standardized administration was found to be necessary.

It should be noted that Jenna enjoyed the tasks on the DAS-II. After the examiner had done all the subtests applicable, for both the typical School-Age battery and several out-of-level subtests, and after spending two hours in the testing session with only one five-minute break, Jenna asked if she could do more. When she was told that she had done most of what was available that day, she asked the examiner to return some other day and let her "play some more."

Initial Test Behaviors

Jenna was first observed in her language class. She was introduced to the examiner and willingly gave her name. The examiner engaged her in conversation, and traded seats with Jenna at her request. She appeared comfortable as she was observed and did not display any inappropriate behaviors because of the extra person's presence. At the end of the speech lesson, she was asked to accompany the examiner, along with her aide, to a separate testing room. She at first declined, saying she did not want to go. With minimal encouragement, and positive verbal reinforcement, she did come to the testing room. Her aide took with her, from the speech room, a set of plastic stickers that have been used as motivators during the language class. They were to be used, if necessary, during the formal testing. Once in the testing room, Jenna was friendly and cooperative. To "break the ice," Jenna was administered a portion of the Kaufman Survey of Early Academic and Language Skills (K-SEALS). This test is an individually administered, nationally normed measure of children's language (expressive and receptive skills), and pre-academic skills (knowledge of numbers, number concepts, letters, and words). The test was administered only to acquaint Jenna with the testing situation and to briefly assess how she would do on the standardized administration of the DAS-II. The K-SEALS is not normed for a child of Jenna's age, having data only for children up to 6 years 11 months. No attempt was made to calculate a score from this test, since that would be impossible. Jenna seemed to enjoy the tasks on this test, and was pleased by her performance. From the results of that administration, it was determined that the administration of the DAS-II was appropriate and it was begun.

Intellectual Assessment

The Differential Ability Scales–Second Edition (DAS-II) has a number of clusters measuring diverse abilities. Each cluster can be examined to assess how Jenna is able to best demonstrate her intellectual abilities. Interpretation begins first with the overall General Conceptual Ability (GCA) score. It must be examined to determine its reliability and accuracy in describing Jenna's ability. After a decision about the GCA's usefulness is made, one can proceed to interpret the relevant cluster scores and finally the individual subtests themselves. The results below reflect Jenna's performance on the standard School-Age battery.

On this administration of the DAS-II, Jenna obtained a Verbal cluster score in the range of 63 to 80, a Nonverbal Reasoning score in the range of 69 to 83, and a Spatial cluster score in the 61 to 73 range, which resulted in an obtained GCA score of 66. The differences found both between the cluster scores and between the subtests that make up the individual clusters were small and nonsignificant,[2] suggesting that the GCA is a valid measure of Jenna's overall ability. Higher than only about 1 percent of the children her own age, Jenna's ability is most likely (95 percent chance) to be in the range of 62 to 73. Using the DAS-II classification

---

[2]A significant difference is one that is too large to be at all likely to occur just from chance variation.

Differential Ability Scales–Second Edition (DAS-II) Cluster Scores

(Each has a mean of 100 and a standard deviation of ±15)

	Standard Score[a]	Percentile Rank[b]	95% Intervals[c]	Between Cluster Difference	Within Cluster Difference	Classification
Verbal	68	2	63 to 80	No	No	Very Low
Nonverbal Reasoning	74	4	69 to 83	No	No	Low
Spatial	65	1	61 to 73	No	No	Very Low
Working Memory	61	1	57 to 69		No	Very Low
General Conceptual Ability	66	1	62 to 73			Very Low
Special Nonverbal Composite	66	1	62 to 73			Very Low

[a]Please see the description of test scores attached to this report.

[b]This is the percent of children her age whose scores Jenna tied or exceeded. A percentile rank of 20, for example, would mean that she scored as high as or higher than 20% of children her age.

[c]Test scores can never be perfectly accurate. This interval shows how much scores are likely to vary 95% of the time just by chance.

system, this would identify Jenna's present level of cognitive ability as being in the Very Low to Low range.

Jenna was able to demonstrate her intelligence equally well, whether through acquired verbal concepts and knowledge, nonverbal inductive reasoning, or complex visual spatial processing. Because of Jenna's language difficulties, one may wish to consider the Special Nonverbal Composite (SNC), which removes from the computation of ability the verbally loaded subtests. When this is done, Jenna obtains a SNC score of 66, with a range of 62 to 73. These scores do not differ from the scores obtained using the standard GCA. There did not appear to be an overall impact due to language skills on this administration of the DAS-II.

The individual subtest scores that Jenna receives on any given administration of a test are considered "obtained" scores and may not represent her "true" score or ability. Obtained scores are expected to fluctuate from one administration of a test to the next and therefore some test of significance must be done to determine if a child's individual subtest scores are higher or lower than the "average." Typically, the best representation of Jenna's ability at the subtest level will be the total

Subtest Analysis (Subtests Have a Mean of 50 and a Standard Deviation of ±10)

Mean Core T = 32	T Score	Critical Value	Actual Difference	Significance	Frequency[a]
Word Definition (*Gc*)	31	7	−1		
Verbal Similarities (*Gc*)	30	8	−2		
Matrices (*Gf*)	35	7	3		
Sequential & Quantitative Reasoning (*Gf*)	33	6	1		
Recall of Designs (*Gv*)	30	7	−2		
Pattern Construction (*Gv*)	29	5	−3		
Recall of Objects– Immediate (*Glr*)	36	9	4		
Recall of Objects– Delayed (*Glr*)	34				
Recall of Digits Forward (*Gsm*)	40	7	8	High	15%
Recall of Sequential Order (*Gsm*)	22	7	−10	Low	15%
Recall of Digits Backward (*Gsm*)	29	7	−3		

[a]How often differences that large or larger occurred among the children on whom the DAS-II was normed.

of all the scores she obtained, not any one of the scores (the highest or the lowest). To determine if a Jenna's individual subtest scores do in fact deviate from the average (mean), a statistical procedure is used which compares each subtest score to "critical values." These values represent the amount of change any one subtest score can be expected to deviate just by chance. If a particular score deviates from the mean of the test by an amount greater than the critical value, then it may be considered to be a strength (High) or a weakness (Low).

All of Jenna's Core subtest scores from the School-Age battery grouped closely about her own mean of 32. For the diagnostic subtests administered to Jenna, she demonstrated a strength (High) on the Recall of Digits Forward subtest and a weakness (Low) on the Recall of Sequential Order subtest. Although these subtest scores are respectively considered a personal strength and a personal weakness for Jenna, the magnitude of the differences from the mean score is not unusual, being found in greater than 15 percent of the population.

When we examine each of the areas assessed by the DAS-II, the following is found:

Verbal Ability (SS = 68, PR = 2, Range = 63 – 80): The Verbal cluster is made up of the Word Definitions and Verbal Similarities subtests. There was no significant difference between Jenna's subtest scores on this cluster. The cluster itself is a measure of complex, verbal mental processing, which includes acquired concepts, verbal knowledge, and reasoning. Jenna's expressive language skills appeared to be equally developed on these tasks, whether the task asked her to utilize her verbal skills to describe word meanings in long descriptive sentences (e.g., "What is a *pencil*?" or "What does *delay* mean?") (Word Definitions *T* score = 31) or to utilize verbal skills to correctly assign three different words into one meaningful classification or category using typically a single word (e.g., "*dog* and *cat* and *mouse*?" or "*hope* and *fear* and *love*?" (Verbal Similarities *T* score = 30).

On the Word Definitions subtest, Jenna typically showed an understanding of the word but was unable to correctly give a verbal description to its meaning. For one word, she answered by using a gesture. Again, her understanding of the words and the language seems to exceed her ability to adequately verbally express her understanding. When categorizing words into functional groups (Verbal Similarities), she showed some distractibility to the task. She needed to be refocused a number of times, but in each case she was able to attend to the questions asked and to make an attempt at the answer. She was able to categorize a number of the items presented into logical groupings. To further assess her verbal skills, she was administered the out-of-level Naming Vocabulary subtest (Naming Vocabulary *T* score = 32). Here she was shown pictures of objects and asked to simply name them. Her score was not significantly different from the other verbal subtests. She was also administered the Verbal Comprehension subtest (Verbal Comprehension *T* score = 42) where she is asked to demonstrate understanding of increasingly difficult directions. This subtest assesses understanding of language through a receptive mode. None of the items required Jenna to respond orally. She demonstrated understanding of basic body parts, and was able to follow directions that had her giving certain unnamed objects to the examiner based upon their function. She did equally well on the more difficult items that asked her to give certain items that were named by their class or function. For example, shown a number of toys and asked to "Give me all the animals" she was able to correctly choose the three items from a group of 8 items. She showed understanding of common prepositions such as behind, to, stand up, under. As the directions became more complex in their nature and often involved two or three steps, she consistently had difficulty.

Nonverbal Reasoning Ability (SS = 74, PR = 4, Range = 69–83): The Nonverbal Reasoning cluster is made up of the Matrices and Sequential and Quantitative Reasoning subtests. The cluster is a measure of nonverbal, inductive reasoning requiring complex mental processing. It required Jenna to identify elements in pictures, to form and test hypotheses about relationships, and to apply the relationship to new material. Both subtests use colored pictures and a multiple-choice format. Jenna again demonstrated no significant difference between the two subtests (Matrices *T* score = 35; Sequential and Quantitative Reasoning = 33).

To further assess her nonverbal skills, she was administered the out-of-level subtest of Picture Similarities. Here she was given a card with a picture on it and then shown four pictures. Jenna was to show her understanding of the similarity between the card and one of the four pictures by placing her card on the correct picture. Most of the item content is representational, using colored pictures. She did best on those matches that involved common objects or matching designs by their shape or pattern, but when the similarity progressed to include quantitative measures, she was unable to do them. The score she obtained on this subtest was not different from the scores obtained on the standard School-Age subtests (Picture Similarities *T* score = 41).

Spatial Ability (SS = 65, PR = 1, Range = 61–73): Jenna also did equally well on the Spatial cluster, which is made up of Recall of Designs and Pattern Construction scores. This cluster is a measure of complex visual spatial processing. It requires the ability to perceive and to remember spatial relationships.

On the Recall of Designs subtest (*T* score = 30) she was shown line drawings for five seconds and then asked to reproduce them with paper and pencil. She showed both minor distortions and some loss of important elements in her design reproductions. The Pattern Construction subtest (*T* score = 29) required her to use spatial skills to recreate pictured designs using two- and three-dimensional tiles and blocks. She was able to copy the designs when using the solid colored, two-dimensional foam tiles but had greater difficulty when presented with the three-dimensional blocks. The patterns in the booklet are two dimensional while the blocks she used are three dimensional. The tasks required her to create the two dimensions and ignore the third. She often appeared to be "stuck" when the designs did not match the blocks she had. She did not always grasp the idea of turning blocks over to reveal the different patterns on their sides or bottom. On two early three-dimensional designs, Jenna was very flexible in her approach, being willing to quickly and easily find the side of the blocks she needed. She in fact gained maximum credit for completing one design in less than four seconds. As the designs became more complex, she lost her flexibility. For Jenna, the scores from the two subtests showed no significant difference. Once again Jenna performed evenly with no discrepancy between her scores or ability.

Because of the memory component on the Recall of Designs subtest, Jenna was also given the out-of-level Copying subtest. Here, as with the Recall of Designs subtest, she is shown line drawings and asked to draw them, but on this subtest the line drawing stays in her view at all time. There is no memory component on the Copying subtest. Jenna was able to correctly reproduce each of the items that resemble letters or strings of letters with no reversals or distortions. Jenna showed difficulty on those later items that were abstract in nature. The score that Jenna obtained (Copying T score = 27) was not significantly different from her other spatial subtest scores.

Memory Ability: Jenna was administered several diagnostic subtests to assess her memory for both meaningful and non-meaningful stimuli presented visually and aurally. These subtests form three categories:

(a) Short-term memory (Memory Span): On the Recall of Digits Forward subtest she was read a series of increasingly longer non-related numbers (e.g., 4 3 7 1) and asked to repeat them back to the examiner. Before each item was presented, Jenna was reminded to "Listen carefully," and no number was presented until Jenna showed attention. With the numbers read at a rate of two per second so that she could not compensate by repeating the numbers to herself, she was able to remember easily a string of up to three numbers but could do only two out of five of the strings of four numbers. Her score (Recall of Digits Forward T score = 40) was significantly higher than her Mean Core T score and suggests that her auditory short-term memory span is better developed than her other assessed skills.

(b) Short-term memory (Working Memory) (SS = 61, PR = 1, Range = 57 – 69): Two subtests (Recall of Digits Backward and Recall of Sequential Order) were administered to Jenna to assess her abilities in the area of working memory. These working memory tasks required Jenna to listen to a randomly ordered list of words (body parts) or numbers, and to hold that list in short-term memory while manipulating it and putting it into a different order. On this Working Memory cluster, Jenna obtained a score in the Low range. She had particular difficulty in her attempt to name specific body parts from highest to lowest (e.g., foot – head – shoulder → head – shoulder – foot) (Recall of Sequential Order T score = 22) despite her demonstrating during the instructions that she understood the concepts of highest and lowest and that she correctly knew the names for the pictured body parts. It appears that her ability to recall information is impacted by the complexity of the items and by her need to manipulate the items in her head. On the Recall of Digits Backward subtest, Jenna also had difficulty repeating

Jenna's Scores Grouped by Cultural and Linguistic Influences

Low Culture/Low Linguistic		High Culture /High Linguistic	
Matrices	= 35	Verbal Similarities	= 31
Sequential & Quantitative Reasoning	= 33	Word Definitions	= 30
Pattern Construction	= 29		
Recall of Designs	= 30		
Copying	= 27		

dictated digits in reversed order (e.g., 4 7 2 → 2 7 4) (Recall of Digits Backward *T* score = 29). There was no significant difference between Jenna's scores on the two working memory subtests.

(c) Long-term retrieval: On the meaningful, visual-verbal memory task of Recall of Objects, she was shown a page with 20 objects and asked to remember all that she could. Given three trials, she was able to correctly recall 16 items (4, 6, 6 items on successive trials) and after a 15-minute delay was able to recall four items. Her scores on both trials of this subtest (immediate and delayed) were not significantly different from each other, nor were they different from her overall average.

To summarize Jenna's results on the memory subtests, her scores on these subtests suggested that her short-term memory skills, working memory, and long-term retrieval skills are weak but evenly developed within the domain of memory.

Cultural and Linguistic Influences. Finally, to discern whether her problems in language greatly impacted on her cognitive abilities, Jenna's scores were evaluated with regard to their individual cultural and linguistic demands. Specifically, her relevant subtest *T* scores were examined for each group of subtests (Low Culture/Low Linguistic and High Culture/High Linguistic). In this way a comparison can be made between subtests that have little cultural and linguistic demand and those that have high culture and linguistic demands.

As can be seen, on this administration of the DAS-II, there appeared to be no difference between Jenna's performance on those tasks that had low cultural and linguistic demands when compared to those with high culture and linguistic demands.

SUMMARY/DIAGNOSTIC IMPRESSION

Jenna is a first-grade student with a complicated educational and developmental history. She has shown delays in the acquisition of early academic skills as well as in several areas of social and communications skills. Overall, Jenna appears to be a youngster with cognitive abilities that are very evenly developed. Her scores and performances were in the Very Low to Low range using the DAS-II classification system. This examiner has attempted to account for each of the suspected strengths and weaknesses that have been reported by other evaluators. Given the nature of the DAS-II, the overall even performance by Jenna on this administration, and the absence of any divergent scores, this administration of the DAS-II and the resultant scores are felt by this examiner to be an accurate reflection of her current levels of cognitive abilities.

Given the nature of Jenna's cognitive abilities and the current levels of her adaptive behaviors, it appears that the diagnostic label of Mental Retardation is appropriate at this time. The results of this evaluation should be shared with the school multidisciplinary team and may, when combined with other information, aid in the development of appropriate educational recommendations. A parent support group is recommended for Mr. and Mrs. D. so that they can meet with parents whose children are facing similar challenges.

CASE REPORT 3
COGNITIVE EVALUATION

Name: Allison Atkins
Parents: Alice and Alan Atkins
Address: Moose Road, Millburgh NH
Birth date: 4/11/01   Age: 5:9 (5 years, 9 months)
Test date: 1/22/07   School: Veterans Memorial School
Teacher: Mary Murdoch   Grade: K.6

Examiner: Peter Strauss, Ed.D.
REFERRAL

Allison was referred by the Veterans Memorial School team for academic achievement and cognitive assessment to be done by Maryanne Green, case manager, and by me. Information on Allison's skills and progress is also being collected in Speech-Language Therapy, Occupational Therapy, and Kindergarten class. Allison has reportedly been making very slow progress in mastering basic, beginning academic skills in Kindergarten class.

Allison is identified as having a "speech or language impairment" and receives special instruction under an Individualized Education Program (IEP), which calls for 7½ hours a week of Kindergarten Class instruction, 2½ hours a week of Special Education instruction in academics, 1½ hours a week of Speech-Language Therapy, and 1 hour a week of Occupational Therapy.

Winifred Daniels, special education teacher, administered the AGS *Early Screening Profiles* for Allison in April 2006, when Allison's age was 4 years, 11 months (4:11) and she was attending the preschool program at Little Learners Children's Center. Ms. Daniels reported a standard score for the Cognitive subscale of the Cognitive/Language Profile of 111, stanine 6, High Average, for Allison's age.[3] However, Allison's score for the Language subscale was much lower: standard score 88, stanine 3, Below Average for her age. Ms. Daniels commented that, "Allison often paused before giving answers. It is this examiner's opinion that she needed the time to process. At times questions had to be repeated. . . . Allison has made a lot of gains in speech and attention since I first met her. It is nice to see such growth. . . . Allison's language delays could impact her classroom performance and should be watched closely. She demonstrated solid cognitive skills, and continued support is recommended in the area of language to ensure she is demonstrating all of her abilities. It is also this examiner's opinion that she should have some weekly support from a special educator during her kindergarten year in the public school." Please see Ms. Daniels's complete report. Allison also had an Occupational Therapy evaluation by Jean Baxter, OTR/L, in November 2004 and a Speech/Language Evaluation by Elizabeth Coltraine, MS, CCC-SLP, in April 2006. Please see their reports. Allison's recent near and far vision and hearing (20 decibel [dB] sweep) screenings were reported to have been within normal limits.

TESTS USED

Appended to this report are a brief description of the Differential Ability Scales (DAS-II) subtests that Allison took, an explanation of the scoring system used, and a table of Allison's test scores. Please note that, throughout the report, I am reporting test scores as *percentile ranks* and *stanines* as described on p. i of the Appendix. *Please note that these are not the verbal labels furnished by the test publisher for the DAS-II.*[4] Other scoring systems, not used in this report, are described on the last page of the Appendix, so the reader can easily substitute the publisher's clas-

---

[3] Please see p. i of the Appendix to this report for a description of the test scores.

[4] The numbers in the first column of each table are the standard scores, scaled scores, or *T* scores from the tests. The numbers in the third column are the percentile ranks corresponding to those scores. The final columns are the stanine equivalents for those scores. *What differs from the test manuals are the verbal labels (e.g., "Low Average") given with the stanine scores.* The last page of the Appendix shows the verbal labels used by the publisher of the DAS-II.

sification systems for the stanine labels I have used. *The verbal labels of the stanines are not necessarily the same classification labels supplied with the tests.* The different tests Allison has taken use many different scoring systems, so the same scores may be called different things, hence my translation of all test scores into a single system so that the same score is always given the same classification label in all reports.

Test Conditions

Allison and I worked together for 90 minutes with one short break in the small testing office. Physical conditions were good. Light, air, and temperature were comfortable. We used kindergarten-size table and chairs. There was very little outside noise.

Marian Haste kindly accompanied Allison from her classroom to the testing room in the opposite end of the building. Ms. Haste and Maryanne Green introduced me to Allison, and Ms. Green talked with Allison about the importance of working hard and doing her very best on the tests.

I explained that the purpose of the evaluation was to help Allison's teachers learn more about the best ways to teach Allison. Everyone is better at some things than at others, and the tests could help determine which were which for Allison. Allison's teachers do not want to waste Allison's time teaching things Allison already knows, and they do want to be sure to teach things Allison does not know yet. Therefore, both right and wrong answers on the tests are valuable. I also explained that there would be some items that would be too easy (*basal* items), designed primarily for younger students, and some that would be much too difficult (*ceiling* items), designed primarily for older students. Those items are included to make sure we do not miss any extreme strengths or weaknesses.[5] I also warned Allison that I was not allowed to indicate whether specific responses were right or wrong. Allison appeared to accept the purpose of testing and those odd rules with good grace, and her subsequent handling of easy and difficult items and the infrequency with which she asked about her correctness indicated that she had indeed understood and accepted my explanation.

Allison followed Ms. Green's instructions and gave every sign of working hard on all of the tests. She paid good attention to all instructions and learned from

---

[5]Most tests increase in difficulty from the lowest-numbered to the highest-numbered items and require that the student be given enough easier items to establish a "basal" and enough difficult items to establish a "ceiling," trying to ensure that both weaknesses and strengths have been adequately covered.

experience while she worked. She was obviously pleased by her successes. Allison yawned occasionally. She did not ask for a break, but seemed happy when I suggested one after about 45 minutes. After about 90 minutes, the quality of her work (though not her attention) suddenly dropped, so I ended the testing and awarded her a decorated pencil for working so hard. Ninety minutes with one short bathroom break is a very long time for a kindergarten student to work hard on difficult tasks. Each task was brief, usually no more than five to fifteen minutes, and there was a good deal of variety among tasks, but the total time was still long for a kindergarten student. The novelty of the situation and the constant, undivided attention may have helped Allison sustain her attention. Because she worked so hard and so well, Allison's scores appear to be reasonably valid indications of her current educational functioning levels. Allison conversed easily in response to my questions or comments, but did not initiate much conversation herself.

TEST FINDINGS

Allison's scores are all compared to the scores of other students of her age, which automatically compensates for the varying difficulty levels of the tests. Therefore, Allison might score higher, compared to other students her age, on a difficult test than on an easier one.

A quick look at the right-side column of stanine scores in the table of Allison's Differential Ability Scales (DAS-II) results shows that most of the scores are within or above the broad, average range (stanines 4, 5, and 6—approximately the middle half of scores). Allison clearly has solid cognitive ability for school work.

Verbal Ability Subtests

These are cognitive tests of verbal knowledge, understanding, and reasoning ability, *not* tests of language development. Please see Allison's speech and language reports and IEP progress reports for information about her language development.

Allison scored Average to High Average (stanines 5 and 6)[6] for her age on the Verbal Ability subtests: Naming Vocabulary (naming pictures) and Verbal Comprehension (following complex oral instructions to do things with toys, such as "first put the smallest child on the chair and then give me both blocks"). Her Average (stanine 5) total Verbal score by norms for age 5 on the DAS-II was significantly higher than her Below Average score by norms for age 4 on the

---

[6]Please remember these are stanine classifications.

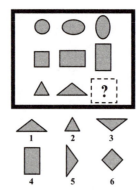

Figure 8.1 Case Studies: Allison Atkins Matrices Example

Language subscale of the Cognitive/Language Profile last spring. Although the DAS-II offers only two verbal ability tests, Allison's responses were consistently accurate and suggested a good command of the language. Allison did not pause more than a second before naming pictures unless she did not know the name of a picture and was trying to think of something to call it.

Nonverbal Reasoning Subtests

On the Nonverbal (fluid) Reasoning[7] subtests, Allison again achieved an Average (stanine 5) score for Picture Similarities (matching pictures on the basis of similar concepts). (An easy item here might be 'a round thing with a round thing' or 'a rectangular thing with a rectangular thing.' A difficult item might be a round analog clock with a rectangular digital clock as the correct choice and other round things as wrong choices.) She did extremely well on the Matrices subtest (choosing the correct picture to complete a logical pattern. Her score was High (stanine 8) for her age on that logical reasoning subtest. This score was a personal strength for Allison, significantly higher than her other scores.[8]

---

[7]"Fluid" reasoning is using flexible reasoning and problem-solving strategies to solve new, unfamiliar problems.

[8]Test scores can never be perfectly accurate. Lucky and unlucky guesses, narrowly beating or exceeding time limits, and other random influences make scores on even the best tests less than totally reliable. A significant difference is one that is too large to occur by pure chance more than a certain percent of the time (usually probability less than .05) unless there were a real difference between the tested abilities. Even significant dif-

Allison's High Average (stanine 6) total score for Nonverbal (fluid) reasoning is a compromise between her Average score for the Picture Similarities and her High score for the Matrices. Her score was identical (by norms for age 5) to Ms. Daniels's score last year for the Cognitive subscale of the Cognitive/Language Profile by norms for age 4. Allison had maintained her strong reasoning abilities compared to other children the same age.

Spatial Ability Subtests

These tests are measures of visual-spatial cognitive abilities, and not just visual perception and perceptual-motor skills. These visual Spatial Ability subtests were a little more difficult for Allison than the Verbal and Nonverbal (fluid) Reasoning subtests. She used her good intelligence, but appeared to have difficulty with the visual perceptual or perceptual-motor demands of some of the tasks. In Pattern Construction, Allison was able to make copies of pictured geometric designs by assembling plastic tiles and plastic cubes with different designs on their faces. She worked with Low Average (stanine 4) speed and accuracy for her age. On the Copying subtest, Allison was able to draw copies of designs, but her accuracy was Below Average (stanine 3) for her age. This score was a personal weakness for Allison, significantly lower than her other scores.

Allison also took a supplementary, Diagnostic subtest that required her to look at an abstract shape and then choose precisely the same shape from six alternatives that were identical except for being rotated or reversed. Her Low Average (stanine 4) score for this matching test was about the same as her Spatial Ability subtest scores. Please see Allison's Occupational Therapy reports.

Total General Conceptual Ability Score

Allison's Average (stanine 5) GCA score on the DAS-II does not give a complete picture of her cognitive abilities. Allison's Verbal Ability and Nonverbal (fluid) Reasoning scores were significantly higher than her Spatial Ability score. Her thinking, reasoning, problem-solving, and verbal intellectual abilities were significantly stronger than her visual-spatial functioning.

---

ferences, however, are not necessarily uncommon. Human abilities normally vary. An uncommon difference is one that did not occur very frequently among the examinees whose scores were used to create the norms for the test.

Additional, Diagnostic Subtests

Allison's scores on the Diagnostic subtests of the DAS-II also revealed a number of interesting characteristics of the way she processes information. On the Recall of Digits Forward subtest, she had a great deal of difficulty repeating series of digits in the same order that I had read them to her. Her score for this test of rote, short-term, auditory memory was Low (stanine 2) for her age and a personal weakness, significantly lower than Allison's other scores.

However, in contrast to this weak rote, auditory memory score, Allison did very well on memory tests with words and visual components. For the Recall of Objects subtest, I showed Allison a page with 20 pictures, named them for her, and gave her 45 seconds to study them. Then I removed the page and asked her to tell me as many of the pictures as she could remember. The order did not matter. I then gave her two more quick looks at the pictures and asked her each time to again tell me as many as she could recall, including ones she had named earlier, again without regard to order. Allison's total score for this visual and verbal memory subtest with real things instead of random numbers was High Average (stanine 6) for her age. About 20 minutes later, I asked Allison to try to tell me the names of the pictures again from memory. Her delayed recall score was about the same as her immediate recall score.

The final memory subtest, Recognition of Pictures, involved no words, just pictures. I would show Allison one or more pictures for five seconds, then turn the page and show her the same picture(s) mixed in with several very similar ones. (For example, I might have shown her a German Shepherd and a Collie and then a page with those pictures plus a Labrador Retriever, a Golden Retriever, and a Rottweiler.) Allison's task was to point to the picture(s) she had seen on the previous page. For credit, she had to indicate every picture from the previous page and none that had not been there. Allison's Very High (stanine 9) score for her age was a personal strength, significantly higher than her other scores.

If her test performance were typical of her usual abilities (something to check in the evaluation-team meeting), it would appear that Allison has a very strong memory when *visual* images are involved, and perhaps when material is *meaningful* to her, whether it is visual or verbal. However, her memory for *meaningless or arbitrary things she heard,* such as random series of numbers, was very weak. This was also the only memory test that required Allison to remember things in *sequence,* which may have contributed to the difficulty she experienced.

Allison also took a supplementary, Diagnostic subtest assessing her beginning math understanding and skills, such as counting, sorting, matching, and comparing. Allison's Below Average (stanine 3) score for her age was a personal weakness, significantly lower than her other scores.

CONCLUSIONS

We know that Allison has strong intellectual ability, at least Average for her age with at least High Average reasoning ability. Her visual-spatial skills were sufficiently weak to pull her Spatial Ability score significantly below her Verbal Ability and Nonverbal (fluid) Reasoning Ability scores. She continued to show her good reasoning ability, and there appeared to have been a significant improvement in language skills.

Not all of Allison's abilities are weak, however, when she uses the visual sensory modality. On the one hand, she has difficulty when she has to perceive rotations and detailed aspects of complex, non-meaningful designs. On the other hand, her memory for meaningful visual images was good to outstanding for her age. Her short-term recall of arbitrary, meaningless series of dictated numbers was very weak in this assessment. The difficulty might have been with the lack of pictures, the lack of meaning, or the requirement that the numbers be recalled in sequence. We may be able to narrow this issue down in the meeting. If we cannot sort it out, and if the issue appears to be important for helping Allison, there are other tests that could be done.

These results need to be coordinated and integrated with Ms. Green's assessment of Allison's academic achievement and with information from Speech-Language Therapy and Occupational Therapy. The only achievement test on this DAS-II was the Early Number concepts, on which Allison had considerable difficulty. Math is an area of academic achievement that depends in part on accurate visual perception and mental visual imagery as well as rote memory for arbitrary or meaningless data (which is what math "facts" seem to be to a beginning student).

If you have any questions about this evaluation, please contact me at the Children's Evaluation Center.

CASE STUDIES: ALLISON ATKINS APPENDICES
SCORES USED WITH ALLISON'S TESTS

(These are not Allison's own scores, just the scoring systems for the tests.)

When a new test is developed, it is normed on a sample of hundreds or thousands of people. The sample should be like that for a good opinion poll: female

314 ESSENTIALS OF DAS-II® ASSESSMENT

and male, urban and rural, different parts of the country, different income levels, and so on. The scores from that norming sample are used as a yardstick for measuring the performance of people who then take the test. This human yardstick allows for the difficulty levels of different tests. The student is being compared to other students on both difficult and easy tasks. You can see from the following illustration that there are more scores in the middle than at the very high and low ends.

Many different scoring systems are used, just as you can measure the same distance as 1 yard, 3 feet, 36 inches, 91.4 centimeters, 0.91 meter, or 1/1760 mile.

STANINES (<u>sta</u>ndard <u>nines</u>) are a nine-point scoring system. Stanines 4, 5, and 6 are approximately the middle half of scores, or average range. Stanines 1, 2, and 3 are approximately the lowest one fourth. Stanines 7, 8, and 9 are approximately the highest one fourth. Throughout this report, for all of the tests, I am using the stanine labels shown below (Very Low, Low, Below Average, Low Average, Average, High Average, Above Average, High, and Very High), even if the particular test may have a different labeling system in its manual.

PERCENTILE RANKS (PR) simply state the percent of persons in the norming sample who scored the same as or lower than the student. A percentile rank of 63 would be high average—as high as or higher than 63 percent and lower than the other 37 percent of the norming sample. It would be in Stanine 6. The middle half of scores falls between percentile ranks of 25 and 75.

STANDARD SCORES ("quotients" on some tests) have an average (*mean*) of 100 and a *standard deviation* of 15. A standard score of 105 would also be at the 63rd percentile rank. Similarly, it would be in Stanine 6. The middle half of these standard scores falls between 90 and 110.

T **SCORES** have an average (*mean*) of 50 and a *standard deviation* of 10. A *T* score of 53 would be at the 62nd percentile rank, Stanine 6. The middle half of *T* scores falls between approximately 43 and 57.

Test Taken by Allison
Differential Ability Scales, 2nd ed. (DAS-II). Colin D. Elliott, Harcourt Assessment, 2007, Upper Early Years Level

The DAS-II is an individual cognitive abilities test, developed and improved from the British Ability Scales and the DAS, for students of ages 2 through 17. It includes verbal, nonverbal (fluid) reasoning, nonverbal/spatial, and special diagnostic tests. The DAS-II probably measures intellectual ability better than many competing tests because the special diagnostic tests are not included in the verbal, nonverbal, spatial, and total scores and because it does measure fluid reasoning ability. The

There are 200 &s, so each && = 1%

Stanine	1 Very Low 4%	2 Low 7%	3 Below Average 12%	4 Low Average 17%	5 Average 20%	6 High Average 17%	7 Above Average 12%	8 High 7%	9 Very High 4%
(&)	& &&&&&&&	&&&&&&& &&&&&&&	&&& &&&&&&& &&&&&&&	&&&&&&& &&&&&&& &&&&&&&	&&&&& &&&&&&& &&&&&&& &&&&&&& &&&&&&&	&&&&&&& &&&&&&& &&&&&&&	&&& &&&&&&& &&&&&&& &&&&&&&	&&&&&&& &&&&&&&	& &&&&&&&
Percentile	1–4	4–11	11–23	23–40	40–60	60–77	77–89	89–96	96–99
Standard Score	–73	74–81	82–88	89–96	97–103	104–111	112–118	119–126	127–
T-Score	–32	33–37	38–42	43–47	48–52	53–57	58–62	63–67	68–

DAS-II was carefully normed on a stratified, random, national sample of 3,480 children. It is designed to be interpreted by both individual subtests and clusters of subtests, not merely by the total score, which is an important consideration for students with unusual patterns of strengths and weaknesses. Different subtests are used at the lower early years, upper early years, and school-age levels.

Verbal Subtests

Verbal Comprehension: Following oral instructions to point to or to move pictures and toys.
Naming Vocabulary: Naming pictures.

Nonverbal/Spatial Subtests

Copying: Drawing pencil copies of abstract, geometric designs.
Pattern Construction: Copying designs with colored tiles or patterned cubes. There are time limits and bonus points for fast work. An alternative "untimed" procedure uses time limits, but no speed bonuses.

Nonverbal (Fluid) Reasoning Subtests

Picture Similarities: Multiple-choice matching of pictures on the basis of relationships, both concrete (e.g., two round things among other shapes) and abstract (e.g., map with globe from among other round things).
Matrices: Solving visual puzzles by choosing the correct picture or design to complete a logical pattern.

School Readiness Subtests

Early Number Concepts: Oral math questions with illustrations—counting, number concepts, and simple arithmetic.
Matching Letter-Like Forms: Multiple-choice matching of shapes that are similar to letters.
Phonological Processing: Rhyming, blending, deleting, and segmenting sounds in spoken words.

Other Diagnostic Subtests

Recall of Digits Forward: Repeating increasingly long series of digits dictated at two digits per second.

Recognition of Pictures: Seeing one, two, or three pictures for five seconds or four pictures for ten seconds and then trying to find those pictures within a group of four to seven similar pictures.

Recall of Objects–Immediate: Viewing a page of 20 pictures, hearing them named by the evaluator, trying to name the pictures from memory, seeing them again, trying again to name all the pictures, and repeating the process once more. The score is the total of all the pictures recalled on each of the three trials, including pictures recalled two or three times.

Recall of Objects–Delayed: Trying to recall the pictures again on a surprise retest 15 to 20 minutes later.

SCORES NOT USED WITH THE TESTS IN THIS REPORT (GIVEN FOR REFERENCE)

(These are not Allison's own scores, just the scoring systems for the tests.)

When a new test is developed, it is *normed* on a *sample* of hundreds or thousands of people. The sample should be like that for a good opinion poll: female and male, urban and rural, different parts of the country, different income levels, etc. The scores from that norming sample are used as a yardstick for measuring the performance of people who then take the test. This human yardstick allows for the difficulty levels of different tests. The student is being compared to other students on both difficult and easy tasks. You can see from the illustration below

	There are 200 &s. Each && = 1%.			-&& && &&&&&&& &&&&&&& &&&&&&& &&&&&&& && &&&&&&& &&&&&&& && &&&&&&& &&&&&&& &&&&&&& &&&&&&& &&&&&&& &&&&&&& &&&&&&& &&&&&&& && &&&&&&& && &&&&&&& &&&&&&& & & && &&		&	
			&& &&&&&&& &&&&&&&		&& &&&&&&& &&&&&&& &&&&&&&		
		& &&&&&&& & & & &			& &&&&&&& &&	& &&&&&&& && & & & &	
Percent in each	2.2%	6.7%	16.1%	50%	16.1%	6.7%	2.2%
Standard Scores	–69	70–79	80–89	90–109	110–119	120–129	130–
T scores	–29	30–36	37–42	43–56	57–62	63–69	70–
Percentile Ranks	–02	03–08	09–24	25–74	75–90	91–97	98–
DAS-II Classification	**Very Low**	**Low**	**Below Average**	**Average**	**Above Average**	**High**	**Very High**

that there are more scores in the middle than at the very high and low ends. Many different scoring systems are used, just as you can measure the same distance as 1 yard, 3 feet, 36 inches, 91.4 centimeters, 0.91 meter, or 1/1760 mile.

PERCENTILE RANKS (PR) simply state the percent of persons in the norming sample who scored the same as or lower than the student. A percentile rank of 50 would be Average—as high as or higher than 50 percent and lower than the other 50 percent of the norming sample. The middle half of scores falls between percentile ranks of 25 and 75.

STANDARD SCORES ("quotients" on some tests) have an average (*mean*) of 100 and a *standard deviation* of 15. A standard score of 100 would also be at the 50th percentile rank. The middle half of these standard scores falls between 90 and 110.

T **SCORES** have an average (*mean*) of 50 and a standard deviation of 10. A *T* score of 50 would be at the 50th percentile rank. The middle half of *T* scores falls between approximately 43 and 57.

CASE REPORT 4

Name: John Sample   School: Anytown Elementary
Date of Birth: 02–11–1999   Chronological Age: 7 years 11 months
Grade: 2   Date of Evaluation: 01–11–2007
School Psychologist: Amy Tester, Ed.S.
Date of Report: 01-18-2007

Reason for Referral

The Student Assistance Team referred John for a comprehensive psychoeducational evaluation to determine why he has not responded to the reading interventions provided as part of his regular instructional program. The team would like to be able to identify additional targeted instructional recommendations as a result of the evaluation.

Relevant Background Information

John is in second grade at Anytown Elementary School. His language appears appropriate for his age. He uses complete sentences to describe his experiences and chooses words that convey his ideas. During math activities, he frequently raises his hand to answer the teacher's questions. When working with small groups of classmates on math, he takes on a leadership role. However, John does not display the same enthusiasm for reading. During reading activities, his teacher frequently reminds him to lift up his head from his desk and to turn to the appropriate page in his book. His teacher is concerned that his reading skills are lower than the skills of the majority of his classmates. She has observed that John struggles to name high frequency words. He attempts to use segmentation and blending to name unfamiliar words and he reads fewer words correctly within a minute than the other children in his second-grade class.

In an effort to improve his reading, his teacher and the reading specialist provided supplemental instruction focused on segmentation and blending of simple consonant-vowel-consonant words. John demonstrated minimal improvements in number of words read correctly based on these interventions. The Student Assistance Team reviewed John's progress and decided to request additional assessment of John's reading skills.

The school psychologist, as a member of the Student Assistance Team, administered several subtests from the *Process Assessment of the Learner—Second Edition (PAL-II)*. These subtests provided information about John's skills on auditory and visual components of reading and about his ability to name aloud stimuli quickly and accurately. The results on the subtests *Syllables, Phonemes, Rimes, Pseudoword Decoding, Receptive Coding, RAN-Letters, RAN-Words,* and *RAN-Digits* indicated he struggled to segment spoken words into syllables and into phonemes. He performed significantly below expectations in naming the portion of the syllable that is left (e.g., *end*) when the initial phoneme (e.g., *b*) or phonemes (e.g., *bl*) of the syllable is/are omitted. In using phonological decoding skills to read nonsense words, he named simple consonant-vowel-consonant words with short vowel sounds. He did well on tasks that required him to name quickly and accurately letters and letter groups and single-digit and double-digit numbers. He named few whole words quickly and accurately.

Based on this information, the members of the Student Assistance Team requested a comprehensive psychoeducational evaluation in an effort to identify targeted interventions to improve John's achievement of reading skills.

Tests Administered

Differential Ability Scales—Second Edition (DAS-II)
Wechsler Individual Achievement Test—Second Edition (WIAT-II)

Results

The examiner administered several tests to evaluate John's cognitive ability and academic achievement. The DAS-II assessed John's ability to receive, perceive, process, and remember information. The WIAT-II assessed his achievement of skills in reading, written expression, and mathematics.

Complex Mental Processing

On the DAS-II, John was given a number of "core" subtests that assess his ability to perform complex mental processing involving conceptualization and transformation of information. These subtests yield three cluster scores measuring Verbal, Nonverbal Reasoning and Spatial abilities.

John's Verbal Ability cluster score of 102 is within the Average range and equal to or better than those of approximately 55% of his same-age peers in the standardization sample. John's performance was consistent on the two subtests that assessed verbal ability. He was able to define words presented orally by the examiner (Word Definition T Score = 52) and to identify the common concept linking three words (Verbal Similarities T Score = 50).

John's Spatial Ability cluster score of 102 shows that he is also within the Average range on tasks that required complex visual-spatial processing. Once again, his score was equal to or better than the scores of approximately 55% of others his age in the standardization sample. His performance also was consistent on the two subtests that assessed visual-spatial ability. He performed within the Average range on a task that measured his ability to recall briefly exposed abstract designs by drawing them with pencil and paper (Recall of Designs T Score = 51). His performance was also within the Average range on a task that measured his ability to use blocks to construct patterns demonstrated by the examiner or presented in a picture (Pattern Construction T Score = 52).

In contrast with John's average performance on verbal and visual-spatial tasks, he performed in the Below Average range on tasks that measured Nonverbal Reasoning Ability (standard score = 89). This score equaled or exceeded the scores of approximately 23% of others his age in the standardization sample. The 13-point difference between verbal and nonverbal reasoning and between spatial and nonverbal reasoning is statistically significant, but relatively common. A difference of this magnitude occurred in 10–15 percent of children John's age in the standardization sample. Given that the identified difference occurs with relative frequency, we will need other confirmatory evidence before we can conclude that John's nonverbal reasoning abilities are a weakness relative to his verbal and visual-spatial abilities.

On the two subtests assessing nonverbal reasoning, his performance was comparable. His ability to perceive and apply relationships among abstract figures (Matrices T Score = 43) and to perceive sequential patterns (Sequential and Quantitative Reasoning T Score = 44) was at the low end of the average range.

John's DAS-II Core Subtest Scores

Differential Ability Scales-Second Edition (DAS-II)			
Composite / Cluster / Core Subtest	Standard Score (Mean=100)	T Score (Mean= 50)	Percentile Rank
General Conceptual Ability	97		42
Verbal Ability	102		55
Word Definitions		52	58
Verbal Similarities		50	50
Nonverbal Reasoning Ability	89		23
Matrices		43	24
Sequential and Quantitative Reasoning		44	27
Spatial Ability	102		55
Recall of Designs		51	54
Pattern Construction		52	58

The items for both tasks are presented visually with little verbal instruction. Nevertheless, internal verbal mediation of the problems is an important component enabling the child come to a correct solution.

Because John's Nonverbal Reasoning Ability score is significantly lower than his scores on the Verbal and Spatial clusters, his overall General Conceptual Ability score of 97 (average range) does not give a complete picture of his abilities in complex mental processing.

Other Diagnostic Ability Tests

To further assess John's abilities to receive, perceive, process, and remember information, the school psychologist administered the "diagnostic" subtests from the DAS-II. On the Working memory cluster, John earned a standard score of 93. Although this score suggests that John's ability to process information that is temporarily being held within short-term memory is within the Average range, the score does not completely summarize his working memory ability. This is because his performance was significantly better on the subtest Recall of Digits Backward (T Score = 52) than on Recall of Sequential Order (T Score = 40). Both tasks required John to listen to a list of verbally presented words and/or numbers and to hold the list in short-term memory while the list is worked on and put in a different order. Recall of Digits Backward is entirely verbal. On the Recall of Sequential Order subtest, the examiner presents lists of body parts verbally. However, the child needs to visualize the body in order to recall the body parts in correct sequence. John's below-average score on this subtest sug-

John's DAS-II Diagnostic Subtest Scores

Differential Ability Scales–Second Edition (DAS-II)			
Cluster/Diagnostic Subtest	Standard Score (Mean = 100)	T Score (Mean = 50)	Percentile Rank
Working Memory	**93**		**32**
Recall of Sequential Order		40	16
Recall of Digits Backward		52	58
Processing Speed	**89**		**23**
Speed of Information Processing		51	54
Rapid Naming		38	12
Other Diagnostic Subtests			
Recall of Objects–Immediate		40	16
Recall of Objects–Delayed		41	18
Recall of Digits Forward		53	62
Recognition of Pictures		54	66
Phonological Processing		51	54

gests that, while he can adequately handle purely verbal working memory tasks, he may have more difficulty with tasks that require the integration of verbal and visual-spatial information. This low subtest score is consistent with John's somewhat below-average score on the Nonverbal Reasoning cluster.

On the Processing Speed cluster, John also earned a score in the below-average range (standard score = 89), suggesting that he is relatively slow in processing information. Once again, however, there was a statistically significant difference between his scores on the two subtests that form the cluster. His performance was average for his age on the Speed of Information Processing subtest (T Score = 51). This task assesses the speed of children in scanning a page to make visual, quantitative comparisons, and is entirely nonverbal. Responses consist of brief marks made with a pencil on a test booklet. The second subtest in this cluster is Rapid Naming, on which John earned a T Score of 38, which is below-average for his age. The tasks on this subtest require the child to retrieve names of colors and animals as quickly as possible. The tasks are visually presented, but require a verbal response from the child, who names the colors and the animals in the pictures. This subtest therefore requires some degree of integration of visual and verbal processing. John performed better when the task required him to perform *simple* mental operations such as naming the colors only, OR naming the animals only. His performance was significantly weaker on a more *complex* task which required him to look at pictures of colored animals (for example, red dog, blue cow) and to name the color first, and then the name of the animal. Once again, the pattern of John's scores on the Processing Speed subtests is very consistent with his scores on the Nonverbal Reasoning and Working memory clusters—he experiences difficulties on tasks that require verbal-visual integration.

Further support for this hypothesis about John's difficulties came from the Recall of Objects subtest. His scores were within the Below Average range on Recall of Objects—Immediate (T Score = 40) and Recall of Objects—Delayed (T Score = 41). His score on Recall of Objects—Immediate was significantly lower than the mean of his T Scores on the "core" subtests, indicating a probable specific cognitive weakness. The Recall of Objects subtest measures visual-verbal memory. Twenty colored pictures are presented on a card for 45 seconds, and the child is asked to remember as many pictures as he or she can. There are two further trials, with briefer presentations of the same pictures. Finally, the Delayed Recall trial comes later as a surprise, with the child being asked to remember what was on the card, but not being allowed to see it again. Successful performance requires verbal encoding, rehearsal and retrieval strategies as well as visualization of the array of pictures.

John's performance was within the Average range on Recall of Digits Forward (T Score = 53), a measure of short-term auditory sequential recall. No visualization is required on this subtest. Also within the Average range was his ability to remember and recognize visual images (Recognition of Pictures; T Score = 54). This subtest measures short-term visual recognition rather than visual recall and requires detailed discrimination. No verbalization is required on this subtest. We conclude from these subtests, together with John's average scores on the Verbal cluster and on the Spatial cluster, that whenever he is required to process information within one sensory modality (verbal or visual), he performs at an average level for his age.

John's score on the Phonological Processing subtest was within the Average range (T Score = 51). This subtest consists of four tasks measuring Rhyming, Blending, Deletion, and Phoneme Identification and Segmentation. Analysis of his performance on these tasks indicates John did well on rhyming. He also did well on blending syllables (e.g., Mon–day) and phonemes (e.g., o–n). He performed below average in deletion (e.g., say Mon–day without Mon). This may reflect a weakness in analytic skill that indicates if he has an "ear" for sounds within words. He also struggled to name phonemes and segments of words he heard. Segmentation of orally presented words is a fundamental skill needed for spelling.

Summary

In processing information, John responds effectively when tasks are presented verbally and when the tasks require a verbal response. He is able to hold verbal information in short-term memory and to repeat or transform the information. Similarly, he responds effectively when tasks are presented visually and when he is asked to recall information he saw or organize visual information and objects in space. In comparison, he struggles to respond effectively on tasks that require integration of visual and verbal processing. This probably impacts his performance on reading tasks which require him to translate printed words (visual modality) into spoken words (verbal modality).

Academic Achievement

The WIAT-II was administered to assess John's achievement of skills in reading, writing, and mathematics. Consistent with teacher observations, John performed better on mathematics subtests than on reading and writing subtests. His standard score of 100 for mathematics was within the Average range and equaled or exceeded the scores of approximately 50% of others his age in the standardization sample. He earned a standard score of 106 for Numerical Operations which required him to solve written mathematics problems. His score was 96 on Mathematics Reasoning which assessed his ability to reason mathematically when problems were presented with verbal and visual prompts. Although he performed within the Average range on both mathematics subtests, it is noteworthy that John's score was slightly lower on Mathematics Reasoning which required processing of auditory and visual information.

On the Reading Composite, John earned a standard score of 69. Within the Extremely Low range, this score equaled or exceeded the scores of approximately 2% of others his age in the standardization sample. Put another way, his performance is in the lowest 2 percent of children of his age. His best performance in reading was on Pseudoword Decoding which required him to pronounce nonsense words that are phonetically regular. Although his score was below average on this task, he was able to sound out unfamiliar letter combinations, following regular rules of phonemic analysis, and blend the segments to name the words. His score was significantly lower on Word Reading which required him to iden-

John's WIAT-II Scores

	Wechsler Individual Achievement Test-Second Edition		
Composite/Subtests	Standard Score (Mean = 100)	Percentile Rank	Abil/Ach Disc. Sig?
Reading	**69**	**2**	**Y**
Word Reading	58	0.3	Y
Pseudoword Decoding	86	18	Y
Reading Comprehension	72	3	Y
Written Language	**83**	**13**	**Y**
Spelling	79	8	Y
Written Expression	90	25	N
Mathematics	**100**	**50**	**N**
Numerical Operations	106	66	N
Mathematics Reasoning	96	39	N

tify beginning and ending sounds, blend two word parts he heard to name a word and point to a letter symbol based on a letter sound said by the examiner. For Reading Comprehension, he struggled to read sentences given picture clues. His performance is consistent with information from the *Process Assessment of the Learner–Second Edition*.

John's score for Written Language was within the Low Average range. He scored in the Average range on Written Expression, which required him to generate a list of words to match a prescribed category and to combine multiple sentences into one meaningful sentence. In contrast, he scored within the Borderline range in spelling dictated letter blends and words. This is consistent with weaknesses in segmentation identified on earlier assessments.

Summary

John is a seven-year-eleven-month-old student in the second grade at Anytown Elementary School. His achievement in mathematics is at the expected rate, and is consistent with his GCA score of 97 on the DAS-II. On the WIAT-II, he scored within the Average range for mathematics. He is performing significantly below grade level expectations in reading, and his scores for reading and written expression are substantially lower than would be expected given his average intellectual ability. Following interventions in the classroom, the Student Assistance Team referred John for a comprehensive psychoeducational evaluation.

John's achievement in reading and writing is affected by weaknesses at the acquisition phase of learning. In collecting information, he demonstrated weaknesses in auditory-visual information processing. He struggles to allocate attention when information is presented both verbally and visually. This weakness affects the accuracy of the information he stores in his memory and the accuracy of the information he retrieves. Overall, he struggles with tasks that demand integration between verbal and visual processing.

RECOMMENDATIONS

The Individualized Education Program Committee will make decisions regarding John's eligibility and need for direct specialized instruction. Regardless of the setting, instruction for John must focus on improving his basic skills in reading and writing. In providing instruction, his teachers will consider his ability to perform effectively when tasks are presented either verbally or visually and his lowered performance on tasks that require integration of verbal-visual processing. A multi-sensory approach to reading instruction should be considered for John (see, for example, Judith R. Birsh (1999). *Multisensory Teaching of Basic Language Skills.* Baltimore, MD: Brookes; and Janet Townend & Martin Turner (2000). *Dyslexia in Practice: A Guide for Teachers.* New York: Kluwer).

Here are some immediate recommendations for teaching: To improve John's phonological awareness, focus on syllables. Ask him to

(a) find a word hidden in a longer word. For example, Say **ball.** Is the word **ball** hidden in **baseball? ballgame? cowboy? bolt?**

(b) say the syllable missing from a word he hears. For example, Say **forgotten.** Now say **gotten.** What is missing?

(c) say a word without a part of the word. For example, say **destiny.** Now say it without **des.**

(d) say a new word by substituting a given syllable for another. For example, Say **sunshine.** Now don't say it with **shine** say it with **day.**

To improve reading and spelling, provide explicit instruction on translating printed words into spoken words (see e.g., Berninger, *Process Assessment of the Learner: Talking Letters*). Ask John to look at a sheet with letters and pictures that begin with each letter. The teacher points to the letter, names the letter and asks John to repeat this. Then the teacher names the picture and makes the sound at the beginning of the picture. Use this strategy to teach John to sound out words and to listen for the sounds in dictated words.

Use the Looking Game to focus his attention on each letter in a word by sweeping your finger under the word from left to right. Cover up the word with a blank card and ask him to spell the word. If he does not spell the word correctly, show the word and point out the letters he missed. For example, bat, nap, jet, kid, cot, but).

Use the Sound Game to focus his attention on the number of phonemes in a word. For example, ask John to say bed. Then ask him to "say it again but don't say /b/." Use blocks or chips to identify the number of phonemes in a word. For example, for bed, place 3 blocks horizontally in front of John. As you say each phoneme, point to the corresponding block. Then remove the block corresponding to the deleted phoneme and pronounce the remaining sounds pointing to the corresponding block as you say the phoneme. (see Berninger, 1998, *Guides for intervention: Reading Writing*).

Appendix A

Upper Early Years Interpretive Worksheet

Step 1: Provisionally evaluate the GCA, SNC, and Core Clusters

If the GCA or SNC is below 70, administer, score and evaluate an adaptive behavior checklist

Step 2: For the Core Clusters, Evaluate Between-Cluster Differences

    A. Identify any significant differences between DAS-II Clusters (Verbal vs. Nonverbal Reasoning vs. Spatial)
    B. Identify the base-rate frequency of any observed significant differences

If differences are significant and unusual, tentatively focus interpretation on Clusters rather than on the GCA
If differences are significant but not unusual, consider whether to focus interpretation on Clusters or on the GCA

Step 3: For the Core Clusters, Evaluate Within-Cluster Differences

    A. Identify any significant Within-Cluster differences between subtest T scores
    B. Identify the base-rate frequency of any observed significant differences

If differences are significant and unusual, focus interpretation on narrow abilities rather than on the Cluster
If differences are significant but not unusual, consider whether to focus interpretation on narrow abilities or on the Cluster

Step 4: Evaluate GCA—Diagnostic Cluster Differences

    A. Identify any significant differences between the GCA and each Diagnostic Cluster
    B. Identify the frequency of any observed significant differences

Interpret Diagnostic Clusters in light of this information

Step 5: For the Diagnostic Clusters, Evaluate Within-Cluster Differences

    A. Identify any significant Within-Cluster differences between subtest T scores
    B. Identify the base-rate frequency of any observed significant differences

If differences are significant and unusual, focus interpretation on narrow abilities rather than the Cluster
If differences are significant, but not unusual, consider whether to focus interpretation on narrow abilities or on the Cluster

Step 6: Narrow Ability Hypotheses

    A. Identify the narrow abilities assessed and any relevant differences between them

Step 7: Evaluate Subtest Variability (Core and Diagnostic subtests)

    A. Identify any significant subtest differences from the Mean Core T Score
    B. Identify the base-rate frequency of any observed significant differences

Step 8: Evaluate Shared Ability Hypothesis

    A. Identify any relevant shared ability groupings

Step 9: Evaluate Cultural and Linguistic Influences

    A. Generate hypotheses based upon how the person does in relationship to both cultural and linguistic demands of each subtest

Step 10: Evaluate relevant subtest comparisons

    A. Generate and test hypotheses based upon relevant subtest comparisons.

Step 11: Evaluate Qualitative Responses and Observed Behaviors

    A. Generate and test hypotheses based upon the scores and also on relevant behaviors and observations

Step 12: (Optional) Compare DAS-II with Achievement Scores

Step 13: Evaluate all of this information and integrate it into a cohesive description of the examinee's cognitive functioning as revealed by the DAS-II

Step 14: Integrate this understanding with background information, previous testing, and concurrent testing

Step 1. Provisionally evaluate the GCA, SNC, and Core Clusters

	Score	(circle one) 90% or 95% confidence	PR	Classification
GENERAL CONCEPTUAL ABILITY (GCA):		-		
SPECIAL NONVERBAL COMPOSITE (SNC):		-		
VERBAL (V):		-		
NONVERBAL REASONING (NVR):		-		
SPATIAL (Sp):		-		

Step 2a. Are there any significant differences _between_ the three Core Clusters?

	Difference	Significant (.01)	Significant (.05)	Not Significant	Is Difference Significant?	
V ( ) vs. NVR ( )		19+	15-18	0-14	Yes	No
V ( ) vs. Sp ( ):		15+	13-14	0-11	Yes	No
NVR ( ) vs. Sp ( ):		17+	13-16	0-12	Yes	No

◆ Step 2a Decision		
Is at least one of the three comparisons marked "Yes"?	YES	NO

If the answer is NO, there are no significant differences between the cluster scores		You may interpret the GCA. **Skip to Step 3a**

If the answer is YES, there are significant differences between the cluster scores		**Go to Step 2b**

Step 2b. Are significant differences _between_ Core Clusters unusually large?

Significant Differences	Direction of Difference	Extreme 15%	Extreme 10%	Extreme 5%	Extreme 2%	Extreme 1%	Is difference unusually large? (10% or less)	
V vs. NVR	V > NVR	16	19	24	30	37	Yes	No
Difference =	V < NVR	13	18	24	30	35		
V vs. Sp	V > Sp	16	19	25	30	38	Yes	No
Difference =	V < Sp	15	19	23	30	36		
NVR vs. Sp	NVR > Sp	15	19	25	33	38	Yes	No
Difference =	NVR < Sp	16	19	24	30	32		

	Step 2b Decision		
	Is at least one of the three comparisons marked "Yes"?	YES	NO

If the answer is NO, there are significant BUT usual differences between the cluster scores	⇨	You may interpret the GCA with caution, but consider interpreting clusters

If the answer YES, there are significant AND unusual differences between the cluster scores	⇨	Interpret the GCA, but only with extreme caution, and consider interpreting clusters

Step 3a: Identify any significant differences _within_ DAS-II Core Clusters

	Difference	Significant (.01)	Significant (.05)	Not Significant	Is difference significant?	
VC ( ) vs. NV ( ):		15+	11-14	0-10	YES	NO
PSim ( ) vs. Mat ( ):		16+	12-15	0-11	YES	NO
PCon ( ) vs. Copy ( ):		10+	8-9	0-7	YES	NO

	Step 3a Decision (repeat for each of the three clusters before continuing to Step 4)	

For each comparison marked NO, there is no significant difference between the subtest scores within the cluster	⇨	Interpret each Cluster with no significant differences. **Then skip to Step 4a**

For each comparison marked YES, there is a significant difference between subtest scores within the cluster	⇨	**Go to Step 3b**

3b. Are significant differences _within_ Core Clusters unusually large?

Significant Differences	Direction of Difference	Extreme 15%	Extreme 10%	Extreme 5%	Extreme 2%	Extreme 1%	Is difference unusually large? (10% or less)	
VC vs. NV	VC > NV	8	10	13	19	32	YES	NO
( ) vs. ( )	VC < NV	9	12	15	17	19		
PSim vs. Mat	PSim > Mat	11	14	18	24	27	YES	NO
( ) vs. ( )	PSim < Mat	12	14	18	22	25		
PC vs. Copy	PC > Copy	9	12	16	23	27	YES	NO
( ) vs. ( )	PC < Copy	9	12	15	21	25		

◆ Step 3b Decision for each cluster	
Is at least one of the three comparisons marked "Yes"?	YES NO

If the answer is NO, there are significant BUT usual differences between subtest scores <u>within</u> one or more clusters	⇨ You may interpret the cluster with caution, but consider interpreting subtests

If the answer is YES, there are significant AND unusual differences between subtest scores <u>within</u> the cluster	⇨ Interpret the cluster, but only with extreme caution, and consider interpreting subtests

Step 3c. Determine Normative Strengths and Weaknesses in the Ability Score Profile

Cluster Ability	Interpretable? (Y/N)	Standard Score	Normative Weakness <85	Within Normal Limits 85-115	Normative Strength >115
Verbal					
Nonverbal Reasoning					
Spatial					

4a. Are there any significant differences _between_ the GCA and the Diagnostic Clusters?

	Difference	Significant (.01)	Significant (.05)	Not Significant	Is difference significant?	
GCA ( ) vs. SchR ( ):		12+	9 -11	0 - 8	Yes	No
GCA ( ) vs. WM ( ):		12+	9 -11	0 - 8	Yes	No
GCA ( ) vs. PS ( ):		15+	11 -14	0 -10	Yes	No

Step 4a Decision		
Is either one of the two comparisons marked "Yes"?	YES	NO

If the answer is NO, there are no significant differences between GCA and the Diagnostic cluster scores	⇒	**Skip to Step 5a**

If the answer is YES, there is at least one significant difference between the GCA and the Diagnostic cluster scores	⇒	**Go to Step 4b**

⇓

4b. Are significant differences _between_ GCA and the Diagnostic Clusters unusually large?

Significant Differences	Direction of Difference	Extreme 15%	Extreme 10%	Extreme 5%	Extreme 2%	Extreme 1%	Is difference unusually large? (10% or less)	
GCA vs. SchR	GCA > SchR	11-13	14-16	17-21	22	23+	YES	NO
Difference =	GCA < SchR	11-13	14-17	18-21	22-26	27+		
GCA vs. WM	GCA > WM	12-14	15-19	20-25	26-29	30+	YES	NO
Difference =	GCA < WM	12-14	15-19	20-27	29-32	33+		
GCA vs. PS	GCA > PS	16-19	20-25	26-33	34-38	39+	YES	NO
Difference =	GCA > PS	16-19	20-27	28-37	38-41	42+		

Step 4b Decision		
Is either one of the comparisons marked "Yes"?	YES	NO

If the answer is NO, there is at least one significant BUT usual difference between the GCA and the Diagnostic cluster scores		You may interpret the discrepant cluster(s) with extreme caution

If the answer YES, there are significant AND unusual differences between the GCA and the Diagnostic cluster score(s)	⇒	You may interpret the discrepant cluster(s) with caution

⇓

Step 5a: For the Diagnostic Clusters, are there any significant differences _within_ clusters?

	Difference	Significant (.01)	Significant (.05)	Not Significant	Is the difference significant?	
Working Memory						
RSO ( ) vs. RDb ( ):		12+	9 -11	0-8	YES	NO
Processing Speed						
SIP ( ) vs. RN ( ):		14+	11-13	0-10	YES	NO
School Readiness						
ENC ( ) vs. MLLF ( ):		14+	11 -13	0-10	YES	NO
ENC ( ) vs. PhP ( ):		11+	8 -10	0-7		
MLLF ( ) vs. PhP ( ):		13+	10 -12	0-9	YES	NO

 Step 5a Decision (repeat for each cluster before continuing to Step 5b or 6)

For each comparison marked NO, there is no significant subtest difference within the cluster	⟹	Interpret the Clusters with no significant subtest differences and go to **Step 6**

For each comparison marked YES, there is a significant difference between subtest scores within the cluster	⟹	**Go to Step 5b**

Step 5b. For the Diagnostic Clusters, are significant differences _within_ the clusters unusually large?

Significant Differences	Direction of Difference	Extreme 15%	Extreme 10%	Extreme 5%	Extreme 2%	Extreme 1%	Is difference unusually large? (10% or less)	
Working Memory								
RSO vs. RDb	RSO > RDb:	11-13	14-17	18-21	22-25	26+	YES	NO
Difference =	RSO < RDb:	10	11-15	16-21	22-26	27+		
Processing Speed								
SIP vs. RN	SIP > RN:	11-13	14-16	17-23	24-32	33+	YES	NO
Difference =	SIP < RN:	11-12	13-16	17-21	22-24	25+		
School Readiness								
ENC vs. MLLF	ENC > MLLF:	11-13	14-18	19-24	25-26	27+	YES	NO
Difference =	ENC < MLLF:	11-12	13-17	18-22	23-26	27+		
ENC vs. PhP	ENC > PhP:	11-13	14-18	19-23	24-27	28+	YES	NO
Difference =	ENC < PhP:	9-10	11-13	14-17	18	19+		
MLLF vs. PhP	MLLF > PhP:	14-16	17-22	23-26	27-29	30+	YES	NO
Difference =	MLLF < PhP:	9-11	12-15	16-19	20-22	23+		

◆ Step 5b Decision		
Is at least one of the comparisons marked "Yes"?	YES	NO

If the answer is NO, there are significant BUT usual differences between subtest scores within one or both clusters	⇨	You may interpret the cluster(s) with caution but consider Narrow Abilities

If the answer is YES, there are significant AND unusual differences between the cluster subtest scores	⇨	Interpret individual clusters, but only with extreme caution. Examine Narrow Abilities.

Step 5c. Determine Normative Strengths and Weaknesses in the Ability Score Profile

Cluster Ability	Interpretable? (Y/N)	Standard Score	Normative Weakness <85	Within Normal Limits 85-115	Normative Strength >115
Working Memory					
Processing Speed					
School Readiness					

Step 6. DAS -II Subtests Broad and Narrow Abilities

	Narrow Abilities
Verbal Ability (Gc)	
Verbal Comprehension	Listening Ability
Naming Vocabulary	Lexical Knowledge
Nonverbal Reasoning Ability (Gf)	
Picture Similarities	Induction
Matrices	Induction
Spatial Ability (Gv)	
Pattern Construction	Spatial Relations
Pattern Construction - Alternative	Spatial Relations
Copying	Visualization
Matching Letter-like Forms	Visualization
Retrieval (Glr)	
Recall of Objects - Immediate	Free-recall Memory
Recall of Objects - Delayed	Free-recall Memory
Memory (Gsm)	
Recall of Digits Forward	Memory Span
Recall of Digits Backward	Working Memory
Recall of Sequential Order	Working Memory
Processing Speed (Gs)	
Speed of Information Processing	Scanning
Rapid Naming	Complex
Auditory Processing (Ga)	
Phonological Processing	Phonemic Coding
Additional	
Early Number Concepts	Lexical Knowledge / General verbal knowledge / Piagetian reasoning

Adapted from Table 2.1, p. 19, Introductory and Technical Handbook (Elliott, 2007).

Step 6. (continued) Identify the narrow abilities assessed and any relevant differences between them

Narrow Ability (subtests): Definition[1]

Free Recall Memory (Recall of Objects – Immediate and Recall of Objects – Delayed): Ability to recall, without associations, as many unrelated items as possible, in any order, after a large collection of items is presented. [Note that Recall of Objects employs both visual and verbal input, not just visual.]

Induction (Picture Similarities, Matrices, Sequential and Quantitative Reasoning): Ability to discover the underlying characteristic (e.g., rule, concept, principle, process, trend, class membership) that underlies a specific problem or a set of observations, or to apply a previously learned rule to the problem. Reasoning from specific cases or observations to general rules or broad generalizations. Often requires the ability to combine separate pieces of information in the formation of inferences, rules, hypotheses, or conclusions.

Language Development (Word Definitions, Verbal Similarities): General development or understanding and application of words, sentences, and paragraphs (not requiring reading) in spoken native language skills to express or communicate a thought or feeling.

Lexical Knowledge (Naming Vocabulary): Extent of vocabulary (nouns, verbs, or adjectives) that can be understood in terms of correct word (semantic) meanings. Although evidence indicates that vocabulary knowledge is a separable component from LD, it is often difficult to disentangle these two highly corrected abilities in research studies.

Listening Ability (Verbal Comprehension): Ability to listen and understand the meaning of oral communications (spoken words, phrases, sentences, and paragraphs). The ability to receive and understand spoken information.

Memory Span (Recall of Digits Forward): Ability to attend to, register, and immediately recall (after only one presentation) temporally ordered elements and then reproduce the series of elements in correct order.

Perceptual Speed (Speed of Information Processing, Rapid Naming): Ability to rapidly and accurately search, compare (for visual similarities or differences) and identify visual elements presented side-by-side or separated in a visual field.

> *Scanning (Ps)* ability to scan, compare, and look up visual stimuli

> *Complex (Pc)* ability to perform visual pattern recognition tasks that impose additional cognitive demands such as spatial visualization, estimating and interpolating, and heightened memory span loads.

Phonetic Coding (Phonological Processing): Ability to code, process, and be sensitive to nuances in phonemic information (speech sounds) in short-term memory. Includes the ability to identify, isolate, blend, or transform sounds of speech.

Piagetian Reasoning (Early Number Concepts): Ability to demonstrate the acquisition and application (in the form of logical thinking) of cognitive concepts as defined by Piaget's developmental cognitive theory. These concepts include seriation (organizing material into an orderly series that facilitates understanding of relationships between events), conservation (awareness that physical quantities do not change in amount when altered in appearance), classification (ability to organize materials that possess similar characteristics into categories), etc.

Quantitative Reasoning (Sequential and Quantitative Reasoning): Ability to inductively and/or deductively reason with concepts involving mathematical relations and properties.

Spatial Relations (Pattern Construction, Pattern Construction – Alternative): Ability to rapidly perceive and manipulate (mental rotation, transformations, reflection, etc.) visual patterns or to maintain orientation with respect to objects in space. Spatial Relations may require the identification of an object when viewed from different angles or positions. Differs from Visualization primarily by an emphasis on fluency.

Visual Memory (Recall of Designs, Recognition of Pictures): Ability to form and store a mental representation or image of a visual shape or configuration (typically during a brief study period), over at least a few seconds, and then recognize or recall it later (during the test phase).

Visualization (Copying, Matching Letter-Like Forms): The ability to apprehend a spatial form, object, or scene and match it with another spatial object, form, or scene with the requirement to rotate it (one or more times) in two or three dimensions. Requires the ability to mentally imagine, manipulate or transform objects or visual patterns and to predict how they would appear under altered conditions (e.g., parts are moved or rearranged). Differs from Spatial Relations primarily by a de-emphasis on fluency.

Working Memory (Recall of Digits Backward, Recall of Sequential Order): Ability to temporarily store and perform a set of cognitive operations on information that requires divided attention and the management of the limited capacity resources of short-term memory.

[1] CHC definitions adapted from http://www.iapsych.com/chcdef.htm

Step 7. Are single subtest T scores significantly different from Mean Core T?

Mean Core T: _____	Circle one (GCA or SNC)	T Score	Difference from Mean	Difference required	High/ Low (H / L) (+ / -)	Frequency (Table B.8)
Verbal Comprehension(Gc)				7		
Naming Vocabulary (Gc)				8		
Picture Similarities(Gf)				7		
Matrices (Gf)				8		
Pattern Construction (Gv)				6		
Copying (Gv)				7		
Recall of Objects-Immediate (Glr)				11		
Recall of Digits Forward (Gsm)				8		
Recognition of Pictures (Gv)				10		
Early Number Concepts (Gc/Gf)				9		
Matching Letter-like Forms (Gv)				9		
Recall of Sequential Order (Gsm)				7		
Speed of Information Processing (Gs)				8		
Recall of Digits Backward (Gsm)				9		
Phonological Processing (Ga)				7		
Rapid Naming (Gs)				10		

Step 8a. Determine Probable and Possible DAS II Early Years Shared Abilities

Early Years Shared Ability	Shared Ability Subtests (includes out-of-level subtests) Enter H, L, +, or − in each box.

Verbal Conceptualization

H / L **or** + / −

VC	NV	ENC

Formulation and Testing of Hypotheses

H / L **or** + / −

VC	PS	PC	Mat

Use of Verbal Mediation to Solve Nonverbal Problems

H / L **or** + / −

PS	PC	Mat

Verbal Comprehension:

H / L **or** + / −

VC	ENC	RSO

Verbal Expression:

H / L **or** + / −

NV	ROi	RDf	RSO	RDb	PhP	RN

Visual Analysis of Pictures:

H / L **or** + / −

VC	PS	Mat	ROi	RPic

Visual Analysis of Figures or Designs:

H / L **or** + / −

PS	PC	Mat	Copy	MLLF

Spatial Visualization and Orientation:

H / L **or** + / −

PC	Copy	MLLF

Visual Verbal Integration:

H / L **or** + / −

PS	Mat	ROi	RSO

Short-term Memory: (general):

H / L **or** + / −

ROi	RDf	RPic	RSO	RDb

Auditory Short-term Memory:

H / L **or** + / −

RDf	RSO	RDb

Visual Short-term Memory:

H / L **or** + / −

ROi	RPic

Verbal Long -term Information Retrieval:

H / L **or** + / −

NV	ENC	RN

Visual/holistic Information Processing:

H / L **or** + / −

PS	PC	Mat	Copy	RPic	MLLF

Sequential Information Processing:

H / L **or** + / −

VC	ROi	RDf	RSO	SIP	RDb	RN

PC = Pattern Construction; Mat = Matrices; VC = Verbal Comprehension; NV = Naming Vocabulary; PS = Picture Similarities; Copy = Copying; ENC = Early Number Concepts; RDf = Recall of Digits – Forward; RPic = Recognition of Pictures; ROi = Recall of Objects – Immediate; PhP = Phonological Processing; RSO = Recall of Sequential Order; RDb = Recall of Digits – Backward; SIP = Speed of Information Processing; RN = Rapid Naming

H = A score that is significantly greater than the mean Core T score.
+ = A score that is greater than the mean Core T score BUT does not reach a level of significance.

L = A score that is significantly lower than the mean Core T score.
- = A score that is less than the mean Core T score BUT does not reach a level of significance.

Step 8b (optional). Early Years Shared Ability formulae for converting sums of T scores to Deviation Scores (Mean = 100, SD = 15)

Early Years Shared Ability	Subtests	Sum of T scores[1]	Multiplier	Additive	Score	.05 SEm
Verbal Conceptualization	VC, NV, ENC		0.60	10.07		8.11
Formulation and Testing of Hypotheses	VC, PS, PC, Mat		0.51	-1.02		7.53
Use of Verbal Mediation to Solve Nonverbal Problems	PS, PC, Mat		0.64	3.53		8.19
Verbal Comprehension:	VC, ENC, RSO		0.64	4.23		7.78
Verbal Expression:	NV, ROi , RDf, RSO, RDb, PhP, RN		0.32	-12.96		6.20
Visual Analysis of Pictures:	VC, PS, Mat, ROi, RPic		0.44	-10.20		8.48
Visual Analysis of Figures or Designs:	PS, PC, Mat, Copy, MLLF		0.41	-2.98		6.68
Spatial Visualization and Orientation:	PC, Copy, MLLF		0.62	7.21		6.73
Visual Verbal Integration:	PS, Mat, ROi, RSO		0.58	-16.42		9.48
Short-term Memory: (general):	ROi, RDf, RPic, RSO, RDb		0.44	-10.97		7.50
Auditory Short-term Memory:	RDf, RSO, RDb,		0.68	-1.44		7.40
Visual Short-term Memory:	ROi, RPic		0.91	8.71		11.76
Verbal Long-term Information Retrieval:	NV, ENC, RN		0.69	-2.91		9.56
Visual/holistic Information Processing:	PS, PC, Mat, Copy, RPic, MLLF		0.35	-5.77		6.54
Sequential Information Processing:	VC, ROi, RDf, RSO, SIP, RDb, RN		0.33	-16.35		6.46

PC = Pattern Construction; Mat = Matrices; VC = Verbal Comprehension; NV = Naming Vocabulary; PS = Picture Similarities; Copy = Copying; ENC = Early Number Concepts; RDf = Recall of Digits – Forward; RPic = Recognition of Pictures; ROi = Recall of Objects – Immediate; PhP = Phonological Processing; RSO = Recall of Sequential Order; RDb = Recall of Digits – Backward; SIP = Speed of Information Processing; RN = Rapid Naming

[1]All subtests in a shared ability grouping must have been administered in order to use the individual formulae.

Step 9. Evaluate Possible Linguistic and Cultural influences on the DAS-II Subtests

DAS-II Subtest	*T* Score	Linguistic / Cultural Influence	Cell Standard Score[1]
Matrices			
Sequential & Quantitative Reasoning			
Pattern Construction		Low / Low	
Recall of Designs			
Matching Letter-like Forms			
Copying			
Recall of Digits Backward		Low / Medium	
Speed of Information Processing			
Recall of Digits Forward		Low / High	
Picture Similarities			
Recognition of Pictures		Medium / Low	
Recall of Objects-Immediate			
Early Number Concepts			
Rapid Naming		Medium / Medium	
Recall of Sequential Order			
Phonological Processing		Medium / High	
Verbal Comprehension		High / Medium	
Naming Vocabulary			
Verbal Similarities		High / High	
Word Definitions			

Adapted from Flanagan, D. P., Ortiz, S. O., & Alfonso, V. (2007). Essentials of Cross-Battery Assessment, Second Edition. New York: John Wiley & Sons.

---

[1]To calculate the Cell Standard Score (Mean = 100, SD = 15), find the *Average T score* for each cell (add *T* scores and divide by the number of subtests in the cell), round the *Average T score*, and then convert the *Average T score* to a standard score using the following formula:

$$SS = \left(\frac{Average\ T\ Score - 50}{10} \right) \times 15 + 100$$

For example, if the 2 subtests, Verbal Similarities and Word Definitions, in the High/High cell had *T* scores of 30 and 42 respectively, the *Average T score* would be 36

$$(30+42)/2 = 36$$

Enter this *Average T score* into the first part of the formula results in:

$$\left(\frac{36 - 50}{10} \right) = \left(\frac{-14}{10} \right) = -1.4$$

Multiply -1.4 by 15:

$$-1.4 \times 15 = -21.0$$

Now add 100:

$$-21 + 100 = 79$$

The 2 subtests that form the High/High cell, with *T* scores of 30 and 42 respectively, when combined, would be the equivalent of a Standard Score of 79.

Step 10. Additional subtest pair comparisons

Comparison	Difference	Difference needed for significance	Possible implication
RDf vs. RDb (....) vs. (....)		8	Non-meaningful auditory memory span versus Non-meaningful auditory working memory
RDf vs. RSO (....) vs. (....)		8	Non-meaningful auditory memory span versus Meaningful auditory/visual working memory
RDf vs. RPic (....) vs. (....)		12	Non-meaningful auditory memory span versus Visual memory
RDf vs. RDes (....) vs. (....)		9	Non-meaningful auditory memory span versus Non-meaningful visual memory
RDb vs. RSO (....) vs. (....)		8	Non-meaningful auditory working memory versus Meaningful auditory/visual working memory
ROi vs. ROd (....) vs. (....)		11	Meaningful visual memory immediate versus Meaningful visual memory delayed
ROi vs. RDf (....) vs. (....)		10	Meaningful visual memory immediate versus Non-meaningful auditory memory span
ROi vs. RDb (....) vs. (....)		14	Meaningful visual memory versus Non-meaningful auditory working memory
RDes vs. RPic (....) vs. (....)		12	Non-meaningful visual memory versus Meaningful visual memory
SIP vs. RN (....) vs. (....)		10	Processing Speed Cluster: If significant difference is evidenced, examine ROi vs. RN comparison
ROi vs. RN (....) vs. (....)		12	* Make this comparison only if the SIP vs. RN is significant. RN could involve Glr

Step 11. Method of Input and Output for DAS-II Subtests

	Input			Output	
	Auditory	Visual		Verbal	Motor
		Meaningful	Symbolic		
Verbal Subtests					
Verbal Comprehension	v	v			v
Naming Vocabulary		v		v	
Word Definitions	v			v	
Verbal Similarities	v			v	
Nonverbal/Spatial Subtests					
Picture Similarities		v	v		v
Copying		v	v		v
Recall of Designs		v	v		v
Pattern Construction			v		v
Nonverbal (Fluid Reasoning) Subtests					
Matrices			v	v	v
Sequential and Quantitative Reasoning		v		v	v
Diagnostic Subtests					
Early Number Concepts	v	v		v	v
Matching Letter-Like Forms			v		v
Recall of Digits Forward	v		v	v	
Recall of Digits Backward	v		v	v	
Recall of Sequential Order	v	v		v	
Recognition of Pictures		v			v
Recall of Objects-Immediate		v		v	
Recall of Objects-Delayed		v		v	
Rapid Naming		v		v	
Phonological Processing	v	v		v	
Speed of Information Processing		v			v

Appendix B

School-Age Interpretive Worksheet

Step 1: Provisionally evaluate the GCA, SNC, and Core Clusters

If the GCA or SNC is below 70, administer, score and evaluate an adaptive behavior checklist

Step 2: For the Core Clusters, Evaluate Between-Cluster Differences

A. Identify any significant differences between DAS-II Clusters (Verbal vs. Nonverbal Reasoning vs. Spatial)
B. Identify the base-rate frequency of any observed significant differences

If differences are significant and unusual, tentatively focus interpretation on Clusters rather than on the GCA.
If differences are significant but not unusual, consider whether to focus interpretation on Clusters or on the GCA

Step 3: For the Core Clusters, Evaluate Within-Cluster Differences

A. Identify any significant Within-Cluster differences between subtest T scores
B. Identify the base-rate frequency of any observed significant differences

If differences are significant and unusual, focus interpretation on narrow abilities rather than on the Cluster
If differences are significant but not unusual, consider whether to focus interpretation on narrow abilities or on the Cluster

Step 4: Evaluate GCA—Diagnostic Cluster Differences

A. Identify any significant differences between the GCA and each Diagnostic Cluster
B. Identify the frequency of any observed significant differences

Interpret Diagnostic Clusters in light of this information.

Step 5: For the Diagnostic Clusters, Evaluate Within-Cluster Differences

A. Identify any significant Within-Cluster differences between subtest T scores
B. Identify the base-rate frequency of any observed significant differences

If differences are significant and unusual, focus interpretation on narrow abilities rather than the Cluster
If differences are significant, but not unusual, consider whether to focus interpretation on narrow abilities or on the Cluster

Step 6: Narrow Ability Hypotheses

A. Identify the narrow abilities assessed and any relevant differences between them

Step 7: Evaluate Subtest Variability (Core and Diagnostic subtests)

A. Identify any significant subtest differences from the Mean Core T Score
B. Identify the base-rate frequency of any observed significant differences

Step 8: Evaluate Shared Ability Hypothesis

A. Identify any relevant shared ability groupings

Step 9: Evaluate Cultural and Linguistic Influences

A. Generate hypotheses based upon how the person does in relationship to both cultural and linguistic demands of each subtest

Step 10: Evaluate relevant subtest comparisons

A. Generate and test hypotheses based upon relevant subtest comparisons.

Step 11: Evaluate Qualitative Responses and Observed Behaviors

A. Generate and test hypotheses based upon the scores and also on relevant behaviors and observations

Step 12: (Optional) Compare DAS-II with Achievement Scores

Step 13: Evaluate all of this information and integrate it into a cohesive description of the examinee's cognitive functioning as revealed by the DAS-II

Step 14: Integrate this understanding with background information, previous testing, and concurrent testing

343

Step 1. Provisionally evaluate the GCA, SNC, and Core Clusters

	Score	(circle one) 90% or 95% confidence	PR	Classification
GENERAL CONCEPTUAL ABILITY (GCA):		-		
SPECIAL NONVERBAL COMPOSITE (SNC):		-		
VERBAL (V):		-		
NONVERBAL REASONING (NVR):		-		
SPATIAL (Sp):		-		

Step 2a. Are there any significant differences _between_ the three Core Clusters?

	Difference	Significant (.01)	Significant (.05)	Not Significant	Is difference significant?
V ( ) vs. NVR ( ):		17+	13-16	0-12	Yes No
V ( ) vs. Sp ( ):		16+	12-15	0-11	Yes No
NVR ( ) vs. Sp ( ):		14+	10-13	0-9	Yes No

◆ Step 2a Decision

	YES	NO
Is at least one of the three comparisons marked "Yes"?	YES	NO

If the answer is NO, there are no significant differences between the cluster scores		You may interpret the GCA. **Skip to Step 3a**

If the answer is YES, there are significant differences between the cluster scores		**Go to Step 2b**

Step 2b. Are significant differences _between_ Core Clusters unusually large?

Significant Differences	Direction of Difference	Extreme 15%	Extreme 10%	Extreme 5%	Extreme 2%	Extreme 1%	Is difference unusually large? (10% or less)	
V vs. NVR	V > NVR	13	16	21	27	30	Yes	No
Difference =	V < NVR	13	16	21	27	31		
V vs. Sp	V > Sp	14	18	23	30	34	Yes	No
Difference =	V < Sp	13	17	23	30	36		
NVR vs. Sp	NVR > Sp	12	15	20	26	30	Yes	No
Difference =	NVR < Sp	12	15	19	25	31		

◆ Step 2b Decision		
Is at least one of the three comparisons marked "Yes"?	YES	NO

If the answer is NO, there are significant BUT usual differences between the cluster scores	⇨	You may interpret the GCA with caution, but consider interpreting clusters

If the answer is YES, there are significant AND unusual differences between the cluster scores	⇨	Interpret the GCA, but only with extreme caution, and consider interpreting clusters

⇩

Step 3a: Identify any significant differences _within_ DAS-II Core Clusters

	Difference	Significant (.01)	Significant (.05)	Not Significant	Is difference significant?	
Verbal WD ( ) vs. VS ( ):		16+	12-15	0-11	YES	NO
Nonverbal Reasoning Mat ( ) vs. SQR ( ):		12+	9-11	0-8	YES	NO
Spatial RDes ( ) vs. PC ( ):		11+	8-10	0-7	YES	NO

◆ Step 3a Decision (repeat for each of the three clusters before continuing to Step 4)	

For each comparison marked NO, there is no significant difference between the subtest scores within the cluster	⇨	Interpret each Cluster with no significant differences. **Then skip to Step 4a**

For each comparison marked YES, there is a significant difference between subtest scores within the cluster	⇨	**Go to Step 3b**

Step 3b. Are significant differences _within_ Core Clusters unusually large?

Significant Differences	Direction of Difference	Extreme 15%	Extreme 10%	Extreme 5%	Extreme 2%	Extreme 1%	Is difference unusually large? (10% or less)	
Verbal								
WD vs. VS	WD > VS	8	10	14	19	21	Yes	No
Difference =	WD < VS	8	10	13	16	18		
Nonverbal Reasoning								
Mat vs. SQR	Mat > SQR	9	11	14	17	20	Yes	No
Difference =	Mat < SQR	9	11	14	20	24		
Spatial								
RDes vs. PC	RDes > PC	9	12	15	19	23	Yes	No
Difference =	RDes < PC	9	11	15	20	25		

Step 3b Interpretive Decision for each cluster		
Is at least one of the three comparisons marked "Yes"?	YES	NO

If the answer is NO, there are significant BUT not unusual differences between subtest scores <u>within</u> one or more clusters	⇨	You may interpret the cluster with caution, but consider interpreting subtests

If the answer is YES, there are significant AND unusual differences between subtest scores <u>within</u> the cluster	⇨	Interpret the cluster, but only with extreme caution, and consider interpreting subtests

Step 3c. Determine Normative Strengths and Weaknesses in the Ability Score Profile

Cluster Ability	Interpretable? (Y/N)	Standard Score	Normative Weakness <85	Within Normal Limits 85-115	Normative Strength >115
Verbal					
Nonverbal Reasoning					
Spatial					

Step 4a. Are there any significant differences _between_ the GCA and the Diagnostic Clusters?

	Difference	Significant (.01)	Significant (.05)	Not Significant	Is difference significant?	
GCA ( ) vs. WM ( ):		12+	9 - 11	0 - 8	Yes	No
GCA ( ) vs. PS ( ):		15+	11 - 14	0 - 10	Yes	No
GCA ( ) vs. SchR ( ):		12+	9 - 11	0 - 8	Yes	No

◆ Step 4a Interpretive Decision

Is either one of the three comparisons marked "Yes"?	YES	NO

If the answer is NO, there are no significant differences between GCA and the Diagnostic cluster scores	⇨	**Skip to Step 5a**

If the answer is YES, there is at least one significant difference between the GCA and the Diagnostic cluster scores	⇨	**Go to Step 4b**

⇩

Step 4b. Are significant differences _between_ GCA and the Diagnostic Clusters unusually large?

Significant Differences	Direction of Difference	Extreme 15%	Extreme 10%	Extreme 5%	Extreme 2%	Extreme 1%	Is difference unusually large? (10% or less)	
GCA vs. WM	GCA > WM	12-14	15-19	20-25	26-29	30+	Yes	No
Difference =	GCA < WM	12-14	15-19	20-27	29-32	33+		
GCA vs. PS	GCA > PS	16-19	20-25	26-33	34-38	39+	Yes	No
Difference =	GCA > PS	16-19	20-27	28-37	38-41	42+		
GCA vs. SchR	GCA > SchR	11-13	14-16	17-21	22	23+	Yes	No
Difference =	GCA > SchR	11-13	14-17	18-21	22-26	27+		

◆ Step 4b Interpretive Decision

Is any one of the comparisons marked "Yes"?	YES	NO

If the answer is NO, there is at least one significant BUT usual difference between the GCA and the Diagnostic cluster scores	⇨	You may interpret the discrepant cluster(s) with caution

If the answer is YES, there are significant AND unusual differences between the GCA and the Diagnostic cluster score(s)	⇨	You may interpret the discrepant cluster(s) with extreme caution

⇩

Step 5a: For the Diagnostic Clusters, are there any significant differences _within_ clusters?

	Difference	Significant (.01)	Significant (.05)	Not Significant	Is the difference significant?
Working Memory					
RSO ( ) vs. RDb ( ):		10+	8-9	0-7	YES NO
Processing Speed					
SIP ( ) vs. RN ( ):		14+	10-13	0-9	YES NO
School Readiness					
ENC ( ) vs. MLLF ( ):		14+	11-13	0-10	YES NO
ENC ( ) vs. PhP ( ):		11+	8-10	0-7	YES NO
MLLF ( ) vs. PhP ( ):		13+	10-12	0-9	YES NO

◆ Step 5a Interpretive Decision (repeat for each cluster before continuing to Step 5b or 6)

For each comparison marked NO, there is no significant subtest difference within the cluster	⇨	Interpret the Clusters with no significant subtest differences and go to **Step 5c**

For each comparison marked YES, there is a significant difference between subtest scores within the cluster	⇨	**Go to Step 5b**

⇩

Step 5b. For the Diagnostic Clusters, are significant differences _within_ the clusters unusually large?

Significant Differences	Direction of Difference	Extreme 15%	Extreme 10%	Extreme 5%	Extreme 2%	Extreme 1%	Is difference unusually large? (10% or less)	
Working Memory								
RSO vs. RDb	RSO > RDb:	9-10	11-14	15-20	21-24	25+	Yes	No
Difference =	RSO < RDb:	9-10	11-13	14-18	19-20	21+		
Processing Speed								
SIP vs. RN	SIP > RN:	11-13	14-17	18-23	24-29	30+	Yes	No
Difference =	SIP < RN:	11-13	14-17	18-21	22-26	27+		
School Readiness								
ENC vs. MLLF	ENC > MLLF	11-13	14-18	19-24	25-26	27+	Yes	No
Difference =	ENC < MLLF	11-12	13-17	18-22	23-26	27+		
ENC vs. PhP	ENC > PhP	11-13	14-18	19-23	24-27	28+	Yes	No
Difference =	ENC < PhP	9-10	11-13	14-17	18	19+		
MLLF vs. PhP	MLLF > PhP	14-16	17-22	23-26	27-29	30+	Yes	No
Difference =	MLLF < PhP	9-11	12-15	16-19	20-22	23+		

◆ Step 5b Interpretive Decision		
Is at least one of the comparisons marked "Yes"?	YES	NO

If the answer is NO, there are significant BUT usual differences between subtest scores within one or both clusters		You may interpret the cluster(s) with caution but consider Narrow Abilities **(Step 6)**

If the answer is YES, there are significant AND unusual differences between the cluster subtest scores		Interpret individual clusters, but only with extreme caution. Examine Narrow Abilities **(Step 6)**

⇩

Step 5c. Determine Normative Strengths and Weaknesses in the Ability Score Profile

Cluster Ability	Interpretable? (Y/N)	Standard Score	Normative Weakness <85	Within Normal Limits 85-115	Normative Strength >115
Working Memory					
Processing Speed					
School Readiness					

⇩

Step 6. Identify the narrow abilities assessed and any relevant differences between them

School-age Abilities and Subtests	Narrow Abilities
Verbal Ability (Gc)	
Word Definitions	Language Development / Lexical Knowledge
Verbal Similarities	Language Development
Nonverbal Reasoning Ability (Gf)	
Matrices	Induction
Sequential and Quantitative Reasoning	Induction /Quantitative Reasoning
Spatial Ability (Gv)	
Pattern Construction	Spatial Relations
Pattern Construction - Alternative	Spatial Relations
Recall of Designs	Visual Memory
Retrieval (Glr)	
Recall of Objects - Immediate	Free-recall Memory
Recall of Objects - Delayed	Free-recall Memory
Memory (Gsm)	
Recall of Digits Forward	Memory Span
Recall of Digits Backward	Working Memory
Recall of Sequential Order	Working Memory
Processing Speed (Gs)	
Speed of Information Processing	Perceptual Speed: Scanning
Rapid Naming	Perceptual Speed: Complex
Auditory Processing (Ga)	
Phonological Processing	Phonemic Coding

Adapted from Table 2.1, p. 19, Introductory and Technical Handbook (Elliott, 2007).

Step 6 (continued). Identify the narrow abilities assessed and any relevant differences between them

Narrow Ability (subtests): Definition[1]

Free Recall Memory (Recall of Objects – Immediate and Recall of Objects – Delayed): Ability to recall, without associations, as many unrelated items as possible, in any order, after a large collection of items is presented. [Note that Recall of Objects employs both visual and verbal input, not just visual.]

Induction (Picture Similarities, Matrices, Sequential and Quantitative Reasoning): Ability to discover the underlying characteristic (e.g., rule, concept, principle, process, trend, class membership) that underlies a specific problem or a set of observations, or to apply a previously learned rule to the problem. Reasoning from specific cases or observations to general rules or broad generalizations. Often requires the ability to combine separate pieces of information in the formation of inferences, rules, hypotheses, or conclusions.

Language Development (Word Definitions, Verbal Similarities): General development or understanding and application of words, sentences, and paragraphs (not requiring reading) in spoken native language skills to express or communicate a thought or feeling.

Lexical Knowledge (Naming Vocabulary): Extent of vocabulary (nouns, verbs, or adjectives) that can be understood in terms of correct word (semantic) meanings. Although evidence indicates that vocabulary knowledge is a separable component from LD, it is often difficult to disentangle these two highly corrected abilities in research studies.

Listening Ability (Verbal Comprehension): Ability to listen and understand the meaning of oral communications (spoken words, phrases, sentences, and paragraphs). The ability to receive and understand spoken information.

Memory Span (Recall of Digits Forward): Ability to attend to, register, and immediately recall (after only one presentation) temporally ordered elements and then reproduce the series of elements in correct order.

Perceptual Speed (Speed of Information Processing, Rapid Naming): Ability to rapidly and accurately search, compare (for visual similarities or differences) and identify visual elements presented side-by-side or separated in a visual field.

　Scanning (Ps) ability to scan, compare, and look up visual stimuli

Complex (Pc) ability to perform visual pattern recognition tasks that impose additional cognitive demands such as spatial visualization, estimating and interpolating, and heightened memory span loads.

Phonetic Coding (Phonological Processing): Ability to code, process, and be sensitive to nuances in phonemic information (speech sounds) in short-term memory. Includes the ability to identify, isolate, blend, or transform sounds of speech.

Piagetian Reasoning (Early Number Concepts): Ability to demonstrate the acquisition and application (in the form of logical thinking) of cognitive concepts as defined by Piaget's developmental cognitive theory. These concepts include seriation (organizing material into an orderly series that facilitates understanding of relationships between events), conservation (awareness that physical quantities do not change in amount when altered in appearance), classification (ability to organize materials that possess similar characteristics into categories), etc.

Quantitative Reasoning (Sequential and Quantitative Reasoning): Ability to inductively and/or deductively reason with concepts involving mathematical relations and properties.

Spatial Relations (Pattern Construction, Pattern Construction – Alternative): Ability to rapidly perceive and manipulate (mental rotation, transformations, reflection, etc.) visual patterns or to maintain orientation with respect to objects in space. Spatial Relations may require the identification of an object when viewed from different angles or positions. Differs from Visualization primarily by an emphasis on fluency.

Visual Memory (Recall of Designs, Recognition of Pictures): Ability to form and store a mental representation or image of a visual shape or configuration (typically during a brief study period), over at least a few seconds, and then recognize or recall it later (during the test phase).

Visualization (Copying, Matching Letter-Like Forms): The ability to apprehend a spatial form, object, or scene and match it with another spatial object, form, or scene with the requirement to rotate it (one or more times) in two or three dimensions. Requires the ability to mentally imagine, manipulate or transform objects or visual patterns and to predict how they would appear under altered conditions (e.g., parts are moved or rearranged). Differs from Spatial Relations primarily by a de-emphasis on fluency.

Working Memory (Recall of Digits Backward, Recall of Sequential Order): Ability to temporarily store and perform a set of cognitive operations on information that requires divided attention and the management of the limited capacity resources of short-term memory.

[1] CHC definitions adapted from http://www.iapsych.com/chcdef.htm

Step 7. Are single subtest T scores significantly different from Mean Core T?

Mean Core T: _____	Circle one (GCA or SNC)	T Score	Difference from Mean	Difference required	High/ Low (H / L) (+ / -)	Frequency (Table B.8)
Word Definition (Gc)				7		
Verbal Similarities (Gc)				8		
Matrices (Gf)				7		
Sequential & Quantitative Reasoning (Gf)				6		
Recall of Designs (Gv)				7		
Pattern Construction (Gv)				5		
Recall of Objects-Immediate (Glr)				9		
Recall of Digits Forward (Gsm)				7		
Recognition of Pictures (Gv)				13		
Recall of Sequential Order (Gsm)				7		
Speed of Information Processing (Gs)				7		
Recall of Digits Backward (Gsm)				7		
Phonological Processing (Ga)				9		
Rapid Naming (Gs)				10		

Step 8a. Determine Probable and Possible DAS II School-Age Shared Abilities

School-age Shared Ability	Shared Ability Subtests (includes out-of-level subtests) Enter H, L, +, or − in each box. (See below for definitions)

Formulation and Testing of Hypotheses

H / L **or** + / −

VS	SQR	PC	Mat

Use of Verbal Mediation to Solve Nonverbal Problems

H / L **or** + / −

SQR	PC	Mat

Verbal Comprehension:

H / L **or** + / −

WD	RSO

Verbal Expression:

H / L **or** + / −

WD	VS	ROi	RDf	RSO	RDb	PhP	RN

Visual Analysis of Figures or Designs:

H / L **or** + / −

PC	Mat	RDes

Visual Verbal Integration:

H / L **or** + / −

SQR	Mat	ROi	RSO

Short-term Memory: (general):

H / L **or** + / −

RDes	ROi	RDf	RPic	RSO	RDb

Auditory Short-term Memory:

H / L **or** + / −

RDf	RSO	RDb

Visual Short-term Memory:

H / L **or** + / −

ROi	RPic

Verbal Long -term Information Retrieval:

H / L **or** + / −

WD	VS	RN

Knowledge of Quantitative Concepts:

H / L **or** + / −

SQR	SIP

Visual/holistic Information Processing:

H / L **or** + / −

PC	RDes	RPic

Sequential Information Processing:

H / L **or** + / −

ROi	RDf	RSO	SIP	RDb	RN

WD= Word Definitions, VS = Verbal Similarities, Mat = Matrices, SQR = Sequential & Quantitative Reasoning, RDes = Recall of Designs, PC = Pattern Construction, VC = Verbal Comprehension, NVoc = Naming Vocabulary, PSim = Picture Similarities, Copy = Copying, ENC = Early Number Concepts, MLLF = Matching Letter-Like Forms, RDig = Recall of Digits, RO = Recall of Objects, SIP = Speed of Information Processing, RPic = Recognition of Pictures

H = A score that is significantly greater than the mean Core *T* score.
+ = A score that is greater than the mean Core *T* score BUT does not reach a level of significance.
L = A score that is significantly lower than the mean Core *T* score.
− = A score that is less than the mean Core *T* score BUT does not reach a level of significance.

Step 8b (optional). School-age shared ability formulae for converting sums of _T_ scores to Deviation Scores (Mean = 100, SD = 15)

School-Age Shared Ability	Subtests	Sum of T scores[1]	Multiplier	Additive	Score	.05 SEm
Formulation and Testing of Hypotheses	VS, SQR, PC, Mat		.46	7.94		6.18
Use of Verbal Mediation to Solve Nonverbal Problems	SQR, PC, Mat		.59	12.15		5.96
Verbal Comprehension	WD, RSO		.87	13.11		8.34
Verbal Expression	VS, WD, ROi, RDf, RSO, RDb, PhP, RN		.27	-7.59		5.45
Visual Analysis of Figures and Designs	PC, Mat, RDes		.60	9.64		6.68
Visual Verbal Integration	SQR, Mat, ROi, RSO		.42	-4.33		6.59
Short-Term Memory (general)	RDes, ROi, RDf, RPic, RSO, RDb		.35	-5.89		6.15
Auditory Short-Term Memory	RDf, RSO, RDb		.59	10.92		5.7
Visual Short-Term Memory	ROi, RPic		.91	9.38		11.51
Verbal Long-Term Information Retrieval	VS, WD, RN		.64	3.35		9.45
Knowledge of Quantitative Concepts	SQR, SIP		.93	6.97		7.52
Holistic Information Processing	PC, RDes, RPic		.63	6.09		8.05
Sequential Information Processing	ROi, RDf, RSO, SIP, RDb, RN		.36	-7.94		5.46

PC = Pattern Construction; Mat = Matrices; RDes = Recall of Designs; WD= Word Definitions; VS = Verbal Similarities; SQR =Sequential & Quantitative Reasoning; RDf = Recall of Digits – Forward; RPic = Recognition of Pictures; ROi = Recall of Objects – Immediate; ROd = Recall of Objects – Delayed; PhP = Phonological Processing; RSO = Recall of Sequential Order; RDb = Recall of Digits – Backward; SIP = Speed of Information Processing; RN = Rapid Naming

[1] All subtests in a shared ability grouping must have been administered in order to use the individual formulae.

Step 9. Evaluate Possible Linguistic and Cultural influences on the DAS-II Subtests

DAS-II Subtest	*T* Score	Linguistic / Cultural Influence	Cell Standard Score[1]
Matrices			
Sequential & Quantitative Reasoning			
Pattern Construction		Low / Low	
Recall of Designs			
Matching Letter-like Forms			
Copying			
Recall of Digits Backward		Low / Medium	
Speed of Information Processing			
Recall of Digits Forward		Low / High	
Picture Similarities			
Recognition of Pictures		Medium / Low	
Recall of Objects-Immediate			
Early Number Concepts			
Rapid Naming		Medium / Medium	
Recall of Sequential Order			
Phonological Processing		Medium / High	
Verbal Comprehension		High / Medium	
Naming Vocabulary			
Verbal Similarities		High / High	
Word Definitions			

Adapted from Flanagan, D. P., Ortiz, S. O., & Alfonso, V. (2007). Essentials of Cross-Battery Assessment, Second Edition. New York: John Wiley & Sons.

---

[1]To calculate the Cell Standard Score (Mean = 100, SD = 15), find the *Average T score* for each cell (add *T* scores and divide by the number of subtests in the cell), round the *Average T score*, and then convert the *Average T score* to a standard score using the following formula:

$$SS = \left(\frac{Average\ T\ Score - 50}{10} \right) \times 15 + 100$$

For example, if the 2 subtests, Verbal Similarities and Word Definitions, in the High/High cell had *T* scores of 30 and 42 respectively, the *Average T score* would be 36

$$(30+42)/2 = 36$$

Enter this *Average T score* into the first part of the formula results in:

$$\left(\frac{36-50}{10} \right) = \left(\frac{-14}{10} \right) = -1.4$$

Multiply -1.4 by 15:

$$-1.4 \times 15 = -21.0$$

Now add 100:

$$-21+100 = 79$$

The 2 subtests that form the High/High cell, with *T* scores of 30 and 42 respectively, when combined, would be the equivalent of a Standard Score of 79.

Step 10. Additional subtest pair comparisons

Comparison	Difference	Difference needed for significance	Possible implication
RDf vs. RDb (....) vs. (....)		8	Non-meaningful auditory memory span versus Non-meaningful auditory working memory
RDf vs. RSO (....) vs. (....)		8	Non-meaningful auditory memory span versus Meaningful auditory/visual working memory
RDf vs. RPic (....) vs. (....)		12	Non-meaningful auditory memory span versus Visual memory
RDf vs. RDes (....) vs. (....)		9	Non-meaningful auditory memory span versus Non-meaningful visual memory
RDb vs. RSO (....) vs. (....)		8	Non-meaningful auditory working memory versus Meaningful auditory/visual working memory
ROi vs. ROd (....) vs. (....)		11	Meaningful visual memory immediate versus Meaningful visual memory delayed
ROi vs. RDf (....) vs. (....)		10	Meaningful visual memory immediate versus Non-meaningful auditory memory span
ROi vs. RDb (....) vs. (....)		14	Meaningful visual memory versus Non-meaningful auditory working memory
RDes vs. RPic (....) vs. (....)		12	Non-meaningful visual memory versus Meaningful visual memory
SIP vs. RN (....) vs. (....)		10	Processing Speed Cluster: If significant difference is evidenced, examine ROi vs. RN comparison
ROi vs. RN (....) vs. (....)		12	* Make this comparison only if the SIP vs. RN is significant. RN could involve Glr

Step 11. Method of Input and Output for DAS-II Subtests

	Input			Output	
	Auditory	Visual		Verbal	Motor
		Meaningful	Symbolic		
Verbal Subtests					
Verbal Comprehension	v	v			v
Naming Vocabulary		v		v	
Word Definitions	v			v	
Verbal Similarities	v			v	
Nonverbal/Spatial Subtests					
Picture Similarities		v	v		v
Copying		v	v		v
Recall of Designs		v	v		v
Pattern Construction			v		v
Nonverbal (Fluid Reasoning) Subtests					
Matrices			v	v	v
Sequential and Quantitative Reasoning		v		v	v
Diagnostic Subtests					
Early Number Concepts	v	v		v	v
Matching Letter-Like Forms			v		v
Recall of Digits Forward	v		v	v	
Recall of Digits Backward	v		v	v	
Recall of Sequential Order	v	v		v	
Recognition of Pictures		v			v
Recall of Objects-Immediate		v		v	
Recall of Objects-Delayed		v		v	
Rapid Naming		v		v	
Phonological Processing	v	v		v	
Speed of Information Processing		v			v

References

Alfonso, V. C., Flanagan, D. P., & Radwan, S. (2005). The impact of the Cattell-Horn-Carroll theory on test development and interpretation of cognitive and academic abilities. In D. P. Flanagan & P. L. Harrison (Eds.), *Contemporary intellectual assessment: Theories, tests, and issues* (2nd ed., pp. 185–202). New York: Guilford Press.

Alfonso, V. C., & Pratt, S. I. (1997). Issues and suggestions for training professionals in assessing intelligence. In D. P. Flanagan, J. L. Genshaft, & P. L. Harrison (Eds.), *Contemporary intellectual assessment: Theories, tests, and issues* (pp. 326–344). New York: Guilford Press.

American Association on Intellectual and Developmental Disabilities (AAIDD) Web site. Retrieved June 12, 2008 from http://www.aamr.org/Policies/faq_intellectual _disability.shtml.

American Psychiatric Association. (2000). *Diagnostic and statistical manual of mental disorders* (4th ed., text revision). Washington, DC: Author.

Bakker, D. J. (2006). Treatment of developmental dyslexia: a review. *Pediatric Rehabilitation, 9,* 3–13.

Bakker, D. J., Van Strien, J. W., Licht, R., & Smit-Glaudé, S. W. D. (2007). Cognitive brain potentials in kindergarten children with subtyped risks of reading retardation. *Annals of Dyslexia, 57,* 99–111.

Bayley, N. (2006). *Bayley scales of infant and toddler development* (3rd ed.). San Antonio, TX: Harcourt Assessment.

Beitchman, J. H., Wilson, B., Brownlie, E. B., Walters, H., & Lancee, W. (1996). Long-term consistency in speech/language profiles: 1. Developmental and academic outcomes. *Journal of the American Academy of Child and Adolescent Psychiatry, 35,* 804–814.

Belk, M. S., LoBello, S. G., Ray, G. E., & Zachar, P. (2002). WISC-III administration, clerical, and scoring errors make by student examiners. *Journal of Psychoeducational Assessment, 20*(3), 290–300.

Binet, A., & Simon, T. (1916/1980). *The development of intelligence in children:* with marginal notes by Lewis M. Terman and preface by Lloyd M. Dunn. (E. S. Kite, Trans.) Facsimile limited edition issued by Lloyd M. Dunn. Nashville, TN: Williams Printing Co. (Original work published 1916.)

Birsh, J. R. (1999). *Multisensory teaching of basic language skills.* Baltimore, MD: Paul H. Brookes Publishing Company.

Bishop, D. V. (1992). The underlying nature of specific language impairment. *Journal of Child Psychology and Psychiatry, 33,* 3–66.

Bonafina, M. A., Newcorn, J. H., McKay, K. E., Koda, V. H., & Halperin, J. M. (2000). ADHD and reading disabilities: A cluster analytic approach for distinguishing subgroups. *Jounal of Learning Disabilities, 33,* 297–307.

Bracken, B. A. (1988). Ten psychometric reasons why similar tests produce dissimilar results. *Journal of School Psychology, 26*(2), 155–166

Bracken, B. A. (2006). Bracken Basic Concept Scale (3rd ed.). San Antonio, TX: Harcourt Assessment.

Bracken, B. A. (2007). Creating the optimal preschool testing situation. In B. A. Bracken

& R. Nagle (Eds.), *Psychoeducational assessment of preschool children* (4th ed., pp. 137–153). Mahwah, NJ: Erlbaum.

Bracken, B. A., & Walker, K. C. (1997). The utility of intelligence tests for preschool children. In D. P. Flanagan, J. L. Genshaft, & P. L. Harrison (Eds.), *Contemporary intellectual assessment: Theories, tests, and issues* (pp. 484–502). New York: Guilford Press.

Braden, J. P., & Athanasiou, M. S. (2005). A comparative review of nonverbal measures of intelligence. In D. P. Flanagan & P. L. Harrison (Eds.), *Contemporary intellectual assessment Theories, tests, and issues* (2nd ed., pp. 557–577). New York: Guilford Press.

Braden, J. P. (Ed.) (2000). *Journal of Psychoeducational Assessment, 18* (3), September. The entire issue is devoted to nonverbal assessment of intelligence.

Briscoe, J., Gathercole, S. E., & Marlow, N. (2001). Everyday memory and cognitive ability in children born very prematurely. *Journal of Child Psychology and Psychiatry, 42,* 749–754.

British Psychological Society. (1999). *Dyslexia, literacy, and psychological assessment.* Report by a working party of the Division of Educational and Child Psychology. Leicester, England: Author.

Brody, S. (Ed.) (2001). *Teaching reading: Language, letters, and thought* (2nd ed.). Milford, NH: LARC Publishing.

Bryant, B. R., Wiederholt, J. L., & Bryant, D. P. (2004). *Gray Diagnostic Reading Test* (2nd ed.). Austin, TX: Pro-Ed.

Carroll, J. B. (1993). *Human cognitive abilities: A survey of factor-analytic studies.* Cambridge, England: Cambridge University Press.

Carroll, J. B. (2005). The three-stratum theory of cognitive abilities. In D. P. Flanagan & P. L. Harrison (Eds.), *Contemporary intellectual assessment Theories, tests, and issues* (2nd ed., pp. 41–68). New York: Guilford Press.

Cattell, R. B. (1941). Some theoretical issues in adult intelligence testing. *Psychological Bulletin, 38,* 592.

Cattell, R. B. (1971). *Abilities: Their structure, growth, and action.* Boston: Houghton-Mifflin.

Cattell, R. B. (1987). *Intelligence: Its structure, growth and action.* Amsterdam: North-Holland.

Cattell, R. B., & Horn, J. L. (1978). A check on the theory of fluid and crystallized intelligence with description of new subtest designs. *Journal of Educational Measurement, 15,* 139–164.

Cohen, J. (1988). *Statistical power analysis for the behavioral sciences* (2nd ed.). Hillsdale, NJ: Erlbaum.

Daniel, M. H. (1986, April). *Construct validity of two-dimensional and three-dimensional block design.* Paper presented at the annual convention of the National Association of School Psychologists, Hollywood, FL.

Daniel, M. H. (1999). Behind the scenes: Using new measurement methods on the DAS and KAIT. In S. E. Embretson & S. L. Hershberger (Eds.), *The new rules of measurement: What every psychologist and educator should know* (pp. 37–63). Mahwah, NJ: Erlbaum.

Doll, B., & Boren, R. (1993). Performance of severely language-impaired students on the WISC-III, language scales, and academic achievement measures. In B. A. Bracken & R. S McCallum (Eds.), *Journal of Psychoeducational Assessment, WISC-III monograph, 11* (pp. 77–86). Brandon, VT: Clinical Psychology Publishing Company.

Dumont, R., Cruse, C., Price, L., & Whelley, P. (1996). The relationship between the Differential Ability Scales and the WISC-III for students with learning disabilities. *Psychology in the Schools. 33,* 203–209.

Dumont, R., Farr, L. P., Willis, J. O., & Whelley, P. (1998). 30-second interval performance on the Coding subtest of the WISC-III: Another case of WISC folklore? *Psychology in the Schools, 35*(2), 111–117.

Dumont, R., & Willis, J. O. (1995). Intrasubtest scatter on the WISC-III for various clinical samples vs. the standardization sample: An examination of WISC folklore. *Journal of Psychoeducational Assessment, 13,* 271–285.

Dumont, R., & Willis, J. O. (2002). Mnemonics for five issues in the identification of learning disabilities taken from the three synoptic gospels of the New Testament of the King James version of the Bible first by Keith Stanovich and later, in imitation, by John Willis and Ron Dumont. Retrieved June 12, 2008, from Dumont-Willis on the Web site: http://alpha.fdu.edu/psychology/mnemonics_ for_ five_ issues.htm

Dumont, R., Willis, J. O., Farr L. P., McCarthy, T., & Price, L. (2000). The relationship between the Differential Ability Scales (DAS) and the Woodcock-Johnson Revised-Cognitive (WJ-R COG) for a sample of referred children. *Journal of Psychoeducational Assessment, 18,* 27–38.

Dunn, L. M. & Dunn, D. M. (2006). *Peabody Picture Vocabulary Test* (4th ed.) (PPVT-4). Circle Pines, MN: Pearson Assessment.

Elliott, C. D. (1983). *British Ability Scales*. Windsor, England: NFER-Nelson.

Elliott, C. D. (1990a). *Differential Ability Scales administration and scoring manual*. San Antonio, TX: The Psychological Corporation.

Elliott, C. D. (1990b). *Differential Ability Scales introductory and technical handbook*. San Antonio, TX: The Psychological Corporation.

Elliott, C. D. (1997). The Differential Ability Scales. In D. P. Flanagan, J. L. Genshaft, & P. L. Harrison (Eds.), *Contemporary intellectual assessment* (ch. 10, pp. 183–208). New York: Guilford Press.

Elliott, C. D. (2001). Application of the Differential Ability Scales (DAS) and the British Ability Scales (2nd ed.) (BAS-II) for the assessment of learning disabilities. In A. S. Kaufman & N. L. Kaufman (Eds.), *Specific learning disabilities and difficulties in children and adolescents: Psychological assessment and evaluation* (pp. 178–217). New York: Cambridge University Press.

Elliott, C. D. (2005). The Differential Ability Scales. In D. P. Flanagan & P. L. Harrison (Eds.), *Contemporary intellectual assessment: Theories, tests, and issues* (pp. 402–424). New York: Guilford.

Elliott, C. D. (2007a). *Differential Ability Scales 2nd edition administration and scoring manual*. San Antonio, TX: Harcourt Assessment.

Elliott, C. D. (2007b). *Differential Ability Scales 2nd edition introductory and technical handbook*. San Antonio, TX: Harcourt Assessment.

Elliott, C. D. (2007c). *Differential Ability Scales 2nd edition normative data tables manual*. San Antonio, TX: Harcourt Assessment.

Embretson, S. E., & Hershberger, S. L. (Eds.) (1999). *The new rules of measurement: What every psychologist and educator should know*. Mahwah, NJ: Erlbaum.

Embretson, S. E., & Reise, S. P. (2000). *Item response theory for psychologists*. Mahwah, NJ: Erlbaum.

Evans, J. J., Floyd, R. G., McGrew, K. S., & Leforgee, M. H. (2002). The relations between measures of Cattell-Horn-Carroll (CHC) cognitive abilities and reading achievement during childhood and adolescence. *School Psychology Review, 31*(2), 246–262.

Farrall, M. L. (2004). The Myth of the WISCIII/WISC-IV Retest: The Apples and Oranges Effect. Retrieved October 27, 2007, from Dumont-Willis on the Web site: http://alpha.fdu.edu/psychology/melissa_farrall_WISCIV.htm

Fiorello, C. A., Hale, J. B., McGrath, M., Ryan, K., & Quinn, S. (2002). IQ interpretation for children with flat and variable test profiles. *Learning and Individual Differences, 13,* 115–125.

Flanagan, D. P. (2001). *Assessment Service Bulletin Number 1: Comparative features of major intelligence batteries: Content, administration, technical features, interpretation, and theory.* Itasca, IL: Riverside Publishing.

Flanagan, D. P., Andrews, T. J., & Genshaft, J. L. (1997). The functional utility of intelligence tests with special education populations. In D. P. Flanagan, J. L. Genshaft, & P. L. Harrison (Eds.), *Contemporary intellectual assessment: Theories, tests, and issues* (pp. 457–483). New York: Guilford Press.

Flanagan, D. P., & Kaufman, A. S. (2004). *Essentials of WISC-IV assessment.* New York: Wiley.

Flanagan, D. P., & McGrew, K. S. (1997). A cross-battery approach to assessing and interpreting cognitive abilities: Narrowing the gap between practice and cognitive science. In D. P. Flanagan, J. L. Genshaft, & P. L. Harrison (Eds.), *Contemporary intellectual assessment* (ch. 17, pp. 314–325). New York: Guilford Press.

Flanagan, D. P, McGrew, K. S., & Ortiz, S. O. (2000). *The Wechsler Intelligence Scales and Gf-Gc theory: A contemporary approach to interpretation.* Boston: Allyn & Bacon.

Flanagan, D. P., & Ortiz, S. O. (2001). *Essentials of Cross-Battery Assessment.* New York: Wiley.

Flanagan, D. P., Ortiz, S. O., & Alfonso, V. (2007). *Essentials of Cross-Battery Assessment (2nd ed.).* New York: Wiley.

Flanagan, D. P., Ortiz, S. O., Alfonso, V. & Mascolo, J. T. (2002). *Achievement test desk reference (ATDR): Comprehensive assessment and learning disability.* Boston: Allyn & Bacon.

Flanagan, D. P., Ortiz, S. O., Alfonso, V., & Mascolo, J. T. (2006). *Achievement test desk reference (ATDR-II): A guide to learning disability identification* (2nd ed.). Hoboken, NJ: Wiley.

Floyd, R. G., Evans, J. J., & McGrew, K. S. (2003). Relations between measures of Cattell-Horn-Carroll (CHC) cognitive abilities and mathematics achievement across the school-age years. *Psychology in the Schools, 60*(2), 155–171.

Flynn, J. R. (1984). The mean IQ of Americans: Massive gains 1932 to 1978. *Psychological Bulletin, 95,* 29–51.

Flynn, J. R. (1987). Massive IQ gains in 14 nations: What IQ tests really measure. *Psychological Bulletin, 101,* 171–191.

Flynn, J. R. (1998). IQ gains over time: Toward finding the causes. In U. Neisser (Ed.), *The rising curve: Long-term gains in IQ and related measures* (pp. 25–66). Washington, DC: American Psychological Association.

Galton, F. (1886). Regression towards mediocrity in hereditary stature. *Journal of the Anthropological Institute, 15,* 246–263.

Gardner, H. (1983). *Frames of mind: The theory of multiple intelligences.* New York: Basic Books.

Goldman, J. J. (1989). On the robustness of psychological test instrumentation: Psychological evaluation of the dead. In Glenn G. Ellenbogen (Ed.), *The primal whimper: More readings from the Journal of Polymorphous Perversity.* New York: Ballantine, Stonesong Press.

Hale, J. B., & Fiorello, C. A. (2004). *School neuropsychology: A practitioner's handbook.* New York: Guilford Press.

Hale, J. B., Hoeppner, J. B., & Fiorello, C. A. (2002). Analyzing Digit Span components to assessment of attention processes. *Journal of Psychoeducational Assessment, 20* (2), 128–143.

Harcourt Assessment. (2007a). DAS-II FAQs. Retrieved September 1, 2007, from https://harcourtassessment.com/HAIWEB/Cultures/en-us/Productdetail.htm?Pid=015–8338–820&Mode=resource&Leaf=015–8338–820_1

Harcourt Assessment. (2007b). DAS-II update letter. Retrieved September 1, 2007, from https://harcourtassessment.com/hai/images/harcourtsite/Products/DAS-II/DAS-II_Errata_Ltr.pdf

Harrison, P., & Oakland, T. (2003). *Adaptive Behavior Assessment System* (2nd ed.) (ABAS: II). San Antonio, TX: Pearson.

Holland, A. M., & McDermott, P. A. (1996). Discovering core profile types in the school-age standardization sample of the Differential Ability Scales. *Journal of Psychoeducational Assessment, 14,* 131–146.

Horn, J. L. (1988). Thinking about human abilities. In J. R. Nesselroade & R. B. Cattell (Eds.), *Handbook of multivariate psychology* (rev. ed., pp. 645–685). New York: Academic Press.

Horn, J. L. (1991). Measurement of intellectual capabilities: A review of theory. In K. S. McGrew, J. K. Werder, & R. W. Woodcock (Eds.), *Woodcock-Johnson Technical Manual* (pp. 197–232). Chicago: Riverside.

Horn, J. L. (1994). The theory of fluid and crystallized intelligence. In R. J. Sternberg (Ed.), *The encyclopedia of human intelligence* (pp. 443–451). New York: Macmillan.

Horn, J. L., & Blankson, B. (2005). Foundations for better understanding of cognitive abilities. In D. P. Flanagan & P. L. Harrison (Eds.), *Contemporary intellectual assessment* (2nd ed., pp. 41–68). New York: Guilford Press.

Horn, J. L., & Cattell, R. B. (1966). Refinement and test of the theory of fluid and crystallized intelligence. *Journal of Educational Psychology, 57,* 253–270.

Horn, J. L., & Noll, J. (1997). Human cognitive capabilities: Gf-Gc theory. In D. P. Flanagan, J. L. Genshaft, & P. L. Harrison (Eds.), *Contemporary intellectual assessment: Theories, tests, and issues* (pp. 53–91). New York: Guilford Press.

Hunt, E. (1980). Intelligence as an information-processing concept. *British Journal of Psychology, 71*(4), 449–474.

Johnson, B. D., Altmaier, E. M., & Richman, L. C. (1999). Attention deficits and reading disabilities: Are immediate memory defects additive? *Developmental Neuropsychology, 15,* 213–226.

Joseph, R. M., Tager-Flusberg, H., & Lord, C. (2002). Cognitive profiles and social-communicative functioning in children with autism spectrum disorder. *Journal of Child Psychology and Psychiatry, 43,* 807–821.

Kamphaus, R. W., & Reynolds, C. R. (1987). *Clinical and research applications of the K-ABC.* Circle Pines, MN: American Guidance Service.

Katzir, T., Kim, Y-S., Wolf, M., Morris, R., & Lovett, M. W. (2008). The varieties of pathways to dysfluent reading: Comparing subtypes of children with dyslexia at letter, word, and connected text levels of reading. *Journal of Learning Disabilities, 41,* 47–66.

Kaufman, A. S. (1976). A new approach to the interpretation of test scatter on the WISC-R. *Journal of Learning Disabilities, 9,* 739–744.

Kaufman, A. S. (1979). *Intelligent testing with the WISC-R.* New York: Wiley Interscience.

Kaufman, A. S. (1994). *Intelligent testing with the WISC-III.* New York: Wiley Interscience

Kaufman, A. S., & Kaufman, N. L. (1983). *The Kaufman Assessment Battery for Children.* Circle Pines, MN: American Guidance Service.

Kaufman, A. S., & Kaufman, N. L. (2004a). *Kaufman Assessment Battery for Children* (2nd ed.). Circle Pines, MN: Pearson Assessment.

Kaufman, A. S., & Kaufman, N. L. (2004b). *Kaufman Test of Educational Achievement* (2nd ed.). Circle Pines, MN: American Guidance Services.

Keith, T. Z. (1990). Confirmatory and hierarchical confirmatory analysis of the Differential Ability Scales. *Journal of Psychoeducational Assessment, 8,* 391–405.

Kelman, M., & Lester, G. (1997) *Jumping the queue: An inquiry into the legal treatment of students with learning disabilities.* Cambridge, MA: Harvard University Press.

Korkman, M., Kettunen, S., & Autti-Ramo, I. (2003). Neurocognitive impairment in early adolescence following prenatal alcohol exposure of varying duration. *Child Neuropsychology, 9,* 117–128.

Lahey, M., & Edwards, J. (1999). Naming errors of children with specific language impairment. *Journal of Speech, Language, and Hearing Research, 42,* 195–205.

Lambert, N., Nihira, K., & Lel, H. (1993). *AAMR Adaptive Behavior Scales-School* (2nd ed.). Austin, TX: Pro-Ed.

Lichtenberger, E. O., Mather, N., Kaufman, N. L., & Kaufman, A. S. (2004). *Essentials of assessment report writing.* New York: Wiley.

Luria, A. R. (1973). *The working brain* (B. Haigh, Trans.). London: Penguin Books.

Manier, D. (2006). Descrambling dyslexia: The neuroscience of a developmental reading disorder. *PsycCRITIQUES, 51,* 34.

Mather, N., & Jaffe, L. (2002). *Woodcock-Johnson III: Recommendations, reports, and strategies.* New York: Wiley.

Mayes, S. D., Calhoun, S. L., & Crowell, E. W. (1998). WISC-III freedom from distractibility as a measure of attention in children with and without attention deficit hyperactivity disorder. *Journal of Attention Disorders, 2,* 217–227.

McBride, G. M., Dumont, R., & Willis, J. O. (2004). Response to response to intervention legislation: The future for school psychologists. *The School Psychologist, 58* (3), 86–91, 93.

McCallum, S., Bracken, B., & Wasserman, J. (2001). *Essentials of nonverbal assessment.* New York: Wiley.

McCarthy, R. & Warrington, E. K. (1990). *Cognitive neuropsychology: A clinical introduction.* London: Academic Press.

McDermott, P. A., Fantuzzo, J. W., & Glutting, J. J. (1990). Just say no to subtest analysis: A critique on Wechsler theory and practice. *Journal of Psychoeducational Assessment, 8,* 290–302.

McGrew, K. S. (1994a). The achievement content criticism of the Woodcock-Johnson and Woodcock-Johnson-Revised: A myth. *Communiqué, 22*(8), 13–15.

McGrew, K. S. (1994b). School psychologists vs school proceduralists: A response to Willis and Dumont. *Communiqué, 22*(8), 13–15.

McGrew, K. S. (1997). Analysis of the major intelligence batteries according to a proposed comprehensive Gf-Gc framework. In D. P. Flanagan, J. L. Genshaft, & P. L. Harrison (Eds.), *Contemporary intellectual assessment* (ch. 9, pp. 151–179). New York: Guilford Press.

McGrew, K. S. (2004). Institute for Applied Psychometrics Cattell-Horn-Carroll (CHC) Definition Project. Retrieved June 12, 2008 from http://www.iapsych.com/chcdef.htm.

McGrew, K. S., & Flanagan, D. P. (1998). *The intelligence test desk reference (ITDR): Gf-Gc Cross-Battery Assessment.* Boston: Allyn & Bacon.

McGrew, K. S., Flanagan, D. P., Keith, T. Z., & Vanderwood, M. (1997). Beyond *g:* The impact of *Gf-Gc* specific cognitive abilities research on the future use and interpretation of intelligence tests in the schools. *School Psychology Review, 26,* 189–210.

McGrew, K. S., Werder, J. K., & Woodcock, R. W. (1991). *WJ-R technical manual: A reference on theory and current research to supplement the WJ-R Examiner's Manuals.* Chicago: Riverside Publishing.

O'Leary, C. M. (2004). Fetal alcohol syndrome: Diagnosis, epidemiology, and developmental outcomes. *Journal of Pediatric Child Health, 40,* 2–7.

Pennington, B. F., Groisser, D., & Welsh, M. C. (1993). Contrasting cognitive deficits in attention-deficit/hyperactivity disorder versus reading disability. *Developmental Psychology, 29,* 511–523.

Pfungst, O. (1911). *Clever Hans (The horse of Mr. von Osten): A contribution to experimental animal and human psychology* (Trans. C. L. Rahn). New York: Henry Holt. (Originally published in German, 1907.)

Piasta, S. B., & Wagner, R. K. (2008). Dyslexia: Identification and classification. In

E. L. Grigorenko & A. J. Naples (Eds.), *Single word reading: Behavioral and biological perspectives* (pp. 309–326). Mahwah, NJ: Erlbaum.

Psychological Corporation. (2001). *Wechsler Individual Achievement Test* (2nd ed.) (WIAT-II). San Antonio, TX: Author.

Rasch, G. (1960). *Probabilistic models for some intelligence and attainment tests.* Copenhagen: Danish Institute for Educational Research.

Rath, L. K. (2001). Phonemic awareness: Segmenting and blending the sounds of language. In S. Brody (Ed.), *Teaching reading: Language, letters & thought* (pp. 64–105). Milford, NH: LARC Publishing.

Raven, J. C. (1939). *Progressive Matrices.* London: Lewis.

Reynolds, C. R. (1990). Conceptual and technical problems in learning disability diagnosis. In C. R. Reynolds & R. W. Kamphaus (Eds.) *Handbook of psychological and educational assessment of children: Intelligence and achievement* (ch. 24). New York: Guilford Press.

Reynolds, C. R. (1997). Forward and backward memory span should not be combined for clinical analysis. *Archives of Clinical Neuropsychology, 12,* 29–40.

Reynolds, C. R., & Kamphaus, R. W. (2003). *Reynolds Intellectual Assessment Scales.* Lutz, FL: Psychological Assessment Resources.

Reynolds, C. R., & Kamphaus, R. W. (Eds.) (2003). *Handbook of psychological and educational assessment of children: Intelligence, aptitude and achievement.* New York: Guilford Press.

Roberts, R. D., Beh, H. C., & Stankov, L. (1988). Hick's Law, competing tasks, and intelligence. *Intelligence, 12,* 101–120.

Roid, G. H. (2003). *Stanford-Binet Intelligence Scales* (5th ed.). Itasca, IL: Riverside Publishing.

Roid, G. H., & Miller, L. J. (1995, 1997). *Leiter International Performance Scale-Revised.* Wood Dale, IL: Stoelting Co.

Rose, J. C., Lincoln, A. J., & Allen, M. H. (1992). Ability profiles of developmental language disordered and learning disabled children: A comparative analysis. *Developmental Neuropsychology, 8,* 413–426.

Rourke, B. P., Del Dotto, J. E, Rourke, S. B., & Casey, J. E. (1990). Nonverbal learning disabilities: The syndrome and a case study. *Journal of School Psychology, 28,* 361–385.

Saklofske, D. H., Prifitera, A., Weiss, L. G., Rolfhus, E., & Zhu, J. (2005). Clinical interpretation of the WISC-IV FSIQ and GAI. In A. Prifitera, D. H. Saklofske, & L. G. Weiss (Eds.), *WISC-IV clinical use and interpretation: Scientist practitioner perspectives* (pp. 33–65). New York: Academic Press.

Sattler, J. M. (2008). *Assessment of children: Cognitive foundations* (5th ed.). San Diego: Jerome M. Sattler, Publisher.

Sattler, J. M., Dumont, R., Willis, J., & Salerno, J. D. (2008). Differential Ability Scales–Second Edition (DAS-II). In J. M. Sattler, *Assessment of children: Cognitive foundations* (5th ed., pp. 605–675). San Diego: Jerome M. Sattler, Publisher.

Sattler, J. M., & Evans, C. A. (2006). Visual impairments. In J. M. Sattler, *Assessment of Children: Behavioral and clinical foundations* (5th ed., pp. 464–477). San Diego: Jerome M. Sattler, Publisher.

Sattler, J. M., Hardy-Braz, S. T., & Willis, J. O. (2006). Hearing impairments. In J. M. Sattler, *Assessment of Children: Behavioral and clinical foundations* (5th ed., pp. 478–492). San Diego: Jerome M. Sattler, Publisher.

Sattler, J. M. & Hoge, R. (2006). *Assessment of children: Behavioral, social and clinical foundations* (5th ed.) San Diego: Jerome M. Sattler, Publisher.

Schlachter, T., Dumont, R., & Willis, J. O. (2008). Stability of DAS to DAS-II scores for a sample of children with ADHD. Manuscript in progress.

Shanahan, M. A., Pennington, B. F., Yerys, B. E., Scott, A., Boada, R., Willcutt, E. G., Olson, R. K., & DeFries, J. C. (2006). Processing speed deficits in attention-deficit/

hyperactivity disorder and reading disability. *Journal of Abnormal Child Psychology, 34,* 585–602.

Sherr, F. (July 18, 2006). Personal communication.

Schrank, F. A., Flanagan, D. P., Woodcock, R. W., & Mascolo, J. T. (2001). *Essentials of WJ III cognitive abilities assessment.* New York: Wiley.

Snow, C. E., Burns, M. S., & Griffin, P. (Eds.) (1998). *Preventing reading difficulties in young children.* Washington, DC: National Academy Press.

Sparrow, S., & Gurland, S. T. (1998). Assessment of gifted children with the WISC-III. In A. Prifitera & D. H. Saklofske (Eds.), *WISC-III clinical uses and interpretation: Scientist-practitioner perspectives* (pp. 59–72). San Diego, CA: Academic Press.

Sparrow, S. S., Cicchetti, D. V., & Balla, D. A. (2005). *Vineland Adaptive Behavior Scales* (2nd ed.). Circle Pines, MN: American Guidance Service.

Spearman, C. E. (1904). "General intelligence," objectively determined and measured. *American Journal of Psychology, 15,* 201–293.

Spearman, C. E. (1927). *The abilities of man: their nature and measurement.* New York: Macmillan.

Springer, S. P., & Deutsch, G. (1989). *Left brain, right brain* (3rd ed.). San Francisco: W. H. Freeman & Co Ltd.

Stankov, L. (1983). Attention and intelligence. *Journal of Educational Psychology, 75,* 471–490.

Swanson, H. L., Mink, J. & Bocian, K. M. (1999). Cognitive processing deficits in poor readers with symptoms of reading disabilities and ADHD: More alike than different? *Journal of Educational Psychology, 91,* 321–333.

Terman, L. M., & Merrill, M. A. (1960). *Stanford-Binet Intelligence Scale.* Boston: Houghton-Mifflin.

Titchener, E. B. (1924). *A text-book of psychology.* New York: Macmillan.

Townend, J. E., & Turner, M. (2000). *Dyslexia in practice.* New York: Kluwer Academic/Plenum.

Trainor, P. (April 19, 2008). Personal communication.

U.S. Congress. (1973). Public Law 93-112. The Rehabilitation Act.

U.S. Congress. (1975). Public Law 94-142. Education for All Handicapped Children Act (EHA).

U.S. Congress. (1990). Public Law 101-476. Individuals with Disabilities Education Act (IDEA).

U.S. Congress. (1997). Public Law 105-17. Individuals with Disabilities Education Act amendments.

U.S. Congress. (2001). Public Law 107-110. *No child left behind act of 2001.*

U.S. Congress. (2004). Public Law 108-446. Individuals with Disabilities Education Improvement Act of 2004 (IDEA 2004 or IDEIA).

U. S. Department of Health, Education, and Welfare. (1975). *A practical guide to measuring project impact on student achievement.* Washington, DC: U.S. Government Printing Office.

Wagner, R. K., Torgesen, J. K., & Rashotte, C. A. (1999). *Comprehensive Test of Phonological Processing.* Austin, TX: Pro-Ed.

Watkins, M. W., Greenawalt, C. G., & Marcell, C. M. (2002). Factor structure of the Wechsler Intelligence Scale for Children (3rd ed.) among gifted students. *Educational and Psychological Measurement, 62,* 164–172.

Wechsler, D. (1926). On the influence of education on intelligence as measured by the Binet-Simon tests. *Journal of Educational Psychology, 17,* 248–257.

Wechsler, D. (1939). *The measurement of adult intelligence.* Baltimore: Williams & Wilkins.

Wechsler, D. (1943). Nonintellective factors in general intelligence. *Journal of Abnormal and Social Psychology, 38,* 101–103.

Wechsler, D. (1949). *Wechsler Intelligence Scale for Children*. San Antonio, TX: The Psychological Corporation.

Wechsler, D. (1950). Cognitive, conative, and non-intellective intelligence. *American Psychologist, 5,* 78–83.

Wechsler, D. (1951). Equivalent test and mental ages for the WISC. *Journal of Consulting Psychology, 15,* 381–384.

Wechsler, D. (1991). *Wechsler Intelligence Scale for Children* (3rd ed.). San Antonio, TX: The Psychological Corporation.

Wechsler, D. (1997). *Wechsler Adult Intelligence Scale* (3rd ed.). San Antonio, TX: The Psychological Corporation.

Wechsler, D. (2002). *Wechsler Preschool and Primary Scale of Intelligence* (3rd ed.). San Antonio, TX: Harcourt Assessment.

Wechsler, D. (2003). *Wechsler Intelligence Scale for Children* (4th ed.). San Antonio, TX: Harcourt Assessment.

Wechsler, D., Kaplan, E., Fein, D., Kramer, J., Morris, R., Delis, D., & Maerlender, A. (2003). *Wechsler Intelligence Scale for Children* (4th ed.), Integrated. San Antonio, TX: The Psychological Corporation.

Willcutt, E. G., Pennington, B. F., Boada, R., Ogline, J. S., Tunick, R. A., Chhabildas, N. A., & Olson, R. K. (2001). A comparison of the cognitive deficits in reading disability and attention-deficit/hyperactivity disorder. *Journal of Abnormal Psychology, 110,* 157–172.

Williams, K. T. (2006). *Expressive Vocabulary Test* (2nd ed.). Circle Pines, MN: Pearson Assessment.

Willis, J. O. (2001). Scoring errors necessitate double-checking protocols. *Today's School Psychologist, 4*(5), 7.

Willis, J. O., & Dumont, R. (1994). Reaction to McGrew: In God we trust, all others bring your data. *Communiqué, 22*(8), 13–15.

Willis, J. O., & Dumont, R. (2002). *Guide to identification of learning disabilities* (3rd ed.). Peterborough, NH: Authors. [johnzerowillis@yahoo.com]

Willis, J. O., & Dumont, R. (2006). And never the twain shall meet: Can response to intervention and cognitive assessment be reconciled? *Psychology in the Schools, 43*(8), 901–906.

Willis, U. (June 12, 2008). Personal communication.

Wolf, M. (1997). A provisional, integrative account of phonological and naming-speed deficits in dyslexia: Implications for diagnosis and intervention. In B. Blachman et al. (Eds.), *Foundations of reading acquisition and dyslexia: Implications for early intervention* (pp. 67–92). Mahwah, NJ: Erlbaum.

Wolf, M., & Bowers, P. (1999). The double deficit hypothesis for the developmental dyslexias. *Journal of Educational Psychology, 91*(3), 415–438.

Wolf, M., & Denckla, M. B. (2005). *Rapid Automatized Naming and Rapid Alternating Stimulus Test*. Austin, TX: Pro-Ed.

Woodcock, R. W. (1990). Theoretical foundations of the WJ-R measures of cognitive ability. *Journal of Psychoeducational Assessment, 8*(3), 231–258.

Woodcock, R. W. (1993). An information processing view of Gf-Gc theory. *Journal of Psychoeducational Assessment, Monograph Series: Advances in Psychoeducational Assessment: Woodcock-Johnson Psychoeducational Battery-Revised,* 80–102.

Woodcock, R. W. (1999). What can Rasch-based scores convey about a person's test performance? In S. E. Embretson & S. L. Hershberger (Eds.), *The new rules of measurement: What every psychologist and educator should know* (pp. 105–127). Mahwah, NJ: Erlbaum.

Woodcock, R. W., & Dahl, M. N. (1971). *A common scale for the measurement of person ability and test item difficulty* (AGS Paper No. 10). Circle Pines, MN: American Guidance Service.

Woodcock, R. W., & Mather, N. (1989). *WJ-R Tests of Cognitive Ability-Standard and Supplemental Batteries: Examiner's manual.* Chicago: Riverside Publishing

Woodcock, R. W., McGrew, K. S., & Mather, N. (2001). *Woodcock-Johnson III.* Itasca, IL: Riverside Publishing.

Wundt, W. (1858–1862). *Beiträge zur Theorie der Sinneswahrnehmung.* Cited in E. G. Boring (1950), *A history of experimental psychology* (2nd ed.). New York: Appleton-Century-Crofts.

Annotated Bibliography

ARTICLES, BOOKS, AND CHAPTERS

Alessi, G. (1988). Diagnosis diagnosed: A systematic reaction. *Professional School Psychology,* *3*(2), 145–151.

A provocative and important article. Why do we often diagnose children as having SLD when there are many other factors that should be explored? Examiners readily acknowledge in theory, but almost never cite in practice such causes of underachievement as poor instruction, defective school management policies, or inadequate curriculum.

Alfonso, V. C., & Pratt, S. I. (1997). Issues and suggestions for training professionals in assessing intelligence. In D. P. Flanagan, J. L. Genshaft, & P. L. Harrison (Eds.), *Contemporary intellectual assessment: Theories, tests, and issues* (pp. 326–344). New York: Guilford Press.

Administration errors unfortunately abound. Training programs carry a heavy responsibility for correcting and preventing such errors.

American Psychiatric Association. (2000). *Diagnostic and statistical manual of mental disorders* (4th ed., Text Revision) (DSM-IV-TR). Washington, DC: American Psychiatric Association.

The new revision of the Diagnostic and Statistical Manual of the American Psychiatric Association. DSM-IV-TR *diagnoses are often required of psychiatrists, other physicians, and clinical psychologists for hospital admissions, epidemiological reports, research, and third-party insurance payments, which makes them important. The* DSM-IV-TR *is largely silent on the questions of etiology, dynamics, course, prognosis, and treatment, and it accomplishes diagnosis primarily through lists of symptoms. There is no necessary relationship whatsoever between the diagnostic categories of the* DSM-IV-TR *and the educational handicaps of the Regulations. The presence or absence of a* DSM-IV-TR *condition does not in any way imply the presence or absence of an educational handicap identifiable under the Regulations. The often ignored Cautionary Statement in the manual makes clear this distinction between DSM-IV-TR diagnosis and legal judgments, such as determining disabilities. Nonetheless, there is a strong argument that one should be able to specify a* DSM-IV-TR *diagnosis as the "condition" for identification of Serious Emotional Disturbance just as we believe it is essential to specify the disorder in one or more basic psychological processes when identifying a specific learning disability.*

Ames, L. B. (1968). A low intelligence quotient often not recognized and the chief cause of many learning difficulties? *Journal of Learning Disabilities, 1,* 735–739. See McLeod (1968) for an opposing viewpoint (with which we agree).

Ames writes, "The so-called Law of Parsimony advises never to seek a complicated explanation of a phenomenon when a simpler one will suffice. Applied to the many school learning problems which plague education today, this principle could substantially reduce the number of children suffering from what is now called learning disability. . . . There is a very large percentage of the school population in this country (it might be as high as 15 percent) who will have difficulty in school simply because of their low intelligence" (p. 735). Be sure to see McLeod's thoughtful (and, we believe, correct) comment on the Law of Parsimony for identification of specific learning disabilities.

Binet, A., & Simon, T. (1916/1980). *The development of intelligence in children:* with marginal notes by Lewis M. Terman and preface by Lloyd M. Dunn. (E. S. Kite, Trans.). Facsimile limited edition issued by Lloyd M. Dunn. Nashville, TN: Williams Printing Co. (Original work published 1916.)

American Guidance Service distributed copies of this facsimile edition, which Professor Dunn had printed from Lewis Terman's personal copy of the original book (a gift to Terman from Henry Goddard dated 6.10.16; Goddard wrote the introduction), including Professor Terman's handwritten marginal notes. This book is well worth the effort to locate a copy.

Bracken, B. A. (1988). Ten psychometric reasons why similar tests produce dissimilar results. *Journal of School Psychology, 26*(2), 155–166.

If you ever administer more than one test to a child you have discovered that not all tests give the same results. Dr. Bracken explains 10 of the most common reasons for such dissimilar results.

Brody, S. (Ed.) (2001). *Teaching reading: Language, letters, and thought* (2nd ed.). Milford, NH: LARC Publishing [P. O. Box 801, Milford, NH 03055 (603.624.1292) http://www.larc publishing.com]

Explores reading practices grounded in research with practical strategies to: enhance language-acquisition; develop phonemic-awareness; systematically improve decoding, advanced letter-cluster identification, and fluency; expand vocabulary and background knowledge; construct deep understanding of complex concepts; and increase pleasure reading. Explains when and how to implement effective instruction. Chapters include: reading theory & practice, emergence of language, the phonemic awareness bridge, decoding strategies, automaticity & fluency, spelling & reading connections, understanding texts & literature, background knowledge, vocabulary depth & breadth, writing to increase comprehension, testing reading & its subskills, and assessment informing lesson plans. [Disclosure: Willis wrote one chapter in this book.]

Carroll, J. B. (1993). *Human cognitive abilities: A survey of factor-analytic studies.* Cambridge, England: Cambridge University Press.

The foundation of the Carroll leg of the Cattell-Horn-Carroll tripod and the empirical foundation for CHC theory and application, this is the periodic table of cognitive elements.

Clements, S. D. (1966). *Minimal brain dysfunction in children.* Public Health Service Report No. 1415, NINDB Monograph No. 3. Washington, DC: U.S. Department of Health, Education, and Welfare.

Interesting historical note. Some hot, new issues may be hot, but not new.

Cohen, S. A. (1971). Dyspedagogia as a cause of reading retardation: Definition and treatment. In B. Bateman (Ed.), *Learning Disorders* (Vol. 4, pp. 269–291). Seattle, WA: Special Child.

Dyspedagogia may be a very seriously under-diagnosed condition.

Daniel, M. H. (1999). Behind the scenes: Using new measurement methods on the DAS and KAIT. In S. E. Embretson & S. L. Hershberger (Eds.) *The new rules of measurement: What every psychologist and educator should know* (pp. 37–63). Mahwah, NJ: Erlbaum.

Item Response Theory is now the basis for the construction of most new tests, but its application is more explicit in the DAS-II than in most other instruments. A basic understanding of Item Response Theory and its application really is something "every psychologist and educator should know."

Daniel, M. H. (1997). Intelligence testing: Status and trends. *American Psychologist, 52,* 1038–1045.

In this review, Daniel presents his views on the current status of three types of intelligence assessments: psychometric, neurological-processing, and dynamic. The psychometric approach has seen a shift toward a multi-factorial model of intelligence with acceptance of a hierarchical model of intelligence with a general factor at the apex. Daniel suggested that for practical reasons the study of intelligence needs to expand the research beyond the broad general ability and investigate the relation of more specific abilities to various learning domains. Construct validity and cross-battery equivalence of scores across tests is also important. The neuropsychological-processing model of assessment is described in terms of PASS theory in which the constructs are considered overlapping processing areas. Daniel's suggestion is that studies of what constructs are being measured by these tests is needed, especially because there is some evidence that the processes purported to be measured on tests from this approach do not differ from psychometric factors. The third type of assessment, dynamic, concentrates on person's ability to learn rather than the structure of cognitive abilities. These tests are still in the developmental stages and more has to be known about these assessments. Daniel discussed the future of intelligence testing and the importance of expanding the domain of intelligence to other areas.

DiCerbo, K. E., & Barona, A. (2000). A convergent validity study of the Differential Ability Scales and the Wechsler Intelligence Scale for Children-Third Edition with Hispanic children. *Journal of Psychoeducational Assessment, 18,* 344–352.

Both the DAS and WISC-III were administered to a sample of 24 English-speaking Hispanic children between the ages of 9 and 11. Global and factor scores for both tests were compared and a relationship between the WISC-III and DAS was indicated, providing evidence for the convergent validity of both tests in assessing English-speaking Hispanic children residing in the United States.

Dumont, R., Cruse, C. L., Price, L., & Whelley, P. (1996). The relationship between the Differential Ability Scales (DAS) and the Wechsler Intelligence Scale for Children-Third Edition (WISC-III) for students with learning disabilities. *Psychology in the Schools, 33,* 203–209.

A sample of 53 public school children who were receiving triennial reevaluations was administered the DAS approximately three years after having been administered the WISC-III. The mean DAS GCA was 87.17 and the mean WISC-III FSIQ was 89.73; there was no statistical difference between these two scores. The DAS Spatial and Verbal Cluster scores were not significantly different from the WISC-III Verbal and Performance IQ scores. The DAS Nonverbal Reasoning Cluster score was significantly below the Verbal and Performance IQ scores on the WISC-III. In addition, 47% of the children in the sample were found to have the same intelligence classification on the DAS as they did three years prior on the WISC-III. The DAS underestimated the classification of 34% of the sample and overestimated the classification of 19% of the children. When reporting the WISC-III FSIQ at 95% confidence, only 4% of the students were found to be misclassified. Hence when the ranges of FSIQ and GCA were considered 96% of the cases were in agreement three years later. The DAS is highly correlated with the WISC-III in a sample of learning disabled children three years apart. When confidence intervals are considered, classifications are very similar between the two groups of scores and any differences were typically related to the Nonverbal Reasoning Cluster.

Dumont, R., & Willis, J. O. (2003). Issues regarding the supervision of assessment. *The Clinical Supervisor, 22,* 159–176.

This article examines what is needed for the responsible supervision and practice of assessment in psychology. It presents, through a series of questions, important issues to be considered in the evaluation and supervision process.

Dumont, R., & Willis, J. O. (1995). Intrasubtest scatter on the WISC-III for various clinical samples vs. the standardization sample: An examination of WISC folklore. *Journal of Psychoeducational Assessment, 13,* 271–285.

"WISC Folklore" is Dumont's term for firmly entrenched beliefs that guide examiners' misinterpretations of WISC findings. See McGrew (1994) for an example of Woodcock-Johnson folklore.

Dumont, R., & Willis, J. O. (2003) Mnemonics for five issues in the identification of learning disabilities taken from the three synoptic gospels of the New Testament of the King James Version of the Bible first by Keith Stanovich and later, in imitation, by John Willis and Ron Dumont. Retrieved February 23, 2008 from http://alpha.fdu.edu/psychology/mnemonics_for_five_issues.htm.

The list includes Stanovich's Matthew Effects and Dumont and Willis's Mark Penalty.

Dumont, R., Willis, J. O., Farr, L. P., McCarthy, T., & Price, L. (2000). The relationship between the Differential Ability Scales (DAS) and the Woodcock-Johnson Tests of Cognitive Ability-Revised (W-J COG) for students referred for special education evaluations. *Journal of Psychoeducational Assessment, 18,* 27–38.

The DAS and WJ-R COG were administered to children referred for special education after pre-referral intervention. The mean GCA on the DAS was 94.15 and the mean BCA for the WJ-R COG was significantly higher at 96.95. The DAS Nonverbal Reasoning Cluster was also significantly lower the WJ-R COG BCA score. The Spatial Cluster and Verbal Clusters on the DAS were not significantly different from the WJ-R BCA. DAS Gc subtests of Word Definitions and Similarities correlated with WJ-R Picture Vocabulary. DAS Gf subtests of Matrices and Sequential & Quantitative Reasoning correlated with WJ-R Analysis-Synthesis. DAS Gv subtests of Recall of Designs and Pattern Construction did not correlate highly with WJ-R Visual Closure but instead correlated higher with Analysis-Synthesis. DAS Gsm subtest of Recall of Digits correlated highest with WJ-R Memory for Sentences. DAS Recall of Objects-Immediate and Delayed did not correlate significantly with any other WJ-R subtest.

Dunham, M., McIntosh, D., & Gridley, B. E. (2002). An independent confirmatory factor analysis of the Differential Ability Scales. *Journal of Psychoeducational Assessment, 20,* 152–163.

This study investigated the structure of the DAS using confirmatory factor analysis with 130 normal school-aged children. The author tested several models a one-factor model, the model suggested by the test's author and two models which include the diagnostic tests with the six core subtests. The one factor model did not adequately represent the data. The model proposed by Elliot was clearly supported by factor analysis. The last two models were proposed by Keith (1990) based on logical analysis of previous research. The first of these models in which Recall of Digits had a moderately high loading on the second order g factor suggested that it could be used as a contribution to the GCA. The last model replicates Keith's (1990) model. The present study found it only reasonably good fit to the data. Results of this study are consistent with the model proposed by Elliot and the authors recommend continuing to use the test as originally proposed by Elliot with the diagnostic subtests interpreted separately.

Elliot, S. N. (1990). The nature and structure of the DAS: Questioning the test's organizing model and use. *Journal of Psychoeducational Assessment, 8,* 406–411.

This opinion paper provides a critique of the DAS. The author states 1) memory subtests are relegated to minor and undefined roles, 2) diagnostic subtests in general are unconnected to the overall GCA and their role in diagnosis is unclear, 3) achievement subtests correlate moderately highly with the GCA but lack a strong clear role, 4) differentiation of cognitive abilities over the course of development is not well-established theoretically. Practical concerns related to the test include the need for more analyses with regards to racial bias in the manual, direct comparisons of diagnostic accuracy in differentiation between handicapped and non-handicapped students, information about the expected discrepancies for groups, and what profiles can be determined reliability and are useful for intervention planning.

Elliott, C. D. (1990). The nature and structure of children's abilities: Evidence from the Differential Ability Scales. *Journal of Psychoeducational Assessment, 8,* 376–390.

A paper about the DAS by the test author which presents its relatively high levels of reliable specific variance (which is required for identifying reliable differences in a cognitive profile), its focused composite scores including a measure of psychometric g in the GCA, measures of Verbal and Nonverbal Ability at the preschool level and Verbal, Nonverbal Reasoning, and Spatial Ability at the school-age level. Since there was no support for a memory factor in the confirmatory factor analysis, this was not retained and the six subtests that loaded highly on g were retained to make the GCA. Abilities become more differentiated with age and subtests become more independent and specific with age. The factor structure is supported by previous findings on the organization of abilities and by statistical analyses. Lastly, Colin Elliott addressed all of the concerns of S. N. Eliot (1990) and refuted many of them with facts provided in the Technical Manual.

Eysenck, H. J., vs. Kamin, L. J. (1981). *The intelligence controversy.* New York: Wiley-Interscience.

The "vs." is the correct citation. Eysenck, a professor of psychology at the University of London and former student of the late Cyril Burt, wrote a strong argument that it "seems very unlikely that the heritability of intelligence in modern Western countries would be lower than 70 percent or higher than 85 percent" (p. 52). Kamin, the Princeton University professor of psychology who reported that Cyril Burt had invented much of the data upon which his famous studies of intelligence were based, wrote a powerful argument for environmental influence on intelligence. "There are not even adequate grounds for dismissing the hypothesis that the heritability of IQ is zero" (p. 154). Only after their contributions had been edited for publication did the authors have the opportunity to see one another's essays and write the rebuttals which conclude the volume.

Flanagan, D. P., Ortiz, S. O., & Alfonso, V. C. (2007). *Essentials of cross-battery assessment* (2nd ed.). New York: Wiley.

The most recent and most complete treatment of the McGrew, Flanagan, and Ortiz Integrated Cattell-Horn-Carroll Approach to Cross-Battery Assessment with sections on the Cross-Battery Approach, evaluation of specific learning disabilities, case reports, and CHC classifications of many tests and subtests. The book includes a CD with three very useful programs for test classification and interpretation of tests, cultural and linguistic issues, and assessment of specific learning disabilities. See also the Official Site of the CHC Cross-Battery Approach by Dawn P. Flanagan and Samuel O. Ortiz at http://facpub.stjohns.edu/~ortizs/cross-battery/ (Retrieved February 29, 2008).

Flanagan, D. P., Ortiz, S. O., Alfonso, V., & Mascolo, J. T. (2006) *Achievement test desk reference (ATDR-II): A guide to learning disability identification* (2nd ed.). Hoboken, NJ: Wiley.

A serious treatment of achievement tests from the standpoint of CHC theory. Realization of the full potential of a cognitive ability test grounded in CHC requires integration with achievement tests within the same theoretical framework, an integration facilitated by this text. [A computerized version of the book's test classification according to CHC theory is available for download at: http://alpha.fdu.edu/psychology/ATDR.htm.]

Galton, F. (1886). Regression towards mediocrity in hereditary stature. *Journal of the Anthropological Institute, 15,* 246–263.

Galton's description and explanation of the phenomenon now usually called regression toward the mean. Some members of school special education evaluation teams continue to be surprised that predicted aca-

demic achievement is not identical to the cognitive ability score used to make the prediction. We urge you to be tactful and explain to your colleagues that the idea is pretty new: it was not developed until '86.

Glutting, J. J., McDermott, P. A., & Konold, T. R. (1998). More ups and downs of subtest analysis: Criterion validity of the DAS with an unselected cohort. *School Psychology Review, 27,* 599–612.

Evaluation of the criterion-related validity of unusual subtests profiles from the DAS. Three methods were used to identify unusual profiles: multivariate-nomothetic, univariate-nomothetic, and univariate-ipsative each with prevalence rates <= 5%. A large sample of 1200 children obtained from a validation study of the Adjustment Scales for Children and Adolescents was used to identify 60 children with unusual profiles and matched to controls by the demographic characteristics and overall IQs. The two groups were compared across a variety of external criteria: (a) propensity for placement in special education, (b) three norm-referenced measures of achievement, and (c) six behavioral indices evaluated through standardized teacher ratings. Results showed no group differences across all criteria, regardless of the method used to identify unusual subtest profiles.

Goldman, J. J. (1989). On the robustness of psychological test instrumentation: Psychological evaluation of the dead. In Glenn G. Ellenbogen (Ed.), *The primal whimper: More readings from the Journal of Polymorphous Perversity.* New York: Ballantine, Stonesong Press.

Although lighthearted, this article actually points to very important considerations of adequacy of test floors. See http://alpha.fdu.edu/psychology/McGee.htm (Retrieved March 7, 2008).

Hale, J. B., Fiorello, C. A., Dumont, R., Willis, J. O., Rackley, C., & Elliott, C. E. (in press). Differential Ability Scales–Second Edition (Neuro)Psychological Predictors of Math Performance for Typical Children and Children with Math Disabilities. *Psychology in the Schools*

Using regression commonality analysis, this study of 371 typical children and 42 children with math learning disabilities (MLD) examined DAS-II basic (neuro)psychological processes in the prediction of WIAT-II Numerical Operations and Math Reasoning performance. Although DAS-II predictors accounted for substantial amounts of achievement variance in typical children (range 46% to 58%), they accounted for less variance in the MLD group (range 33% to 50%), and this loss of predictive validity was especially pronounced when one interprets the DAS-II General Conceptual Ability (GCA) score instead of subcomponent factor or subtest scores. Consistent with neuroimaging studies of children with disabilities, predictor combinations were different for children with MLD, suggesting that differences in, or the absence of, typical predictor-outcome relationships may serve as a foundation for developing specific interventions to address the cognitive and learning deficits experienced by children with MLD.

Holland, A. M., & McDermott, P. A. (1996). Discovering core profile types in the school-age standardization sample of the Differential Ability Scales. *Journal of Psychoeducational Assessment, 14,* 131–146.

The cognitive subtest profiles of the 2,400 children ages 6 to 17 years who comprised the DAS normative sample were sorted using multistage hierarchical cluster analyses with independent replications. Seven core profile types were discovered and described in terms of prevalence and characteristics. Discussion in the article shows how typology provides clinicians and researchers necessary contrasts against which to evaluate claims regarding the distinctiveness and potential diagnostic and treatment utility of specific profiles.

Hughes, T. L., & McIntosh, D. E. (2002). Differential Ability Scales: Profiles of preschoolers with cognitive delay. *Psychology in the Schools, 39,* 19–29.

This study was an examination of DAS cluster score profiles for children who were diagnosed as preschools as either having or not having a cognitive delay. Cluster analyses resulted in distinctive profiles for each group which were distinct from one another. The groups identified included a Pre-math group defined as children with limited development in skills needed for pre-math tasks including lower scores on Copying, Recall of Digits, and Early Number Concepts. Another group had difficulties with Receptive Language including vocabulary development, language comprehension and use of verbal mediation identified with lower scores in Verbal Comprehension and Early Number Concepts. Another group was identified as Pre-Math / Visual Memory which had a similar profile as Pre-Math group with an added weakness in visual memory in Recall of Objects. The authors conclude by describing particular interventions that can be used with various groups of children.

Joseph, R. M., Tager-Flusberg, H., & Lord, C. (2002). Cognitive profiles and social-communicative functioning in children with autism spectrum disorder. *Journal of Child Psychology and Psychiatry, 43,* 807–821.

A high rate of uneven cognitive development across verbal and nonverbal abilities as measured by the DAS was found in this sample of children with autism spectrum disorder

Kamphaus, R. W., & Reynolds, C. R. (1987). *Clinical and research applications of the K-ABC.* Circle Pines, MN: American Guidance Service.

This was the essential adjunct to the original Kaufman Assessment Battery for Children with many innovative approaches to test interpretation that served as early models for best current practices.

Kaufman, A. S. (1976). A new approach to the interpretation of test scatter on the WISC-R. *Journal of Learning Disabilities, 9,* 739–744.

Kaufman startled many practitioners and trainers when he revealed that wide scatter of subtest scaled scores on the WISC-R was much more common than most WISC-R experts realized or believed. This article and Kaufman's repetition of the information in the Intelligent Testing volumes for the WISC-R, WISC-III, and WISC-IV contributed to the appropriate attention now paid by better examiners and publishers to base rates for scatter, discrepancies, and other test results.

Keith, T. Z. (1990). Confirmatory and hierarchical confirmatory analysis of the Differential Ability Scales. *Journal of Psychoeducational Assessment, 8,* 391–405.

Analyses found that the constructs measured by the DAS are quite consistent across overlapping age ranges. Hierarchical confirmatory factory analysis confirmed that the DAS provides a good measure of g, general intelligence across the two batteries and measures a 5 subscale hierarchical model which includes Verbal (Word Definitions, Similarities, Recall of Objects), Nonverbal Reasoning (Pattern Construction & Recall of Designs), Memory (Recall of Digits), Gf (Matrices and Sequential & Quantitative) and Speed (Speed of Information Processing). Fit statistics suggest that this final model provides an excellent fit for ages 6 to 17. This model is quite consistent with the model proposed by the author and publisher of the instrument. For preschool age children, the final model has subtests grouped into 3 factors: Verbal (Verbal Comprehension and Naming Vocabulary), Nonverbal Reasoning (Picture Similarities, Recognition of Pictures, Copying, and Pattern Construction), and Quantitative (Recall of Digits and Early Number Concepts). These results are also consistent with the structure of the test.

Keith, T. Z., Quirk, K. J., Schartzer, C., & Elliott, C. D. (1999). Construct bias in the Differential Ability Scales? Confirmatory and hierarchical factor structure across three ethnic groups. *Journal of Psychoeducational Assessment, 17,* 249–268.

This study examines the DAS's construct bias for children from three major ethnic groups and across the entire age range as well as determine the nature of the constructs measured across these three groups. Both purposes were accomplished through hierarchical, multisample confirmatory factor analysis of the DAS standardization data. Results suggested that the DAS measures the same constructs for all three ethnic groups across the four age levels studied; the DAS, therefore, shows no construct bias across groups. Furthermore, the hierarchical factor structure of the instrument is consistent with the structure of the DAS's Cluster and composite scores, thus supporting construct validity.

Maller, S. J. (2003). Intellectual assessment of deaf people: A critical review of core concepts and issues. In Marschark, M. (Ed.) *Oxford handbook of deaf studies, language, and education* (p. 451–463). Cary, NC: Oxford University Press.

Some of the issues discussed by Maller include technical characteristics of tests (e.g., differential item function) and threats to validity such as unknown effects of translating test instructions into American Sign Language and lack of examiner knowledge of deaf persons and various forms of communication.

Mather, N., & Jaffe, L. (2002). *Woodcock-Johnson III: Recommendations, reports, and strategies.* New York: Wiley.

An extraordinarily thorough and helpful treatment of the WJ III, including many very useful forms, sample reports, 158 pages of specific, practical recommendations, and 85 pages of detailed explanations of teaching strategies, which evaluators can (and should) use in their reports. Even if you never use the WJ III, this book is extremely useful with any interpretation of assessment.

McIntosh, D. E. (1999). Identifying at-risk preschoolers: The discriminant validity of the Differential Ability Scales. *Psychology in the Schools, 36,* 1–10.

Thirty-two at-risk preschoolers and 30 typical preschoolers were administered the DAS. Results indicated that the DAS was an excellent measure to use when trying to differentiate between at-risk and normal preschoolers. The DAS could reliably identify, better than chance, whether a child was at-risk or not. Specifically, the GCA score was found to be approximately 77% accurate in correctly classifying at-risk from normal preschoolers. In addition, the use of the DAS in an abbreviated format by selecting specific core and/or diagnostic subtests during the preschool screening process was strongly supported.

McIntosh, D. E., Brown, M. L., & Ross, S. L. (1995). Relationship between the Bracken Basic Concept Scale and the Differential Ability Scales with an at-risk sample of preschoolers. *Psychological Reports, 76,* 219–244.

Thirty-five at-risk preschoolers (a somewhat small sample size with restricted range) were administered the Upper Preschool battery of the DAS and the Bracken Basic Concept Scale. Pearson coefficients showed a .70 correlation between the Bracken Total Test score and the DAS GCA, the Verbal and Nonverbal Cluster scores had correlations of .60 and .59 with the Bracken Total Test score, respectively. The School Readiness composite from the Bracken showed the highest correlations of the various Bracken subtest scores with the DAS GCA and two clusters. The authors conclude that the Bracken could be used as a screening measure of intelligence with at-risk preschoolers. The notable finding that the Bracken Total test score has a similar relation to both the Verbal and Nonverbal clusters of the DAS was attributed to the Bracken possibly measuring both Verbal and Nonverbal ability.

McIntosh, D. E., & Gridley, B. E. (1993). Differential Ability Scales: Profiles of learning-disabled subtypes. *Psychology in the Schools, 30,* 11–24.

Cluster analysis of a sample of 83 school children with learning disabilities from the standardization sample yielded six distinct homogeneous subgroups. The first subgroup, Generalized, had below average GCAs and Spatial ability scores in the average range but core and diagnostic subtest scores that were depressed with the Word Reading and Spelling subtests the lowest and significantly lower than the GCA. The High Functioning group had average GCAs (highest of the subgroups) and Word Reading and Spelling subtest scores significantly lower than GCAs. The Normal group had average GCAs and the lowest scores on Recall of Objects. The Underachievement group had profiles similar to Normal group but below average GCAs. The Borderline/Generalized group had GCAs in the low or borderline ranges with low scores appearing to be related to overall low functioning rather than to specific learning disabilities. The Dyseidetic group had GCAs in the below average range with a significant discrepancy between GCA and Verbal Ability scores. The authors conducted a three step-wise discriminate analyses, one with diagnostic subtests only, one with achievement subtests and one with both diagnostic and achievement subtests. Accuracy of prediction was highest (78.31%) when the achievement and diagnostic subtests were considered simultaneously. As a group, the lowest subtest scores were on Recall of Objects and Picture Recognition indicating that the children with learning disabilities, as a group, had poor short-term visual memory skills.

McIntosh, D. E., Mulkins, R., Pardue-Vaughn, L., Barnes, L. B., & Gridley, B. E. (1992). The canonical relationship between the Differential Ability Scales Upper Preschool Verbal and Nonverbal Clusters. *Journal of School Psychology, 30,* 355–361.

A sample of 77 preschoolers was administered the Upper Preschool battery of the DAS. One significant canonical correlation was found and a linear combination of the Nonverbal and Verbal clusters shared about 45% of their variance. Redundancy analyses showed that on average 35% of the total variance accounted for in the Verbal cluster is accounted for by the Nonverbal linear combination and 32% of the Nonverbal cluster can be accounted for by the Verbal linear combination. Examination of the squared structure coefficients (bivariate correlations with the variable and the linear composite) showed that 85% of the variance in Naming Vocabulary and 71% of the variance in Verbal Comprehension scores are accounted for by the Verbal Cluster. Picture Similarities, and Pattern Construction have about 77% of their variance accounted for by the Nonverbal cluster. The Nonverbal cluster also accounts for 55% of the variance in Copying subtest scores. In all, the analyses show that there are two distinct clusters (Verbal and Nonverbal), but these clusters share some variance. Hence, these findings justify use of the GCA as well as the use of all three clusters.

McIntosh, D. E., Wayland, S. J., Gridley, B., & Barnes, L. B. (1995). The relationship between the Bracken Basic Concept Scale and the Differential Ability Scales with a preschool sample. *Journal of Psychoeducational Assessment, 13,* 39–48.

Sixty preschool children were administered the Upper Preschool battery of the DAS and the Bracken Basic Concept Scale. Low correlations were found between the Bracken and Recall of Objects and Recognition of Pictures on the DAS. Moderate correlations were found between the Bracken subtests and Matching Letter-Like Forms and Recall of Digits on the DAS. Pearson correlations showed a .80 correlation between the Bracken Total Test score and the GCA on the DAS. Bracken Total score had a correlation of .67 with the Verbal Cluster of the DAS and a .73 correlation with the Nonverbal Cluster of the DAS. The School Readiness composite from the Bracken Test showed the highest correlation (.78) among the Bracken subtests with the DAS GCA. The authors conclude that the Bracken measures both verbal and nonverbal abilities and that the Bracken can be used as a screening measure of intelligence with at-risk preschoolers (in particular the School Readiness composite). A concern about this study is its use of bivariate correlations to make conclusions.

McLeod, J. (1968). Reading expectancy from disabled readers. *Journal of Learning Disabilities, 1,* 97–105. See Ames (1968).

McLeod writes, "A respect for the law of parsimony is a characteristic of science, but educational psychology's penchant for simple answers to questions of complex human behavior, particularly in the area of learning disability, has tended toward paucity rather than parsimony of explanation" (p. 97). We could not agree more.

National Research Council. (2002). *Mental retardation: Determining eligibility for Social Security benefits.* Committee on Disability Determination for Mental Retardation. Daniel J. Reschly, Tracy G. Myers, & Christine R. Hartel, editors. Division of Behavioral and Social Sciences and Education. Washington, DC: National Academy Press.

Despite the apparently narrow focus of the title, this volume is an excellent compendium of recent information about the diagnosis of mental retardation, produced by the 16-member Committee of the Na-

tional Research Council. There are informative chapters on intellectual assessment, adaptive behavior assessment, the relationship of intelligence and adaptive behavior, and differential diagnosis. Highly recommended for evaluators and teams making identifications of mental retardation or differential identifications of mental retardation and specific learning disabilities. Online at :http://lab.nap.edu/ nap-cgi/discover.cgi?term=mental%20retardation &restric=NAP

Neisser, U. (Ed.) (1998). *The rising curve: Long-term gains in IQ and related measures.* Washington, DC: American Psychological Association.

Very stimulating discussions of the Flynn effect (including a chapter by Flynn himself), racial differences on intelligence tests, and the "hypothesis of dysgenic trends."

O'Neill, A. M. (1995). *Clinical inference: How to draw meaningful conclusions from tests.* New York: Wiley.

A valuable antidote to the increasing mechanization and depersonalization of assessment.

Riccio, C. A., Ross, C. M., Boan, C. H., Jemison, S., & Houston, F. (1997). Use of the Differential Ability Scales (DAS) Special Nonverbal Composite among young children with linguistic differences. *Journal of Psychoeducational Assessment, 15,* 196–204.

The Special Nonverbal Composite (SNC) of the DAS was administered to children ages 3:6 to 6:0 who were identified as Deaf/Hearing Impaired, as Developmentally Delayed, as having Specific Language Impairment, as having Limited English Proficiency or English as a second language. Additionally there was a control group of children that had no identified concern. Results indicated that SNC scores obtained for children in the English as a second language or limited English proficiency group were comparable to those obtained by the control group. While children in the Specific Language Impairment and Deaf/Hearing Impaired groups obtained lower scores. However their scores were still significantly higher than those obtained by the children in the Developmentally Delayed group. While the SNC of the DAS appears to be a good measure for children with linguistic differences, the specific language impaired and deaf/hearing impaired groups did score lower than the control group. These results suggest that performance on these subtests may be influenced by language ability—but there is still clear differentiation between these groups and children with developmental delay.

Sattler, J. M. (2008). *Assessment of children: Cognitive foundations* (5th ed.). San Diego: Jerome M. Sattler, Publisher. http://www.sattlerpublisher.com/

Latest edition of the classic text in psychological assessment with valuable chapters on general assessment topics, such as statistics, writing reports, and general domains of assessment, as well as specific chapters on particular tests and many extremely useful tables. The long chapter on the DAS-II was written by Prof. Sattler with Ron Dumont and John Willis. Dumont and Willis contributed to some other chapters as well.

Sattler, J. M., & Dumont, R. P. (2004). *Assessment of children: WISC-IV and WPPSI-III supplement.* San Diego: Jerome M. Sattler, Publisher.

Additional, detailed information on these two tests.

Sattler, J. M., & Evans, C. A. (2006). Visual impairments. In J. M. Sattler & R. Hoge, *Assessment of Children: Behavioral and clinical foundations* (5th ed., pp. 464–477). San Diego: Jerome M. Sattler, Publisher.

Assessment of children with visual impairments requires specialized skills and knowledge. This chapter provides very useful information as well as urging collaboration with an expert, such as a teacher of the blind and visually impaired.

Sattler, J. M., Hardy-Braz, S. T., & Willis, J. O. (2006). Hearing impairments. In J. M. Sattler & R. Hoge, *Assessment of Children: Behavioral and clinical foundations* (5th ed., pp. 478–492). San Diego: Jerome M. Sattler, Publisher.

Assessment of children who are deaf or hard of hearing requires specialized skills and knowledge and understanding of various aspects of deaf culture or cultures. This chapter provides very useful information as well as urging collaboration with an expert, such as a teacher of the blind and visually impaired.

Sattler, J. M., & Hoge, R. (2006). *Assessment of children: Behavioral, social and clinical foundations* (5th ed.). San Diego: Jerome M. Sattler, Publisher.

Comprehensive treatment of educational and psychological assessment of children emphasizing particular disabilities, behavior assessment, and other clinical topics. We consider it an absolutely essential reference, along with the companion Cognitive Applications. The valuable appendices include many extremely helpful semistructured interviews. [Disclosure: Dumont and Willis contributed to some chapters.]

Stone, B. J. (1992). Joint confirmatory factor analyses of the DAS and WISC-R. *Journal of School Psychology, 30,* 185–195.

Using a sample of 115 children the factor structure of both tests were examined. Elliott's verbal, nonverbal, spatial, and diagnostic model provided significantly better fit to the data than alternative models— a single-factor model that was based on Spearman's General factor and both a two-factor Verbal and Performance model and a three-factor Verbal, Performance, and Freedom from Distractibility model.

Stone, B. J. (1992). Joint factor analyses of the DAS and WISC-R. *Diagnostique, 17,* 176–184.

A joint factor analysis was performed with the DAS and WISC-R. A four factor solution was observed, with four factors accounting for 63% of the total variance. The first factor was named Verbal-conceptual and had high loadings from all of the verbal tests from the WISC-R and DAS as well as the nonverbal reasoning tests and Recall of Objects from the DAS. The second factor was considered a visual-spatial factor and consisted of Picture Completion, Picture Arrangement, Block Design, and Object Assembly from the WISC-R and Matrices, Pattern Construction, and Recall of Digits from the DAS. The third factor was an attention-quantitative factor and included Arithmetic and Digit Span from the WISC-R and Sequential and Quantitative Reasoning, Matrices, and Recall of Digits from the DAS. The fourth factor was considered processing speed and included Coding from the WISC-R and Speed of Information Processing from the DAS. The author concluded that results supported separating the DAS core and diagnostic subtests, as all of the tests with high g loadings were on the first factor. The lowest loadings were on the processing speed tasks. Second, he concluded that both the DAS and WISC-R contained a highly g loaded verbal composite and a lower g loaded nonverbal composite. The factor structures of the WISC-R and DAS were supported by this study.

Sonuga-Barke, E. J. S., Dalen, L., Daley, D., & Remington, B. (2002). Are planning, working memory, and inhibition associated with individual differences in preschool ADHD symptoms? *Developmental Neuropsychology, 2,* 255–272.

The association between individual differences in symptoms of ADHD and performance on tasks of executive functioning (planning, working memory, and inhibition) was explored in a sample of 160 preschool children. The executive functioning measures were reliable and correlated with age and IQ as measured by the BAS. Once age and IQ was controlled, planning and working memory were correlated with each other but not with inhibition. There was no association between ADHD and working memory or planning. There was significant negative association between ADHD and conduct problems and inhibition. Specific deficiencies in inhibition control rather than general executive function deficits are associated with ADHD in the preschool period.

Terman, L. M. (1916). *The measurement of intelligence.* Boston: Houghton-Mifflin. [Terman's translation, revision, expansion, and American norming of the Binet-Simon scales.]
This is how the whole business got started in the United States.

Titchener, E. B. (1924). *A text-book of psychology.* New York: Macmillan.
Titchener translates Wilhelm Wundt's (1858–1962) selbstbeobachtung as "introspection" or "a looking-within" (p. 20 in the 1924 edition of the 1909 revision of the 1896 Outline of Psychology). This was an important method of experimental psychology consisting in part of analyzing complex perceptions into discrete sensations. Sensations of cold and pressure, for example, yield a perception of wetness. A balloon filled with cold water will feel wet even if the surface is entirely dry. We mention this because of our belief that taking a new test before you become familiar with it is a good way not only to begin learning the test, but also to help yourself understand the task demands and thinking processes involved.

U.S. Congress. (2001). No child left behind act of 2001 (P.L. 107-110). Retrieved February 23, 2008 from http://www.ed.gov/policy/elsec/leg/ esea02/index.html.
This reauthorization of the Elementary and Secondary Education Act imposes sweeping mandates on most U. S. public schools, one of which, most germane to this discussion, requires annual testing in reading, writing, and math. Although the quality and difficulty levels of the tests developed or adopted by the individual states vary, the flurry of testing does produce one more source of historical information about a student's educational progress.

U.S. Congress. (2004). Individuals with Disabilities Education Improvement Act of 2004 (P. L. 108-446). Retrieved February 29, 2008 from http://idea.ed.gov/download/ statute.html.
The latest revision of the Education of all Handicapped Children Act of 1975 makes substantial changes in the rules for identifying specific learning disabilities.

Vernon, P. E. (1950). *The structure of human abilities.* London: Methuen.
First factor analysis performed on a cognitive test (Thurstone's primary mental-ability test). Results indicated that that subtests intercorrelated and could yield two group factors verbal-educational and spatial-mechanical. A hierarchical model of cognitive ability from first-order primary abilities to second-order group factors to third-order general factors was developed on this test.

Willis, J. O., & Dumont, R. (2006). And never the twain shall meet: Can response to intervention and cognitive assessment be reconciled? *Psychology in the Schools, 43* (8), 901–908.
This is the concluding article in a two-issue discussion in Psychology in the Schools of Response to Intervention edited by Nadeen Kaufman and Nancy Mather. "Arguments between Response to Intervention (RTI) with Curriculum-Based Measurement (CBM) and traditional, individual psychoeducational assessments encourage a false dichotomy between alternatives that are not mutually exclusive, but complementary. This article discusses strengths and weaknesses of both approaches, touches on current legislative issues, and suggests that judicious, appropriate use of both types of assessment enhances the value of each. Initial identification of students who might need specialized instruction is better done with CBM than with individual psychoeducational assessments. RTI approaches would usually be more efficient than individual assessments and should reduce the need for such assessments. However, when RTI does not solve the problem or there are multiple, severe, and complex referral concerns, individual psychoeducational assessments are still essential."

Wundt, W. (1858–1862). *Beiträge zur Theorie der Sinneswahrnehmung.* Cited in E. G. Boring (1950), *A history of experimental psychology* (2nd ed.). New York: Appleton-Century-Crofts.
Everything you ever wanted to know about introspection in experimental psychology. See Titchener (1924).

Youngstrom, E. A., Kogos, J. L., & Glutting, J. J. (1999). Incremental efficacy of Differential Ability Scale factor scores in predicting individual achievement criteria. *School Psychology Quarterly, 14,* 26–39.
Blocked entry hierarchical regressions were used to investigate the relative contribution of the GCA score compared to the three factor scores from the clusters. GCA was entered first as a single block and then the three clusters were entered together in the second block. The GCA explained 27–36% of the variance in achievement outcomes. As a group the three clusters accounted for an additional 2.02 to 4.17% of the variances. All had small effect sizes. Further, these effects did not depend on whether a student was in special education or general education. The authors conclude by saying that the GCA is the most efficient predictor of academic achievement and relying on the clusters does not provide additional information that has practical utility.

SOME OF THE TESTS MENTIONED IN CHAPTERS

Bracken, B. A. (2006). *Bracken Basic Concept Scale* (3rd ed.). San Antonio, TX: Harcourt Assessment.
The receptive scale (BBSC-3:R) is a multiple-choice test on which the child points to the one of four pictures that best illustrates each concept named by the examiner (e.g., Show me which picture has the most puppies). The expressive scale (BBSC-3:R) asks the child to name similar pictures illustrating the same concepts. The author describes a "basic concept" as ". . . a word, in its most elementary sense, that is a label for one of the basic colors, comparatives, directions, materials, positions, quantities, relationships, sequences, shapes, sizes, social or emotional states and characteristics, textures, and time. Basic concepts of basic in the sense that they represent the most rudimentary concepts in these specific categorical areas". These concepts are especially important for understanding instructions routinely spoken by teachers. The BBCS-3 was normed on 640 English-speaking children of ages 3-0 through 6-11 (160 per year of age), who were able to take the test without modifications, in an otherwise representative, stratified, national sample. Scores are provided at three-month intervals.

Bryant, B. R., Wiederholt, J. L., & Bryant, D. P. (2004). *Gray Diagnostic Reading Test* (2nd ed.) (GDRT-2). Austin, TX: Pro-Ed.
A revision of the Gray Oral Reading Test-Diagnostic, the GDRT-2 includes four core subtests (Letter/Word Identification, Phonetic Analysis, Reading Vocabulary, and Meaningful Reading) and three supplemental subtests (Listening Vocabulary, Rapid Naming, and Phonological Awareness). The GDRT-2 was normed in 2001–2002 on 1,018 students of ages 6 through 18

Dunn, L. M., & Dunn, D. M. (2006). *Peabody Picture Vocabulary Test* (4th ed.) (PPVT-4). Circle Pines, MN: Pearson Assessment.
The PPVT-4 measures single-word, receptive or listening vocabulary by presenting the student with spoken words and, for each word, showing the student four pictures from which to chose the best match for the word. The test was normed along with the EVT on a large, representative, national sample [720 children of ages 2½ through 5; 1,900 children of ages 6 though 18; and 920 adults of ages 19 to 81+] and serves its very narrow purpose very well. Because the PPVT-4 and EVT-2 were normed on the same sample, precise statistics are available for comparing a student's scores on the two tests.

Kaufman, A. S., & Kaufman, N. L. (2004). *Kaufman Assessment Battery for Children* (2nd ed.) (KABC-II). Circle Pines, MN: Pearson Assessment.

The KABC-II is a major revision of an innovative cognitive ability test. It uses different combinations of subtests at different ages from three through eighteen to test up to five areas of cognitive ability. The KABC-II may be interpreted by Luria's theory as a measure of Sequential and Simultaneous (or Successive) processing, Planning, and Learning for a Mental Processing Index (MPI) or by Cattell-Horn-Carroll (CHC) theory as a measure of Short-Term Memory (Gsm), Visual-Spatial Thinking (Gv), Fluid Reasoning (Gf), Long-Term Storage and Retrieval (Glr), and Comprehension-Knowledge (Gc) for a Fluid-Crystalized Index (FCI). There is also an optional Nonverbal Index based on tests that use little oral language. The KABC-II was normed on a nationwide sample of 3,025 individuals of ages 3 through 18.

Lambert, N., Nihira, K., & Lel, H. (1993). *AAMR Adaptive Behavior Scales–School* (2nd ed.) (ABS-S:2). Austin, TX: Pro-Ed.

Part One assesses Independent Functioning, Physical Development, Economic Activity, Language Development, Numbers and Time, Prevocational/ Vocational Activity, Self-Direction, Responsibility, and Socialization. Part Two assesses Social Behavior, Conformity, Trustworthiness, Stereotyped and Hyperactive Behavior, Self-Abusive Behavior, Social Engagement, and Disturbing Interpersonal Behavior. The scale was normed on "more than 2,000 persons from 31 states with developmental disabilities attending public schools and more than 1,000 students who have no disabilities."

Reynolds, C. R., & Kamphaus, R. W. (2003). *Reynolds Intellectual Assessment Scales* (RIAS). Lutz, FL: Psychological Assessment Resources.

The RIAS includes two verbal, two nonverbal, and two memory subtests. All of the subtests were developed from well-known and researched formats from earlier tests, but the combination of these subtests into these particular scales is unique. The RIAS was normed on a nationwide, random, stratified sample of 2,438 persons ranging in age from 3 to 94.

Roid, G. H. (2003). *Stanford-Binet Intelligence Scales* (5th ed.) (SB5). Itasca, IL: Riverside Publishing.

This is the latest version of the oldest modern individual intelligence test. It is divided in two ways. There are verbal and nonverbal (really less verbal) scales, each of which includes five factors: Fluid Reasoning, Verbal Knowledge, Quantitative Reasoning, Visual-Spatial Processing, and Working Memory. The scores can be reported by the two scales and/ or the five factors. It was normed on 4,800 individuals of ages 2 past 80, with 400 at each year of age from 2 through 16.

Roid, G. H., & Miller, L. J. (1997). *Leiter International Performance Scale-Revised* (LIPS-R). Wood Dale, IL: Stoelting.

The revised Leiter is an almost utterly nonverbal set of test batteries administered by pantomime and demonstration with almost no verbal instructions to the student and no verbal responses from the student. The Visualization and Reasoning Battery, normed on 1,719 students uses pictures and abstract designs to test a variety of thinking processes from simple matching of identical pictures to mental visualization of two- and three-dimensional figures to complex, nonverbal analogies. The Attention and Memory Battery, normed on 763 of the same students, uses visual materials and paper-and-pencil tests to measure attention, concentration, and memory. Each subtest begins with items for teaching and practice to avoid the need for verbal instructions. Figuring out the tasks is part of the challenge of this scale. There are also parent, teacher, and self rating scales for typical behavior, normed on 785, 173, and 208 students, and an examiner rating scale for the student's behavior during the test session normed on 1,719 students.

Sparrow, S. S., Cicchetti, D. V., & Balla, D. A. (2005). *Vineland Adaptive Behavior Scales* (2nd ed.) (VABS-II). Circle Pines, MN: American Guidance Service.

The Vineland Adaptive Behavior Scales are not "tests," but questionnaires completed by teachers or parents or by an evaluator working with a parent or other care-taker (Survey Interview Form). They include domains of Communication, Daily Living Skills, Socialization and, for younger students, Motor Skills, with subdomains within each domain. There is also a Maladaptive Behavior scale for the Interview forms. The Interview forms were normed on a representative, national sample of 1,085 children ages 0 through 4 years, 2,290 children ages 5 through 21 years, and 320 persons ages 22 to 90 years.

Wagner, R. K., Torgesen, J. K., & Rashotte, C. A. (1999). *Comprehensive Test of Phonological Processing* (CTOPP). Austin, TX: Pro-Ed.

The CTOPP, with different forms for ages 7–24 and 5–6, uses a variety of tasks to assess a student's ability to perceive and manipulate the sounds that make up words. The CTOPP was normed in 1997–98 on 1,656 individuals around the U.S. Many of the tasks are presented by tape recordings.

Wechsler, D. (2003). *Wechsler Intelligence Scale for Children* (4th ed.) (WISC-IV). San Antonio, TX: The Psychological Corporation.

The WISC-IV is an individual test that does not require reading or writing. "Verbal" subtests are oral questions requiring oral answers. "Perceptual Reasoning" subtests are nonverbal problems, some of which are timed and one of which allows bonus points for extra fast work. "Working Memory" subtests require remembering data (e.g., repeating dictated digits) or remembering and mentally manipulating data (e.g., repeating dictated digits in reversed order). "Processing Speed" subtests measure speed on fairly simple paper-and-pencil tasks. Two supplemental subtests (no more than one per scale) can be substituted for standard subtests in total scores if absolutely necessary. Process subtests are never used for calculating total scores. Subtest scores and total scores are based on the scores of the 2,200 children originally tested in a well-designed, nationwide sample.

Wechsler, D., Kaplan, E., Fein, D., Kramer, J., Morris, R., Delis, D., & Maerlander, A. (2003). *WISC-IV Integrated.* San Antonio, TX: The Psychological Corporation.

The WISC-IV Integrated provides additional subtests and procedures to explore further an examinee's performance on the regular WISC-IV subtests. These include multiple-choice versions of some of the subtests, normed so that an examinee would ordinarily obtain approximately the same score on each version; separate norms for components of subtests; norms for certain categories of observations; and additional subtests. The WISC-IV Integrated was normed on a smaller sample of children (730) than the rest of the WISC-IV (2,200).

Williams, K. T. (2006). *Expressive Vocabulary Test* (2nd ed.) (EVT-2). Circle Pines, MN: Pearson Assessment.

The EVT measures single-word, expressive or speaking vocabulary by presenting the student with pictures, and at the lower end, asking the child to name the picture, and for most of the test, asking the student to give another name for the picture after the examiner has given one name for it (e.g., the examiner shows a picture of a cottage and says, "House. Tell me another word for 'house.'" The test was normed along with the EVT on a large, representative, national sample [720 children of ages 2½ through 5; 1,900 children of ages 6 though 18; and 920 adults of ages 19 to 81+] and serves its very narrow purpose very well. Because the PPVT-4 and EVT-2 were normed on the same sample, precise statistics are available for comparing a student's scores on the two tests.

Wolf, M., & Denckla, M. B. (2005). *Rapid Automatized Naming and Rapid Alternating Stimulus Test* (RAN/RAS). Austin, TX: Pro-Ed.

The tests include four rapid automatized naming tests (Letters, Numbers, Objects, Colors) and two rapid alternating stimulus tests (2-Set Letters and Numbers; 3-Set Letters, Numbers, and Colors). Norms are based on scores of 1,461 children and adolescents in 26 states, of ages five through 18.

Woodcock, R. W., McGrew, K. S., & Mather, N. (2001). *Woodcock-Johnson Tests of Cognitive Ability and Achievement* (WJ III). Itasca, IL: Riverside Publishing.

The WJ III is explicitly designed to assess an examinee's abilities on many specific Cattell-Horn-Carroll Gf-Gc (CHC) "cognitive factors," not just a total score or a few factors. The Cognitive, Diagnostic Supplement, and Achievement batteries provide 53 tests organized by CHC broad and narrow abilities. Examiners are permitted to select tests for specific assessment purposes and, since the tests do not appear to have all been administered in the same sequence to all examinees in the standardization samples, there appears to be no danger of test difficulty being altered by taking tests out of their normal contexts (which is a potential concern when subtests are plucked from most assessment measures). Tests can also be combined into a General Intellectual Ability (GIA) score of 7 or 14 tests and into several Cognitive Categories. Achievement tests are organized into academic domains (reading, writing, math, oral language) and abilities (skills, applications, and fluency). The WJ III was normed on 8,818 children and adults (4,783 in grades kindergarten through 12) in a well-designed, national sample. The same persons also provided norms for the WJ III tests of cognitive ability and academic achievement, so the ability and achievement tests can be compared directly, and cognitive and achievement tests can be combined to measure CHC factors.

Index

About the CD-ROM

INTRODUCTION

This appendix provides you with information on the contents of the CD that accompanies this book. For the latest information, please refer to the ReadMe file located at the root of the CD.

SYSTEM REQUIREMENTS

Make sure that your computer meets the minimum system requirements listed in this section. If your computer doesn't match up to most of these requirements, you may have a problem using the contents of the CD.

For Microsoft Windows (including 98/Me/2000/XP/Vista):

- Microsoft Excel 2003 or higher

- Microsoft Word 2003 or higher

- A CD-ROM drive

For Macintosh:

- Microsoft Excel 2003 or higher

- Microsoft Word 2003 or higher

- A CD-ROM drive

NOTE: Many popular **spreadsheet** programs are capable of reading Microsoft Excel files. However, users should be aware that some of the formatting and functionality might be lost when using a program other than Microsoft Excel.

ALSO NOTE: The "save" command will not work on this CD. To save data, or individual subject information, you must use the "save as" command, supply a new file name, and save the file to your hard drive. The read-only status of this CD ensures that the file cannot be saved except when re-named and saved to your hard drive. This will also ensure that the original file remains intact and ready for data entry each time it is used and that the original material cannot be corrupted or lost accidentally.

USING THE CD

To view the interface on the CD, follow these steps:

1. Insert the CD into your computer's CD-ROM drive.

Note to Windows users: The interface won't launch automatically if you have AUTORUN disabled. In that case, click Start—>Run. In the dialog box that appears, type D:\start.exe. (Replace D with the proper letter if your CD drive uses a different letter. If you don't know the letter, see how your CD drive is listed under My Computer.) Click OK.

Note to Mac users: The CD icon will appear on your desktop; double-click the icon to open the CD and double-click the "Start" icon.

2. The CD-ROM interface will appear. The interface provides a simple point-and-click way to use and explore the programs on the CD.

WHAT'S ON THE CD

The following sections provide a summary of the software and other materials you'll find on the CD. There are three types of files: Microsoft Word documents, Microsoft Excel Templates, and Adobe Reader PDF files.

Files:

Microsoft Word documents

The CD contains several Microsoft Word files that can be opened so you can add DAS-II evaluation results. Other Word files can be printed out to use as appendices to your evaluation reports.

One or both of the two pages of Statistics Explanations can be appended to an evaluation report.

Some readers may find the Alternative Report Forms helpful for creating user-friendly reports for parents and teachers. There are also School-Age and Upper Early Years Cluster Description and Scores forms that allow you to report scores with explanations of Cattell-Horn-Carroll (CHC) classifications.

The School Age and Early Years Interpretive Worksheets allow you to follow the steps in the recommended interpretive sequence.

Adobe pdf Files

The CD includes 10 pdf-file tables of KTEA-II and WJ III achievement test scores predicted (taking into account regression toward the mean), from DAS-II General Conceptual Ability, Special Nonverbal Composite, Verbal Ability, Nonverbal Reasoning, and Spatial Ability scores. If you wish to compare KTEA-II or WJ III achievement scores to predicted achievement scores, you can look up the predicted scores in these tables.

There are also three pdf-file tables of DAS-II Extended Scores for GCA, SNC, and Verbal, Nonverbal, and Spatial cluster scores. All of these pdf files are derived from actual DAS-II norms and are presented by the generous permission of Pearson Assessment.

Excel Template

DAS II Computer Assistant

This CD-ROM contains a spreadsheet file (***DAS-II Computer Assistant***) *written and programmed in Microsoft Excel that allow readers to enter specific test data and information and have them analyzed. The automated worksheet is provided on the CD for your convenience in applying the principles described in the book. It is meant to facilitate and automate the analysis and interpretation of obtained data. The* ***DAS-II Computer Assistant*** *template DOES NOT convert raw scores to ability scores, nor ability scores to T scores. This program does not convert raw scores or ability scores to any metric. Users of this* *program are responsible for following the test publisher's administration and scoring guidelines. All scores entered into these programs must be derived from the norms and procedures provided by the test publisher.*

Before using the template, users should first score the DAS-II and compute all relevant *T* scores, cluster scores, and GCA and SNC scores. These scores can then be entered into the appropriate cells of the template. Preprogrammed formulae on the spreadsheet take the data entered and apply DAS-II interpretive principles to conduct the analyses.

Figure 1

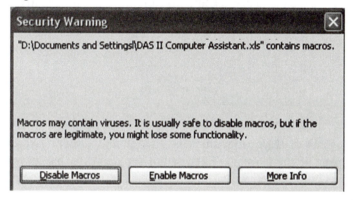

If, when the program is opened, a security warning similar to that in Figure 1 appears, click on the button to enable macros. Not doing so may reduce the functionality of the program. You will see this option only if you have the security setting in Excel at "medium" or a higher level. If your setting is "low," you will not see this screen upon opening.

The template is protected to avoid overwriting cells that contain the program formulae. If you attempt to enter information into a cell that has been protected, you will receive a warning, similar to that shown in Figure 2, indicating that the cell is protected and therefore read-only.

Figure 2

You do not need a password to use the template. There are only two pages on which you need to enter data (Input page Early Years or Input page School-Age). These pages are accessed by clicking on the color-coded tabs found at the bottom of the template (Figure 3). Clicking on any of the tabs will reveal the page for those tabs.

Figure 3

Depending upon your own computer screen, some tabs may not be visible. If this is the case, you can either click on the arrows in the lower left hand section of the tab menu or click and drag on the separator bar in the right hand section of the tab menu (Figure 4).

Figure 4

After scoring a DAS-II, you may enter the T scores and Standard scores on the Input page of the template. Each cell of the template that allows for data entry is color coded with red font. The easiest way to navigate through cells requiring data entry (or deletion) is by simply using the Tab key on your keyboard. Note that on the Early Years input page (Figure 5), there is a radio button control for choosing either the Lower or Upper Early Years battery.

Figure 5

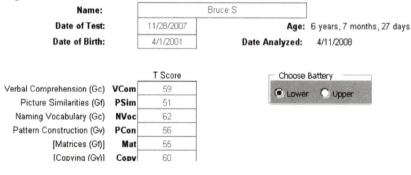

Be sure that all data already in the template are either changed or deleted for each of your individual cases. Neglecting to delete or change data can result in inaccurate interpretations. Once you have completed inputting your DAS-II data and deleting data in any unused input cells, the template automatically transfers those data to appropriate sections on the other tabs. Figure 6 shows some of the results on the Record form Early Years tab. Note that data have been transferred and additional results added.

Figure 6

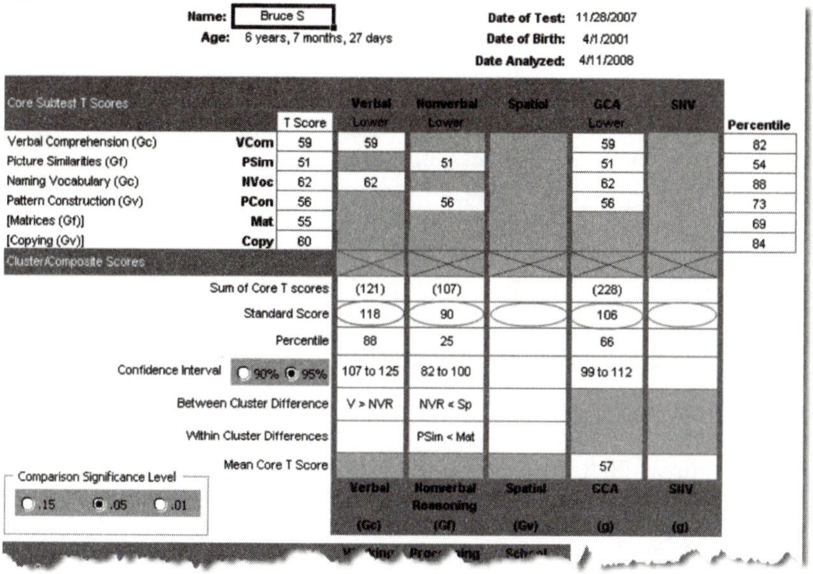

Name: Bruce S
Age: 6 years, 7 months, 27 days
Date of Test: 11/28/2007
Date of Birth: 4/1/2001
Date Analyzed: 4/11/2008

Core Subtest T Scores		T Score	Verbal Lower	Nonverbal Lower	Spatial	GCA Lower	SNV	Percentile
Verbal Comprehension (Gc)	VCom	59	59			59		82
Picture Similarities (Gf)	PSim	51		51		51		54
Naming Vocabulary (Gc)	NVoc	62	62			62		88
Pattern Construction (Gv)	PCon	56		56		56		73
[Matrices (Gf)]	Mat	55						69
[Copying (Gv)]	Copy	60						84
Cluster/Composite Scores								
Sum of Core T scores			(121)	(107)		(228)		
Standard Score			118	90		106		
Percentile			88	25		66		
Confidence Interval		90% / 95%	107 to 125	82 to 100		99 to 112		
Between Cluster Difference			V > NVR	NVR < Sp				
Within Cluster Differences				PSim < Mat				
Mean Core T Score						57		
			Verbal (Gc)	Nonverbal Reasoning (Gf)	Spatial (Gv)	GCA (g)	SNV (g)	

Comparison Significance Level: .15 / .05 / .01

On the Record form pages, for both the Early Years and School-Age Batteries, there are three radio button controls that allow you to choose confidence intervals of either 90 or 95%, comparison significance levels of either .15, .05, or .01, and GCA or SNC Mean Core *T* scores. Results from the ***DAS-II Computer Assistant*** template generally follow the guidelines presented in this book. However, the template does not follow each individual interpretative step sequentially, instead incorporating all the steps throughout the pages.

Each of the separate template pages can be printed by choosing Print from the File Menu.

TOOLS

The following applications are on the CD:

Adobe Reader - Adobe Reader is a freeware application for viewing files in the Adobe Portable Document format.

Shareware programs are fully functional, trial versions of copyrighted programs. If you like particular programs, register with their authors for a nominal fee and receive licenses, enhanced versions, and technical support.

Freeware programs are copyrighted games, applications, and utilities that are free for personal use. Unlike shareware, these programs do not require a fee or provide technical support.

GNU software is governed by its own license, which is included inside the folder of the GNU product. See the GNU license for more details.

Trial, demo or evaluation versions are usually limited either by time or functionality (such as being unable to save projects). Some trial versions are very sensitive to system date changes. If you alter your computer's date, the programs will "time out" and no longer be functional.

TROUBLESHOOTING

If you have difficulty using any of the materials on the companion CD, try the following solutions:

Disable any antivirus software that you may have running. Programs sometimes mimic virus activity and can make your computer incorrectly believe that it is being infected by a virus. (Be sure to enable antivirus software later.)

Close all running programs. The more programs you are running, the less memory is available to other programs.

Reference the ReadMe: Refer to the ReadMe file located at the root of the CD-ROM for the latest product information (if any) at the time of publication.

Customer Care

If you have trouble with the CD-ROM, please call the Wiley Product Technical Support phone number at (800) 762-2974. Outside the United States, call 1 (317) 572-3994. You can also contact Wiley Product Technical Support at http://support.wiley.com. John Wiley & Sons will provide technical support only for installation and other general quality control items. For technical support on the applications themselves, consult the program's vendor or author.

To place additional orders or to request information about other Wiley products, please call (877) 762-2974.